JUDGING AT THE INTERFACE

This book explores how the Permanent Court of International Justice, the International Court of Justice, the European Court of Human Rights, and investment treaty tribunals have used deference to recognise the decision making authority of States. It analyses the approaches to deference taken by these four international courts and tribunals in 1,714 decisions produced between 1924 and 2019 concerning alleged State interferences with private property. The book identifies a large number of techniques capable of achieving deference to domestic decision-making in international adjudication. It groups these techniques to identify seven distinct 'modes' of deference reflecting differently structured relationships between international adjudicators and domestic decision-makers. These differing approaches to deference are shown to hold systemic significance. They reveal the shifting nature and structure of adjudication under international law and its relationship to domestic decision making authority.

Esmé Shirlow is an Associate Professor at the Australian National University (ANU). She has served as an assistant to a number of investment treaty tribunals, and advises parties to investment treaty claims and in proceedings before the International Court of Justice. Prior to joining the ANU, she worked in the Australian Government's Office of International Law. Dr Shirlow completed her PhD as a Dickson Poon Scholar at King's College London, for which she was awarded the King's Elsevier Outstanding PhD Thesis Prize. She completed her LL.M. at the University of Cambridge, where she was awarded – among other prizes – the BRD Clarke Prize for Best Overall Performance in the LL.M., the Clive Parry Prize for Best Result in International Law, and the Whewell Scholarship in International Law.

Judging at the Interface

DEFERENCE TO STATE DECISION-MAKING AUTHORITY IN INTERNATIONAL ADJUDICATION

ESMÉ SHIRLOW
Australian National University

CAMBRIDGE
UNIVERSITY PRESS

CAMBRIDGE
UNIVERSITY PRESS

University Printing House, Cambridge CB2 8BS, United Kingdom

One Liberty Plaza, 20th Floor, New York, NY 10006, USA

477 Williamstown Road, Port Melbourne, VIC 3207, Australia

314–321, 3rd Floor, Plot 3, Splendor Forum, Jasola District Centre, New Delhi – 110025, India

79 Anson Road, #06–04/06, Singapore 079906

Cambridge University Press is part of the University of Cambridge.

It furthers the University's mission by disseminating knowledge in the pursuit of education, learning, and research at the highest international levels of excellence.

www.cambridge.org
Information on this title: www.cambridge.org/9781108490979
DOI: 10.1017/9781108867108

First published 2021

A catalogue record for this publication is available from the British Library.

ISBN 978-1-108-49097-9 Hardback

For David, with gratitude.

Contents

Figures

Tables

Foreword by Judge James Crawford

State sovereignty, 'the fundamental principle ... on which the whole of international law rests',[1] has long exerted a significant constraint on international lawyers. Seen as the State's plenary and exclusive legal competence (externally as well as internally), sovereignty is at once the vehicle enabling the creation of international law and the outer limit of its reach. Both attributes were affirmed by the first permanent international court in its early days, which shows the importance paid to international dispute settlement institutions for as long as the system of international law creation and enforcement remains substantially decentralised. The key question is that of the relationship between international and domestic legal competence, and to what extent it entails a pattern of deference. It is that question that Esmé Shirlow examines in this work.

There are two types of risk with such a challenging project. The first relates to focus. Some studies of this kind craft elaborate theoretical accounts of the normative vices and virtues of various models already identified; others engage in a scrupulous analysis of the textual and contextual data extracted from the body of case law. Yet both approaches are likely to present a distorted image of the subject under scrutiny. The second risk, associated with the first, concerns lighting, or colouring. It may be tempting to treat indeterminate concepts such as 'deference' in dispositive terms, painting a black-and-white image of instances in which the concept is either observed or not; this might help to handle an otherwise untameable concept and to fit practice into preconstructed charts and tables. Yet such an approach ignores subtle variations in the use of the concept and different shades of the case law.

[1] Military and Paramilitary Activities in and against Nicaragua (*Nicaragua* v. *United States of America*), Merits, Judgment, ICJ Reports 1986, p. 14 (para. 263).

Dr Shirlow skilfully avoids both these risks, adopting instead a more nuanced approach both as regards her methodology and her conclusions. With respect to methodology, the study scrutinises an impressive pool of case law from four judicial regimes, extrapolating elaborated yet recognisable patterns on the question of deference. With respect to substance, Dr Shirlow insightfully traces the doctrinal and theoretical underpinnings of each of these identified patterns, assessing the implications of the various approaches to deference for the structure of the international legal system.

In his Lalive Lecture delivered a decade ago, David Caron pictured international courts as partners with domestic organs – notably domestic courts – in upholding the rule of law, and hailed the margin of appreciation and the degree of discretion as avenues to acknowledge the States' role in this collective enterprise.[2] The functions of international courts had long been at the heart of his interests, as a key to appreciate their performance and interactions with other institutions, international and domestic. Dr Shirlow builds upon his collaborative view of international and domestic institutions and demonstrates that international and domestic decision-making are not – or do not need to be – antagonistic but instead can complement one another, benefitting from their relative strengths.

In doing so she affirms that the concept of decision-making authority, and of sovereignty upon which it rests, constantly evolves. She reminds us as international lawyers – whether government officials, international adjudicators, academics, or practitioners – of our shared duty to help it ensure that it evolves in desirable directions.

James Crawford

International Court of Justice

[2] D Caron, 'International Courts and Tribunals: Their Roles amidst a World of Courts' (2011) 26 *ICSID Review Foreign Investment Law Journal* 1, 12.

Acknowledgements

I would like to dedicate this book to my doctoral supervisor, Professor David D. Caron, who passed away unexpectedly in the final months of the doctoral candidacy from which this book emerged. I have found constant cause to remember David as I completed this project. David referred to unfinished projects as 'bulbs' waiting to be planted, tended, and ultimately brought to flower. It gives me great sadness to know that David will not see this final version of my dissertation, now book – a bulb that he helped me to plant and cultivate. I am grateful for his faith in me and my ideas, as well as his encouragement of my personal and professional development. David leaves a significant intellectual legacy but, above all else, I will remember him for his warm character, wisdom, and generosity. I learned much from his example and feel privileged to have known him.

This book grew out of doctoral research completed at King's College London, and was made possible by the encouragement, friendship and support of so many. I would like to thank, in particular, my second supervisor, Dr Florian Grisel, for his constant guidance and encouragement. Our many conversations have informed my approach and improved my analysis immeasurably. Florian has also provided vital guidance and support as I have transitioned to my faculty position and it has been a privilege to learn from his example as a scholar, teacher, and friend. I had underestimated on starting my PhD the true significance of quality supervision and consider myself very lucky to have had the benefit of two exceptional supervisors. I am grateful also to Mr Dickson Poon, and the Dickson Poon School of Law, for providing me with a generous scholarship without which it would not have been possible to complete the work underpinning this book.

I have been privileged to have had several professional opportunities that have informed the development of the ideas in this book. I worked at the

Australian Attorney-General's Department's Office of International Law prior to undertaking my doctoral studies and thereafter continued my work with the Office in a consultancy capacity during the first two years of my PhD. My work at the Office informed my choice of topic and provided a valuable opportunity to see the practical impact of the issues I was researching. I am grateful to the many colleagues I worked with, and particularly to John Atwood and Bill Campbell AO QC, from whom I learnt a great deal about both public international law and public service. I am also grateful to the members of the investor-State tribunals for which I have acted as an assistant during the writing of this work. I learnt much about the mechanics of arbitral decision-making from these appointments and am extremely grateful for these opportunities. I have also been fortunate to work in a number of advisory roles in investment treaty claims during the writing of this work, alongside, in particular, Sam Wordsworth QC and Professor Chester Brown. These two incredibly gifted and generous lawyers have taught me much, and I am grateful to have had opportunities to learn from them. Finally, I had the opportunity to teach at both King's College London and the Australian National University during the writing of my doctorate and then book. Teaching has clarified elements of my thinking, and also provided a welcome distraction during long months of coding.

I have benefitted immensely from the support, guidance, and kindness of so many during the writing of this book. My family – Megan, Gwen, and Bob – have provided much-needed support (and some helpful distractions!) as I completed this work. I am especially grateful to my mother, Dr Megan Shirlow, who has been a constant source of inspiration for me. She believed in me before all others and encouraged me to become the best version of myself that I could be. She has provided steadfast care and support to both myself and my sister through the most difficult of circumstances, and I consider myself incredibly lucky to have her in my life.

Many others, too numerous to mention, have provided invaluable personal and academic support and to all of them I remain indebted. Special thanks go to Dr Eva Klambauer, Rosie Goldfeder, Dr Gwen Shirlow, and Angela Van who have offered enduring friendship and support for many years across different continents. My thanks also to Dr Will Bateman for his continued encouragement of this project since I joined the ANU. I am particularly grateful also to Dr Jonathan Bonnitcha, Professor Chester Brown, Dr Florian Grisel, Professor Bruno Simma, Professor Jorge Viñuales, Jack Wass, Professor Philippa Webb, Sam Wordsworth QC, and the two anonymous Cambridge University Press peer reviewers for reading and providing extremely constructive feedback on drafts of my book at varying stages of completion. I benefitted greatly from their keen attention to detail, constructive comments and comprehensive knowledge of international and public law. Their comments helped me to improve and strengthen my arguments and analysis. I am also grateful to be able to include a foreword by Judge James Crawford with this work. James supervised my LL.M. dissertation at the University of Cambridge and encouraged me to undertake doctoral study under David's supervision. It feels especially fitting to include this foreword as a link to the individuals and experiences so formative to my work and thinking.

The editorial team at Cambridge University Press, and especially Tom Randall, Gemma Smith, Subathra Manogaran, and Helen Baxter have provided valuable support and guidance during the preparation of this manuscript and have been particularly patient as I endeavoured to draw the project to a close among bushfire- and pandemic-related disruptions. I am grateful, too, to Sebastian King who provided astute proofreading assistance during the final production stages.

Finally, I am grateful to my husband, Andrew Bekkema. Without his unwavering support and encouragement, this book would not have been possible. Andrew has consistently encouraged me to reach further and dream brighter. He provides a source of inspiration for me every day and has provided me with the courage and support necessary to both embark on and finish this project.

Table of Cases

Note: This book uses the following in-text footnote citation system for cases: *Abbreviated case name, decision type, decision date in the format DD-MMM-YYYY (regime)*, pinpoint.

PERMANENT COURT OF INTERNATIONAL JUSTICE

INTERNATIONAL COURT OF JUSTICE

INVESTMENT TREATY ARBITRATION

EUROPEAN COURT OF HUMAN RIGHTS

Table of Treaties, Resolutions, and Declarations

Abbreviations

ACtHR	African Court on Human and Peoples' Rights
BIT	Bilateral investment treaty
CDDH	Council of Europe Steering Committee for Human Rights
CoE	Council of Europe
Dissent/SO	Dissenting/Separate Opinion
ECHR	European Convention for the Protection of Human Rights and Fundamental Freedoms
ECJ	European Court of Justice/Court of Justice of the European Union
ECtHR	European Court of Human Rights
ELR	Exhaustion of local remedies
FET	Fair and equitable treatment
GC	Grand Chamber of the European Court of Human Rights
IACtHR	Inter-American Court of Human Rights
ICJ	International Court of Justice
ICSID	International Centre for Settlement of Investment Disputes
ICSID-AF	Additional Facility Rules of the International Centre for Settlement of Investment Disputes
ISDS	Investor-State dispute settlement (treaty-based)
LCIA	London Court of International Arbitration
MoA	Margin of appreciation
NAFTA	North American Free Trade Agreement
P1-1	Article 1 of Protocol 1 to the European Convention for the Protection of Human Rights and Fundamental Freedoms
PCA	Permanent Court of Arbitration
PCIJ	Permanent Court of International Justice
SCC	Stockholm Chamber of Commerce

UK	United Kingdom of Great Britain and Northern Ireland
UN	United Nations
UNCITRAL	United Nations Commission on International Trade Law
USA, US	United States of America
VCLT	Vienna Convention on the Law of Treaties
WTO	World Trade Organization

Introduction

Deference and the International Adjudication of Private Property Disputes

While working as a government lawyer in 2011, my team received a letter advising that the Philip Morris tobacco company had decided to sue Australia under a bilateral investment treaty. The company contended that Australia's tobacco plain packaging requirements breached its intellectual property rights, entitling it to billions of dollars in compensation under international law. This news was not particularly shocking to the small team of which I was part, which had been assembled within the government's Office of International Law to respond to these types of claim. The news *was* shocking, however, to the wider Australian public. Over the ensuing months, public disbelief became better-articulated in the press: how can an international tribunal sit in judgment over a measure that the Australian parliament had decided was in the public interest after extensive scientific enquiry and public consultation? Could an international tribunal really reverse the finding of Australia's highest court that the legislation was lawful?

These concerns about the appropriate reach of international law and about the appropriate relationship between international adjudicators and domestic decision-makers are longstanding. In 1927, for example, an Australian professor, William Sutton Cumbrae-Stewart KC, contended that: '[T]he League of Nations is doomed to failure if it attempts too much in the way of being busy about other people's business.'[1] Some thirty-five years later, an American professor, Richard A. Falk, echoed this sentiment, observing that: '[I]nternational law, in contrast to domestic law, is much like a Victorian lady and must depend upon an excess of self-restraint to achieve virtue.'[2] Such concerns have gained traction in recent years as the expansion of international law has prompted qualitatively different and quantitatively increased opportunities

[1] Brisbane Telegraph (1927).

[2] Falk (1964), pp. 53–4.

for overlap and interaction between domestic and international decision-making.

International adjudication remains a central focus in these debates. In more recent times, Australia's 2011 Trade Policy Statement, for instance, indicated 'Australia's view that domestic courts, not investment tribunals, are the appropriate bodies to resolve investment disputes between domestic states and foreign investors.'[3] Lord Sumption in 2013 similarly argued that the European Court of Human Rights ('ECtHR') 'undermines the democratic process'.[4] And a key concern reported by stakeholders in the European Union's 2016 consultation process on the proposed Transatlantic Trade and Investment Partnership concerned the relationship between domestic judicial systems and investor-State dispute settlement.[5] Such concerns have produced mounting calls for the abolition of certain international adjudicative mechanisms entirely or modifications to how international adjudicators decide disputes.[6] Deference is also increasingly invoked as a tool capable of responding to the perceived 'legitimacy crisis' affecting international adjudication.[7] This is unsurprising given that deference is a key means by which international adjudicators recognise, accommodate, and constrain State decision-making authority. This book focuses on this role of deference in settling the interface between domestic and international decision-making authority.

FRAMING THE INTERFACE BETWEEN DOMESTIC AND INTERNATIONAL DECISION-MAKING

This book investigates how courts in four international regimes use deference to recognise the decision-making authority of domestic actors in cases concerning alleged State interferences with private property. The book focuses principally on two interrelated questions. It first considers when and how international adjudicators defer to States. Second, it analyses the implications of deference in international adjudication and of differences in approaches to deference in different times and contexts. I use these cross-cutting enquiries to develop a theory of deference as an adjudicative practice. To make this

3 Trakman (2012), p. 981. See: Australia, Department of Foreign Affairs and Trade (2011). Similar concerns have been raised by other States, see for example: United States of America, Department of State (2005); Republic of South Africa, Department of Trade and Industry (2013); Embassy of the Netherlands in Jakarta, Indonesia (2014).

4 Sumption (2013), p. 11.

5 European Commission (2015), p. 3.

6 See, further, Caron and Shirlow (2018); Kyriakou (2007).

7 See, especially, Burke-White (2008a); Vadi and Gruszczynski (2013); Dzehtsiarou and Greene (2011); Kwiecien (2012); Leonhardsen (2012); Henckels (2013), p. 200; Roberts (2011).

investigation of deference in international adjudication manageable, the book explores how the Permanent Court of International Justice, the International Court of Justice, the European Court of Human Rights, and investment treaty tribunals have used deference to recognise the decision-making authority of domestic actors in international cases concerning alleged State interferences with private property rights. The cases form a particularly useful empirical focus and backdrop for the broader conceptual questions explored in the book. They have been adjudicated under international law for a long period of time and in different regimes and therefore lend themselves to comparative analysis. Furthermore, property claims – as explored in more detail in what follows – very frequently raise State requests for deference because they concern matters in respect of which States might expect to hold authority to make final decisions.

The book identifies a large number of techniques capable of achieving deference to domestic decision-making in international adjudication. It groups these techniques to identify seven distinct 'modes' of deference. These modes reflect relationships between international adjudicators and domestic decision-makers of submission, deferral, abstention, restraint, reference, respect, and control/dismissal. I demonstrate that distinct structures of authority underlie these seven modes of deference. The seven modes of deference differ structurally depending on whether they rely on a view of decision-making authority as conclusive, suspensive, or concurrent. Adjudicators adopting a conclusive view of decision-making authority favour categorical approaches to deference: one actor's decision controls the outcome of another actor's decision-making process. Suspensive authority, by contrast, precludes the exercise of one actor's authority in favour of another, either for a limited period of time or in respect of particular subjects. Concurrent authority arises where two decision-makers work in tandem, their decision-making processes being viewed as complementary rather than incompatible or exclusive. The book shows that these differing structures of authority underpin international adjudicative approaches to deference. These three structures of authority, in turn, reflect three distinct theoretical paradigms concerning the relationship between the international and domestic legal orders. Whereas the conclusive views of authority underlying the modes of deference as submission and control reflect a monist view of this relationship, the suspensive views of authority underlying the modes of deferral and abstention reflect dualist paradigms, and the concurrent views underpinning the modes of restraint, reference, and respect reflect pluralist approaches. Differing approaches to deference in different regimes and time periods thus hold systemic significance. Studying deference in international adjudication from this perspective brings into focus the shifting nature and structure of adjudication under public international law and its relationship to domestic decision-making authority.

This is by no means the first study of deference in international adjudication. Several scholars have examined how international adjudicators attribute weight to domestic decisions including through deferential proportionality balancing or reasonableness review,[8] restrictive interpretation of treaties,[9] and margin of appreciation ('MoA') analysis.[10] These studies have each been informed by differing research goals and methodologies, encompassing doctrinal,[11] normative,[12] and statistical approaches.[13] The present study complements and extends these previous studies in three principal ways. First, it moves past the question of whether international adjudicators *should* give deference to domestic decisions, to consider instead how they structure and analyse deference in practice. The book works from theory to practice to policy, rather than adopting an inverse, more normative approach. Second, instead of studying the approach of an individual regime to deference, the book compares the approaches taken to deference by adjudicators in four regimes.[14] To do so, I adopt an inductive approach to identifying deference in international adjudicative reasoning, eschewing a search for formal labels and doctrines that have formed the focus of studies of deference in existing scholarship to instead identify instances of deference from a more conceptual and inclusive perspective. In so doing, the book brings into focus the function(s) of deference in international adjudication and the impact of institutional setting on that function. Finally, the book elaborates temporal developments in approaches to deference. These dynamic qualities of deference have not previously been empirically investigated and there is thus little understanding of whether approaches to deference have changed as international law has developed. Existing studies of deference have instead treated it as a fixed phenomenon.[15] By contrast, this book examines whether – and how – approaches to deference change over time. This illuminates the dynamic properties of deference and the changing relationship between

8 Henckels (2014); Vadi and Gruszczynski (2013); Roberts (2011); Vadi (2018).
9 Van Harten (2013); Crema (2010); Orakhelashvili (2003).
10 Legg (2012); Duhaime (2014); Arai-Takahashi (2002).
11 See, for example, Gruszczynski and Werner (2014).
12 See, for example, Henckels (2014).
13 See, especially, Van Harten (2013).
14 Knight (2018) undertakes such a study across domestic common law regimes to develop a useful taxonomy of the approaches to deference adopted therein.
15 Some authors identify diachronic shifts, but tend not to draw broader implications from those changes. See, for example, Kratochvil (2011).

domestic decision-making and international adjudication. With this focus, the book demonstrates how deference mediates contestations and fluctuations in the interfaces between domestic and international decision-making authority. It demonstrates, in particular, that the domestic/international interface is both contested and in flux and is likely to remain so into the future.

A *An Interface Contested*

Conflict permeates law. It prompts litigation, but the management or settlement of conflict also runs through much of what law does. Several core conflicts confront international adjudicators, particularly those deciding private property claims. These include conflicts between individuals and the State, the local and global and conflicts between the protection of private property and other public interests. International adjudication may either settle these conflicts or provide an arena for their continued discussion. Deference performs a key function in these conflicts, because it determines who plays a role in settling them. Deference provides a tool to mediate, in particular, conflicting claims to national and international decision-making authority in respect of these issues. This book tracks the approaches adopted by international adjudicators to settling such conflicting claims to authority. I organise approaches to deference in international private property decisions into a taxonomy of seven distinct 'modes' of deference, to argue that different approaches to deference in international litigation signal fundamentally distinct views of the role of domestic decision-making authority under international law. I use this framework to track how international adjudicators invoke deference to settle conflicts about the interface between international and domestic decision-making authority. This analysis highlights approaches to deference variously favouring submission, cooperation, complementarity, and supremacy. It illuminates how deference performs the role of 'frontier management'[16] in international adjudication, constructing and regulating the interface between particular political and legal communities and sources of law.

This book focuses on how international courts and tribunals deciding claims relating to alleged State interferences with private property have used deference to manage these conflicts. The book focuses on this subset of international cases for a number of reasons, explored more fully in Chapter 2. A key reason for selecting this focus is that private property cases are particularly likely to raise the conflicts that may generate calls for deference. While private property is protected by various rules of international law, it

[16] Walker (2013), p. 103.

subsists physically within a territorial space. This makes it a matter particularly apt for national regulation. In fact, territory, in turn, is 'an organizing principle for political and legal authority'[17] and is central to the notion of State sovereignty. Sovereignty reflects that the State is 'master of its own territory', holding exclusive powers to allocate, regulate, and administer property within that territory.[18] 'Sovereignty' can be examined from two perspectives. 'Internal sovereignty' refers to the power or authority of States to regulate their own institutions.[19] Internal sovereignty signifies a State's 'absolute and perpetual power' over its territory and nationals.[20] From this internal perspective, the 'sovereign' is the entity with the final right to decide matters in a given territory or concerning particular individuals.[21] 'External sovereignty' refers to the independence of the State in its relations with other States or external entities.[22] It generates a 'right to be left alone',[23] permitting the State to decide 'without interference from organizations or individuals external to the jurisdiction'.[24] Whereas 'internal sovereignty' describes a State's *authority* to decide, 'external sovereignty' delineates whether it may exercise that authority *autonomously*. Holistically, then, sovereignty can be said to designate the extent of a State's *autonomous authority* to decide.[25] Both facets of sovereignty describe the relationship of States to other entities.[26] The relational quality of sovereignty means that it 'is acted upon, asserted, developed and limited within the context of a relationship with others'.[27] International adjudication provides a key forum for this 'contestation of sovereignty'.[28] The decisions of international adjudicators impact the extent of State decision-making authority and therefore both construct and constrain State sovereignty.

Most theories of property draw on this close connection between property and sovereignty. For some theorists, private property is a foundation of

17 Brölmann (2007), p. 86.
18 Wortley (1956), p. 588. See, also, *Norwegian Loans (Dissent/SO-Lauterpacht), 6-Jul-1957 (ICJ)*, p. 52.
19 See, especially, McRae (1971), p. 82; Jennings (2002), p. 32; Hart (1994), p. 223; Schrijver (2000), p. 65.
20 Bodin (1576). See, also, Kwiecien (2012), p. 52; Crawford (2014), p. 72.
21 Crawford (2014), p. 71; Wildhaber (1983), p. 441.
22 McRae (1971), p. 82; Olivier (1988), p. 86; Hart (1994), p. 223; Kwiecien (2012), p. 52.
23 Kumm (2016), p. 239. See, also: Hathaway (2008); McRae (1971), p. 81; Schrijver (2000), p. 71.
24 Drezner (2001), p. 323.
25 See, similarly: Jackson (2003), p. 790; Grieves (1969), p. 2.
26 Kwiecien (2004), p. 88; Romano (2007), p. 793; Schrijver (2000), p. 71; McRae (1971), p. 83; Henkin (1990), p. 97; Kelsen (1960), p. 637; McCorquodale (2006); Fassbender (2003), p. 115; Wildhaber (1983), p. 441.
27 McCorquodale (2006).
28 Legg (2012), p. 58.

civilisation: State sovereignty arises to protect and preserve private property rights.[29] Locke, for example, derived State sovereignty from a pact to escape a state of nature that threatened the rights of life, liberty, and property.[30] For Locke, the first two rights were predicated on property rights, leading to the conclusion that: '[G]overnment has no other end but the preservation of Property.'[31] For other theorists, private property is distributed by the sovereign and so follows and derives from the State. Hobbes[32] and Austin[33] thus conceptualised the State as the entity with exclusive power to grant and recognise property rights. Private property might instead be linked to individual – rather than State – identity. Some theorists, for example, argue that a person has no concrete existence until they exercise their will on the outside world, making the creation of property a fundamental form of self-expression.[34] These theories indicate that questions of sovereignty are likely to be deeply implicated in private property cases. This is particularly so where private property cases are litigated internationally. The international adjudication of private property disputes deterritorialises the State's regulatory authority over property.[35] As such, and as developed further in what follows, international private property disputes are particularly likely to evoke claims of sovereign control and requests for deference to domestic decision-making authority. The international litigation of other rights might, of course, produce similar claims. To that extent, the conceptual analysis and framework presented in this book is likely to be generalisable to these other contexts. Private property disputes are simply used to illustrate the contours and role of deference in international adjudication, with this focus also keeping the empirical components of the book methodologically sound (and feasible)

The connection between deference, authority, and sovereignty explains in part why studies of deference have thus far been distinctly normative and hotly contested. As Chapter 1 argues, deference is a tool through which the concept of sovereignty is operationalised in international adjudication.[36] Ostensibly technical debates about deference reflect more fundamental debates about the delineation of sovereignty in the international system. As Part II shows,

29 See, for example: de Vattel (1797); Ederington (1997), p. 266; Cohen (1927).

30 Locke (1988), pp. 115–16, 315.

31 Ibid, para. 94.

32 Hobbes (1996), p. 164.

33 Austin (1885), p. 839.

34 Radin (1982), p. 972.

35 See, similarly, Brölmann (2007), pp. 86, 94; Sassen (2015), p. 61; *Barcelona Traction (Dissent/SO-Padilla Nervo), 5-Feb-1970 (ICJ)*, p. 249.

36 On making sovereignty 'actionable', see, further, Viñuales (2014), p. 317; von Rosenvinge (2010), p. 2; Franck (1990), p. 26.

studying approaches to deference across different adjudicative regimes offers a means by which 'the space left for sovereignty in different legal contexts can be specifically compared'.[37]

B *An Interface in Flux*

This study builds on existing contributions, but addresses deference from a different perspective. Instead of considering a particular type or manifestation of deference in international adjudication, it considers instead the concept of deference and its function in international adjudication. It links deference to authority to highlight the different structures of authority represented by deferential reasoning. Linking deference to authority gives greater significance to differences in how deference is analysed by adjudicators operating in different times and regimes. It also provides a framework through which different approaches to deference can be conceptually analysed and understood. The linkage between deference and authority, coupled with the empirical study undertaken in Part II, reveals that approaches to deference differ depending on how international adjudicators conceptualise the structure of their relationship to domestic decision-makers. Whereas some adjudicators conceptualise the relationship between domestic and international decision-making in conclusive or suspensive terms, others conceptualise a shared and cooperative space of concurrent decision-making authority. These forms of authority are introduced in Part I and subsequently developed through the empirical study reported in Part II. That Part identifies 'conclusive', 'suspensive' and 'concurrent' views of authority through analysis of the seven different modes of deference that are present in international adjudicative reasoning in private property claims. It demonstrates that instead of distinguishing 'deferential' from 'non-deferential' approaches to international review, it is more fruitful to consider different approaches to deference as reflections of underlying international adjudicative assessments of domestic decision-making authority and of the structure of the domestic/international interface.

This book does not propose to settle the contested interface between the domestic and international orders. Nor does it endorse a particular doctrinal approach to deference. The objective is instead conceptual, empirical, and explanatory. The book focuses on *who* is able to exercise their authority to determine key issues relevant to the outcome of international disputes and *what tools* are used to recognise that authority. The book develops a framework

[37] Viñuales (2014), p. 323.

to inform ongoing debates about the appropriate role of deference to domestic decision-making in international law. It moves beyond advocating a particular approach to settling conflicting claims to authority, to examine instead deference in different times and contexts. The book tracks international adjudicative approaches to deference from 1924 to 2019. It demonstrates that deference operates as a fundamental and inherent component of international adjudication. Despite this continuity, approaches to deference have been subject to constant change. Deference functions as a lever to make international law responsive to a broader and ongoing dialogue about the appropriate relationship between international adjudication and State decision-making autonomy and authority. Deference thus supports dynamism and flexibility in international law. International adjudicators use deference to claim decision-making authority and to recognise the decision-making authority of States. In spite of this, existing studies have treated deference as a fixed phenomenon, studying '*the*' approach to deference taken by a specific international adjudicative mechanism.[38] Few studies track approaches to deference over time, much less to consider what this reveals about the changing nature of international adjudication. This book extends understandings of deference through a comparative study analysing its incidence across a ninety-five-year period in adjudicative decisions from four international regimes. This brings into focus the systemic role of deference in international adjudication. This temporal and cross-institutional empirical analysis of deference is the first of its kind.

Deference reveals how international adjudication is evolving. Deference tracks both the development of international law and opposition to it. As international law evolves, so do perceptions of the proper relationship between domestic decision-makers and international adjudicators. This book uses deference to tell this story of international adjudication and its shifting relationship to domestic legal orders. Tracking evolution in approaches to deference brings into focus shifts in international adjudicative perceptions of the roles and competence of international adjudicators vis-à-vis domestic decision-makers. As conceptualisations of sovereignty evolve, so do approaches to deference. Deference widens and narrows as international adjudicative confidence 'simultaneously undergo[es] erosion with respect to many issues and reinforcement with respect to others'.[39] The book thus examines how adjudicators use deference to readjust the relationship between international and domestic decision-making authority dynamically over time and in different

38 See, for example, Van Harten (2013), p. 48; Henckels (2015); Legg (2012).

39 Rosenau (1997), p. 5.

regimes. This has practical implications. The book identifies the structural frameworks used by adjudicators to analyse questions of deference and brings into focus the underlying assumptions and theoretical paradigms that inform the approaches adopted in individual cases. This analysis has important consequences for the theory and practice of international law. The identification of how international adjudicators approach the issue of deference may assist litigants to international private property cases.[40] It may also assist States to structure domestic decision-making to better attract deference from international adjudicators. It may further inform system design, illuminating the features of international regimes that impact the analysis of deference in individual cases. The analysis of deference in these pages therefore raises questions of governance and institutional design, related to the allocation and contestation of authority in the international system.

My aim in this book is to highlight the role of deference in international adjudication as a tool for flexible interface management. Deference draws attention to the role of international adjudicators in settling contested questions about the authority of international and domestic decision-makers in respect of private property. This facilitates an investigation into whether international courts and tribunals adopt the restrained and deferential persona envisaged by Falk, bowing their heads to States by deferring to domestic decisions or whether they have instead become bothersome and 'nosy neighbours', as Cumbrae-Stewart feared, twitching their curtains to intervene and control how States regulate in their territories.

STRUCTURE AND APPROACH

The book is divided into three parts.

Part I introduces a conceptual framework for analysing deference, and the methodological approach informing the analysis of deference in Part II. The part consists of three chapters. Chapter 1 introduces the notion of deference and links it to the concept of authority. Characterising deference as a recognition of another actor's decision-making authority underpins the book's core conceptual contribution. Linking deference to authority provides a conceptual framework for analysing possible justifications for deference. It further explains why deference takes different structures, explaining why deference can be more or less categorical. Chapter 2 introduces the focus of the study. The chapter introduces the four courts and tribunals subject to

40 While respondent States are particularly likely to seek deference, individuals may also seek deference to State decisions.

detailed empirical study in Part II: the Permanent Court of International Justice ('PCIJ'), the International Court of Justice ('ICJ'), the European Court of Human Rights ('ECtHR') and investment treaty tribunals.[41] The remainder of the book explores how these adjudicators defer to domestic decision-making in international private property cases. Chapter 3 introduces the empirical, comparative, and inductive research methodology underpinning the analysis in Part II. While a methodology chapter is perhaps not common in international law monographs, the perspective taken in Chapter 1 as to the nature of deference necessarily influences how it is identified and analysed in Part II. Chapter 3 bridges the book's conceptual and empirical analyses.

Part II investigates how adjudicators in the selected regimes structure deference, and the implications of deference for their relationship to domestic decision-makers. Chapter 4 presents a framework for the qualitative analysis of deference in Part II. The chapter introduces the range of approaches used by international adjudicators to recognise the decision-making authority of domestic actors in international private property cases. The chapter organises these approaches into a taxonomy of seven modes of deference, developed on the basis of a comprehensive inductive review of 1,714 majority and dissenting decisions from 889 proceedings of the four courts and tribunals under investigation. The chapter draws on Chapter 1 to argue that deference in international adjudication is underpinned by three distinct views of authority. Chapters 5 to 7 introduce these perspectives on the interfaces between domestic and international authority and the approaches to deference that they produce. These chapters illustrate how international adjudicators use deference to demarcate zones of exclusive, suspensive, and shared decision-making authority between international and domestic actors.

Part III examines what the varying modes of deference and differing approaches to authority reveal about international adjudicative understandings of the relationship between domestic and international decision-making authority and the national and international legal orders. Chapter 8 draws on Part I's qualitative schema to investigate the frequency of different structures of deference and authority in the analysed decisions. This chapter highlights that deference is ubiquitous in international adjudicative decision-making,

[41] Whether investment treaty arbitration is a 'regime' has been contested. See, further: Salacuse (2010), p. 430; Pauwelyn (2014), p. 12. It is nonetheless treated in what follows as a field suited to collective study. This reflects the approach adopted in the bulk of scholarship considering investment arbitration and is, moreover, considered particularly appropriate – as Chapter 2 explains – given the focus of this particular study. Part II examines approaches of institutionally different investment tribunals to the issue of deference.

but that the balance between international supervision and domestic authority is drawn differently across different times and by different international adjudicators. Deference manifests in neither a constant nor uniform form. Chapter 9 examines the structural and systemic function of deference in international adjudication. It develops a conceptual cartography of deference, arguing that different approaches to deference structure relationships between international and domestic actors variously as horizontal, vertical, or overlapping. Chapter 10 connects theory to practice, to draw out key lessons from the preceding analysis for policy-makers, adjudicators, and litigants. It proposes a theory of deference founded on practice, but capable of continued evolution.

The Conclusion draws the discussion in the preceding chapters together.

PART I

CONCEPTUAL FRAMEWORK AND METHODOLOGICAL APPROACH

This part develops a conceptual and methodological framework to organise the subsequent discussion and to situate the project in relation to existing studies. Chapter 1 defines deference. The chapter draws on theories of authority to conceptualise deference as the recognition of decision-making authority on the basis of 'second-order reasons'. It introduces the concept of 'second-order reasons' and examines the range of second-order reasons that may prompt deference in international adjudication. These include 'instrumental', 'prudential', and 'non-instrumental' second-order reasons, which the chapter examines in turn. Chapter 2 introduces the focus and approach of the study. Existing studies of international adjudicative deference have focused on specific approaches to deference adopted by particular international courts or tribunals. This book instead studies deference comparatively, to explore its systemic implications in international adjudication. Chapter 2 explains why the study focuses on decisions determining private property claims by four international courts and tribunals. Chapter 3 introduces the methodology informing the comparative and empirical study reported in Part II. It presents a theory of international adjudication and explains how an empirical study of adjudicative reasoning can remain 'internal' to the discipline of law despite borrowing methodological techniques and theories from 'external' disciplines.

1

Defining Deference: The Connection between Deference and Authority

This chapter introduces the concept of deference and illustrates how it functions in international adjudication. Section 1.1 links the concept of 'deference' to that of 'authority'. It explains that 'authority' refers to an actor's ability to induce deference from another actor. This section uses accounts of authority to extend existing analyses of adjudicative deference. Linking adjudicative deference to authority provides a conceptual framework to expand the analysis of possible reasons for deference and further explains why different adjudicators may structure deference more or less categorically. The section introduces the concept of 'second-order reasons' and examines four accounts of authority based on different categories of second-order reason. It uses this analysis to explore why international adjudicators might defer to domestic decision-making authority when deciding international private property claims. Section 1.2 examines how theories of authority impact the 'degrees' of deference. Some theoretical accounts conceptualise authority as conclusive or suspensive, and thus their application in adjudicative reasoning might prompt categorical approaches to deference (defer/not defer). Other approaches to conceptualising authority, by contrast, accommodate more flexible analysis (more/less deference). Section 1.2 examines these structural approaches to authority, and their impact on deference in turn, and also distinguishes deference from related concepts. This conceptual framework informs the empirical analysis of deference in Part II. That part examines the varying approaches taken by international adjudicators to these conceptual features of deference.

1.1 TOWARDS A CONCEPT OF DEFERENCE: LINKING DEFERENCE AND AUTHORITY

Deference is a multifaceted concept with 'a somewhat chameleonic character'.[1] Diverse analytical techniques have been grouped at various times (and to

[1] Elliott (2015a).

differing extents) under the rubric of 'deference'.[2] The different definitions of 'deference' in existing literature reflect that much existing scholarship has focused on specific manifestations of deference. This has caused some scholars to lament that 'the imprecise way in which [the term 'deference'] is often used has begun to rob it of utility'.[3] Studies of international adjudicative deference have nevertheless coalesced around analysing, critiquing, or endorsing particular doctrinal approaches to deference. Scholars studying the approaches of the ECtHR, for example, focus on the 'margin of appreciation' ('MoA'),[4] and scholars examining investment treaty arbitration focus predominantly on 'standards of review' analysis.[5] These accounts are pragmatic and partial. They focus on *conceptions* of deference, rather than the concept of deference itself.[6]

Compared to these 'conceptions' of deference, a 'concept' of deference provides a 'meta-definition' capable of encompassing 'as many of the different *conceptions*' of deference as possible.[7] This section advances one such conceptual approach to defining deference, arguing that deference equates to a recognition of another actor's decision-making authority. In cases brought before international adjudicators, there will be a range of issues for the adjudicator to decide. 'Deference' refers to the techniques used by adjudicators to recognise domestic decision-making authority to decide, or to play a role in deciding, what the conclusion to any of these issues might be.[8] 'Deference' thus refers to techniques used by international adjudicators to recognise a domestic actor's superior 'authority' to decide issues relevant to the settlement of the dispute brought before the international adjudicator.[9] Subsection 1.1.1 introduces the notion of 'authority' and examines how it is linked to deference. Subsections 1.1.2 to 1.1.4 introduce different accounts of authority. Each such account supplies a different basis on which one actor might recognise, and thus defer to, another actor's authority.

2 See, for differing definitions of 'deference', Cheyne (2014), p. 38; Henckels (2014), p. 113; Greener (2002), p. 737; Candia (2014), p. 5; Gerards (2011), p. 87; Contreras (2012); O'Donnell (1982), p. 475; Young (2010), p. 737; Clayton (2006); Anthony (1998); de Ville (2006); Pappas (2008); Harowitz (2008).

3 Elliott (2015b), p. 79.

4 See, especially, Legg (2012); O'Donnell (1982).

5 See, especially, Henckels (2015); Gruszczynski and Werner (2014); Vadi (2018).

6 On the distinction between 'concepts' and 'conceptions' see, further, Gallie (1956), p. 169; Harowitz (2008), p. 1072; Calvert and Hayes (2012), pp. 18–19; Alexander and Schauer (1997), p. 1363.

7 Thomas (2013), p. 6; Beck (2007), p. 633.

8 Henckels (2014), p. 115; Greer (2010), p. 6; Clayton (2004), p. 38; Ostrovsky (2005), p. 48.

9 See, similarly, Elliott (2013).

1.1.1 *Deference and the Concept of Authority*

Theories of authority explain why a person should follow the decisions of another in circumstances in which they are not coerced or persuaded to do so. Coercion causes an actor to submit to the decisions of another due to fear of the consequences of not doing so.[10] This distinguishes coercion from authority: whereas coercion prompts obedience, authority prompts *deference*.[11] Authority provides a *justification* for acting in a certain way and so will prompt *principled* and *voluntary* obedience to the decisions of another.[12] Pocock illustrates this vividly, observing that '[a] slave or a serf is flogged into obedience, not deference'.[13] Authority also differs from persuasion. Whereas persuasion prompts an actor to accede to the views of another because they independently agree that they are correct,[14] authority elicits deference to another's views 'even in the absence of substantive agreement'.[15] A very well-behaved child might, for example, disagree with its parent that it should go to bed at 7pm, but might nonetheless comply with that direction out of deference to its parent's authority. 'Authority', as thus understood, describes 'the ability of one actor to use institutional and discursive resources to induce deference from others'.[16] An actor may thus recognise another actor's authority by 'deferring' to that actor, thereby permitting the actor to exercise its authority to make decisions free in whole or part from the influence or control of another actor. 'Deference' thus refers to a response to a recognised claim to authority.

This distinction between persuasion and authority is important in adjudication. Differing from persuasion, authority prompts deference to another actor on the basis of 'second-' rather than 'first-' order reasons.[17] First-order reasons are reasons related to the merits of deciding (or not deciding) in a particular way.[18] For the child, a relevant first-order reason for going to bed at 7pm might be that they have to wake up at 4am to catch the train to school. Recognising this, the child might be *persuaded* that the appropriate course of action would be to go to bed early so as to avoid being tired in the morning. Similarly, the

10 Weber and Roth (1979), p. 53; Dick (1978), p. 376; Schauer (2004), p. 1567; Hart (1994), p. 20; Harowitz (2008), p. 1076.

11 Arendt (2006), p. 93; Hurd (1999), pp. 380–3; Franck (2006b), p. 93; Bodansky (2007).

12 See, similarly, Bodansky (2007); Pocock (1976), p. 516.

13 Pocock (1976), p. 516.

14 See, especially, Arendt (2006), p. 93; Dick (1978), p. 377; Schauer (2004), p. 1571; Harowitz (2008), p. 1074; Young (2010), p. 818.

15 Venzke (2013a), p. 383.

16 Barnett and Finnemore (2004), p. 5. See, similarly, Raz (2009), p. 136; Westlund (2013), p. 457; Cunliffe and Reeve (1999), p. 461.

17 Legg (2012), p. 37.

18 Ibid, p. 21; Raz (1999), p. 41.

fact that the child prefers to travel by train rather than the 8am bus might provide a first-order reason for the child to go to bed early in order to catch the train on time. For international adjudication, such 'first-order' reasons might include, for example, assessment of 'a dispute's impact on the individual's concerns, the facts of the dispute, and the particular justifications for the respondent state's approach'.[19] An adjudicator thus does not exhibit 'deference' merely by recording a finding that corresponds to a litigant State's 'decision' that its actions were consistent with international law.[20] Such an adjudicator may merely have been persuaded by its own appraisal of the first-order reasons for decision (the facts of the dispute) that the State is correct in its view that it has not breached international law.[21]

The adjudicator in such circumstances exhibits deference only if it allows its appraisal of these first-order reasons (the facts) to be influenced by 'second-order reasons'. Second-order reasons are 'reasons to act or to refrain from acting on one's own assessment of the first-order balance of reasons'.[22] They operate as 'content-independent' reasons to reach a particular decision, having 'nothing to do with the substance or merits of the mandated action'.[23] A child might, for example, defer to their parent's request to go to bed at 7pm (second-order reasons), even if their appraisal of first-order reasons might justify a different conclusion (for example, because they want to watch a television show that begins at 8pm, hate catching the train to school or feel like staying at home tomorrow instead). Although these first-order reasons might provide the child a reason to stay up late, the parent's request to the child generates second-order reasons that take priority and exclude action on the basis of these first-order reasons for decision. Similarly, an adjudicator might recognise a State's greater expertise in assessing whether its conduct was in some way justified by, for example, a public purpose. The adjudicator exhibits deference by referring to this second-order reason (expertise) in appraising the first-order reasons for decision (the facts, including justifications for the State's conduct).[24] In such circumstances, an adjudicator would decide a case not because another actor's decisions are perceived to be *correct* (first-order reasons) but rather due to a perception

[19] Legg (2016), p. 253.

[20] Cf, especially, Gruszczynski and Vadi (2014), p. 168; Fukunaga (2012), p. 570.

[21] This explains why some scholars argue that there is no scope for deference in adjudication, because courts should operate on the basis of persuasion rather than deference: Allan (2006), p. 675.

[22] Legg (2012), p. 18. See, also, Raz (1999), p. 41.

[23] Dan-Cohen (1994), p. 27.

[24] The range of second-order reasons that may prompt deference in international adjudication are introduced in the subsections that follow.

that another actor has greater competence and is *more likely* to reach a correct decision than the adjudicator (second-order reasons).

This is not to suggest that a formal 'transfer' of authority between the domestic and international actor is taking place wherever an international adjudicator defers to a State's decision. States do transfer decision-making authority to international courts and tribunals when they consent to those institutions hearing claims against them. But adjudicators do not 'take away' additional State authority by declining to defer to them. The practice of deference is, instead, a less formal authority practice. Where an international adjudicator identifies a domestic decision that may be relevant to the case before it, it must thereafter decide whether it should rely on its own authority to decide the dispute or should instead defer to the authority of another actor in making that determination. Where the decisions of multiple actors overlap, deference assists those actors to manage their relative claims to authority and ultimately helps to determine whose authority is recognised (and to what extent). Deference therefore impacts not the *conferral* of authority, but rather its *recognition* by other actors.

Different theories of authority (and deference) differ not in analysing this structural quality of authority, but rather in identifying the second-order reasons that ought to prompt deference to authority in any given case. Different theories give different roles for deference by recourse to instrumental, prudential, or non-instrumental second-order reasons for action and belief. Existing literature on deference in international adjudication has focused on instrumental second-order reasons for deference,[25] in part because such accounts have largely not drawn on the broader conceptual relationship between authority and deference. The categories of second-order reason that prompt deference under different theories of authority are thus introduced and considered in more detail in turn in the following three subsections.

1.1.2 *Deference and Instrumental Second-Order Reasons*

There are two principal accounts of why an actor might be treated as an authority capable of prompting *instrumental* deference. These are the 'service' and 'leader' conceptions of authority. According to these accounts of authority, deference follows a recognition by one decision-maker that another actor has the best claim as between the two to either the competence (service account) or legitimacy (leader account) to decide certain questions.

[25] See, especially, Henckels (2015), pp. 34–43; Cheyne (2014), pp. 40–1; Gruszczynski and Vadi (2014), p. 166; Vadi (2018), pp. 195–201; Legg (2012), pp. 25–6, 145–74.

Competence and legitimacy supply instrumental second-order reasons for deference because they serve as a form of shortcut reasoning to improve decision-making in situations of empirical or normative uncertainty.[26] The idea is that where a matter is empirically unclear or normatively contested, an international adjudicator will increase its chances of making decisions that are 'substantively good' and/or 'normatively legitimate' by deferring to domestic actors with greater competence or legitimacy in respect of those matters.[27] The instrumental utility of recognising another actor's authority is appraised differently depending on the theory of authority adopted. Subsections 1.1.2.1 and 1.1.2.2 present the two instrumental accounts of authority. Under the 'service' conception introduced in Subsection 1.1.2.1, an actor's empirical epistemic authority (its expertise/competence) offers an instrumental second-order reason for deference. By contrast, under the 'leader' conception, introduced in Subsection 1.1.2.2, the actor's normative epistemic authority (its legitimacy) provides the reason for deference.

1.1.2.1 The 'Service' Conception of Authority: Deference to Empirical Epistemic Authority

Under a 'service' conception of authority, deference follows the recognition of another actor's superior competence. The relative competence of another actor may derive from their subject matter expertise or knowledge, their 'steadier, less biased will' or their lower processing costs (for example, better resources).[28] These features generate 'empirical epistemic authority' (competence). As Hershovitz explains, a service conception of authority posits that 'we will do better by following an authority than by working out what to do on our own'.[29] In deciding whether to hold a picnic, for example, a person might place trust in a meteorological report about weather patterns rather than looking skywards on the day of the event. Deference to the meteorological expert is justified because it offers the individual a better means of achieving their own pre-existing goals (a dry picnic) than would acting independently (trying to work out what the cloud patterns mean without expert assistance).

Deferring to actors with empirical epistemic authority (expertise/competence) *serves* others by making them more able to reach 'correct' decisions. As

26 Hershovitz (2003), p. 213.

27 Ibid, p. 216; Elliott (2013), p. 11; Harowitz (2008), p. 1085; Daly (2012), p. 73; Enoch (2014), pp. 234–5.

28 Raz (2009), pp. 136–7.

29 Hershovitz (2003), p. 206.

Young explains, where a decision-maker is better able or equipped to decide an issue, a failure by an adjudicator to defer to them would:

> [A]t worst, run the risk of replacing the correct answer . . . with [the adjudicator's] own incorrect assessment. At best, it would give rise to inefficiency, with the [adjudicator] replicating the reasoning of the [other decision-maker], reaching the same conclusion.[30]

Deference to empirical epistemic authority is particularly appropriate in situations of empirical uncertainty, including in relation to technical or scientific questions. Faced with such situations, an international adjudicator might defer to another decision-maker considered to be an 'expert' on those subjects to enhance their chances of obtaining a 'correct' answer.[31]

Under a 'service' conception of authority, then, deference arises because one decision-maker perceives that: (i) a range of answers could be given to a particular question; (ii) some of those answers are likely to be more correct (better) than others; and (iii) another decision-maker is in some way better placed to identify correct answers.[32] The service conception of authority means that, all other things being equal,[33] '[t]he less-well-equipped the court is [to make the decision], the greater the degree of deference; the better

[30] Young (2009), pp. 563.

[31] See, for example, Harowitz (2008), pp. 1065–6; Henckels (2014), p. 123; Young (2009), pp. 565–6; Van Harten (2013), pp. 80–1; Allison (1994), p. 370; Rivers (2006), p. 200; Fahner (2016), p. 62; Puthuppally (2014), p. 93.

[32] Bodansky (1999), p. 620. Those denying a role for deference typically proceed from a different perspective, positing there to be one 'right' answer to the issues in dispute, with deference undermining the court's ability to provide this right answer. See, especially, Allan (2006), p. 678; Green (2010), p. 86; Letsas (2007); Benvenisti (1999), p. 844. Dworkin's 'right answer' thesis, for example, may prompt such a view. According to his theory of law as integrity, there will be only one tenable interpretation of the law, its being the role of the court/tribunal to provide that interpretation: Dworkin (1986), pp. 255–6. Cf, however, Allars (1994) (arguing that Dworkin's theory was developed by reference to private law cases and does not reflect the approach of administrative tribunals to issues of deference in domestic public law cases: pp. 199–200). This view links also to rejections of deference on the basis that it results in moral relativism: van der Vyver (1998), p. 46. As Legg explains, however, such a view 'relies on an overly narrow understanding of universality', which requires tribunals to 'interpret and substantiate a single, uniform meaning of the human rights at issue': Legg (2012), pp. 39–40. There can be universal values without those values manifesting in the same way in all contexts: Walker (2013); Donoho (2001). Deference can be consistent with this latter understanding of universalism, insofar as it maintains consistency at the level of value but permits differences at the point of application: Legg (2012), pp. 44, 58.

[33] Particular subjects may hold higher stakes and therefore prompt greater deference, given that '*wrong* answers can be especially hazardous in particular cases': Harowitz (2008), p. 1092. See, similarly, Galligan (1986), p. 368.

equipped, the less the deference.'[34] In effect, and as Soper explains, this is 'no different from relying on a calculator or computer; deference is justified in exactly the way that one justifies using any tool as the best means of achieving one's predetermined ends'.[35]

An actor's empirical epistemic authority might be assessed from one of two perspectives. They might be considered to be an expert because they *personally* have the skills or expertise to make a particular decision. This approach to assessing competence would require that personal expertise be proved for each decision-maker in each case before deference will follow.[36] While theoretically such an analysis of relative competence would yield conceptually stronger analyses of deference, it may not always be practicable. This is especially so for adjudicative analyses of deference, in which the theory of authority must be mediated against what analysis is possible for judges in practice. As Makela notes, for example, such an approach could mean that deference would 'fall and rise' as an ever-changing comparison between the specific competencies of individual adjudicators and individual decision-makers.[37] It would also raise issues of resourcing as well as more fundamental questions of propriety: are adjudicators equipped to make such fine-grained analyses of individual expertise and, even if they are, should they? These practicalities mean that, in most legal systems, adjudicators establish the empirical epistemic authority of other actors by reference to presumptions, usually referring to the other actor's institutional structure. Domestic institutions, for example, divide roughly between 'administrative', 'executive', 'legislative', and 'judicial' structures. Each institutional type is comparatively stronger at making particular types of decision than others. In an ideal system, these institutions would 'dovetail' with one another to leverage their respective strengths and minimise their respective weaknesses.[38] Deference provides a means by which the strengths and weaknesses inherent in institutional design can be appraised and accommodated on a case-by-case basis.

Superior empirical epistemic authority (expertise/competence) may derive from an institution's structural and procedural features. The adversarial structure of adjudication or the limited investigative powers of a court might, for instance, hamper its capacity to locate and review relevant sources of information. Courts also have restrictive rules of evidence and procedure, which may

[34] Dyson (2006), p. 108.
[35] Soper (2002), pp. 35–6.
[36] Vaughan (2013), p. 419; Allan (2006), p. 692; Krotoszynski Jr (2002), p. 737; Hershovitz (2003), p. 207.
[37] Makela (2013), p. 352.
[38] Hart Jr and Sacks (1994), p. 158.

'have the effect of limiting both the range of claims and the type of information which the courts receive'.[39] Rules on standing and access before courts might further limit the range of individuals who can provide input into a judicial decision. Legislatures and administrators might, by contrast, have access to a wider range of views that will allow them to reach empirically better decisions. An adjudicator might also operate under contracted timeframes within which to appraise the information to which it does have access.[40]

These procedural qualities of adjudication may mean that certain questions will be more suited to settlement through other institutional structures. The bilateral and adversarial decision-making procedures of courts, for example, may make them 'ill equipped to examine or to address polycentric or policy questions which necessarily involve the weighing of multiple interests'.[41] Legislatures and administrators might, by contrast, have access to a wider range of views that will allow them to reach empirically better decisions.[42] The reactive procedures of courts, too, may make them ill adapted to address issues that require 'analysis, action, review, and possibly readjustment'.[43] Legislatures, by contrast, may be better able to review the societal impacts of particular decisions or appraise their necessity.[44] Domestic administrative bodies (and often legislatures as well) may also be better able than courts to continually monitor a situation, gather evidence about it or seek information from more diverse stakeholders.[45] Legislatures and administrators might, for instance, be better able than courts to solicit expert opinions to guide complex decision-making choices. They might also generate greater expertise by dealing repeatedly with similar subject matters, as opposed to the more generalised jurisdiction of courts.[46] The service conception would privilege decision-making through those structures that have the greatest likelihood of producing a correct decision.

Different institutions also employ different reasoning processes. This may mean that some institutions are institutionally better adapted than others to deal with particular types of subject. Habermas, for example, suggests that the separation of powers between various institutional types reflects a 'distribution of the possibilities for access to different sorts of reasons'.[47] Whereas

39 Carolan (2009), p. 153.

40 Shany (2005), p. 918; Jowell (2003), p. 73; Raine (2013), p. 102.

41 Carolan (2009), p. 154. See, similarly, Harris (2003), p. 641

42 Galligan (1986), pp. 243–4.

43 Carolan (2009), p. 155.

44 Parker (2013), p. 1331.

45 Fredman (2006), p. 56; Carolan (2009), p. 144.

46 Galligan (1986), p. 249.

47 Habermas (2015), p. 192.

a legislature may be able to reason using normative, pragmatic, or empirical reasons, the judiciary is largely confined to legal discourse.[48] A legislature might therefore have greater empirical epistemic authority than the judiciary to provide answers to questions best determined through political, normative, or moral debate. Equally, different institutions have differing levels of access to, and capacity to appraise, sensitive or scientific information. Such features make some institutions better adapted to make particular decisions than others. Administrative or legislative decision-makers might be better able than adjudicators, for example, to make scientific determinations, national security assessments, or health or economic policy decisions.[49]

Proximity may also impact empirical epistemic authority. International adjudicators may be less 'acquainted with local issues, sensitivities and traditions' than domestic decision-makers.[50] They may be hampered in evaluating local circumstances, including because they are less proximate to relevant data or evidence that domestic decision-makers may be in a comparatively better position to collect and analyse.[51] This may be compounded by resourcing constraints, which may prompt international adjudicators to defer fact-heavy assessments to comparatively better-resourced domestic decision-makers.[52] Cultural distance may also make international adjudicators less adept at interpreting and applying domestic law than domestic institutions.[53] Conversely, systemic position means international adjudicators typically have greater institutional expertise in interpreting and applying international law.[54] They may also hold greater empirical epistemic authority in relation to questions requiring decision from a steadier or less biased vantage point.[55] That is, their lack of proximity may insulate them from the political context of a dispute and associated 'volitional defects' stemming from cultural prejudice or pressure from proximity.[56] Adjudicators, also, will typically have 'a greater institutional capacity for

48 Ibid, p. 192. See, also, Dworkin (1977).
49 Daly (2012), pp. 91–4; Legg (2012), p. 153; Puthuppally (2014), p. 88.
50 Henckels (2013), p. 205. See, also, McGoldrick (2016), p. 35; Shany (2005), p. 918; Nollkaemper (2011), p. 29. As Chapter 2 explains, however, this depends on the identity and experience of adjudicators.
51 Kanetake (2016a), p. 21; Henckels (2014), p. 123; Gross and Ni Aolain (2001), p. 638.
52 Shany (2005), p. 918; Chen (2012), p. 29; Henckels (2013); Gruszczynski and Werner (2014), p. 2; Helfer (2008), p. 128.
53 Schill (2012), p. 24; Katselas (2012), p. 142; Oesch (2003), pp. 642–3; Nollkaemper (2013a), p. 543.
54 Legg (2012), p. 167; Daly (2012), p. 242; Young (2005), p. 160.
55 Føllesdal (2013a), p. 295; Henckels (2013).
56 Tasioulas (2010), p. 101.

independence, impartiality, and procedural rigour' than other institutions.[57] This may make them better-adapted to make decisions necessitating decision-making from an impartial or unbiased perspective.

Institutional features and placement thus mean that some institutions are better adapted to make particular decisions than others. Deferring to such institutions in situations of uncertainty allows adjudicators to benefit from such expertise. Such deference reflects a view that one institution's decisions on a given matter are *more likely*, all things considered, to be correct than the adjudicator's decision on that matter. Thus, even where another decision-maker might be an expert, an adjudicator under the 'service' conception of authority would be justified in declining to offer them deference where the adjudicator is a *better* expert or where there is no evidence that the decision has drawn on the other actor's relevant expertise.

Some scholars argue that the empirical epistemic authority deficiencies of international adjudicators should be addressed not through deference to other actors but by structural alterations to international adjudicative mechanisms.[58] This could include, for example, greater use of expert evidence or third-party submissions and appointment of national judges or judges with specific technical skills.[59] Redressing all empirical epistemic authority imbalances would, however, collapse institutional types, risking a loss also of the comparative strengths of different institutions for different tasks.[60] Such redress might be more possible (and appropriate) in certain regimes. A potential advantage of submitting a dispute to an international investment tribunal, a Chamber of the ICJ, or a court on which the State can appoint an ad hoc judge is, for example, some capacity to control the expertise of adjudicators relative to the issues in dispute. It is likely not possible to use such appointment procedures to overcome *all* empirical epistemic authority deficits, particularly those that stem from the adjudicative – rather than administrative or legislative – structure of such bodies. Such debates nevertheless indicate that the role to be played by empirical epistemic authority in the analysis of deference will differ in each legal system depending on the structural and procedural features of the adjudicator, their perception of their own expertise vis-à-vis other actors and the way in which they appraise the roles of different institutional types. This is developed further in Part II.

57 Carolan (2009), p. 155.
58 Young (2010), p. 822; Higgins (1968), p. 82.
59 Fahner (2013), p. 489; Føllesdal (2013a); Puthuppally (2014), p. 84; Franck (2006a), p. 504.
60 Daly (2012), p. 118; Pratt (2018), p. 562.

1.1.2.2 The 'Leader' Conception of Authority: Deference to Normative Epistemic Authority

A 'leader' conception of authority is based on a view that some issues have no 'right' answer. There may be no 'expert' capable of settling a matter that is deeply controversial or empirically unsolvable.[61] For such matters, the service conception of authority does not explain why one person should defer to the judgments of another. Yet, some actor must be given the power to settle these issues because 'walking away and waiting for agreement are both impossible or impractical'.[62] Where unanimity is impossible, authority supplies a means of coordinating action.[63] The leader conception recognises that, even if people do not agree on the answers, they may nonetheless agree on a process to settle these questions.[64] That is, an actor might be given authority to *lead* others by being given a 'right to decide' these issues.[65] As Hershovitz illustrates:

> Considerations of safety and efficiency demand that people drive on the same side of the road, but it does not matter much if it is the left or the right. An entity that has the ability to enforce a solution may be a legitimate authority regarding which side of the road people drive on, despite its lack of expertise or any claim to better judgment.[66]

Some actors may thus hold 'normative', rather than 'empirical', epistemic authority. Whereas deference to empirical epistemic authority (expertise/competence) follows from an adjudicator deciding that it *cannot* determine a question as well as another actor, deference to normative epistemic authority (legitimacy) is based on an assessment that the adjudicator *should not* determine it. Empirical epistemic authority is authority 'about facts, about what is the case'.[67] An actor with empirical epistemic authority is *an authority* about a matter.[68] Normative epistemic authority, by contrast, is authority 'about action, about what one ought to do'.[69] The actor deferred to is *in authority*.[70] Normative epistemic authority gives people 'reasons for action' and empirical epistemic authority provides 'reasons for belief'.[71]

[61] Soper (2002), pp. 48–9.
[62] Ibid, pp. xi–xii.
[63] Finnis (2011), p. 232.
[64] Wittgenstein (2010), para. 241.
[65] Soper (2002), pp. 43–5. See, also: Dick (1978), p. 376; Bodansky (2012).
[66] Hershovitz (2003), pp. 207–8.
[67] Soper (2002), p. 35; Raz (2009), pp. 154–5.
[68] Dick (1978), p. 377.
[69] Soper (2002), p. 35; Raz (2009), pp. 154–5.
[70] Dick (1978), p. 377.
[71] Raz (2009), pp. 142, 154–5.

The distinction between empirical and normative epistemic authority explains why authority cannot in all cases be equated with legitimacy. Under a 'service' conception, a non-legitimate actor may exercise authority due to its expertise or competence. However, if *legitimate* authority is valued, as it is in a 'leader' conception, then it may not be sufficient for an actor merely to be competent to settle a given question. Instead, it may need to meet additional procedural or substantive standards for its decisions to be treated as legitimate and therefore authoritative. The leader conception thus equates 'authority' with 'legitimacy'.[72] Theories of legitimacy therefore offer a means of identifying bases for deference under a leader account of authority. The following paragraphs examine the relationship between deference in a leader account of authority and three dominant theories of legitimacy: source-based, procedural and substantive legitimacy.

1.1.2.2.1 SOURCE-BASED LEGITIMACY Accounts of legitimacy that are source-based treat those actors that have a 'right to rule' as legitimate authorities.[73] The origin of such a right can differ. It may derive from a religious theory, from tradition, or from the consent of those subject to it.[74] State consent is, for example, considered to be a necessary, but not always sufficient, basis for the legitimacy of international organisations or adjudicators.[75] Similarly, within a domestic system legitimate authority might stem from a constitution, such that certain institutions may generate deference from other actors in recognition of their constitutional or legislative mandate.[76] An international adjudicator might thus defer to a domestic actor because it recognises that actor's right to rule due to its source-based legitimate authority. It might emphasise, for example, that a particular decision warrants deference because it emanates from a 'sovereign State' or from an actor that has been accorded constitutional powers to make particular decisions.

1.1.2.2.2 PROCEDURAL LEGITIMACY A procedural account of legitimacy would accord authority by reference to the qualities of the decision-maker or its decision-making process. Decisions might be legitimate if made by

72 Weber (1947). See, further, Hurd (1999), p. 400; Wheatley (2011), p. 533; Caporaso (2000), p. 6.
73 Thomas (2014), p. 735; Tyler (2006), p. 376; Buchanan and Keohane (2006), p. 405; Shany (2016); Hurd (1999), p. 381.
74 d'Aspremont and de Brabandere (2011), p. 190; Bodansky (1999), pp. 605, 612; Wolfrum (2008), p. 6.
75 Hathaway (2008), p. 23; Besson (2009), p. 371; Bodansky (2012); Peters and Schaffer (2013), p. 324.
76 van Coller (2006), pp. 469–70; de Ville (2004), p. 589; Young (2009), p. 554; Sumption (2011), p. 313.

a decision-maker with due process, fairly, consistently, or through a procedure allowing for participation, accountability or the giving of reasons.[77] Such decisions may be considered legitimate because they 'come into being in accordance with the right process'.[78] Democratic decision-making processes may, for instance, offer a source of legitimate authority. Democratic processes recognise equal decision-making authority for those enjoying franchise and so might be considered particularly legitimate processes for making decisions about questions with no empirically 'correct' answer.[79] This is because they respect the equal claim of all citizens to the empirical epistemic authority (expertise/competence) to decide empirically unsolvable questions.[80]

Legal theory has long grappled with how procedural, particularly democratic, legitimacy should inform comparative assessments of authority for judicial as compared to other actors.[81] Waldron, for example, argues that adjudication 'disenfranchises ordinary citizens' because it privileges decision-making by 'unelected and unaccountable judges'.[82] This leads Waldron to reject strong-form judicial review, endorsing adjudicative deference to more democratic decision-makers.[83] Democratic theory can also, however, highlight situations in which democratic authority may be insufficient to justify deference.[84] Democratic decision-making might, for example, impact those outside the democratic process by regulating boundary-crossing or extraterritorial conduct or foreigners' rights.[85] Similarly, a decision might discriminate against a minority group that has not been adequately represented in a democratic process.[86] Ultimately, analysis of the comparative democratic strengths of adjudicative decision-making as compared to decision-making through other institutional types depends on the decision at stake and the concept of democracy adopted.[87] Waldron's view relies, for example, on an understanding of democracy valuing deliberation through

77 Franck (1988), p. 706; Hurd (1999), pp. 67–73; Shany (2016); Wolfrum (2008), p. 6; Daly (2012), p. 114; Bodansky (2012); Thomas (2014), p. 739; Dyzenhaus (1998), p. 35.

78 Franck (1988), p. 706

79 Hershovitz (2003), p. 214; Daly (2012), pp. 114–15; Tremblay (2005), pp. 632–3; Bodansky (1999), p. 621.

80 Davis (1996), p. 126. See, also: Dyson (2006), p. 103; Young (2010), p. 825; Benhabib (2009), p. 693.

81 See, especially, Waldron (1993). For consideration of this debate vis-à-vis international courts, see, von Staden (2012).

82 Waldron (2006), p. 1353.

83 Waldron (2013), p. 167.

84 See, especially, Ely (1980).

85 Fahner (2013), pp. 486–7; Franck (1990), p. 455; Schill (2012), p. 23; Shany (2005), p. 920.

86 Ely (1980); Legg (2012), pp. 72–3; Benvenisti (1999), pp. 72–3.

87 See, further, Cotula (2017); Lazarus and Simonsen (2015).

majority rule. Heightened scrutiny of decisions affecting minorities or political outsiders similarly interprets democratic legitimacy as requiring that individuals have the opportunity to participate in decision-making processes impacting them: where they do not, the legitimacy of the procedure may dissipate, rendering deference to decisions emanating from that procedure less justifiable.[88] Other theorists, by contrast, characterise judicial institutions as a component of a democratic 'dialogue' between the various arms of government.[89] Under these accounts, the reasons for an adjudicator to defer to another arm of government on procedural legitimacy grounds may be less compelling for certain types of decisions.

A question left open in the preceding discussion is the extent to which deference to democratic authority is appropriate at the international level. Under Waldron's account, deference might be especially valued in the context of international adjudication: international courts have been routinely criticised as undemocratic due to geographical and cultural distance from the populations their decisions impact.[90] Such distance makes international courts even less subject to democratic control than domestic courts. Some scholars, however, reject *any* role for deference to democratic authority in international adjudication. They argue it privileges particular political values in an avowedly liberal, and ideologically neutral, international legal order.[91] The strength of such arguments depends on the particular international regime at issue. The European Convention on Human Rights ('ECHR'), for example, expressly privileges democratic values.[92] Other international regimes operate with less express objectives, or in respect of less democratic States. It might therefore be expected that the ECtHR would be more likely than other international courts to treat democratic decision-making as authoritative. Even if a regime privileges democracy, however, international adjudicative appraisal of the democratic credentials of individual domestic actors might nevertheless be problematic, including because international adjudication is considered either ill-equipped or not an appropriate forum for such assessments.[93]

88 Cotula (2015), p. 131.

89 Fredman (2006), pp. 53–4; Dworkin (1996), p. 7; Young (2017).

90 Crawford and Brownlie (2012), p. 669; Føllesdal (2013a), p. 287; Bellamy (2014), p. 1020.

91 Pirker (2014), p. 66; Roberts (2011), p. 178; Shany (2005), p. 920.

92 The Convention refers to democracy in the preamble, in Articles 9–11, and in Articles 2(3) and 4 of Protocol 4. Applicant States must also meet democratic criteria to be admitted to the Council of Europe: European Convention on Human Rights and Fundamental Freedoms (1950/1953) ETS 5; Protocol 4 to the European Convention for the Protection of Human Rights and Fundamental Freedoms (1963/1968) ETS 46.

93 Raine (2013), p. 105; Gerards (2011), p. 118; Schill (2012), p. 24; Daly (2012), pp. 133–4.

1.1.2.2.3 SUBSTANTIVE LEGITIMACY Finally, legitimate authority might derive from a more substantive vision of legitimacy. Substantive theories of legitimacy look beyond legal pedigree and process to consider instead the normative features of decisions.[94] Using this account of authority, a deferring actor comes closer to engaging with first-order reasons for decision than it might under other accounts of authority. The deferring actor, nevertheless, does not engage in its own assessment of the merits of a given decision: it instead defers to another actor's decision, provided that it has confidence that the actor (or its decision) has complied with particular substantive criteria in exercising its authority. This might include, for example, an assessment of whether the decision solves a particular problem or otherwise reflects values such as equality, fairness, justice, reasonableness, or respect for human rights.[95] Accounts privileging substantive legitimacy operate at the intersection of the leader and service conceptions of authority. Plato's vision of rule by experts recognises, for example, that those holding normative epistemic authority (legitimacy) may also be those with greater empirical epistemic authority (expertise/competence).[96] For Plato, expertise could therefore be a source of legitimacy. This connection between competence and legitimacy prompts Raz to reject the leader conception as a viable separate account. He argues instead that:

> If the primary point of authority . . . is to improve conformity with reason, it is implausible to think that someone who contributes not at all in that respect, someone who in fact makes us act more against reason than we would do had we not tried to follow him, can have legitimate authority.[97]

While the two instrumental accounts of authority have been examined separately so far, they may thus overlap or be contested in practice. Deference may be attributed to an entity because it is recognised to have *both* better expertise *and* legitimacy than the deferring decision-maker.[98] To generate deference, a decision-maker might thus need to demonstrate that it is both a more expert and legitimate than the adjudicator.[99] It might alternatively be necessary for a decision-maker to claim multiple types of legitimacy such that, for example, procedural *and* substantive criteria are used to assess its legitimate authority and thus the extent of deference due to its decisions.[100] This indicates that

94 See, further, Franck (1990), p. 17; Bodansky (2012); Land (2015); Grossman (2009), pp. 115–17; Thomas (2013), p. 751; Scharpf (2002), p. 11; Buchanan (2003).

95 Bodansky (1999), p. 612; Wolfrum (2008), p. 6; Thomas (2014), p. 751; Shany (2016); Franck (1990), p. 18; Buchanan and Keohane (2006); Scharpf (2002), p. 11.

96 Plato (2011) Book III: 410; Book IV: 473; Book VI: 484.

97 Raz (2009), p. 157.

98 See, further, Peter (2019).

99 Brown (2014), p. 67.

100 Christiano (2010), p. 121.

expertise and legitimacy may be assessed from several differing perspectives. The propensity of international adjudicators to distinguish these bases for instrumental deference is examined in more detail in Part II.

1.1.3 *Deference and Prudential Second-Order Reasons*

Deference may also operate based on prudential second-order reasons, including prudential reasons related to an adjudicator's own interests. An adjudicator may defer to a State, for example, because deference offers it a means to secure power or personal advantage. Deference in international adjudication may follow from a prudential assessment that acknowledging State decision-making authority will lead to stability or enhanced legitimacy for the international adjudicator or the regime in which it operates.[101] Deference may thus be used by international adjudicators as a tool of legitimation to build, maintain or defend their legitimacy.[102] The linkage between legitimacy, authority and deference, along with the possibility that deference may be invoked strategically, explains why deference has been so central in debates about the legitimacy of international regimes. Indeed, the claim is often made that more deferential approaches could address the 'legitimacy crisis' faced by international adjudicators.[103]

The scope for deference to be used strategically by international adjudicators has been frequently suggested but under-analysed in the literature.[104] Strategic uses of deference have, however, been the subject of detailed studies of interpersonal and professional communications. These studies indicate that 'deference behaviors affect how others perceive a communicator', such that deference may operate as a form of social influence.[105] As Colwell observes, as a relational tool: 'Acts of deference communicate one person's yielding of their own will, ideas, or interests to those of another, and by doing so, highlight the power and prestige differences between them.'[106] Deference may thus operate as a symbol

[101] See, similarly, Bickel (1962).

[102] See, generally, on judicial legitimation strategies, Madsen (2015); Hurrelmann et al. (2005), pp. 121–2. On the importance of legitimacy (and allegations of illegitimacy) in political discourse and its impact on regime efficiency see, especially, Caron (1993), pp. 557–61; Ashforth and Gibbs (1990).

[103] See, further, Henckels (2014), p. 114; Petersmann (2014); Vadi and Gruszczynski (2013), p. 622; Leonhardsen (2014), pp. 136–9; Paine (2015); Atik (2003); Ghouri (2014), p. 3.

[104] See, for example, Kratochvil (2011), p. 335; Gerards (2011), p. 106; Candia (2014), p. 9; Henckels (2014), p. 115; Arai-Takahashi (2002), p. 232. See, however, in a domestic context, Bickel (1962).

[105] Fragale et al. (2012), p. 374.

[106] Colwell (2007), p. 443.

of 'appeasement',[107] conveying 'acceptance of one's position in the hierarchy and assur[ing] others that there is no intent to mount a challenge to the order'.[108] Empirical studies of peer-to-peer interactions confirm this function, indicating that deference 'is most frequently displayed by those individuals most concerned with preserving their status and rank'.[109]

Deference might therefore be used strategically by international adjudicators to avoid contestation or backlash from States. International adjudicators derive their competence from State consent and also typically rely on voluntary compliance by States with their rulings.[110] Adjudicators seeking to solidify their position may deploy the language of deference to 'soften' their decisions and to protect themselves from criticisms of 'judicial activism'.[111] Madsen, for example, argues that an international adjudicator might defer more readily to those States responsible for originating political backlash against the regime in which the international adjudicator is situated.[112] A new adjudicator or an adjudicator whose decisions are subject to particular scrutiny may also afford States greater deference so that they can 'fly under the radar' long enough to cement their own authority.[113] The more secure an international adjudicator perceives their authority to be, the more 'emboldened' they may feel in eschewing the language of deference while reviewing State decision-making.[114] The increased scope and impact of international adjudication is particularly likely to influence prudential assessments of the utility of deference. As their rulings affect more subjects and subject matters, international adjudicators may come to need legitimacy in respect of additional constituencies or topics.[115]

107 Fragale et al. (2012), p. 374.

108 Ibid, p. 374. These studies typically focus on verbal markers of deference, which are less apposite in the context of adjudication. Based on verbal markers, however, some studies have suggested that courts like the PCIJ and ICJ have a deferential 'style'. See, for example, Prott (1970), pp. 75–7, 83–5; Hyde (1930), pp. 1, 18; Nafziger (1984), p. 330; Tryon (1912), p. 207. On judicial 'style' see, further, Cardozo (1947), pp. 342–52.

109 Fragale et al. (2012), p. 373.

110 See, further, Lauterpacht (1991), p. 23; Guillaume (1995), p. 850; Müller and Schneider (2007), p. 104; Caron (2007a), p. 410.

111 Arai-Takahashi (2002), p. 232. See, also: Leonhardsen (2014), p. 138; Guzman (2008), pp. 188–9; Bickel (1962), pp. 111–99; El Boudouhi (2015), p. 21; Broude (2016). This links to the point raised in the Introduction and developed in the following chapters: an international adjudicator can accord deference to a State without necessarily finding in favour of the State in respect of the claim as a whole.

112 Madsen (2016).

113 Pauwelyn and Elsig (2012).

114 Ratner (2008), p. 488.

115 See, especially, Thomas (2013), p. 21; Clark (2007); Bodansky (2012); Buchanan and Keohane (2006); Caron and Shirlow (2018).

Another factor affecting deference on prudential grounds is an international adjudicator's level of independence. The independence of international adjudicators is often conceptualised along a spectrum differentiating between adjudicators that operate as 'agents' and those that act as 'trustees'.[116] An 'agent' exercises 'delegated authority on behalf of their principals in pursuit of goals that the principal has defined'.[117] 'Agent' adjudicators are subject to greater controls than 'trustee' adjudicators, there being greater scope for State oversight and override of their decisions.[118] 'Agent' adjudicators might thus use deference prudentially to avoid State challenges to their activities. Trustee adjudicators, by contrast, have more 'open-ended' powers than agents.[119] They enjoy greater independence from their creators, acting as 'trustees of the values that inhere in the treaties that constituted them'.[120] It has been suggested that the ECtHR is a trustee court, whereas investment treaty tribunals operate in a manner more akin to agents.[121] Adjudicators may, however, move across this spectrum in discharging their functions.[122] Adjudicators initially operating as 'agents' might also develop interests over time diverging from those of the principal, making them more akin to a 'trustee'.[123] This indicates that assessments of whether deference is prudentially valuable are likely to differ over time and by regime.

1.1.4 *Deference and Non-Instrumental Second-Order Reasons*

Deference might also operate based on non-instrumental, 'moral', second-order reasons. Such deference does not arise because the deferring actor recognises that another decision-maker might make a *better* decision or because deference is prudentially useful to the deferring actor. It instead operates to express particular attitudes considered to be inherently good, such as attitudes of empathy, respect, trust, gratitude, or identification with a 'community'.[124] As Dan-Cohen illustrates:

[116] See, especially, Alter (2008a), p. 41. Independence could alternatively be analysed using 'constitutional', 'contractual', and 'judicial' models: Stone Sweet and Grisel (2017) or using distinctions between 'community-' and 'party-' originated bodies: Caron (2007a), pp. 403–4; Caron (1991), p. 66.

[117] Yackee (2012), p. 399. See, further, Alter (2008a), p. 40; Bradley and Kelley (2008).

[118] Stone Sweet and Brunell (2013), p. 65; Stone Sweet and Grisel (2014), p. 27; Alter (2008a), p. 34.

[119] Stone Sweet and Brunell (2013), p. 62.

[120] Ibid, p. 62. See, also, Alter (2008a), p. 40.

[121] Ulfstein (2013), p. 852; Kurtz (2013); Franck (2006a), pp. 46–7. Cf, Langford and Behn (2018), p. 559.

[122] Roberts (2013), p. 61; Voeten (2012), pp. 437–8.

[123] Stone Sweet and Grisel (2009), p. 120.

[124] Dan-Cohen (1994), p. 36. Certain approaches to comity may express such attitudes: Endicott (2015).

> Obedience to the law is a due expression of gratitude to the state ... Another prominent source of deference is identification. Obeying the law, for example, is said to be a way of identifying with one's society and expressing one's loyalty to it. Finally, the respect conveyed by deference can be a matter of trust: obedience conveys one's belief that the authority will not lead one astray.[125]

A leading philosophical account of this form of deference is offered by Soper, who argues that deference can signify self-respect, empathy, and respect for others and for community.[126] Thus, a person might defer to another if they can imagine that they would act similarly if placed in the same position as the person to whom they are deferring.[127]

The role of non-instrumental second-order reasons for deference has been largely neglected in scholarship analysing deference in international adjudication. This account of deference indicates, however, that there is likely to be increased deference between linked decision-makers operating under a sense of joint enterprise ('us' as compared to 'we'/'them').[128] Soper's account explains in particular why international adjudicators might defer to State decision-making in crisis scenarios or circumstances of practical constraint.[129] In assessing decisions adopted in such scenarios, adjudicators may exhibit deference by reviewing State measures by reference to what was known at the time of their adoption (*ex tunc*) as opposed to the time of the adjudicator's assessment (*ex nunc*).[130] As the international adjudicator is less constrained than the original decision-maker, such deference does not improve the chances of reaching a *better* decision.[131] It is therefore not based on instrumental second-order reasons. Instead, deference manifests a view that, *in the same circumstance*, the adjudicator would likely have reached similar decisions, it being unfair to judge the State's decisions with the benefit of hindsight or from a position removed from the constraints under which the State operated. Such non-instrumental deference reduces the 'otherness' between the deferor and the deferee, such that 'differences in perspective are reduced to differences in situation'.[132]

125 Dan-Cohen (1994), p. 36. See, also, Brownlee (2004), p. 271.
126 Soper (2002), pp. 157–8, 170, 181–2. Soper also recognises an instrumental function for deference, insofar as it promotes 'harmony' and the 'efficient allocation' of authority. See, also, Schauer (2004), p. 1573.
127 Soper (2002), p. 170.
128 Cf, Slaughter (2003), pp. 193–4, 218.
129 On deference in these situations see, further: Hoexter (2000), pp. 501–2; Lazarus and Simonsen (2015), p. 120; Greer (2000), p. 7; Hilson (2013), p. 265.
130 Brems and Lavrysen (2015), p. 152; Paine (2019), p. 16.
131 Cf, Henckels (2015), p. 140.
132 Berman (2013b), p. 672.

Non-instrumental deference might also reflect other attitudes. It might, for example, be based on second-order reasons of autonomy or subsidiarity. Deference might express the adjudicator's view that '[p]eople are better off . . . if they are able to organize their own affairs and develop and pursue their own conceptions of the good'.[133] It might otherwise reflect values of fairness. When an actor defers to democratic decisions they consider to be wrong, for example, they exhibit respect for the principle of fairness. Deciding for themselves in those circumstances would be equivalent to assuming 'a right to determine how things should go that overrides the equal rights of all the others'.[134] Deference to democratic decisions might thus stem not from instrumental second-order reasons, but instead be motivated by non-instrumental values. An adjudicator might otherwise defer to another actor to express respect or empathy, or to recognise the actor's liberty, right to self-determination, or autonomy.

1.2 DEGREES OF DEFERENCE: THE STRUCTURE OF SECOND-ORDER REASONS

The second-order reasons underlying authority can be exclusionary or non-exclusionary. This means that the structure of authority influences the degree of deference. This section explores this structural feature of authority. The distinction between 'exclusionary' and 'non-exclusionary' second-order reasons is illustrated in Subsection 1.2.1 by reference to the difference between 'ordering' and 'requesting'. Subsection 1.2.2 explores how the structure and content of an international obligation may impact this analysis. As noted earlier, legal obligations supply adjudicators with first-order reasons for decision and (once interpreted) delineate which first-order reasons may be considered relevant to applying a given obligation. As Subsection 1.2.2 explains, where an adjudicator has no jurisdictional competence to consider the first-order reasons for decision, the issue of deference does not arise. An adjudicator is therefore not – properly speaking – 'deferring' merely because they determine that they have no jurisdiction or because they interpret an international legal obligation in a 'State-friendly' way. The adjudicator 'defers' where they allow their appraisal of the first-order reasons for decision to be influenced by the categories of second-order reasons introduced earlier. Where an adjudicator does have jurisdiction to consider first-order reasons, those first-order reasons may cancel out, be balanced alongside or be displaced by second-order reasons prompting deference.

[133] Hershovitz (2003), p. 213–4.
[134] Christiano (2012).

1.2.1 *Deference as an Order or Request*

The impact of the structure of authority on deference can be elaborated by reference to the difference between 'orders' and 'requests'. Orders provide exclusionary reasons for action. They 'replace or cut off the hearer's independent assessment of the merits of the case' and 'replace or exclude their own deliberation over what to do'.[135] By contrast, requests offer non-exclusionary reasons for action: '[C]ountervailing reasons may outweigh the request.'[136] Similar to orders and requests, deference can be based on exclusionary or non-exclusionary (second-order) reasons for action or belief. Where it operates on the basis of exclusionary second-order reasons in a manner akin to an order, deference effectively delegates or entrusts decision-making authority to another actor. The second-order reasons for decision *cut off* the analysis of the first-order reasons for decision.[137] This gives the actor that is deferred to the exclusive capacity to consider the first-order reasons to reach a decision. That actor's decision would then *replace* or *preclude* the capacity of the adjudicator to consider for themselves the balance of first-order reasons.[138] Such deference prompts the adjudicator to disregard 'at least some reasons which are … relevant and would in the absence of the exclusionary reason have sufficed to justify proceeding in some other way'.[139] By contrast, where deference operates on the basis of non-exclusionary second-order reasons in a manner akin to a request, it does not preclude assessment of first-order reasons. Instead, second-order reasons are considered alongside, and may *outweigh*, applicable first-order reasons.[140] A legitimate authority's decision might, under this approach, become 'a very weighty or presumptive force, the strength of which varies according to the force of the underlying reasons that justify the authority's claim to legitimacy'.[141] In this case: '[O]ne's own judgment is not pre-empted, but only balanced against the reasons for deferring to the views of another.'[142]

Theorists differ in how they characterise the structure of the second-order reasons prompting deference. According to Soper, empirical epistemic authority is categorical (someone is either an expert or they are not), whereas normative epistemic authority is less binary (someone may hold more or less

135 Westlund (2013), p. 458. Cf, Hershovitz (2003), p. 204 (orders as 'weightier reasons').
136 Hershovitz (2003), p. 204.
137 Raz (1986), p. 42.
138 Soper (2002), pp. 35–6; Legg (2012), p. 25; Raz (2009), p. 142.
139 Finnis (2011), p. 234. See, also, Raz (1986), p. 46.
140 Soper (2002), pp. 35–6.
141 Grant (2017), p. 519.
142 Soper (2002), p. 45.

legitimacy). As such, for Soper, deference to empirical epistemic authority operates on the basis of exclusionary second-order reasons (akin to an order), but deference to normative epistemic authority prompts reasoning by reference to non-exclusionary second-order reasons (akin to a request).[143] Raz, by contrast, considers that authority operates akin to an order in both forms.[144] As Raz explains: 'Legitimate authorities provide pre-emptive reasons for action, in that the reasons they provide are not to be added to all other relevant reasons when assessing what to do, but should exclude and replace some of those other reasons.'[145] Raz illustrates this view of authority by reference to the doctrine of *res judicata*: the binding (and authoritative) judgment of a court shuts out any further consideration of the facts underlying the cause of action that gave rise to that judgment.[146]

Other scholars adopt less categorical approaches. Daly, for example, considers that someone *can* be more or less expert than others. For a doctor, for instance, 'the weight to be given to the views of the patient will vary' because each patient's expertise will differ.[147] For these scholars, the second-order reasons prompting deference are non-exclusionary. They are weighed *alongside* first-order reasons for a particular decision.[148] In such accounts, the structure of the second-order reasons underlying authority is 'less one of a command that demands blind obedience than a reference point that redistributes argumentative burdens'.[149] Such structures of authority prompt deference in degrees, akin to a request. Hickman, for example, argues that courts should give weight to a legislature's decision if it is on a matter on which the legislature has better expertise than the court.[150] However, as Young explains:

> '[T]his is not to say that the court should adopt the conclusion of the legislature. Instead, the court may require greater evidence that the legislation has failed to find the right balance. The greater weight almost acts like a presumption in favour of legality, which can be rebutted by strong evidence.'[151]

Perry describes such deference as following from 'weight-adjusting' second-order reasons.[152] In such cases, another actor's greater legitimacy or expertise

143 Ibid, pp. 35–6.
144 Raz (1979), pp. 22–5; Raz (2009), pp. 140, 155; Raz (1986), pp. 53–69.
145 Raz (1986), p. 46.
146 Ibid, p. 42.
147 Daly (2012), p. 199.
148 Legg (2012), p. 11.
149 Venzke (2013a), p. 398.
150 Hickman (2005).
151 Young (2017), p. 167.
152 Perry (1989).

for deciding a particular matter might be a factor that weighs in the balance of a court's assessment of the first-order reasons for deciding that matter.

Like these theorists, international adjudicators themselves adopt various approaches to structuring authority, which, in turn, influence their approaches to deference. Second-order reasons prompting deference may exclude *all*[153] or only *some*[154] of the relevant first-order reasons or may instead operate in a non-exclusionary way *alongside* first-order reasons.[155] This explains why deference prompts some international adjudicators to treat State decisions as conclusive or suspensive (akin to an order), whereas others treat them as only persuasive (akin to a request). Further, the different categories of second-order reason capable of prompting deference may be treated variously as exclusionary or non-exclusionary or even cut in opposite directions.[156] Different situations may thus require qualitatively different or weightier second-order reasons to justify deference.[157] How international adjudicators conceptualise authority and the impact of their conceptions of authority on their approaches to deference are considered in more detail in Part II.

1.2.2 *Distinguishing Deference from a Lack of Jurisdictional Competence to Decide a Matter*

Deference must be distinguished from a lack of jurisdictional competence to decide an issue (just as it must be distinguished from persuasion to decide an issue in a particular way). This causes some scholars to distinguish 'deference' from doctrines of jurisdiction and justiciability.[158] De Ville argues, for example, that: '[W]hen a court decides that a matter falls within the competence of the legislature or the executive, the court is not showing deference; it is deciding the law.'[159] De Ville's distinction between jurisdictional restraint and deference relies on a particular understanding of how justiciability and like doctrines operate. Justiciability doctrines are a category of devices that may result in an international adjudicator declining to adjudicate a dispute or aspects of a dispute due to the nature of matters raised.[160] Non-justiciability may flow variously from a finding that:

153 Dan-Cohen (1994), p. 27; Hernández (2014), pp. 169–70.
154 Green (1988), pp. 41–2; Raz (1999), p. 46.
155 von Staden (2016a), p. 1116; Soper (2002), pp. 22–3; Raine (2013), p. 102.
156 This is acknowledged but not addressed in detail in Raz (1999), p. 47.
157 Raz (2009), p. 148.
158 Legg (2012), p. 26; Schill and Briese (2009), p. 74; Henckels (2015), p. 188.
159 de Ville (2004), p. 589. See, similarly, Allan (2006), p. 688.
160 On justiciability, see McGoldrick (2010); Lauterpacht (1933); Brownlie (1967).

(i) the claim fails because the act is not within the court's jurisdiction to assess;
(ii) the applicant is legally entitled to relief, but other branches of government should make that assessment, such that the court should 'stay its hand'; or
(iii) the court should deploy 'extra-constitutional' criteria in order to determine whether the court, or another body, should decide the issue.[161]

These different forms of justiciability reflect different reasons for concluding that it would be improper for an adjudicator to determine a matter. The first approach adopts a perspective that the adjudicator should not determine the matter because it lacks legal competence (jurisdiction) to do so. The second and third approaches, by contrast, are informed by pragmatic or epistemic concerns of competence and propriety. They reflect a view that even if an adjudicator *is* empowered to determine a matter, there might be reasons to suggest that it *should not exercise* that authority.

The first form of justiciability is not a manifestation of deference. It instead merely recognises that a particular issue was never entrusted to an adjudicator to decide and so falls outside of its jurisdiction. This was the effect achieved by early arbitration treaties, which as 'standard practice' excluded matters affecting a State's vital interests, honour, or 'domestic jurisdiction' from international adjudicative jurisdiction.[162] Such treaties gave States broad discretion to regulate particular subjects to the exclusion of adjudicative authority. This, however, did not result from 'deference' but was instead a delineation of the adjudicator's jurisdictional mandate.

The second and third approaches to justiciability can, by contrast, reflect deference. In both circumstances, the adjudicator has jurisdictional competence to decide an issue itself but chooses – for reasons of deference – to adopt or to be guided by another actor's decision on that issue. The adjudicator 'has some continuing authority to act, and does act; only its independent judgment is displaced, not its actual authority'.[163] Justiciability doctrines may thus reflect deference if (i) a matter is within the adjudicator's jurisdictional competence but (ii) second-order reasons prompt the adjudicator to decline to exercise that competence.[164] An adjudicator might determine, for example, that the State has superior competence to decide particular matters otherwise within the

161 Seidman (2004), pp. 448–50. See, also, Bodie (1995); Daly (2012), p. 267.
162 See, further, Juss (1994), p. 231. The scope of jurisdiction may impact deference. This is returned to in Part II.
163 Harowitz (2008), p. 1077.
164 This is developed in Part II.

adjudicator's jurisdiction, prompting the adjudicator to designate those matters as non-justiciable. Such approaches to justiciability reflect deferential reasoning because they express an international adjudicator's perception of 'the nature and limits' of its role, expertise, and function.[165]

For reasons similar to De Ville's, some scholars dispute that deference in the form of 'restraint' is 'deference' at all.[166] These scholars argue that restraint links to the *content* of international obligations, functioning on the basis of first- rather than second-order reasons.[167] They argue that in interpreting an international obligation, the only question an adjudicator should address is whether the relevant conduct falls within the scope of decision-making autonomy left by the relevant provision.[168] Of course, merely because an adjudicator adopts a narrower interpretation of an obligation than is conceivably possible does not necessarily indicate deferential reasoning.[169] Instead, the adjudicator may be merely determining the relevant grounds of review or scope of its jurisdictional mandate (first-order reasons) independently of any assessment of second-order reasons prompting deference.[170] 'Restraint' thus does not in all instances equate to 'deference'.[171]

It is also incorrect, however, to argue that no forms of restraint exhibit deference. Second-order reasons may inform an exercise of restraint. An adjudicator might select a less restrictive understanding of what is required by an international obligation or otherwise select particular first-order reasons as relevant, for example, in order to exhibit respect for – and defer to – domestic decision-making authority. This might prompt the adjudicator to recognise some zone of exclusive domestic decision-making competence in light of a State's superior expertise in that zone relative to the international adjudicator. Such deference differs from a situation in which an international adjudicator interprets an international obligation or its jurisdictional mandate in a manner incidentally allowing greater scope for State decision-making authority. As with justiciability, an exercise of restraint can only properly be characterised as 'deference' where the international adjudicator recognises that it has the competence to decide a particular issue, but chooses to restrict that competence in deference to the State.

165 McGoldrick (2010), p. 985. See, also, Dupuy and Viñuales (2013); Root (1920), p. 181.
166 Henckels (2015), p. 181; Schill and Briese (2009), p. 74; Fahner (2013), p. 494.
167 Fahner (2013), p. 494; Kjos (2016), p. 354.
168 Allan (2006), p. 689.
169 Cf, Van Harten (2013); Mahoney (1990), p. 58; Pauwelyn and Elsig (2012).
170 Daly (2012), p. 259.
171 Restraint may manifest as, inter alia, reticence to develop law or conservative readings of precedent. See, especially, Lauterpacht (1949); Lauterpacht (2010); Kolb (2013), pp. 1145, 1157; Zarbiyev (2012), pp. 250–1. This book does not comprehensively examine 'restraint', focusing instead on 'restraint' only insofar as it is linked to deferential reasoning.

The denial of justice obligation illustrates this relationship between deference and restraint. Denial of justice has typically been interpreted to include a requirement that domestic courts not misapply the law.[172] That obligation may be defined in a manner more or less restrictive of a host State's authority. An adjudicator might decide that domestic courts must not breach domestic law (most restrictive of domestic decision-making authority); commit a 'gross' misapplication of domestic law (less restrictive of domestic decision-making authority); or make decisions that are 'improper and discreditable' or 'shocking' by international standards (least restrictive of domestic decision-making authority).[173] This decision as to the *content* of the obligation stems from an analysis of applicable law and typically occurs independently of the application of any second-order reasons prompting deference.[174] Obligations can be more or less restrictive,[175] but that alone is not an instance of 'deference'. An adjudicator only exhibits deference if it interprets the obligation less restrictively due to a desire not to impinge on domestic decision-making authority. That is, it exhibits deference wherever it modifies the requirements of the obligation on the basis of the second-order reasons discussed in Section 1.1.1. This was the approach taken, for example, in *Arif*, in which an ICSID tribunal held that what is reviewable under a denial of justice obligation might be restricted in scope because of the 'political and international delicacy to disacknowledge the judicial decision of a court of another country'.[176] Thus, a restrictive interpretation might merely show that the adjudicator is of the view that the State's conduct is not caught by the obligation. A restrictive interpretation indicates deference, however, wherever the adjudicator deliberately interprets an obligation to leave scope for autonomous State decision-making on the basis of the second-order reasons canvassed in this chapter.

1.3 CONCLUSIONS

This chapter developed a conceptual framework linking deference to authority and to reasoning based on second-order reasons. It defined deference as arising where an international adjudicator, at least to some degree, 'decline[s]

172 On the requirements for a finding of denial of justice see, further, Paulsson (2005); Borchard (1919), p. 331.

173 Paulsson (2005), p. 73. See, for example, *Azinian, Final Award, 1-Nov-1999 (ICSID-AF)*, paras 102–3; *Mondev, Award, 11-Oct-2002 (ICSID-AF)*, para. 126; *Waste Management (No. 2), Final Award, 30-Apr-2004 (ICSID-AF)*, para. 97.

174 Paulsson (2005), p. 89.

175 See, especially, Bonnitcha (2014).

176 *Arif, Award, 8-Apr-2013 (ICSID)*, para. 431.

to make [its] own independent judgment on a particular issue' in order to respect or recognise the decision-making *authority* of another actor.[177] This is not the same as requiring that the international adjudicator *would* have reached a *different* decision *but-for* deference.[178] Rather, deference operates where the international adjudicator *might* or *could have* rendered a different decision (or a decision with no reference to another actor's authority) but chose – for reasons of deference – not to do so. The chapter introduced key categories of second-order reasons that may prompt deference and examined their impact on its structure and extent.

This conceptual framework informs the empirical study that follows. It indicates that 'deference' is likely to manifest through different reasoning techniques depending on how underlying questions of decision-making authority are contested, negotiated, and settled by relevant decision-makers. It further indicates that different approaches to deference are likely to be favoured at different times and by different decision-makers. This is because legitimacy and expertise, as well as prudential and non-instrumental reasons for deference, are likely to be appraised and valued differently by different adjudicators, in different decision-making regimes, and in different time periods. These issues are considered in Part II. That part builds on this discussion to develop a taxonomy tracking the *concept* of deference developed in this chapter against its various *conceptions* (manifestations) in international private property cases. Chapters 2 and 3 introduce the focus of Part II and the methodology informing it.

177 Clayton (2006), p. 109. See, also, Harowitz (2008), p. 1073; Daly (2012), p. 28.
178 Cf, Henckels (2015), p. 34.

2

Deference in Context: Domestic Authority and International Private Property Claims

The study forming the empirical part of this book is based on a relatively homogenous group of cases from four international courts and tribunals. The empirical study of approaches to deference in this setting is designed to capture the full range of approaches to deference present in a subset of international cases. Property disputes were selected as the focus of this study because property has been a subject of long-term protection under international law, and property disputes are litigated in a range of international regimes. This opens up the possibility for temporal and cross-institutional study. This chapter introduces the setting for the study of deference in Part II. Section 2.1 introduces private property obligations under international law. Section 2.2 introduces the adjudicative regimes selected for detailed study, identifying the elements of unity and plurality that make the approaches to deference adopted by these courts and tribunals a particularly fruitful basis for the comparative study. Section 2.3 concludes.

2.1 HISTORICAL CONTEXT: THE PROTECTION OF PRIVATE PROPERTY UNDER INTERNATIONAL LAW

As compared to other international obligations, international private property protections have a unique historical lineage and pervasiveness. Property was one of the earliest subjects regulated by international law.[1] Some scholars go as far as to argue that 'modern international law developed for the express purpose of protecting private property rights from state interference'.[2] For other scholars, private property rights have no 'history'. Instead, as natural law rights, they are 'universal, both with respect to space

[1] See, especially, Crawford and Brownlie (2012), p. 610; Alvik (2018).

[2] Ederington (1997), p. 264–5. See, also, Crawford and Koskenniemi (2012), pp. 18–19.

and time'.[3] Taking a more positivistic approach, this section charts the development of procedural and substantive private property protections under international law.[4] The section illustrates that international private property protections have not been purposively designed as a unified 'field' of law. They have instead evolved based on developments in various regimes at different times. Rather than offering a comprehensive history, this section outlines the relevant institutional and substantive framework broadly to provide context for the analysis that follows. This historical context reveals the structural development of the international private property protections and adjudicative mechanisms that form the focus of analysis in Part II.

2.1.1 *Diplomatic Protection and Customary International Law Protections of Private Property*

Early international protections of private property developed through the practice of monarchs, feudal lords, and subsequently States affording 'diplomatic protection' to protect their subjects in external territories from treatment that was inconsistent with customary international law.[5] A customary international law 'minimum standard of treatment', for instance, precluded certain acts directed towards foreigners and their property, including denials of justice.[6] Over time, additional customary international law protections crystallised, including prohibitions on the uncompensated expropriation of private property.[7] Foreign individuals or corporations were the early beneficiaries of these international property protections, although some States asserted that customary international law also protected certain resident nationals, including minorities.[8] By the late nineteenth century, the protection of private property through the mechanism of diplomatic protection had become well-established. Throughout this period, States also entered into treaties affording protection to the property of their own nationals and/or recognising additional obligations towards foreigners.[9]

3 Pendas (2012), p. 97. See, also, Tierney (2004), p. 2.

4 The term 'international law' is used throughout this book to refer to those sources listed in Statute of the International Court of Justice (1945) art 38.

5 See, especially, Borchard (1919), p. 13; Root (1910), pp. 521–2; Parlett (2011), pp. 47–9; Vermeer-Künzli (2007), p. 175.

6 See, further, Parlett (2011), p. 88; Borchard (1919), pp. 330–6.

7 On more recent developments, see *Diallo, Preliminary Objections Judgment, 24-May-2007 (ICJ)*, para. 39. See, further, Milano (2005), p. 138.

8 See, further, Barrie (1995), p. 66; Shelton (2007), p. 8.

9 See, further, Barrie (1995), p. 66.

The exercise of diplomatic protection prompted the diplomatic settlement of claims, adjudication of claims before international courts or tribunals, and even at times military intervention.[10] Most early adjudicative mechanisms were given jurisdiction to adjudicate defined and concluded events.[11] Such modes of settlement came under increasing criticism in the 1800s, with a growing perception that these adjudicators 'came to their decisions by compromise ... taking the place of negotiators'.[12] This led to proposals for the creation of a standing international court,[13] which gained sufficient traction by the turn of the century to form a subject of negotiation at the Hague Peace Conferences of 1899 and 1907.[14] Ultimately, however, consensus was not reached during either Conference regarding the mode of electing judges.[15] The Conferences resulted instead in the creation of an arbitral mechanism designated the 'Permanent Court of Arbitration' ('PCA').[16] The PCA was hailed as 'a thoroughly practical beginning' to serve as the 'germ out of which a better and better system will gradually evolve'.[17] Substantively, the Conferences also resulted in the rejection of force as a permissible primary means of collecting contractual debts.[18]

2.1.2 *The Creation of Two World Courts: The Permanent Court of International Justice and the International Court of Justice*

Following World War I, the allied and associated powers negotiated a Covenant for a new international 'League of Nations'.[19] A clause recognising the obligation of States to 'give complete protection to all rights and property legally acquired and held by foreigners', was proposed for inclusion in the Covenant but ultimately not adopted.[20] The Covenant nevertheless recognised rights for certain minorities and inhabitants in 'mandate' territories, as

10 Gathii (2009), p. 357; Lamm (2014), pp. 1–2; Giustini (1986), p. 217; Bilder (2007), p. 200.
11 Parlett (2011), pp. 53–4; Crawford and Koskenniemi (2012), p. 205.
12 Tryon (1912), p. 216.
13 See, generally, Scott (1926), p. 302; Greene (1927), p. 182; Hudson (1928), p. 1; Root (1920), p. 182.
14 See, further, Eyffinger (2007a); Hull (1970); Hudson (1928), p. 3.
15 See, further, Eyffinger (2007b), p. 222; Greene (1931), p. 228; Hudson (1928), p. 3; Caron (2000), p. 17.
16 Hague Convention for the Pacific Settlement of International Disputes (1899/1900) 1 Bevans 230.
17 Hudson (1928), p. 2.
18 Hague Convention (II) Respecting the Limitation of the Employment of Force for the Recovery of Contract Debts (1907/1910) TS 537.
19 Covenant of the League of Nations (1919/1920).
20 Friedman (1953), p. 116.

well as for 'native inhabitants' in territories under foreign control.[21] The recognition of broader rights for *all* minorities was rejected for fear this would 'assail the holy principle of "full internal sovereignty"'.[22] Obligations in mandated territories were considered more politically palatable due to the 'inherently international' character of such territories.[23]

A 'Permanent Court of International Justice' was also established at this time. The Court was a permanent institution closely linked to, but institutionally independent from, the League of Nations.[24] It held both advisory and contentious jurisdiction.[25] The Court's contentious jurisdiction relied on State consent expressed through optional clause declarations, treaty provisions, or special agreements.[26] Many of the declarations conferring jurisdiction on the Court were subject to reservations, excising from the Court's jurisdiction disputes concerning inter alia the vital interests of States or matters falling within their 'domestic jurisdiction'.[27] In spite of a significant number of jurisdictional consents, '[m]ost States parties to the Statute never appeared before the Court in contentious proceedings'.[28] Although formally a 'world court', the Court's jurisdiction was principally invoked by European States.[29] This notwithstanding, the Court was undoubtedly 'more representative of the international community and of the major legal systems of the world than any other international tribunal had ever been before it'.[30]

The jurisdiction of the Court was subject to standing and subject-matter restrictions. Only States or Members of the League of Nations could appear in contentious cases as parties before the Court.[31] Direct individual standing had been proposed, but was ultimately rejected on the basis that 'a State would never permit itself to be sued before a court by a private individual'.[32] Thus, individuals whose property was affected by internationally wrongful conduct could not themselves bring disputes before the Court. Nevertheless, the Court was frequently 'called upon to pass judgment upon the responsibilities of

21 Covenant of the League of Nations (1919/1920) arts 22, 23.
22 Representative of Great Britain (James Headlam-Morley), quoted in Milano (2005), p. 87.
23 Waldock (1965), p. 8.
24 See, further, Kolb (2013), p. 4.
25 Hudson (1931), p. 432.
26 See, generally, Tams (2013); Hill (1932); Rosenne (1997). The principle of *forum prorogatum* may also apply: Fachiri (1932), p. 541.
27 Owen (1968), p. 705.
28 Tams (2013), p. 27.
29 Singh (1989), p. 221; Abi-Saab (1996), p. 307.
30 ICJ Registry (1976), pp. 15–16.
31 Statute of the Permanent Court of International Justice (1920), arts 34–5.
32 League of Nations (2005), p. 207.

States in their relations with private individuals'.[33] Such responsibilities derived from both treaties and rules of customary international law.

From 1933, the political situation in Europe resulted in a 'decline in business' for the PCIJ.[34] The invasion of the Netherlands in 1940 rendered the seat of the Court inaccessible, and the Court ultimately ceased operations.[35]

Negotiations from 1943–5 led to the replacement of the League of Nations by the United Nations, and the disbanding of the PCIJ in favour of a new 'International Court of Justice' ('ICJ').[36] The ICJ inherited the PCIJ's seat and facilities, and a modified version of its Statute and procedural rules.[37] It was also given comparable subject-matter jurisdiction.[38] Despite these continuities, the ICJ differs from the PCIJ. Its jurisdiction covers a more diverse group of States.[39] It also has a closer institutional relationship with the UN than did the PCIJ with the League: whereas the ICJ is the 'principal judicial organ of the United Nations',[40] the PCIJ was institutionally independent from the League of Nations. The ICJ remains the only international court with general subject-matter jurisdiction of potentially unlimited geographical scope.[41]

2.1.3 *The Development of Human Rights Obligations and Creation of Human Rights Courts*

Following World War II, substantive private property protections came also to be linked to the development of international human rights law.[42] In Europe, States negotiated a European Convention on Human Rights ('ECHR').[43] A right of property was not, however, included in the instrument as adopted due to disagreements during drafting as to whether 'property rights were essentially a matter for domestic jurisdiction'.[44] In 1952, States party to the ECHR reached agreement on a Protocol incorporating a right of property

33 Steiner (1936), p. 420. See, further, Schwebel (1996), p. 327; Zyberi (2013), p. 331; Brölmann (2013).

34 Grieves (1969), p. 67.

35 Hudson (1941), p. 1.

36 Charter of the United Nations (1945) 1 UNTS XVI, art 92. See, further, Hernández (2014), p. 37; Kolb (2013), pp. 53–4.

37 See, further, Hudson (1957), p. 573.

38 Charter of the United Nations (1945) 1 UNTS XVI, art 92.

39 Singh (1989), p. 220.

40 Charter of the United Nations (1945) 1 UNTS XVI, art 92.

41 Donoghue (2012), p. 182.

42 See, for example, Charter of the United Nations (1945) 1 UNTS XVI, art 1; Universal Declaration of Human Rights (1948) UNGA Res. 217A(III), art 17.

43 European Convention on Human Rights and Fundamental Freedoms (1950/1953) ETS 5.

44 Allen (2005a), p. 19.

('P1-1').[45] That instrument recognised a right of peaceful enjoyment of possessions, protection from deprivations of property, and protection from the imposition of controls on the use of property. The protections conferred by P1-1 were subject to 'wide-ranging restrictions', in recognition that 'state[s] may have legitimate grounds for interfering with private property'.[46] Property rights were also included in inter-American[47] and African[48] regional conventions on human rights in 1969 and 1981 respectively. These instruments reflected a recognition by States that the treatment of their nationals – including of their property – could be a matter of international, and not only domestic, concern.

Alongside these substantive developments, regional human rights instruments also prompted institutional developments for the international enforcement of private property rights. The ECHR framework, for example, created a dispute settlement mechanism empowered to adjudicate disputes under the Convention.[49] Some States initially opposed the creation of such a mechanism, considering it 'anti-democratic' to give an international body 'authority to interfere in the internal affairs of States'.[50] Nevertheless, following a sufficient number of ratifications, an opt-in Court became operational in 1959. States also created a quasi-judicial 'Commission' empowered to make recommendations on the settlement of inter-State disputes.[51] Both the Commission and States party to the Convention could refer matters to the Court where the relevant respondent State had accepted the Court's jurisdiction. Individuals could also present claims to the Commission if the responding State had opted in to this petition procedure.[52] From 1998, a Protocol terminated the mandate of the Commission and transformed the European Court into a permanent body with compulsory jurisdiction and a right of individual petition.[53] Inter-American and African Courts with similar jurisdictional mandates were established in 1969 and 1998, respectively.[54]

45 Protocol 1 to the European Convention for the Protection of Human Rights and Fundamental Freedoms (1952/1954) ETS 9.

46 Greer (2000), p. 12.

47 American Convention on Human Rights (1969/1978) 1144 UNTS 123, art 21.

48 African Charter on Human and Peoples' Rights (1981/1986) 1520 UNTS 244, art 14.

49 European Convention on Human Rights and Fundamental Freedoms (1950/1953) ETS 5.

50 Council of Europe (1975), pp. 114, 168.

51 European Convention on Human Rights and Fundamental Freedoms (1950/1953) ETS 5, art 31.

52 See, further, Mosler (1963), p. 810; Kjeldgaard-Pedersen (2010), p. 272.

53 Protocol 11 to the European Convention on Human Rights and Fundamental Freedoms (1994/1998) ETS 155.

54 American Convention on Human Rights (1969/1978) 1144 UNTS 123; Protocol to the African Charter on Human and Peoples' Rights on the Establishment of the African Court on Human and Peoples' Rights (1998/2004). These institutions became operational in 1978 and 2006, respectively.

2.1.4 The Arbitration of Private Property Disputes

Throughout the above period, States also referred international private property disputes to arbitral dispute settlement. Bilateral treaties of friendship, commerce and navigation, for example, offered protections to individuals and their property through State–State or individual–State dispute settlement clauses.[55] The World War I peace treaties also established arbitral mechanisms empowered to determine international private property claims related to wartime seizures and expropriations.[56] Several ad hoc commissions were also established with jurisdiction over individual or State claims related to State interferences with private property.[57] A 1922 treaty between Germany and Poland, for example, established a tribunal with jurisdiction over disputes brought by individuals concerning the 'suppression of acquired rights' or discrimination against minorities.[58]

After World War II, States continued to conclude treaties creating ad hoc dispute settlement mechanisms for specific private property violations.[59] From 1959 onwards, States also signed investment treaties, which conferred both substantive and procedural protections on foreign investors against host State interferences with their property or investments. Most investment treaties stipulate broadly analogous protections but are by no means homogenous. They typically impose several obligations on States, including prohibitions of uncompensated expropriation of foreign investment; a requirement to accord investors the minimum standard of treatment under customary international law, 'fair and equitable treatment' ('FET'), and/or 'full protection and security'; and prohibitions on 'arbitrary' or 'discriminatory' impairments.[60] From the mid-1990s onwards, these protections have been increasingly incorporated into investment chapters in free trade agreements.

2.1.5 The Creation of a 'Field' of International Private Property Law?

Some commentators argue that the developments outlined above have created a 'distinct field' of 'international property law',[61] or even a regional custom

55 See, further, Vandevelde (2011); Johnson and Gimblett (2011), p. 668.
56 See, further, Johnson and Gimblett (2011), p. 660; Martin (1947), p. 298. Some scholars dispute that these were 'international' tribunals. See, for example, Kolb (2013); *Anglo-Iranian Oil (Dissent/SO-Winiarski and Badawi Pasha)*, 5-Jul-1951 *(ICJ)*, p. 97. Compare, however, Korowicz (1956), p. 546.
57 See, generally, Feller (1935).
58 See, generally, Korowicz (1956), pp. 533, 548, 554; Kjeldgaard-Pedersen (2014).
59 See, for example, Lillich and Weston (1988); Caron (2007b); Caron (2015).
60 See, further, Bonnitcha (2014).
61 Sprankling (2012).

concerning the protection of private property.[62] A unified 'field' appears, however, to be some way off. Instead, developments in international private property protections have not been 'homogenous or consistent'.[63] International protection has, furthermore, been heavily contested throughout the above period. Many developing States contend, for example, that they are free under customary international law to regulate private property according to their own national laws.[64] Ultimately, this has frustrated efforts to establish universal standards of private property protection.

The historical outline nevertheless highlights the significant qualitative and quantitative changes in the structure and extent of private property protections that have occurred over time. Institutionally, procedural protections have become more numerous, with a proliferation of adjudicative mechanisms empowered to assess State compliance with international private property obligations. Such mechanisms have also become accessible to a larger number of potential claimants. This includes, for instance, expansion of procedural (if not substantive[65]) rights to individuals not merely States, and to nationals in addition to foreigners. Private property protections now also cover more individuals and a larger geographical area. States party to the ECHR, for example, comprise some 800 million individuals.[66] The number of possible beneficiaries of ECHR property protections is even more numerous given that both corporations and foreigners may invoke P1-1. Substantively, there is now also an 'increased density' of private property obligations,[67] including increased 'treatification'.[68] Such obligations cover a wider gamut of State conduct, reflecting a deepening of international law.[69]

Taken holistically, these developments mean that international private property rules are becoming both 'more pervasive' and 'more consequential' in determining the extent of State decision-making authority over private property.[70] While the historical developments discussed above cannot be read

62 Mardikian (2018).

63 Dolzer (2002), pp. 72–3. Developments have also been treaty-based and do not necessarily reflect customary international law. See, especially, Simma and Alston (1988); McLachlan (2008).

64 See, generally, Adede (1977a), pp. 177–8; Friedman (1953), p. 134; Czapiewska (1990), p. 60; Miles (2010), p. 17.

65 On whether private property protections confer 'delegated' as compared to 'direct' rights, see, further, Parlett (2011), pp. 109–10; Douglas et al. (2014). This has consequences in individual cases, but for the present work need not be resolved.

66 Madsen (2016).

67 van den Hout (2008), p. 644.

68 Salacuse (2010), p. 429.

69 Wolfrum (2008), p. 12.

70 Helfer (2003), p. 196.

teleologically as coherent elements of a larger whole, they are nevertheless still best understood by reference to this broader context. States have engaged in continuous and longstanding efforts to delineate the appropriate scope of private property protections under international law. Several themes permeate this history, including ongoing debates as to the extent to which international adjudicators ought to defer to domestic decisions in enforcing these private property rights. It is these debates that have animated the research underpinning this book.

2.2 INSTITUTIONAL CONTEXT: COMPARING ADJUDICATIVE APPROACHES TO DEFERENCE

Existing accounts of deference in international adjudication have typically focused exclusively either on deference in one regime or on one doctrinal approach to deference.[71] Where a comparative element is included, it is typically evaluative: the approaches to deference adopted in a primary regime are appraised by reference to the approaches adopted in domestic[72] or other international[73] regimes. Typically, scholars use such comparison to endorse the transplantation of approaches to deference from one regime into another.[74] Such an approach means that the selected comparators are rarely themselves made the subject of enquiry on the same footing as the primary regime. This book investigates deference from a different perspective. It is based on a comparative empirical study focusing on approaches to deference in the private property case law of the Permanent Court of International Justice ('PCIJ'), the International Court of Justice ('ICJ'), the European Court of Human Rights ('ECtHR'), and investment treaty arbitration. The study adopts a *neutral* comparative approach by applying the same research method to investigate the incidence of deference in the private property decisions of these four international adjudicative bodies.

This section introduces the elements of unity and plurality that makes this comparison meaningful.[75] Subsection 2.2.1 introduces the elements of unity

[71] See, for example, Henrard (2012); Mowbray (2010); Vadi and Gruszczynski (2013); Duhaime (2014). Literature on PCIJ and ICJ approaches to deference is noticeably scarce. See, however, Ragni (2014).

[72] See, especially, Van Harten (2013).

[73] See, for example, Contreras (2012) (comparing ECtHR and IACtHR approaches to the MoA); Candia (2014); Arato (2014), p. 547 (application of the ECtHR's MoA in investment arbitration); Gerards (2011) (comparing ECtHR and ECJ approaches); Vadi (2018), pp. 201–25 (comparing ICJ, WTO, and ECtHR approaches to investment tribunals).

[74] See, for example, Kriebaum (2007), p. 719.

[75] On the requirements of unity and plurality for comparison see, further, Valcke (2004), p. 720; van Reenen (1995a), p. 408.

that make a comparative study of the approaches to deference adopted by the four adjudicative bodies possible. This includes: their structural unity, as international courts and tribunals; their systemic unity, as adjudicative bodies situated in regimes of public international law; and their functional unity, as adjudicative bodies empowered to determine private property claims. Such unities do not generate uniformity, but nonetheless render the four adjudicative bodies comparable for the purposes of analysing their approaches to deference.[76] Subsection 2.2.2 introduces the elements of plurality that provide sufficient differences to make comparative study of these bodies worthwhile. It considers the differences between the PCIJ, ICJ, ECtHR, and investment tribunals in terms of: historical context and institutional structure; geographical coverage; claim structure; sociological environment; and enforcement mechanisms. The subsection argues that these features all hold the potential to impact deference in each regime, therefore supporting the goals of the empirical study reported in Part II.

2.2.1 *Structural and Functional Comparability and International Systematicity*

Comparative scholars debate the appropriate goals of comparison. Pluralist approaches begin from the proposition that 'even when similar concepts are being used across jurisdictions, they may not necessarily play the same role in each'.[77] As such, pluralists emphasise that comparisons must take context into account. For such scholars, comparison seeking to unify and evaluate by reference to external systems is necessarily problematic and undesirable. By contrast, scholars endorsing 'universal' approaches deploy comparative methods to identify convergence in the approaches adopted across separate legal systems or regimes to commonly encountered legal problems. At their extreme, universalist approaches can deny the relevance of context, conceptualising law as a-contextual and ripe for transplantation across systems. Not all universalist approaches, however, deny the importance of context. A functional universalist approach assumes convergence only at the level of function. It presupposes that the legal systems under study encounter a common problem, and investigates the tools used to address that problem, allowing for such tools to be the same or different in each context. Such an approach does not presuppose the similarity

[76] See, for a similar approach to comparison of international institutions, Schermers and Blokker (2011), p. 4 (emphasising the possibility of 'unity within diversity').

[77] McCrudden (2007), p. 374.

of the tools, only the similarity of the function served by them. The comparative study reported in this book adopts such a perspective.

This functional universalist approach does not invoke comparison to evaluate approaches to deference by reference to an 'ideal' approach.[78] Neither does it aim at transposition. I instead analyse the approaches taken to deference in each regime on their own merits to investigate the systemic function played by deference in international adjudication. This approach to comparison has been underutilised. Few works discuss the incidence or theoretical basis of deference across more than two international adjudicative regimes.[79] General treatises on international law are also notably silent on the issue of deference or refer only in passing to specific manifestations of deference without detailed analysis or attempts at conceptual linkages between manifestations of deference in different regimes.[80] To derive systemic observations, a particular view as to the comparability of the four international adjudicative regimes must necessarily be adopted. This subsection examines the similarities of the four selected international courts and tribunals that derive from their shared structural, functional, and systemic features.

2.2.1.1 Structural Comparability

International private property disputes could be settled through a range of mechanisms. Article 33(1) of the UN Charter, for example, envisages the 'pacific settlement of disputes' through 'negotiation, enquiry, mediation, conciliation, arbitration, judicial settlement, resort to regional agencies or arrangements, or other peaceful means'.[81] Not all of these mechanisms share structural unities. They differ according to how much control the parties have over the settlement of their dispute, the role of law in the dispute settlement process, and the extent to which settlement is subject to third-party control.[82] Arbitral and judicial settlement ('adjudication') describe, in essence, a process in which a third-party is empowered to issue a final and binding decision based on law.[83] Adjudication is more binding, and less subject to the control of the

78 On comparison to an ideal type see, further, van Reenen (1995b), p. 177.

79 For a cross-regime account of deference as manifested through standards of review and the MoA, see, Gruszczynski and Werner (2014).

80 See, for example, Crawford and Brownlie (2012); Cheng (2006); Oppenheim et al. (1996).

81 Charter of the United Nations (1945) 1 UNTS XVI art 33(1). See, similarly, Hague Convention for the Pacific Settlement of International Disputes (1899/1900) 1 Bevans 230, arts 2 and 16.

82 See, further, Romano et al. (2014).

83 See, generally, ibid; Bilder (1982), p. 11.

disputing parties, than the other forms of dispute settlement listed in Article 33(1).

The selected courts and tribunals share a structural unity because they comprise instances of 'adjudication' that is 'international' in character. Scholars have long debated the features sufficient to give an adjudicator an 'international' character. Scholars have variously focused on whether adjudicators: derive their mandates from a treaty; are empowered to determine disputes involving State/s; and/or decide by applying international law as the applicable law.[84] Some authors use one of these features exclusively, whereas others apply them in tandem as 'indices' of an adjudicator's 'internationality'.[85] Characterising a body as 'international' by reference to its applicable law rests on a substantive assessment that is empirically more complex to substantiate in an ex ante manner when compared to other, more structural, features. This book therefore understands 'international adjudicators' to be those that exhibit structural unity because they (i) adjudicate disputes; in which (ii) the jurisdictional mandate is conferred by treaty; and (iii) at least one State is a litigating party.

These features make adjudication a particularly likely form of dispute settlement to prompt calls for deferential reasoning.[86] As a 'hard' and 'formal' mode of dispute settlement, adjudication increases the stakes and makes parties more likely to claim decision-making authority in opposition to that of the third-party adjudicator.[87] Where an adjudicator determines disputes involving at least one State as a litigating party, it is particularly likely to have to mediate the interface between international and domestic decision-making authority. States have greater incentives than private parties to raise the issue of deference for consideration given its impact on their decision-making authority. Adjudicators empowered by treaty also confront the issue of deference in a manner structurally different to institutions established under domestic law or contract. An adjudicator empowered by

[84] See, further, Bilder (2007), p. 195; Murphy (2013); Rosenne (1993), p. 298; Malintoppi (2006), p. 136.

[85] Kolb (2013), pp. 73–5.

[86] Approaches to deference in quasi-judicial commissions are outside the scope of this book. There are nevertheless good reasons to expect that comparative study could yield insights into differences in approaches to deference in adjudicative and quasi-judicial settings. Merrills, for example, suggests that the European Commission on Human Rights tended to refer cases with 'serious political implications' to the Committee of Ministers and not the Court for decision: Merrills (1988), p. 4. Such bodies, furthermore, perform an important gatekeeping role, particularly where they determine the admissibility of applications to the court/tribunal: Kingsbury (2011); Madsen (2016); Puig and Brown (2012).

[87] See, further, Esty (2006), pp. 1509–11; Lissitzyn (1951), p. 40; Romano et al. (2014).

an instrument originating in a national legal system has a different juridical basis and qualitatively different connection to the national legal order than an adjudicator empowered by treaty. This is likely to influence its appraisal of instrumental, non-instrumental, and prudential second-order reasons for deference. These structural features indicate that the selected courts and tribunals will encounter comparable issues of deference.

2.2.1.2 Systemic Unity

Comparative projects typically adopt one of two perspectives. They might, first, compare 'different legal systems'. To do so, they adopt an external perspective according to which the legal systems under study are conceived to be separate. A comparative approach could, alternatively, compare different 'fields of law' within a unified – but not necessarily uniform[88] – system. This latter approach presupposes some organic or structural link between the fields under study, and therefore adopts an internal approach to comparison.[89] The selection of one or the other perspective influences the implications that can be drawn from the research. For the study of deference, an external comparison would yield insights into commonalities and differences in adjudicative approaches to deference. An internal comparison, by contrast, would yield insights into the function of deference and the structure of the system of law within which it operates.

Many scholars debate whether international regimes comprise a unified legal 'system' or rather operate as a 'set of self-contained regimes' or even a 'loose agglomeration or anarchy'.[90] Some authors argue,[91] whereas others dispute,[92] that the international legal order is a unified system. Hart developed a particularly influential view of systemic unity, arguing that a legal 'system' is constituted by a unified set of secondary rules of recognition.[93] Dupuy builds on this account for international law, distinguishing between a formal unity of secondary rules,[94] and substantive unity of primary rules[95] or principles.[96] As Delmas-Marty notes, however, this dichotomy between

88 See, especially, Nelken (2013), p. 344.
89 Hey and Mak (2009), p. 287.
90 Han (2006), p. 102; Sands (2002), p. 202.
91 Crawford (2014), para. 237.
92 Jennings (1996), p. 5 ('just a disordered medley').
93 Hart (1994), p. 232.
94 Concerning, for example, interpretation, sources of law, or the consequences of unlawful acts: Dupuy (1999), pp. 793–4.
95 For example, rules of general international law or jus cogens: ibid, pp. 794–5.
96 For example, the principle of sovereignty: ibid, p. 794.

systemic unity and separation risks a 'double deadlock: fusion signals a seemingly utopian and potentially worrisome legal unity, while separation presupposes complete autonomy, which no longer exists'.[97]

In this book, the four selected courts and tribunals are conceptualised as inhabiting a unified (but not necessarily uniform) system of public international law. The view of systematicity adopted sits between Delmas-Marty's poles of fusion and separation. The project eschews a completely 'external' perspective to comparison, and is instead based on the assumption that there is *some* system of public international law. The project does not rely, however, on a particularly rigorous notion of unity. This is because it does not seek to promote the transposition of approaches to deference across the studied regimes. Instead, the project posits only a loose connection between the four regimes under study. To draw inferences across the jurisprudence, it adopts a view of these regimes as 'conceptually related to general international law'.[98] This is a relatively low bar for 'unity', and appears, prima facie at least, to be reasonably uncontroversial for the four regimes under study.[99] As noted above, each of the four regimes comprises adjudicative institutions that are 'international' in character and structurally part of an international legal order. In deciding disputes, these adjudicative bodies also 'speak a language in which the common grammar is international law'.[100] None of the regimes has developed a comprehensive set of unique secondary rules. They instead apply secondary rules derived from general international law.[101] This systemic view forms the basis of the comparative project. It does not, however, deny diversity. It merely adopts a view of public international law as a 'system' that is 'simultaneously homogeneous and heterogeneous, unified but multipolar'.[102]

2.2.1.3 Functional Comparability versus Substantive Uniformity

Some scholars argue that some or all of the four selected adjudicative regimes exhibit substantive uniformity insofar as they apply the same or broadly

97 Delmas-Marty (2009), p. 2.

98 Simma and Pulkowski (2006), p. 500.

99 McLachlan (2008), p. 364; International Law Commission (2006), p. 82. See, similarly, *Bankovic, Admissibility Decision, 12-Dec-2001 (ECtHR-GC)*, para. 57; *Asian Agricultural Products, Award, 27-Jun-1990 (ICSID)*, para. 21; *Brazilian Loans, Judgment, 12-Jul-1929 (PCIJ-A21)*, p. 124.

100 Dupuy (2007), p. 28.

101 See, further, Simma and Pulkowski (2006), pp. 491–3; Simma (1985), pp. 115–17; International Law Commission (2006), pp. 66–8; McLachlan (2005), p. 280.

102 Craven (2003), p. 12.

analogous private property rules.[103] While the obligations applied in the four adjudicative regimes might overlap, however, they are by no means coextensive. These regimes do not, for instance, work by reference to a unified concept of 'property'. Whereas the ECHR protects 'possessions',[104] investment treaties typically protect 'investments',[105] and the doctrine of diplomatic protection under customary international law protects property or vested rights.[106] The precise interests protected in each regime may thus differ. Adjudicators even within the one regime may differ in interpreting the scope of protectable interests.[107] Douglas, for example, identifies in investment treaty jurisprudence four different conceptualisations of the class of protectable interests.[108] This reflects the nebulous character of the concept of 'property'.

The obligations applied in each regime also differ in structure and purpose. Investment treaties, for example, regulate negative externalities associated with domestic decision-making. They purport to protect those external to a political community (foreigners within the State) from the State's adverse conduct.[109] Human rights treaties, by contrast, largely focus on 'social interactions within the State'.[110] They are typically inward facing, aiming to bind the State in respect of the treatment of its own nationals. Whereas the regulation of negative externalities results in outward facing and 'other binding' obligations, the regulation of internal acts prompts inward-facing and 'self-binding' regulation.[111] Such distinctions hold potential implications for deference. Scholars suggest, for example, that inward-facing obligations might generate greater scope for deference than outward-facing obligations.[112] In addition to these structural differences, it is arguable that adjudicators in each of the regimes also apply obligations of a differing character. Human rights, for instance, are often conceptualised as inherent in human beings as an incident of their humanity, whereas investment protections are granted on instrumental grounds, including to increase the flow of foreign investment and to encourage States to internalise regulatory costs.[113]

103 See, especially, Dupuy and Viñuales (2012); Nicholson (1965), p. 397; Vadi (2016), p. 217; Schill (2011), p. 1095; Salacuse (2010), p. 430.
104 The Court has held that P1-1 'is in substance guaranteeing the right of property': *Marckx, Judgment, 13-Jun-1979 (ECtHR)*, para. 63. See, further, Sprankling (2014), p. 36.
105 Investment treaties usually define 'investments' by reference to an indicative list of assets owned or controlled by the investor. See, further, Douglas (2014a).
106 See, generally, van Banning (2002), pp. 11–12.
107 See, generally, ibid, pp. 12–16; Sasson (2010); Sprankling (2014).
108 Douglas (2014a).
109 von Staden (2012), p. 1037.
110 von Bogdandy and Venzke (2014), p. 199.
111 Alter (2008b), p. 37.
112 Jachtenfuchs and Krisch (2016); Føllesdal (2016), p. 162; Shany (2005), p. 936.
113 Dupuy (2009), p. 48; Kriebaum (2014), p. 50; Vadi (2016), p. 217; Paparinskis (2014).

An approach to comparison relying on functional unity rather than substantive uniformity does not, however, require homogeneity among the obligations applied by these adjudicators. Such homogeneity would only be necessary if the empirical study were intended to identify approaches to deference to be transposed across the selected regimes. The aim of this study is, however, different. As Valcke explains, 'comparison can proceed so long as there is a plurality of entities to compare, quite apart from whether these entities turn out to be identical or different'.[114] It is not necessary to conclude that the regimes apply exactly the same private property protections. They need not even operate as a unified regime of 'international property law',[115] or be influenced by one another's approaches.[116] Sufficient unity for a meaningful comparison of the approaches to deference adopted by these adjudicators is supplied by their adjudication of functionally analogous disputes.

All four institutions apply rules of international law designed to provide remedies to individuals who suffer injury as a result of internationally wrongful State conduct interfering with their property rights.[117] This private property caseload is typically concerned with 'normal' or 'day-to-day' conditions.[118] This distinguishes these regimes from bodies dealing exclusively with the protection of property in conflict scenarios. Each regime, moreover, applies rules on property stipulating minimum standards of protection, rather than obligations aiming for harmonisation.[119] This distinguishes these regimes from others including, in particular, regimes of supranational community law.[120] The four adjudicative regimes thus perform a similar function, even if they apply different legal rules to discharge it. Of course, other courts and tribunals – or other international obligations – could have formed the focus of the present study.[121]

114 Valcke (2004), p. 721. Cf, de Ville (2006), p. 122 (comparison as 'the act of composing or unifying two . . . different things').

115 Sprankling (2012).

116 On which, see Cotula (2015), p. 130; Fry (2007), p. 121; Fauchald (2008), p. 342; Miller (2002).

117 See, especially, Simma (2011), p. 576; Dupuy and Viñuales (2012); Dugard (2004), para. 44; Waschefort (2012), p. 62.

118 All four courts/tribunals exercise predominantly prospective jurisdiction (cf, the PCIJ/ICJ special agreements procedure). This distinguishes them from regimes adjudicating disputes over past events in which the State knows at the time of consent which issues will arise (and therefore can better control which issues of domestic decision-making are referred to the adjudicator). See, especially, Caron (2014); Caron (2007a), pp. 404–6.

119 On the possible impact of this feature on deference, see Candia (2014), p. 21 (arguing that harmonisation goals lead to more intrusive review).

120 Supranational courts are also structurally linked to domestic courts, including through doctrines of direct effect and preliminary reference. See, further, Helfer and Alter (2009); Semertzi (2014).

121 Certain other candidates were excluded, including because their connection to private property was less direct (WTO panels and Appellate Body decisions) or the conception of private property applied in the regime focused on community, rather than private, interests

An empirical analysis of deference in the application of all international obligations by all international courts and tribunals would, however, become too fragmented and generalised, and would also introduce too many variables, to be methodologically defensible. It would also be a vast and near-impossible undertaking. As such, a relatively homogenous group of courts/tribunals and obligations structure the present enquiry. There is nonetheless reason to expect that the conceptual framework and findings developed on the basis of this study could be adapted to study approaches to deference in other contexts. This is because the comparative study has been designed to investigate approaches to deference in comparable, but still distinctive, settings. These elements of plurality are introduced below.

2.2.2 *Plurality: Contextual Comparisons*

While adjudicators in the four regimes share unities that make their approaches to deference possible to compare, they also exhibit pluralities that make that comparison particularly worthwhile. The present study focuses on approaches to deference within diverse regimes. Several particular differences that distinguish the four selected adjudicative regimes from one another are especially noteworthy. The selected international courts and tribunals have operated in different temporal, geographic, and social contexts. They also have different claim structures and caseloads, allowing for investigation of approaches to deference in courts and tribunals that adjudicate both inter-State disputes (the PCIJ and ICJ), and individual–State disputes (the ECtHR and investment tribunals). Finally, the selected international courts and tribunals have different enforcement structures and, with that, different relationships to domestic enforcement systems. The following subsections discuss these features, highlighting the particular reasons to expect that they may influence the approaches taken by adjudicators to issues of deference. Table 2.1 provides a simplified snapshot of some of these key differences between the selected adjudicative regimes.

2.2.2.1 Historical Context and Institutional Structure

The selected courts and tribunals have operated in distinct time periods, such that comparative study of their approaches to deference holds particular potential to illuminate the impacts on deference of developments in both

(IACtHR, ACHR). Such adjudicative mechanisms had also determined a lower number of cases than those decided by the four regimes under study. Future analysis could fruitfully examine whether the approach to analysing deference proposed in this book usefully maps to these different contexts.

TABLE 2.1 *Key features of the four adjudicative bodies under review*

	Permanent Court of International Justice	International Court of Justice	European Court of Human Rights	Investment treaty arbitration
Period of operation	1922–46	1946–present	1959–present	Various (the first publicly known claim was filed in 1987)–present
Institutional structure	Permanent; institutionally linked but separate to the League of Nations	Permanent; institutionally linked to the United Nations ('UN')	Permanent; institutionally linked to the Council of Europe ('CoE')	Ad hoc with varying degrees of institutional support
Geographic coverage	Multilateral (theoretically global, but predominantly European)	Multilateral (theoretically global)	Multilateral/regional (CoE Members)	Bilateral/multilateral (significant geographical spread)
Structure of claims	State–State claims	State–State claims	Initially, State–State but, from 1998, individual–State and State–State claims P1-1 claims can be made by both nationals and foreigners	Individual–State claims by foreign 'investors' Some treaties also provide for State–State claims
Jurisdiction	General subject-matter jurisdiction Contentious and advisory jurisdiction	General subject-matter jurisdiction Contentious and advisory jurisdiction	Specialist subject-matter jurisdiction (human rights disputes) Contentious and advisory jurisdiction	Specialist subject-matter jurisdiction (investment disputes) Contentious jurisdiction only

Enforcement	League of Nations oversight of State compliance	UN oversight of State compliance	CoE oversight of State compliance	Varies: enforcement through either the New York or ICSID Convention framework
Judges	Eleven judges and four deputy judges (until 1929), thereafter fifteen judges, with the possibility for appointment of judges ad hoc Judges elected by the League of Nations Assembly and Council for a fixed nine-year term, with the possibility of re-election	Fifteen judges, with the possibility for appointment of judges ad hoc Judges elected by the UN General Assembly and Security Council for a fixed nine-year term with the possibility of re-election	Forty-seven judges, with the possibility for appointment of judges ad hoc. Cases are heard by a single judge; three-judge Committee; seven-judge Chamber; or seventeen-judge Grand Chamber Judges elected by the CoE Parliamentary Assembly for a fixed nine-year term (or until they reach the age of seventy), with no possibility of re-election	Usually three-member panels Appointment of nationals is discouraged in some regimes (ICSID) One arbitrator is typically appointed by each party, with the third elected by the two party-appointed arbitrators

international law and its surrounding sociopolitical context. As Chapter 1 demonstrated, approaches to deference are likely to change over time. Deference is particularly likely to arise where the law is in a state of flux or development. In such circumstances, the authority to interpret obligations will be an active site of negotiation and contestation. A continuously operating adjudicative institution will have more time to develop interpretive authority, and to settle its approach to the delineation of authority in contested areas. By contrast, 'one-time only adjudicators are unlikely to build up the web of doctrine necessary to mediate the complicated relationships' between international and domestic decision-makers.[122] The diverse historical contexts in which the PCIJ, ICJ, ECtHR, and investment treaty tribunals have operated may thus impact their approaches to deference in individual cases.

The PCIJ was 'the first significant court of justice at the international level'[123] and was also one of the first international courts to grapple with issues of deference. The PCIJ also operated at a time when there were few international courts from which it could draw analogy and inspiration. The PCIJ lacked a body of existing international jurisprudence to draw on, giving it significant scope to develop its own approaches to deference. Unlike the PCIJ, the other three selected courts/tribunals remain operational. The ICJ and ECtHR have both now been in operation for over sixty years. It is nevertheless possible that their approaches to deference have evolved over time. Christoffersen and Madsen, for example, argue that the ECtHR has transitioned from an approach favouring 'legal diplomacy' (1950–74), to a 'progressive' jurisprudence (1975–89), a solidified sense of authority (1990–2004), and a recent period of 'critique' (2004–12) and challenge (2012–present).[124] Kolb similarly periodises the ICJ's activities, describing periods of 'dynamism and internationalism' (1947–62), 'proceduralist jurisprudence' (1966–86), and 'renaissance and hyperactivity' (1986–present).[125] Unlike the other three courts, investment treaty tribunals do not operate in a continuous form. They are instead constituted ad hoc for individual disputes and are thus more likely to have to establish afresh in each case their own authority vis-à-vis that of domestic actors.

Permanency also has the potential to alter an adjudicator's perception of its function. Adjudicators operating in a permanent institutional structure may be more likely than ad hoc adjudicators to operate with a long-term vision.[126] They

122 Young (2005), pp. 163–4.

123 Spiermann (2003), p. 399.

124 Christoffersen and Madsen (2013), pp. 236–8.

125 Kolb (2013), pp. 1149–55. See, also: Posner (2004), p. 11; Rosenne (1997), pp. 19–24; Abi-Saab (1996); Spiermann (2003), p. 409.

126 See, further, von Bogdandy and Venzke (2014); Guillaume (1995), p. 859; Bilder (2007), p. 198; Jennings (1998), p. 7; Webb (2013), pp. 149–52.

may, for instance, dedicate comparably greater efforts to law-making as opposed merely to dispute resolution.[127] Potentially, they may also develop approaches to support the ongoing sustainability and adaptability of the regime in which they operate.[128] Adjudicators in courts or tribunals operating over a continuous time period might be expected to generate greater stability and authority than ad hoc adjudicators.[129] Ad hoc adjudicators may, by contrast, adopt bolder, less tentative, approaches to settling disputed claims of authority.[130] Van Harten argues, for example, that ad hoc arbitrators review domestic decision-making in a manner that asserts and expands their own decision-making authority.[131] This prompts some scholars to argue that modifying the structure of investment treaty arbitration to introduce a standing court system might make adjudicators in that regime 'more likely to demonstrate deference to States'.[132] By contrast, others suggest that ad hoc adjudicators are more constrained by States and thus likely to be more deferential so as not to 'upset the countries with nominating authority'.[133] Approaches of adjudicators to deference may thus differ depending on whether they adjudicate disputes within a standing or ad hoc institutional structure.[134]

2.2.2.2 Geographical Coverage

An adjudicator's territorial jurisdiction, which determines the geographical origin of its litigants, may also influence its approach to deference. Regional courts such as the ECtHR (at least until recently) adjudicate disputes involving States with comparably more shared history, culture, and values than non-regional courts and tribunals.[135] States party to disputes before the PCIJ were similarly predominantly European.[136] The impact of such geographical factors on adjudicative reasoning depends on an adjudicator's institutional setting, historical context, and the specific factual issues raised in individual disputes. There is, nevertheless, reason to expect that geographical factors may influence

127 Donoghue (2012), pp. 182–91; Hernández (2014), pp. 93–4; de Visscher (1968), p. 390; von Bogdandy and Venzke (2014), p. 90; Shelton (2008), p. 9.
128 Pauwelyn and Elsig (2012).
129 Webb (2013), p. 148.
130 Ibid, p. 150.
131 Van Harten (2013), p. 162.
132 Rogers (2013), p. 251. See, similarly, Feldman (2017).
133 Stephan (2002), p. 337. See, also, Pauwelyn and Elsig (2012).
134 Permanency may arise on a de facto basis, including through repeat appointments of the same individuals in ad hoc proceedings. See, further, Langford and Behn (2018), p. 565; Kapeliuk (2010); Webb (2013), p. 152.
135 Evenson (2001), p. 222; Sadurski (2009), p. 400.
136 Friedmann (1964), p. 5.

adjudicative approaches to deference. Mountfield argues, for example, that the common democratic structures of States appearing before the ECtHR means that the Court is likely to be particularly 'mindful … that a democratically elected government must be permitted to make and change policy'.[137] Such adjudicators may therefore privilege democracy as an instrumental or even non-instrumental second-order reason for deference. Adjudicators determining disputes involving more geographically diverse States might, by contrast, adopt different interpretive choices. They might, for example, grant greater interpretive leeway to States in order to respect pluralism over homogeneity.

Geographical coverage also influences the epistemic communities and audiences to which adjudicative decision-making is directed. Different stakeholders will differ in their views concerning the role of the adjudicator vis-à-vis the State. Such views may impact adjudicative analyses of deference. As the subject-matter competence of international adjudicators expands, they may, for instance, increasingly need to speak not just to States but also to 'the civil society actors that provide them with cases and buttress their authority'.[138] This may influence, in particular, adjudicative appraisal of prudential second-order reasons for deference.

2.2.2.3 Adjudicators

Different adjudicators work in each of the selected regimes. Even for relatively cohesive bodies such as the PCIJ, ICJ, and ECtHR, the plurality of judges on each court makes it likely that over time different approaches to deference will be favoured. This is because different adjudicators may hold different views of the role of international adjudication vis-à-vis domestic decision-making. The impact of these sociological features on the substance of adjudicative reasoning is difficult to discern accurately. Given that deliberations are confidential, studies typically focus on how judicial backgrounds, particularly nationality, influence voting patterns or case outcomes.[139] Some scholars suggest that ad hoc judges with the nationality of their appointing State are particularly deferential because they tend to vote in support of that State's position.[140] Care must be taken, however, not to

137 Mountfield (2002), p. 146. See, similarly, Ratner (2008), p. 497.

138 von Staden (2016a), p. 1126.

139 See, for example, Grieves (1969), pp. 110–11; Franck (2009), p. 465; Behn et al. (2018); Anand (1963), pp. 30–1; Posner (2004), p. 16. Some studies have investigated the impacts of bloc/allegiance voting, and voting among judges representing States sharing similar political or religious structures: Smith (2004), p. 216; Posner and de Figueiredo (2005), pp. 599–601. See, for more recent sociological work on international adjudicators, Grisel (2017); Grisel (2018). See, also, Sacriste and Vauchez (2007).

140 Lauterpacht (1930), p. 182. Cf, Smith (2004), pp. 199–200; Anand (1963), pp. 30–1; Voeten (2011), p. 63.

conflate deference as a reasoning structure with a favourable outcome for a State.[141] Care must also be exercised in correlating an individual's national or even professional profile with allegiance to a particular State.[142]

There is, nonetheless, reason to expect that sociological factors may influence approaches to deference. Adjudicators may, for example, derive particular approaches to deference through analogy to approaches adopted in the systems in which they received their legal training.[143] Adjudicators may also approach deference differently depending on their professional background. Madsen, for example, suggests that diplomatic experience may make some judges better at 'balancing law and politics' than others.[144] Tumonis similarly argues that academics 'tend to be more activist as international judges, while former diplomats tend to be more restrained and are more responsive to national interests'.[145] Government experience in a particular State may, moreover, prompt an adjudicator to treat the views of that State or of other like States as particularly trustworthy and authoritative.[146] Krisch suggests, for example, that an international judge with domestic judicial training may be more likely to have 'internalized a vision of the domestic constitution as the final point of reference, and of domestic decision-makers and judges as having the final word'.[147] Conversely, an international judge versed in a particular body of domestic law might feel better authorised to interpret that law in place of domestic decision-makers than might a judge with no relevant domestic legal training. Spiermann argues, for example, that the appointment of international adjudicators who previously worked as domestic lawyers or judges may influence an international court's propensity to interpret domestic law without reference to existing domestic interpretations.[148] Judicial skillsets might also impact judicial approaches to deference, including the tendency of judges to engage with complex factual evaluations[149] or with topics requiring specialist knowledge.[150] Judges from different regions may, furthermore, differ in their

141 See, also, Chapter 1. This is developed in Chapters 3 (arguing that this makes it necessary methodologically to look beyond case outcomes to study deference) and 8 (illustrating that deference is also frequently sought by non-State entities in adjudication).
142 Posner (2004), p. 17.
143 Young (2005), p. 162; Anand (1965), p. 805. On the role of domestic analogies in the analysis of deference, see, further, Chapter 9.
144 Madsen (2014), p. 333.
145 Tumonis (2012), p. 131.
146 Føllesdal (2009), p. 296.
147 Krisch (2010), p. 148.
148 Spiermann (2005), p. 349.
149 Emberland (2007), p. 207.
150 Lauterpacht (1991), p. 17; Francioni (1999), p. 20 (considering administrative, criminal, and constitutional law expertise).

appraisal of possible sources of normative epistemic authority such as, for example, democracy.[151]

The institution of ad hoc and national judges supports these hypotheses.[152] The mechanism for States to appoint a judge of their choice or nationality is intended to assuage State concerns that decisions concerning aspects of State sovereignty might be rendered by foreign judges.[153] States historically appointed national ad hoc judges because they had particular expertise or knowledge of relevant domestic law and politics.[154] They could therefore assist other adjudicators by 'explaining some exceptional features of the national legal system not easily understood by foreigners'.[155] They might, moreover, be better acquainted than foreign adjudicators with the 'political, social, cultural and environmental circumstances' of the responding State.[156] Some commentators have even argued that the provision for ad hoc and national judges allowed international courts to cross 'a frontier from outside (the state) to inside (the state) by being transformed metaphorically – "in a sense" – into a national court'.[157] Although a detailed study of the impact of judicial backgrounds on deference is beyond the scope of the present work, these features indicate that deference is particularly likely to differ depending on adjudicative context.

2.2.2.4 Claim Structure and Caseload

The PCIJ, ICJ, ECtHR, and investment treaty tribunals adjudicate disputes exhibiting three distinct claim structures: disputes between States, disputes between a State and its own citizens, and disputes between a State and foreign subjects. These claim structures influence the types of cases filed before these adjudicators, and the total number of private property cases they receive. Empowering individuals to file international claims increases the number of potential claimants and thus an international adjudicator's potential caseload.[158] Individuals may also be more motivated than States to litigate

151 Weeramantry (1996), pp. 2–3.

152 On national and ad hoc judges see, generally, Hurst (1943), p. 322. The capacity to appoint a national arbitrator is unavailable in ICSID arbitration without the consent of the other disputing party: Convention on the Settlement of Investment Disputes between States and Nationals of Other States (1965/1966) 575 UNTS 159 art 39. See, for example, *Urbaser, Decision on Jurisdiction, 19-Dec-2012 (ICSID)*, paras 3–4.

153 See, generally, Anand (1969), p. 100; Hill (1931), p. 670; Smith (2004), pp. 198–201.

154 Kolb (2013), p. 119; Hurst (1943), p. 323; Tryon (1912), p. 205; Bernhardt (1993).

155 Anand (1969), p. 100.

156 Ishikawa (2010), p. 396.

157 Scott (2008), p. 41.

158 Shany (2009a), p. 79; Alter (2011); Keohane et al. (2003), p. 153.

cases concerning their private property.[159] Different claim structures thus influence adjudicative caseloads and the opportunities afforded to each of these courts and tribunals to make decisions about deference. Private litigants may also be more likely to file cases raising issues of deference. Where a case implicates particularly sensitive domestic decision-making functions, State claimants might instead seek a diplomatic settlement. They may be more sensitive to the interests of the responding State, and also eager to avoid exposing themselves to future litigation as a respondent.[160]

It might therefore be expected that investment treaty tribunals and the ECtHR would have both a larger caseload than the PCIJ and ICJ, but also the opportunity to opine on issues of deference more frequently. At the same time, however, a court determining an individual–State dispute might be more hesitant to grant deference, out of a perception that it would upset the procedural equality of the disputing parties by according 'extra weight to the views of one of the parties'.[161] A large caseload may also in itself influence an adjudicator's approach to deference. Alter argues, for example, that adjudicators without a steady flow of cases might 'work harder to please governments, so as to encourage the bringing of more cases'.[162] The success of an international court or tribunal might by contrast prompt a court to defer more readily to States in order to generate efficiencies and effectiveness that, in turn, will boost perceptions of its legitimacy. The diverse claim structures and caseloads of the four selected courts and tribunals thus bring into focus the possible impact of different institutional structures on adjudicative approaches to deference.

2.2.2.5 Remedies and Enforcement

The nature of remedies awarded in each of the four regimes also differs. Investment tribunals typically award compensation in quantitatively larger amounts compared to the PCIJ, ICJ, and ECtHR. Henckels suggests that this feature should impact arbitral analyses of deference, such that '[t]he consequences of a finding of liability should be borne in mind when considering the standard of review that should be employed by an international tribunal'.[163] This might be

159 Alter (2014), p. 5.

160 Ibid, p. 7; Alvarez (2006), p. 480; Alter et al. (2016), p. 22.

161 Vadi and Gruszczynski (2013), p. 623. See, similarly, Allan (2006), p. 676; Fahner (2016), p. 73. The application of an argument to this effect (in relation to investment arbitration) was rejected by a domestic court in 2017. See Charlotin (2017).

162 Alter (2014), p. 7. See, also, Contreras (2012), p. 57; Stone Sweet and Brunell (2013), p. 66; Alvarez (2006), p. 479.

163 Henckels (2014), p. 241.

prompted by prudential reasons, or because the stakes of reaching an incorrect decision in such circumstances are increased such that there is greater scope for epistemic deference.[164] Enforcement structures also differ between the regimes. This may particularly influence prudential appraisals of deference. The enforcement structures for the decisions of investment treaty tribunals differ depending on whether the tribunal is 'territorialised' or 'non-territorialised'.[165] A 'territorialised' investment tribunal has its juridical seat in a domestic legal order.[166] The award resulting from a 'territorialised' investment tribunal is made enforceable through a domestic system.[167] Non-territorialised tribunals, by contrast, operate more autonomously and are more insulated from national control.[168] The awards of non-territorialised tribunals are binding in a manner more akin to the enforcement mechanisms employed by the PCIJ, ICJ, and ECtHR. This book analyses approaches to deference in the decisions of both forms of investment treaty arbitration. The analysis nonetheless distinguishes where relevant between non-territorialised (ICSID) and territorialised (non-ICSID) investment tribunals.

2.3 CONCLUSIONS

This chapter introduced the case study forming the focus of the remaining chapters of the book. The chapter explained why the private property decisions of the PCIJ, ICJ, ECtHR, and investment treaty tribunals offer a particularly fruitful basis for comparative study, and introduced the basis on which that comparative study was developed. The similarities and differences between these adjudicative regimes mean that, while sharing features in common, there is reason to expect that their approaches to deference will differ – either institutionally, or over time. This provides a rich setting for the analysis of deference that follows. Examining approaches to deference in these diverse institutional settings provides a platform for highlighting whether approaches to deference in international adjudication have changed over time or differ depending on institutional setting. The book does not explore these issues causally. Rather, the focus is on distilling different approaches and examining their conceptual structure and the trends pertaining to their use.

164 See, further, Sunstein (2007).
165 See, especially, Kjos (2013), p. 31.
166 Gaillard (2010), p. 277.
167 Kjos (2013), p. 19; Convention on the Recognition and Enforcement of Foreign Arbitral Awards (1958/1959) 330 UNTS 3.
168 Stone Sweet and Grisel (2014), p. 74; Kjos (2013), p. 44.

3

Locating Deference: The Function of Deference in Legal Adjudication

This book investigates how deference is structured in individual cases, and whether the treatment of deference differs by regime or over time. Adjudicative decisions thus form the focus of this study. This focus, however, necessarily entails treating adjudicative decisions as a meaningful source of data. Legal (doctrinal) and social sciences (empirical) research methods provide two competing methodologies through which such a study might be conducted. Section 3.1 explores the relative strengths and weaknesses of empirical and doctrinal approaches, and examines how adjudicative decisions can remain a meaningful source of *legal* data when analysed using an empirical methodology drawn from *non-legal* disciplines. Section 3.2 outlines the methods used to identify deference in the private property decisions of the four selected courts and tribunals. It explains both how cases were selected for analysis, and the approach used to analyse them. Section 3.3 concludes.

3.1 TOWARDS INTERDISCIPLINARITY: COMBINING EMPIRICAL METHODS AND ADJUDICATIVE THEORY

The nature of deference makes adjudicative decision-making a natural site for analysis.[1] International private property rules are typically both flexible and vague. This means that international adjudicators perform a key role in

[1] These questions could be assessed through analysis of treaties, but treaties are typically silent on the deference that should be attributed to domestic decisions or the possibility of domestic decisions. In addition, analysis of treaty provisions would not provide any insights into how such provisions are interpreted and applied by adjudicators in practice. Aspects of these questions could also be answered through interviews or surveys of adjudicators. Adjudicators might, however, offer strategic answers, or otherwise fail to account for approaches with which they are unfamiliar or unaware. At best, such analysis would yield only partial information about how adjudicators approach deference.

interpreting and developing this area of law, and are uniquely positioned to structure the interaction between domestic and international claims to decision-making authority whenever they are called on to apply private property protections. Adjudicative reasoning is, moreover, a particularly good subject for comparative analysis. Law has an inherently 'topical structure',[2] making adjudicative decisions particularly 'amenable to comparison'.[3] Adjudicators also provide carefully crafted reasons for their decisions.[4] Such decisions are not produced in response to particular research questions, constituting instead a 'naturally occurring communication'.[5] These features make adjudicative decisions particularly credible sources of information about adjudicative approaches to deference. It also makes them particularly amenable to temporal and cross-institutional comparison.

Both doctrinal and empirical techniques could provide a means of analysing deference in adjudicative decision-making.[6] These approaches typically differ in the identification and breadth of the data they are used to analyse. A doctrinal study might, for instance, study the approach to deference adopted in particular landmark, frequently cited, or leading cases.[7] This has caused some scholars to argue that doctrinal methods risk becoming 'impressionistic', because they focus on materials that reflect 'the researcher's values, national locus, and imperfect factual knowledge'.[8] Such approaches, moreover, risk sampling on the dependent variable by focusing on cases that have adopted a particular approach to the topic under study.[9] For the study of international law, this approach to analysis poses particular methodological problems. A focus on a small subset of international cases would, in particular, fail to account for the formally non-precedential nature of international adjudicative decisions.[10] It could risk creating the impression that a small subset of cases (or a single case) is representative of a larger corpus of case law.[11] It might further

2 Balkin (1996), p. 220.

3 Friedheim and Kadane (1970), p. 480. See, also, Ulmer (1963), pp. 170–1.

4 Friedheim and Kadane (1970), p. 482.

5 Fragale et al. (2012), p. 379.

6 For comparison of empirical and doctrinal approaches see, generally, Shaffer (2008); Hall and Wright (2008); Webley (2010), p. 926.

7 See, for examples of this approach to analysing adjudicative deference, Henckels (2015), p. 20; Gerards (2011), p. 90. See, more generally, for examples of this approach, Bjørge and Miles (2017); Greer and Wildhaber (2012), p. 656; Yalkin (2009), p. 3; Ulmer (1963), p. 166.

8 Falk (1967), p. 487. See, also, Legg (2012), p. 12.

9 Steininger (2018). See, further, Sadl and Panagis (2015); Lim (2014), p. 524; Jacob (2011), p. 86.

10 On precedent in international adjudication see, generally, Balcerzak (2004), pp. 137–9; Guzman and Meyer (2008), p. 516; Ginsburg (2004), p. 637; Sacerdoti (2011), p. 139.

11 Such approaches are more justifiable in regimes with a system of precedent: Pappas (2008), p. 984.

imply a view that adjudicative approaches are homogenous and connected. International adjudicators have considerable discretion, however, to refer to past cases as they deem fit.[12] This means that international adjudicative decisions hold 'essentially equal value'.[13]

Empirical techniques from social sciences disciplines offer a more systematic and comprehensive means of analysing adjudicative decisions. Such methodologies typically permit analysis of a large corpus of data, supporting the identification of patterns and trends in the case law. The benefits of more systematic methods make understandable the 'empirical turn in international legal scholarship'.[14] Scholars studying international private property regimes, for example, have empirically investigated what motivates States to conclude investment treaties, and the impact of investment treaties on the promotion of foreign direct investment.[15] Scholars have also developed citation analyses of adjudicative jurisprudence,[16] investigated the impacts of extra-legal influences on adjudication,[17] and considered how the features of respondent States impact the outcomes of disputes.[18]

Empirical techniques nonetheless present their own disadvantages when applied to the study of adjudicative decision-making. Social sciences empirical methodologies adopt 'enquiry paradigms'.[19] They eschew analysis of the *legal* quality of legal texts, to explore instead their extra-legal implications and significance.[20] Such studies invariably adopt an 'external' perspective to law.[21] Deriving methodological approaches from other disciplines, they focus on legal texts not from the perspective of legal theory *as law*, but rather from the perspective of social sciences *as fact*.[22] To analyse law *as fact*, such methodologies collapse the boundary between law and other disciplines.[23] They reduce law to an aspect of social interaction, denying for the purposes of empirical study its regulative elements. The treatment of law as a social fact limits the legal implications that can be drawn from empirical studies of law.

12 See, for example, Grisel (2014a), p. 217; Guillaume (2011), p. 13.
13 Hall and Wright (2008), p. 66.
14 Shaffer and Ginsburg (2012), p. 1. See, also, Giorgetti (2013), p. 265.
15 See, for example, Egger and Pfaffermayr (2004); Salacuse and Sullivan (2005); Poulsen and Aisbett (2013).
16 See, for example, Sadl and Olsen (2014), p. 8.
17 See, for example, Van Harten (2012), p. 211; Schultz and Dupont (2015); Posner and de Figueiredo (2005); Smith (2004).
18 See, for example, Behn et al. (2018); Franck (2009).
19 Samuel (2009), pp. 438, 449–50.
20 Bodansky (2006).
21 See discussion in: Dunoff and Pollack (2012), p. 19.
22 Samuel (2009), p. 432; Pollack (2014); Banakar and Travers (2013), p. ix.
23 Hirsch (2005), p. 918; Morgenthau (1940), p. 263; Allott (1999), pp. 1–2.

Empirical studies of law do not 'necessarily entail any claim about the jurisprudential importance of the particular aspects of judicial opinions that a researcher might choose to study'.[24] This means that empirical studies of law risk becoming 'law-blind'.[25] In contrast to empirical studies of law, doctrinal approaches investigate the authoritative nature of legal texts *as law*. Such methodologies use the law to determine the validity of claims made about it.[26] They remain internal to the discipline of law, focusing on the significance of law 'from the perspective of participants in the system'.[27]

Existing empirical analysis of international decisions illustrates this point. Such analysis has to date focused almost exclusively on case outcomes, rather than adjudicative reasoning.[28] Some studies even conflate adjudicative 'deference' in international investment arbitration with investor losses.[29] As Hernández notes, however, an international adjudicator's authority is 'tightly intertwined with the reasons given in its support'.[30] Particularly for a study of an adjudicative device such as deference, outcomes are less important than how and why decisions on deference are made. Focusing solely on case outcomes as data risks missing potentially more interesting and important aspects of international adjudication.

Empirical and doctrinal techniques thus both offer methodological options for the study of adjudicative deference with their own relative strengths and weaknesses. Attempts to combine these methodologies to leverage these strengths and minimise these weaknesses have to date, however, been largely unsuccessful. As Klabbers notes, the use of empirical methodologies to study international law has been 'inevitably, about subjection'.[31] Such methodologies impose the 'vocabulary, methods, theories and idiosyncrasies' from the discipline of social sciences on the discipline of law.[32] Even where

24 Hall and Wright (2008), p. 77.

25 Sylvest (2010), p. 440.

26 Samuel (2009), pp. 432–3.

27 Allott (1999), pp. 1–2. See, also, Samuel (2009), pp. 432–3.

28 See, especially, Wellhausen (2016), p. 129; Langford and Behn (2018), p. 566. Focusing on outcomes is methodologically problematic insofar as outcomes may be oversimplified and also merely reflect the strength of the parties' respective positions: Giorgetti (2013); Posner and de Figueiredo (2005), p. 601; Kapeliuk (2010), p. 71. It is difficult to draw implications from win/loss ratios without a yardstick by which to measure whether a particular 'win' was meritorious, making any analysis particularly subjective. Some scholars, inadvertently illustrating these issues, have attempted to develop 'a legal strength indicator' in order to justify appraising case outcomes: Langford and Behn (2018), p. 573.

29 Langford and Behn (2018).

30 Hernández (2014), p. 99.

31 Klabbers (2009), p. 120.

32 Ibid, p. 120.

interdisciplinarity does not result in subjection, the appeal to social sciences methods has been more 'in the nature of reference rather than integration'.[33] Scholars invoke social sciences methodologies without reflecting on their 'fit' with legal methodologies and theories. This has meant that analysts of legal texts looking for greater rigour at the level of methodology have had to select between 'two equally unappealing options'.[34] They could choose to 'defend the autonomy of international law and its legal methodology' by adopting a society-blind doctrinal approach.[35] Or they could 'let the discipline [of law] be colonized by the theories and empirical methodology of political and social scientists' by adopting a law-blind empirical approach.[36]

There is, however, a third option. To this end, this section develops a methodology for the study of law as a distinct regulative order in an empirical way. The methodology is developed through an integration of empirical social sciences methods with a legal and social sciences theory of international adjudication. This methodology is better adapted than existing empirical and doctrinal methods to analyse the significance of adjudicative approaches to deference. The methodology permits reflection on the legal and political importance of deference and its influence on the recognition of decision-making power and authority between actors in an adjudicative regime. This methodology means that the empirical analysis presented in Part II derives data and conclusions speaking to both the legal and social dimensions of deference, rendering the practice of deference 'intelligible as a sociological phenomenon, but without leaving out law'.[37]

The development of an empirical legal methodology for studying deference begins from the recognition that all doctrinal approaches are, at least in part, empirical. As Holtermann and Madsen observe, the claim that something is law (an 'ought-proposition') relies on an empirically observable fact having taken place (an 'is-proposition').[38] The legal validity of a statute, for example, presupposes the passing of the law by a legislature, which is an empirically observable phenomenon.[39] The 'data' for doctrinal approaches comprises 'legal rules, principles and decisions'.[40] These empirical facts are treated as doctrinally valid sources of data for various reasons, depending on the legal theory informing

33 Tipson (1977), p. 48.
34 Sadl and Olsen (2017), p. 328.
35 Ibid, p. 328.
36 Ibid, p. 328. See, also, Holtermann and Madsen (2016), p. 11.
37 Madsen (2013), p. 22.
38 Holtermann and Madsen (2016), pp. 10–11.
39 Ibid, pp. 19–20.
40 Peters (2013), p. 545.

their analysis. The legal theory informing an empirical study of adjudicative decisions will thus impact the implications that can be drawn from it.

A legal-positivistic empirical study of adjudicative decision-making might reveal trends in adjudicative interpretations of 'the law' on deference. Positivism identifies law by reference to formal source doctrines.[41] For international law, Article 38 of the ICJ Statute is typically taken as the starting point to identify such sources.[42] Article 38 relegates adjudicative decisions to 'subsidiary' status. For positivists, adjudicative decisions do not create law, but only offer a means to identify and interpret primary sources.[43] Given this perspective, a legal-positivistic approach 'takes law as a given . . . and seeks to ascertain what it says'.[44] The nature of authority makes it problematic, however, to treat approaches to deference as merely neutral manifestations of 'the law'. Deference instead reflects dynamics of power and authority with implications stretching beyond formal legal doctrines. A legal-positivistic analysis of deference would not account for these features of deference.

The conceptual approach to deference developed in Chapter 1 indicates that it is not possible to identify *the* approach to deference in international law. Different approaches to deference will instead subsist at different times and in different contexts. It is the comparison of these approaches and analysis of what they represent – rather than the structure of each in isolation – that forms the focus of the present study. An empirical study of adjudicative decisions underpinned by a legal-positivist theory of law would not, therefore, offer broader insights into the dynamics influencing the development of that law. This is because it treats adjudicators as neutral (apolitical) entities discovering, rather than creating, law and in so doing risks becoming society blind. Without a theory of adjudication, however, empirical study of adjudicative decisions would be nothing more than a 'mere piling up of citations'.[45]

Other theories of law recognise greater scope for adjudicators to create and develop law than traditional legal-positivist theories.[46] Some legal-positivists, for example, expand the doctrine of 'sources' to encompass adjudicative decisions as law.[47] Other scholars adopt different theories of international law, entailing recourse to different sources of data. Legal realists, for example,

41 See, further, Morgenthau (1940), p. 265; Orakhelashvili (2008), p. 55; Venzke (2014).

42 Statute of the International Court of Justice (1945).

43 See, generally, Venzke (2016), p. 69; Zammit Borda (2013), p. 652; de Brabandere (2012); Menon (1989), p. 128.

44 Bodansky (2006), p. 285.

45 Berman (2013a).

46 See, further, Besson (2011), p. 46; von Bogdandy and Venzke (2011), p. 981; Reid (1972); Alvarez (2006), p. 461.

47 Levit (2005), p. 127.

identify 'law' by reference to the decisions of adjudicators in practice.[48] Adjudicative decision-making thus forms the primary data under a theory of legal realism. Legal realists also expand the frame of potential data sources, focusing on 'the interplay of law, politics and judicial personality'.[49] Akin to legal realism, process-based theories of adjudication shift the focus of study from an 'exposition of the existing rules of international law', to an analysis of the decision-making process and the factors influencing that process.[50] Such theories offer a better theoretical basis for an empirical and legal study of adjudicative decision-making. Certain process-based theories of adjudication are particularly apt for an empirical study of deference because they focus on the role of authority in adjudicative decision-making. These theories posit that, even if legal-positivists are correct that adjudicative decisions do not formally constitute a source of law, adjudicative decisions may nonetheless operate as authoritative reference points in legal discourse.[51] This is because past decisions set expectations for participants in the system and act as focal points for legal analysis and argument.[52] They impose 'argumentative burdens', casting shadows over legal discourse by requiring engagement with their terms and justification for departure from them.[53]

Process-based theories that conceptualise adjudication as an authoritative decision-making process bring into focus the structures of power and authority underlying adjudicative decision-making. Adjudicators through their decisions articulate 'claims to normative authority'.[54] They do not passively derive rules of law by 'resorting to some pre-existing knowledge'.[55] They instead actively 'influence the construction of the social reality in which they intervene'.[56] Law does not have 'an *a priori* existence which is subsequently reduced into language'.[57] It is, instead, 'permanently reinvented', gaining meaning through interpretation and application.[58] Adjudication is

48 See, further, White (1986), p. 831; Aalberts and Venzke (2017), p. 290; Hall and Wright (2008), p. 76; Llewelyn (1930), pp. 449–50.

49 Telman (2014), p. 246.

50 Dunoff and Pollack (2012), p. 13.

51 See, especially, Venzke (2011), p. 102; Venzke (2012), p. 63.

52 See, generally, Guzman and Meyer (2008), p. 527; Cohen (2015), p. 185; Jacob (2011), p. 1015; Venzke (2011), p. 127; King and Moloo (2014), p. 883; Ginsburg (2004), p. 654; Brunnée and Toope (2000), p. 65; Koh (1997), p. 2646.

53 Venzke (2011), p. 127.

54 Hernández (2014), pp. 169, 192–3.

55 d'Aspremont (2020), p. 328.

56 Ibid, p. 333. See, similarly, Schneiderman (2010), p. 409; Crawford (2014), p. 21; Madsen (2018), p. 5.

57 Cass (1996), p. 359.

58 de Schutter and Tulkens (2008). See, similarly, Venzke (2011), p. 115; d'Aspremont (2020).

a particularly central site for that reinvention because adjudicators hold authority to talk about and construct the law.[59] Through their decisions, adjudicators socialise stakeholders towards particular conceptions of the adjudicator's authority, and particular understandings of the State, the State's role, and the extent of State authority.[60] To do so, they cite past decisions to support their own authority as well as the authority of past decision-makers. Such a theory of adjudication acknowledges greater scope for judicial agency than positivistic theories. It characterises adjudicators not merely as neutral figures applying 'the law', but rather as political actors implicated in its construction.[61]

Deference lends itself well to such analysis. In making decisions on deference, international adjudicators determine where decision-making authority lies in international legal regimes. They assert and revise the bounds of their own authority, and that of others. Coupled with a process-based theory of adjudication, empirical methods can be used to systematically analyse adjudicative decisions on deference *as law*. This treats the law and legal adjudication as distinct from facts and other forms of decision-making. It also, however, eschews the apolitical lens of positivism. It permits analysis of adjudicative decision-making as a political and authoritative practice, with international adjudicators functioning as social and political agents. Connecting adjudication to politics does not, however, require the conflation of international law with that field. Such a theory of adjudication recognises, instead, that international law functions as part of a broader political process, without denying 'the distinctiveness of law as a means of authority and social control'.[62] It recognises that adjudicative decisions manifest the law, but also construct and develop it. By integrating social sciences methods with legal theory, this method leverages the strengths of doctrinal and empirical approaches to studying law.

3.2 IDENTIFYING DEFERENCE IN LEGAL REASONING THROUGH INDUCTIVE ANALYSIS

The vast majority of existing studies of deference in international adjudication have been doctrinal.[63] Existing literature analyses specific devices or doctrines through which deference is – or could be – exhibited. It focuses on particular approaches to deference, which are usually selected because they are

59 Venzke (2011), p. 102; Madsen and Dezalay (2002), p. 189.
60 See, generally, Foucault (2007), p. 49; Holstein and Gubrium (2000), p. 344.
61 See, similarly, Fish (1989), p. 95; Fish (2000), p. 367; Samuel (2009), p. 454.
62 Koh (1997), p. 2627.
63 See, especially, Gruszczynski and Werner (2014); Dothan (2018); Henckels (2014); Legg (2012).

considered to designate deference in particular (often domestic) legal systems.[64] Empirical studies of deference in international adjudication have been similarly focused on specific manifestations or markers of deference. Van Harten's study of deference in international investment arbitration, for example, used text searches of arbitral jurisprudence for '[k]eywords ... to locate situations in which the arbitrators referred to terms and concepts used commonly by courts to show restraint based on the role of another forum'.[65] Such searches included terms that indicate deference in specific domestic contexts, such as 'Lochner', 'Oakes', 'Chevron', 'Brussels regime', and 'Wednesbury'.[66] This, and other existing studies, focus on deferential reasoning that is flagged by adjudicators using certain specific terms or doctrinal labels.[67] International decisions are thus not reviewed for instances of deference, but instead for certain (limited) deference-markers.

The methods adopted in doctrinal and empirical studies have, to date, meant that analysis of deference in international adjudication has been expressly *linguistic*. Such studies investigate similarity at the level of *conception* rather than *concept*. Those courts and tribunals considered to be more deferential will be those which deploy selected terms or doctrines to indicate deferential reasoning. Such approaches preclude accounting for deferential reasoning manifesting under different labels.[68] They also conflate possible differences in reasoning and approach insofar as such differences are labelled using common terms. Instead, however: '[L]abels are less important than the underlying approach or philosophy and its consequences.'[69] Studying deference at the level of concept (function) rather than conception (label), by contrast, better reveals whether systems are converging or diverging at the level of meaning rather than merely expression.[70] It also supports a more holistic study of approaches to deference.

A comprehensive understanding of how 'deference' manifests in international adjudication therefore cannot depend solely on a deductive text search for terms indicating deferential reasoning. Text searches of international decisions for key words taken to designate deferential reasoning can offer only limited guidance as to how international adjudicators approach

64 Gruszczynski and Werner (2014). On the utility of domestic analogies for developing international approaches to deference, see, further, Chapter 9.

65 Van Harten (2014), p. 13.

66 Van Harten (2013), p. ix.

67 See, similarly, Zglinski (2018) (deductive search for 'margin of appreciation').

68 See, more generally, Legrand (1998), p. 519; Nelken (2004), p. 2.

69 Daly (2012), p. 9 quoting Steyn (2005), p. 350.

70 Nelken (2004), p. 9; Bomhoff (2010), p. 115.

issues of deference. Such text searches presuppose how deference is structured and labelled, thereby introducing assumptions as the basis for empirical study that themselves should be empirically verified.[71] They also fail to accommodate the possibility that the incidence of linguistic markers for deference will differ either over time or according to institutional setting. Deductive text searches of ECtHR and investment treaty tribunal decisions for terms that are nowadays understood to designate deferential reasoning, for example, return more results than do searches of PCIJ and ICJ decisions. The term 'margin' (which may indicate a margin of appreciation or discretion), for instance, appears in only one private property decision of the PCIJ/ICJ, and there only to refer to a 'margin of profit'.[72] While there are instances of PCIJ and ICJ private property decisions using the term 'defer', all refer to a deferral of issues to the merits, or to 'deferred' payments. These results could indicate that the ECtHR and investment treaty tribunals are more deferential than the PCIJ or ICJ. They may, instead, indicate that certain courts or tribunals are more likely to construct deferential reasoning using anticipated terms.[73] Such results therefore reveal little without a more comprehensive analysis of how the PCIJ and ICJ account for domestic decision-making authority. A cross-institutional and temporal study of deference must be capable of identifying deference-achieving devices even where they are not labelled as might be expected.

Deductive text searches also risk conflating different approaches to deference that are nevertheless labelled using equivalent terms. A search for the term 'defer' across the corpus of investment treaty arbitration decisions, for example, returns hundreds of results indicating uses of the term to label allocations of decision-making authority. Yet, within these results, the term refers to such allocations in a range of different relationships and forms. This includes references to deference within another international[74] or domestic[75]

[71] One assumption is that the terms used to designate deference in domestic settings are used by international adjudicators. See, especially, Van Harten (2013).

[72] *Factory at Chorzów, Merits Judgment, 13-Sept-1928 (PCIJ-A17)*. Some dissenting and separate opinions used these terms to refer to deferential reasoning. These approaches are discussed in Part II.

[73] A further key difficulty associated with text searches is the short length and opaque reasoning style of some international judgments.

[74] See, for example, *Canfor, Decision on Jurisdiction, 6-Jun-2006 (UNCITRAL)*, para. 84 (deference within a WTO panel/Appellate Body decision); *Yukos, Final Award, 18 July 2014 (PCA/UNCITRAL)*, para. 709 (deference within an ECtHR decision).

[75] *ADF, Award, 9-Jan-2003 (ICSID-AF)*, para. 15 (domestic deference to international awards); *Chevron, Partial Award on Merits, 30-Mar-2010 (UNCITRAL)*, para. 340 (inter-State comity); *Ambiente Ufficio, Decision on Jurisdiction and Admissibility, 8-Feb-2013 (ICSID)*, para. 617 (domestic deference to political decisions).

decision or system; deference to a State in assessing the necessity of measures or the presence of a public interest;[76] deference in treaty interpretation, including deferential interpretation to leave a State policy space[77] deference *to* treaty text[78] and deference (flexibility) *within* treaty text;[79] deference to another international body;[80] deference to the claimant's framing of its case[81] or its business judgments;[82] deference to a contractually selected choice of forum;[83] deference to domestic judicial decisions or proceedings;[84] deference to State law;[85] and deference to domestic administrative proceedings.[86] A search for the term 'comity'[87] returns a similarly diverse set of results, revealing that 'comity' has been invoked as a principle supporting a finding of non-violation;[88] to inform the selection of a standard of proof;[89] and as regulating the relationship between international adjudicators and domestic courts.[90] These results reveal that one term might be deployed to describe reasoning achieving deference in diverse ways. Conversely, different terms

76 See Part II.

77 See Part II. See, for example, *PNG Sustainable Development, Award, 5-May-2015 (ICSID)*, paras 177, 256–7.

78 See, for example, *Tokios Tokelės, Decision on Jurisdiction, 29-Apr-2004 (ICSID)*, para. 25; *Waguih Siag, Decision on Jurisdiction, 11-Apr-2007 (ICSID)*, para. 127.

79 See, for example, *Aguas del Tunari, Decision on Jurisdiction, 21-Oct-2005 (ICSID)*, para. 285; *Caratube, Award, 5-Jun-2012 (ICSID)*, para. 336 (ICSID requirement of 'foreign control' as 'flexible and deferential'). On interpretation of 'foreign control' under the ICSID Convention, see, further, Caron and Shirlow (2019).

80 See, for example, *Electrabel, Decision on Jurisdiction, Applicable Law and Liability, 30-Nov -2012 (ICSID)*, para. 4.15 (deference to earlier arbitral decisions); *Eastern Sugar, Partial Award, 27-Mar-2007 (SCC)*, para. 118 (deference to EU organs). See, further, Shany (2003); Shirlow (2014a).

81 See, for example, *Garanti Koza, Decision on Jurisdiction, 3-Jul-2013 (ICSID)*, para. 85 (claimant requesting deference to its 'view that ICSID Arbitration is more favorable than UNCITRAL Arbitration' for application of a most-favoured nation clause). On such clauses, see, further, Caron and Shirlow (2015).

82 See, for example, *Micula, Final Award, 11-Dec-2013 (ICSID)*, para. 1138.

83 See, for example, *SGS (Pakistan), Decision on Jurisdiction, 6-Aug-2003 (ICSID)*, para. 73; *SGS (Paraguay), Decision on Jurisdiction, 12-Feb-2010 (ICSID)*, para. 183.

84 See Part II.

85 See Part II.

86 See Part II.

87 See, generally, on comity, D'Alterio (2011), pp. 398–9; Paul (1991); Schultz and Ridi (2017); Worster (2008); Eleftheriadis (2010); Endicott (2001); Endicott (2015); Amaza (2012); Shany (2007), p. 166.

88 See, for example, *Al Warraq, Final Award, 15-Dec-2014 (UNCITRAL)*, para. 405; *Railroad Development Corporation, Award, 29-Jun-2012 (ICSID)*, para. 175; *CCL, Jurisdictional Award, 1-Jan-2003 (SCC)*, p. 138.

89 See, for example, *Tokios Tokelės, Award, 26-Jul-2007 (ICSID)*, para. 124.

90 See, for example, *British Caribbean Bank, Award, 19-Dec-2014 (PCA/UNCITRAL)*, paras 187–90, 213–15.

might describe the same phenomenon or function, even within the one regime. Ambrus, for example, argues that 'the terms "standard of proof", "level of scrutiny", and "margin of appreciation" describe the same phenomenon – though from different perspectives'.[91] A comparative and empirical study of deference must thus move beyond labels, to consider instead the function of these devices and linguistic markers.

This book is therefore based on an *inductive* analysis of deference in international private property decisions. The book also adopts a functional rather than linguistic approach to comparison. It focuses on the functional purpose served by deference. Most systems of law rely on a distribution of power between different governmental bodies. Allocations can occur both vertically (for example, local, federal, international) and horizontally (for example, legislative, judicial, executive). Allocations of authority invariably produce overlaps, necessitating devices to determine where final decision-making authority lies. This is the function of deference. This function of deference may be achieved and expressed in diverse ways. To investigate deference functionally, this book proposes a methodological shift from existing analyses. Instead of investigating deference as a doctrine or specific legal rule (conception), it studies deference as a form of legal reasoning (concept). The approach therefore does not presume substantive uniformity in the devices through which deference manifests. It begins instead from a more neutral position assuming only functional unity: that international adjudicators will have developed some method(s) to regulate conflicting claims to authority. This approach to comparison accommodates the possibility that adjudicators may structure and label deference differently.

3.2.1 *Case Selection*

The study of deference reported in Part II focuses on deference in the private property 'decisions' of the PCIJ, ICJ, ECtHR, and investment treaty tribunals.[92] The analysed 'decisions' include decisions in English[93] on

[91] Ambrus (2013), p. 109.

[92] This approach avoids sampling on the dependent variable. Compare, for example, Arnardóttir (2017), p. 22 ('the sample consisted of judgments where the Court expressly dealt with the national margin of appreciation, i.e., where the term "margin of appreciation" came up as a keyword or in free text search').

[93] The review of cases was limited to those in English. The low number of decisions from the selected four regimes that have not been translated into English reduces the likelihood of the analysis missing important differences, but future research could productively explore the possibility of there being differing approaches to deference in English- and non-English proceedings.

provisional measures, jurisdiction, merits, damages, rectification, and supplementation.[94] Dissenting and separate opinions[95] and annulment decisions are also analysed.[96] Decisions on agreed terms and purely procedural (for example, scheduling) decisions are excluded because they are unlikely to address issues of deference.[97]

The study focuses exclusively on 'private property' decisions. An inclusive approach was adopted to identify 'private property' cases for this study.[98] 'Property' was taken to encompass rights or interests that individuals might hold over objects or 'things'.[99] This encompasses both tangible and intangible property, and rights *in rem* or *in personam*.[100] The approach to identifying 'property' was therefore broad and non-technical, encompassing anything claimed to be private property.[101] This open definition supports institutional, temporal, and cross-case comparisons. It reflects that differences in the types of property or interests protected in each regime do not themselves impact the functional role to be played by deference in each setting. A flexible approach to identifying 'private property' cases also supports temporal comparisons. It accommodates changes to the notion of 'property' over time.[102] Property is, after all, 'an expansive and highly adaptable legal category'.[103] It nevertheless retains a recognisable core permitting comparative study.[104]

94 The last two types of decision form an integral part of the decision they supplement or rectify. See, especially, Convention on the Settlement of Investment Disputes between States and Nationals of Other States (1965/1966) 575 UNTS 159, arts 49–51.

95 Each regime permits adjudicators to issue dissenting and separate opinions. Such decisions may elucidate the majority's reasoning and/or influence the development of future approaches to deference. Adjudicators may also be comparatively more willing to discuss issues of deference in dissenting/separate opinions as compared to majority decisions. All declarations, dissents, and separate opinions are designated in what follows as 'dissent/separate opinion' or 'dissent/SO'. On conventions around labelling separate opinions as 'dissenting', 'concurring', 'separate', etc., see, further, Anand (1965); Hussain (1984).

96 On the role of annulment committees, see, especially, Caron (2012).

97 Only unique, non-substantively identical, decisions were analysed. Procedural decisions on stays of proceeding/enforcement were included.

98 'Private' property is that belonging to natural or legal persons.

99 See, especially, Sprankling (2014), pp. 22–3.

100 See, further, ibid, p. 36. On the distinction between contractual and property rights see, generally, Martinkute (2016); Douglas (2014a).

101 Care must thus be taken in deriving conclusions from the data as to the frequency of private property cases. On the difficulties of categorising disputes, see, further, Romano (2002), p. 383.

102 See, generally, van Banning (2002); Poirier (2002), p. 186. See, for example, Frigo (2000), pp. 45–49 (expansion of 'possessions' under P1-1 over time); Sornarajah (1994), p. 190 (expansion of 'investment' over time).

103 Merges (2011), p. 4.

104 Sprankling (2012), p. 31.

All publicly available investment treaty arbitration decisions are treated as private property decisions for the purposes of this study.[105] PCIJ and ICJ private property cases were identified by a review of the documents related to all disputes filed before each Court.[106] Cases in which private property was not mentioned, or only mentioned in passing as an incidental issue, are treated as non-private property cases for these Courts.[107] For the ECtHR, only P1-1 claims are included.[108] The sheer number of P1-1 decisions means that only a sample have been analysed. All Grand Chamber ('GC') P1-1 decisions were included (n = 88), given that the GC only considers cases raising serious issues of 'general importance'.[109] The GC's procedure also 'nearly always includes a public hearing, and is longer and more thorough'.[110] GC decisions thus have 'particular weight within the Convention system'.[111] In addition to these GC decisions, a sample of Committee and Chamber P1-1 decisions was also analysed (n = 383).[112] These decisions were included because many

[105] Investment treaty decisions were treated as 'publicly available' where they were available by January 2020 through italaw.com or the ICSID, International Energy Charter Treaty, PCA, United Nations Conference on Trade and Development, or Stockholm Chamber of Commerce ('SCC') websites. The public disclosure of decisions appears sufficiently random to remove the risk that publication is biased towards decisions with particular qualitative features. As the dataset consists of the entire population of publicly available investment arbitration decisions, Part II reports population – rather than sample – statistics.

[106] Five differently designated proceedings were treated as two 'disputes' to arrive at an overall figure for the number of PCIJ private property disputes (n = 16): (i) 'Certain German Interests in Polish Upper Silesia' and 'Factory at Chorzów'; and (ii) 'The Mavrommatis Jerusalem Concessions', 'The Mavrommatis Palestine Concessions', and 'Readaptation of the Mavrommatis Jerusalem Concessions'.

[107] This process was cross-checked by comparison to categorisations of other scholars. See, in particular, Posner (2004), p. 3; Posner and de Figueiredo (2005), p. 505.

[108] Other ECHR provisions may also be invoked by reference to private property rights (particularly Articles 6, 8, 13 and 14). Where these provisions are invoked by reference to private property they are, however, usually raised in conjunction with a P1-1 claim. Articles 13 and 14, in particular, are treated as complementary to the other Convention rights: Merrills (1988), p. 169. The Court's analysis of P1-1 claims will therefore typically refer also to its analysis of these other provisions insofar as they are relevant to claimed property rights. Such cross-references are incorporated in the empirical study.

[109] European Convention on Human Rights and Fundamental Freedoms (1950/1953) ETS 5, arts 30 and 43.

[110] Costa (2011), p. 176.

[111] de Londras and Dzehtsiarou (2015), p. 533.

[112] To identify this sample, a list of all P1-1 Committee and Chamber decisions as at 1 January 2020 was prepared (n = 2,018). The sample was selected by two methods: (i) a purposive sample, whereby the first decision issued in each calendar year was selected for review; and (ii) a randomised sample, whereby every fifth decision in the list was selected for review. The number of decisions analysed was selected to ensure that the sample was 'representative' of the population. Social sciences sampling techniques suggested that a minimum of 322 decisions

proceedings do not continue past Committee and Chamber level. In addition, where a case is referred from Committee or Chamber level to the GC, the GC frequently adopts Committee and Chamber findings of fact and law without engaging in *de novo* review.[113] All dissenting and separate opinions for the analysed ECtHR decisions were also reviewed (n = 226). The analysis of ECtHR decisions was thus systematic, without being exhaustive. This approach resulted in the collection of 1,714 decisions – comprising 1,212 majority and 502 dissenting or separate opinions – from 889 proceedings decided from 1924 to 2019 (see Table 3.1).

3.2.2 *Case Analysis*

Once the 'private property' cases of each institution had been identified, each decision was assembled in a custom-built NVivo database. Each document was read in its entirety and 'coded'.[114] 'Coding' refers to the labelling of text to

TABLE 3.1 *Database overview*

	Analysed documents		
	Number of private property disputes	Number of private property 'decisions'	Number of dissents, declarations, separate opinions
PCIJ	16	31	58
ICJ	12	21	101
ECtHR Grand Chamber	77	88	157
ECtHR Committee and Chamber	380	383	69
ICSID investment treaty arbitration	229	423	78
Non-ICSID investment treaty arbitration	175	266	39
TOTAL	889	1,212	502

needed to be analysed to have a 95 per cent probability that the sample analysed would represent the population: Guthrie (2010), pp. 54–5.

113 Shelton (2003), p. 123.

114 Coding was completed by one person but discussed with others, allowing for consistency but not multiple perspectives on the data. To ensure consistency, the approach was documented as coding progressed. On such 'memoing', see, further, Ngulube (2015), p. 19; Webley (2010), p. 936.

create an index of terms that are both summative and 'essence-capturing' of the content of the decisions.[115] This approach permitted the reading of each decision in isolation, while also identifying the themes raised in each decision that were like those raised in other decisions. Coding was split into four phases.

In a first phase, 'metadata' was assigned to each decision. This captured information about each decision, including the parties to the dispute, the date of decision, and the adjudicators issuing it. Each document was also indexed using descriptive coding. Text was labelled, for example, as relating to particular procedural, jurisdictional, or merits issues. This process of indexing was completed iteratively, in order to remain responsive to topics raised in the text of the decisions. Coding therefore did not proceed by reference to a list of topics prepared in advance. This approach prompted a closer engagement with the decisions, and provided a means of breaking down and categorising the data by pulling out initial points of interest.[116] All coding during this phase was 'tentative and provisional'[117]: it was intended to organise the data to support later phases of more focused and systematic coding.

The second phase of coding was more targeted. During this phase, attention was directed towards identifying how adjudicators recognised or referred to the decision-making authority of domestic decision-makers. As noted already, the approach to coding adopted in this phase anticipated that adjudicators may allocate domestic decision-making authority without necessarily labelling that analysis using particular, predictable, terms. As such, instead of looking for labels, the approach to coding sought to identify 'indicators' of deference. Codes were derived inductively from the data to summarise adjudicative approaches to deference.[118] The purpose was to 'build concepts out of data ... rather than impose those concepts on the data'.[119] This meant that the coding scheme was not developed in advance. It was instead developed iteratively through the reading and rereading of the decisions. Where new approaches to deference were identified, previously coded decisions were reread to ensure that such approaches were 'new' rather than latent or

115 On 'coding', see, generally, Saldaña (2009), p. 3; Hess (2013), p. 935; Caudle (2010), p. 422; Ngulube (2015), p. 6.

116 Bryman and Burgess (2000), p. 5.

117 Saldaña (2009), p. 81.

118 On such inductive techniques for coding, see, further, Leech and Onwuegbuzie (2007), p. 565; Ayres et al. (2003), p. 874; Berg and Lune (2014), p. 338; White and Marsh (2006), p. 35.

119 Nourse and Shaffer (2014), p. 165.

overlooked in previous coding.[120] This approach required constant reflection and comparison between decisions. This approach supported a deeper engagement with the decisions, and yielded results that would not have been possible had the decisions been reviewed with a preconceived view as to the structure deference ought to take. It instead enabled the identification of unanticipated approaches to deference.

Concretely, this meant that each decision was reviewed to identify where domestic decisions or the possibility of domestic decisions were referred to by adjudicators.[121] Where such text was identified, it was reviewed and coded in response to the following questions:

(i) What doctrines or structures of reasoning are used to attribute weight or relevance to domestic decision-making?
(ii) What rationale(s) are offered for the invocation and/or use of such structures or doctrines (if any)?[122]
(iii) What (if any) source (i.e., treaty rules, general principles etc.) is identified as the basis for those doctrines or of the court or tribunal's approach to domestic decision-making?
(iv) Which domestic decision-makers, or which domestic decisions, are granted or denied deference?

Attention was thus directed towards understanding the features of deference and the factual circumstances within which it arises. This approach reflects social sciences methodologies targeted at generating, rather than testing, theory.[123] The use of 'indicators', rather than particular search terms, stemmed from the expectation that international adjudicators would use various terms and approaches to construct deferential reasoning. Inductive coding was thus informed not by hypotheses, but rather by 'foreshadowing questions'.[124] This reflected the goals of the research. The purpose was not to

[120] Ngulube (2015), p. 8; Saldaña (2009), p. 149.
[121] A broad notion of 'domestic decision' was adopted to capture decisions from all actors capable of binding the State as a matter of public international law, noting that the precise application of principles of attribution may be disputed in practice. This approach identified all adjudicative references to domestic decision-making, including some not relevant to the focus of the project. This included, in particular, references to domestic decisions for the purposes of identifying State practice, *opinio juris*, and general principles of law; as relevant to treaty interpretation; for estoppel-based arguments; or as the basis of domestic analogies.
[122] For example, the role of the court or tribunal, its legitimacy/illegitimacy vis-à-vis domestic actors etc. See, further, Chapter 8.
[123] See, especially, White and Marsh (2006), pp. 30, 34; Walliman (2011), pp. 36–7.
[124] White and Marsh (2006), p. 34.

test a hypothesis that deference *would be* expressed in a particular way, but instead to *discover* how international adjudicators construct deferential reasoning. The use of 'open questions' about how deference would be structured, sourced, and justified, and to which decisions or decision-makers it would attach, guided a flexible analysis, eschewing a more rigid 'mining' of the data in search of particular labels for, or structures of, deference.

Analysis of decisions to identify such indicators was completed in tandem with the development of the conceptual framework reported in Chapter 1. This ensured that the theoretical and empirical components of the project were integrated and informed one another. This distinguishes the enquiry reported in this book from more positivistic or causation-focused studies. As noted in Chapter 2, the intent is not to predict future approaches. Instead, the empirical study has been developed inductively and qualitatively to ground analytical, critical, and in-depth insights into the phenomenon of deference in different institutional settings and time periods.

This method has certain limitations. The analysis of deference in 'decisions', for instance, uses textual references as a proxy for significance.[125] A potential limitation, therefore, arises from the possibility that adjudicators will not expressly address issues of deference. Some adjudicators allude to matters of deference in passing without extrapolating in detail the basis for their approach. Such opacity was most evident in earlier decisions and the decisions of particular adjudicators. It may stem from the approach taken to drafting,[126] or alternatively reflect an unawareness, inability or even caution to articulate the true basis of decision.[127] An adjudicator may also adopt particularly sparse forms of expression to 'appear to speak with authority and conviction'.[128] Failures to mention deference are, however, in themselves worthy of study. Silences reveal that adjudicators consider that they either need not, or *should* not, mention deference as a basis for decision-making. The more accepted deference is, for example, the more likely it is to be implicit and not extensively argued. Similarly, strategic mentions of deferential reasoning – even if, in reality, deference did not influence the adjudicator's analysis of the case – show that the adjudicator considers deference to be a 'satisfactory and publicly acknowledgeable grounds for decision making'.[129] As the analysis is not

125 Baker (2006), pp. 44, 48.
126 On which, see, further, Hernández (2014), pp. 103–5; Bedjaoui (1991), pp. 51–8; Weeramantry (1996), p. 3; Jhabvala (1978), p. 830.
127 Oldfather et al. (2012), pp. 1201, 1212; Fauchald (2008), p. 308; Thirlway (2006), p. 23.
128 Baker (2006), p. 122.
129 Bankowski et al. (1991), p. 17. See, similarly, Hall and Wright (2008), p. 98.

intended to predict future outcomes, it is unnecessary to base the empirical approach on an assumption that adjudicators do what they say they are doing. Instead, the study focuses on *the reasons* provided *to justify* adjudicative decisions about deference to domestic decision-making. The method accounts for the possibility that adjudicators may use one reason to reach a decision, and another to justify it. It treats the giving of reasons as an 'important political act, notwithstanding the fact that such statements might be disingenuous'.[130] The decisions were thus analysed to identify what they reveal about how international adjudicators 'account for, and legitimate, their activities'.[131]

Another potential limitation of an inductive analysis is coding fallibility. To address this potential limitation, qualitative inductive analysis was supplemented with deductive coding. Where particular terms were identified as linked to deferential reasoning, text searches were run across the corpus of decisions for those terms.[132] This included words such as 'defer', 'comity', 'manoeuvre', 'right to regulate', 'margin', 'latitude', 'better placed', 'competent authorities', and 'restraint'. It also included references to specific doctrines or procedures, such as 'exhaustion of local remedies' and 'justiciability'. Such text searches were used as a means of cross-checking that the manual coding of decisions had not missed any references to potentially relevant reasoning structures. For each such text search, results were subsequently reviewed to examine how words were used in context. This supported analysis of whether they indicated an instance of deferential reasoning or instead the use of a term in another (irrelevant) context.[133]

In a third phase, the codes generated in earlier phases were compared, merged into categories, and/or organised into hierarchical lists.[134] This sorted them into meaningful groups describing distinct approaches to deference. The overarching aim in this phase was to identify cross-cutting categories, patterns, themes, and connections in the data. During this phase, focus shifted from individual decisions to the codes which had been generated. Codes were no longer read in the context of the specific case, instead

130 Hurd (1999), p. 391.

131 Silverman (2011), p. 248.

132 On this method of directed content analysis, see, generally, Berg and Lune (2014), p. 338; Leech and Onwuegbuzie (2008), p. 602; Saldaña (2009), p. 120.

133 The term 'defer', for example, was used to refer to a range of different types of deferential reasoning, but also as a way of referring to postponed events or payments.

134 On 'thematic' coding, see, further, Boyatzis (1998), p. 160; Leech and Onwuegbuzie (2007), p. 564; Gerbic and Stacey (2005), p. 46; Vaismoradi et al. (2013), p. 400; Fereday and Muir-Cochrane (2006), p. 89; Boyatzis (1998); Ayres et al. (2003).

being disentangled from their individual context to identify cross-cutting themes. The origin of each code in a data source (decision) became less important than its relationship to other codes. This again was an iterative process, as the generation of themes required revisiting the texts to ensure that the generated themes described the content of the decisions as closely as possible.

Once codes had been sorted into groups and lists, coded content was reread to develop categories capable of describing the full range of approaches to deference used by international courts and tribunals. In this fourth phase, coded data was extracted and read *as a code* rather than as extracts of individual decisions. Based on this analysis of the coded text, codes were again merged and reordered, this time based on conceptual similarities between the approaches to deference identified and coded in the previous phases. Gradually, the categories of deferential reasoning discussed in Part II were identified in the data. Thereafter, a quantitative analysis of these codes and categories was conducted to produce the data reported in Chapter 8.

3.3 CONCLUSIONS

This chapter introduced the theoretical and methodological framework informing the empirical analysis of adjudicative approaches to deference reported in Part II. The chapter introduced the limitations of doctrinal analysis of deference, as well as the difficulties associated with empirical techniques. It emphasised, in particular, the apparent dichotomy in existing literature between 'internal' doctrinal and 'external' empirical analyses of legal reasoning. The chapter examined how empirical methods might be connected to legal theory to chart a third course instead. Recognising that the implications to be drawn from empirical studies of legal reasoning will differ depending on the theoretical paradigms informing them, the chapter introduced a process-based theory of adjudication according to which international adjudication is viewed as an authoritative decision-making practice. It thereafter examined how this theoretical paradigm could be used to underpin an empirical investigation of the legal *and* political implications of deference. In so doing, it generated a framework to support an 'internal' – yet empirical – analysis of adjudicative decision-making. The methodological framework developed in this chapter links to the particular aims and themes underlying the book. It draws on the close connection between deference and authority developed in Chapter 1. It also brings into focus the relationships between deference, authority, and power, as well as the dynamic properties of deference and its legal and political implications. The framework is, nonetheless, capable of more general application. The chapter thus contributes to the broader methodological literature, offering one means of rationalising the application of qualitative and quantitative empirical techniques to analyse international adjudicative decision-making. Part II is based on the application of these techniques.

PART II

DEFERENCE IN THE INTERNATIONAL ADJUDICATION OF PRIVATE PROPERTY DISPUTES

This part examines how the PCIJ, ICJ, ECtHR, and investment treaty tribunals have recognised the decision-making authority of domestic officials in private property cases. The part is based on a comprehensive inductive study of the ways in which international adjudicators conceptualise the effect of domestic decisions in international adjudication by reference to second-order reasons. The analysis is empirical rather than evaluative. The account of deference proceeds separately from any assessment as to the strengths or weaknesses of different approaches, or even of deference itself. The part develops an analytical framework to identify different approaches to deference, and to examine the conceptual assumptions that underpin them. In mapping approaches to deference, and linking them to different conceptual paradigms, Part II provides a framework to explain how deference operates in international adjudication. It uses examples from the analysed cases to illustrate broadly similar approaches to deferential reasoning in international private property cases and to investigate how deference is structured and applied in adjudicative decision-making.

Chapter 4 identifies the recipients of deference, and introduces a taxonomy illustrating how deference manifests in international adjudication. This taxonomy moves beyond a binary distinction between deferential and non-deferential approaches, highlighting the nuances sitting between these poles. The chapter identifies seven different 'modes' of deference in international adjudication. It builds on Chapter 1 by dividing these modes of deference according to whether they represent 'conclusive', 'suspensive', or 'concurrent' views of decision-making authority. These views of decision-making authority, and the approaches to deference underlying them, are introduced in the subsequent chapters of this part, which examine approaches to deference reflecting a view of decision-making authority as conclusive (Chapter 5) or suspensive (Chapter 6), and approaches to deference that treat domestic and international decision-making authority as concurrent (Chapter 7). The main aim of these chapters is to demonstrate that different approaches to deference in international adjudication reflect distinct views as to the interface between domestic and international decision-making. As such, these chapters do not provide an exhaustive account of every instance of each mode of deference. Instead, I have selected illustrative examples to highlight the features of, and differences between, these approaches.

4

Structures of Deference in International Adjudication

This chapter develops an explanatory framework that organises approaches to deference in international adjudication according to how each approach to deference structures the relationship between international and domestic decision-making authority. Section 4.1 introduces the range of domestic decisions referred to by adjudicators in the four regimes. These references to domestic decisions were analysed as part of the empirical study to determine how international adjudicators structure deference to domestic decisions. Section 4.2 introduces the results of this analysis, identifying seven different 'modes' of deference present in international adjudicative decision-making. These modes range from treating domestic decisions as controlling on international adjudicators ('conclusive domestic authority'), to rejections of deference to domestic decisions entirely ('conclusive international authority'). Between these two extremes, deference to domestic decisions also at times results in a suspension of the exercise of international decision-making authority ('suspensive domestic authority'), or in a more concurrent operation of domestic and international decision-making authority ('concurrent authority'). These distinct approaches to deference, and to authority, are introduced in this chapter and explored in more detail in Chapters 5 to 7.

4.1 DEVELOPING A TAXONOMY OF DEFERENCE: IDENTIFYING REFERENCES TO DOMESTIC DECISIONS IN INTERNATIONAL PRIVATE PROPERTY CASES

This book explores deference to the full range of domestic decision-making, including decisions by legislatures, administrators, executive officers, and the courts. This reflects that international adjudicators in international private property decisions are confronted with a range of different domestic decisions to which they might defer. The types of domestic decisions that might attract deference from international adjudicators are introduced in this section. Subsection 4.1.1 examines references to domestic judicial decisions by adjudicators in the four regimes, and Subsection 4.1.2 the references by these adjudicators to domestic regulatory decisions concerning public purposes. Subsection 4.1.3 introduces a further category of domestic decisions referred to by adjudicators in the four regimes, related to the interpretation or application of domestic law. All references to such domestic decisions were used as the basis for identifying adjudicative approaches to structuring and analysing deference. These approaches form the focus of Section 4.2.

4.1.1 *Domestic Judicial Decisions*

International adjudicators in private property cases frequently refer to domestic judicial decisions. Domestic judicial decisions become relevant in international adjudication in several ways. A judicial decision may itself be impugned before an international court or tribunal.[1] In such cases, international adjudicators must determine whether they can review a domestic judicial decision to determine whether it breaches international law. This is primarily a matter of applicable law. As noted in Part I, some obligations are inherently more stringent and controlling of State decision-making than others. Adjudicators may, however, act deferentially by expressly reducing the stringency of an international obligation by reference to second-order reasons to provide greater scope for autonomous State decision-making authority. International adjudicators may also confront requests for deference to domestic judicial proceedings or decisions where the dispute itself concerns non-judicial measures. An impugned measure might, for example, have already been, or could in the future be, reviewed by a domestic court.[2] A domestic court might alternatively have already pronounced on certain matters of fact or law related to the subject matter of the international claim.[3] A judicial decision, or series of judicial decisions, might otherwise have discussed the interpretation or application of law relevant to the

[1] As in the case, for instance, of a denial of justice. On which see, generally, Paulsson (2005). Domestic judicial decisions may also form the basis of expropriation or fair and equitable treatment claims, among others. See, further, Demirkol (2018). See, for example, *Saipem, Award, 30-Jun-2009 (ICSID)*; *GEA, Award, 31-Mar-2011 (ICSID)*; *Deutsche Bank, Award, 31-Oct-2012 (ICSID)*; *Arif, Award, 8-Apr-2013 (ICSID)*. On the capacity for judicial decisions to constitute an expropriation compare, however, Douglas (2014b).

[2] See, for example, *Feldman, Interim Decision on Preliminary Issues, 6-Dec-2000 (ICSID-AF)*; *BG, Final Award, 24-Dec-2007 (UNCITRAL)*; *Azinian, Final Award, 1-Nov-1999 (ICSID-AF)*; *Archer Daniels, Award, 21-Nov-2007 (ICSID-AF)*, paras 96–100.

[3] See, for example, *Binder, Final Award, 15-Jul-2011 (UNCITRAL)*, paras 427–8.

international claim.[4] Deference to domestic judicial decisions or proceedings in these scenarios has been largely underexplored in the literature.[5]

The interactions between international adjudicators and domestic courts are usually only partly, if at all, regulated by applicable treaties or customary international law. The most common rules dealing with the relationship between domestic and international adjudicators tend to confer sequential authority on one decision-maker. Such sequential organisation is, for example, achieved through clauses requiring an exhaustion of local remedies or imposing a fork-in-the-road requirement. To the extent they exist, such rules regulate interactions only partially, leaving open the question as to the ultimate weight to be attributed to domestic judicial decisions by international adjudicators. This means that international adjudicators have significant discretion in determining whether – and to what extent – to defer to domestic judicial decisions. Deference to domestic judicial decisions signals an international adjudicator's awareness of the limits of its authority relative to domestic courts. Such deference may follow from an appraisal of various categories of second-order reason as introduced in Chapter 1. Domestic courts may, for example, be considered to have better authority to interpret and apply domestic law than an international adjudicator.[6] Domestic courts might also be perceived to have better resources to evaluate facts or otherwise be closer to and therefore in a better position to access and appraise evidence.[7] Some commentators also argue that domestic courts might be better placed to assess 'important public policy considerations' because their proceedings are 'ordinarily open to the public' and 'often provide for third-party submissions on public interest matters'.[8] Considerations of authority might even prompt international adjudicators to defer to domestic judicial determinations on international law. Most commentators reject scope for such deference, arguing that domestic courts will typically not be superior decision-makers on such matters when compared to international adjudicators.[9] There may, nonetheless, be some scope for deference, including in relation to domestic

4 See, for example, *Rafig Aliyev, Judgment, 6-Dec-2011 (ECtHR)*, paras 121–8; *Helnan, Decision on Jurisdiction, 17-Oct-2006 (ICSID)*, paras 105–6, 147–8, 162.

5 This reflects that many studies focus expressly only on deference to public purpose determinations. See, for example, Henckels (2015), p. 20.

6 See, for example, Douglas (2003), p. 273; Nollkaemper (2006), p. 318; Jenks (1938), p. 591; Young (2005), p. 207; Kolb (2013), p. 875.

7 Nollkaemper (2011), p. 254. See, similarly, Romano (2013), pp. 563–4; Costa (2011), p. 179; Jennings (1998), p. 13.

8 Trakman (2014), p. 168.

9 Grant (2015), p. 52; Nollkaemper (2011), p. 254; Vadi (2010), p. 98; Young (2005), pp. 203–4. The likelihood of such deference increases where domestic courts are empowered to apply

judicial applications of well-established international obligations, as compared to more abstract interpretations of international law.

4.1.2 *Regulatory Decisions Concerning Public Purposes*

The empirical study revealed that States interfere with private property for a range of claimed public purposes, and that those public purposes may fall within the scope of review in several guises. Public purposes may be relevant to an adjudicator's jurisdiction, be relevant interests in balancing tests, form a requisite component of legal tests applied to determine whether State conduct complies with international law, or operate as exceptions or defences. While decisions as to the scope of review can be determinative of the role played by deference, such decisions are not themselves manifestations of deference.[10] Instead, the matters relevant to an adjudicator's scope of review represent only *first-order* reasons.[11] Given the close relationship between deference and a scope of review encompassing public purposes, however, this subsection briefly reviews the key ways adjudicators considered public purposes to be relevant to international private property obligations in the reviewed private property cases, before considering how deference might be relevant in these assessments.

In several decisions, international adjudicators assessed the relevance and veracity of State claims to have acted for public purposes as a matter relevant to their jurisdiction and/or the admissibility of a private property claim. Adjudicators confronted such public purposes in determining whether 'political' as compared to 'legal' disputes were justiciable, whether matters were within a State's 'reserved' or 'domestic' jurisdiction, and whether a dispute implicated a State's 'inherent right to regulate', 'vital interests', or 'sovereignty'.[12] Where connected to jurisdiction and admissibility, the analysis of public purposes raises two interrelated points of deference. First, it prompts adjudicators to demarcate boundaries between the

international law. See, generally, Gardbaum (2009); Petzold (1993), pp. 61–2; El Boudouhi (2015), p. 17. The role of domestic judicial decisions as a source of international law is beyond the scope of this book. On this relevance of domestic judicial decisions, see, Nollkaemper (2009), p. 19; de Visscher (1968), p. 391; Zammit Borda (2013), p. 658; Jenks (1964), p. 555.

10 Cf. Vadi and Gruszczynski (2013), p. 625; Salazar (2010), pp. 57–8.

11 de Ville (2004), pp. 596, 607. On first-order reasons, see Chapter 1.

12 See, for example, *Certain Property, Preliminary Objections, 10-Feb-2005 (ICJ)*, pp. 12, 16; and *Anglo-Iranian Oil, Preliminary Objection Judgment, 22-Jul-1952 (ICJ)*, pp. 98–101 (domestic jurisdiction); *Abaclat, Decision on Jurisdiction and Admissibility, 4-Aug-2011 (ICSID)*, paras 548–50 (sovereign debt restructuring); *Spyridon, Award, 7-Dec-2011 (ICSID)*, paras 737–40 (public powers regulation, including taxation); *Electricity Company of Sofia and Bulgaria (Dissent/SO-Urrutia), 4-Apr-1939 (PCIJ-A/B77)*, para. 63 ('the working conditions of a public service conceded . . . to a foreign concessionaire').

decision-making authority of international adjudicators and States in respect of public purposes.[13] Second, if public purposes are considered relevant to matters of jurisdiction or admissibility, adjudicators may be more or less deferential in ascertaining the presence of such public purposes and their connection to the dispute before the adjudicator.

Public purposes may also be relevant to appraising the international legality of State conduct. Customary international law, along with most investment treaties, for example, permits States to expropriate foreign property if such expropriation pursues, inter alia, a 'public purpose'.[14] Under the ECHR, States are similarly required to identify a 'general' or 'public' interest to justify any interference with 'possessions'.[15] Analysis of whether a measure breaches an international obligation requiring a State to act 'reasonably' or 'non-arbitrarily', and any rule requiring 'proportionate' conduct, may also entail an assessment of a State's public purposes. Under P1-1, for example, the legality of State interference with property is predicated on an analysis of whether the State struck a 'fair balance' between public purposes and individual rights.[16] Some investment treaty obligations have been similarly interpreted to require States to act proportionately or otherwise to balance investor rights against the public interests of the host State.[17] Thus, adjudicators may weigh public purposes alongside other factors to determine whether a State's conduct has, on balance, breached an international obligation.

[13] On justiciability, see, generally, McGoldrick (2010), p. 985; King (2008), pp. 420–3. On justiciability in international law, see, further, Rosenne (1997), p. 776; Juss (1994), p. 227; de Bustamente y Sirven (1924), p. 249; Merrills (1969); Kolb (2013), p. 332. On the right to regulate, see Titi (2014); Korzun (2017). On 'political' and 'legal' disputes, see Lauterpacht (1933); Bodie (1995). On the 'reserved' domain, see Hull (1970), p. 319; Arangio-Ruiz (1996); Brierly (1925). On when justiciability might reflect deference, see Chapter 1.

[14] See, for example, *Anglo-Iranian Oil (Dissent/SO-Levi Carneiro), 22-Jul-1952 (ICJ)*, p. 159; *Feldman, Award, 16-Dec-2002 (ICSID-AF)*, paras 135–6; *AIG, Award, 7-Oct-2003 (ICSID)*, para. 10.4.1. See, further, Higgins (1982), p. 288; Bring (1980), p. 107; Nicholson (1965), p. 399; López Escarcena (2014), p. 60.

[15] See, for example, *Marckx, Judgment, 13-Jun-1979 (ECtHR)*, para. 64; *Hakansson, Judgment, 21-Feb-1990 (ECtHR)*, paras 44–6; *Akdivar, Judgment, 16-Sept-1996 (ECtHR-GC)*, para. 88. See, generally, Çoban (2004), pp. 194–5; Rook (2001), pp. 78–9. The Court does not distinguish between these terms: *James, Judgment, 21-Feb-1986 (ECtHR)*, para. 43.

[16] See, for example, *Scollo, Judgment, 28-Sept-1995 (ECtHR)*, para. 40; *Herrmann, Judgment, 26-Jun-2012 (ECtHR-GC)*, para. 93. See, further, Rook (2001), p. 69; Allen (2007), p. 296; Mowbray (2010), pp. 290–2. For criticism of this 'fair balance' test, see Allen (2005a), p. 123.

[17] See, for example, *Tecmed, Award, 29-May-2003 (ICSID-AF)*, paras 115–79; *AIG, Award, 7-Oct-2003 (ICSID)*, para. 10.3.1; *Saluka, Partial Award, 17-Mar-2006 (UNCITRAL)*, para. 300. See, further, Titi (2017). This differs from a 'police powers' defence: the purposes 'balanced' comprise a broader category of public interests and typically do not have to satisfy the additional criteria applied to determine whether a public purpose falls within a State's police powers.

Different balancing tests accord different roles to a State's public purposes.[18] A balancing test might attribute particular weight to individual rights such that the 'scales are loaded, yet not conclusively, in favour of rights'.[19] Balancing tests may also differ in structure. They may involve the balancing only of *first-order* reasons, or instead balance *first-* along with *second-* order reasons.[20] In the latter structure, as Legg explains, '[t]he second-order reasons may cancel out, strengthen, or reduce the ordinary weighting of first-order reasons'.[21] Balancing tests also differ in formality. A structured proportionality test, for example, may prompt an adjudicator to consider: the aim of a measure; its suitability, and necessity for that aim; and the ratio between its aim and impact.[22] Other forms of balancing may be less formulaic, involving a more impressionistic examination of the interests at issue.[23] Balancing tests provide a structure for reasoning and do not themselves resolve the question of deference.[24] Deference may, however, inform the adjudicator's selection of the factors to be balanced, or the appraisal of those factors in relation to other reasons for decision. As Webber notes, 'identifying the interests that are to count and determining their weight cannot proceed apolitically and amorally'.[25] The differing structures and focal points of balancing tests also make them more or less searching.[26] This, in turn, impacts the likelihood of deference arising in their application.

Public purposes may also operate as exceptions, justifications, or excuses.[27] Under customary international law, for example, a State is not liable for expropriation if its measures fall within the ambit of its 'police powers'.[28]

18 For a discussion of different structures or focal points for balancing tests, see, further, Engle (2012), p. 8; Montt (2012), p. 207; Legg (2012), p. 185; Arai-Takahashi (2002), p. 193; Kleinlein (2011), pp. 1148, 1170; Crow (2017); Rivers (2006).

19 Greer (2010), p. 10.

20 Alexy (2009), p. 424. See, similarly, Legg (2012), pp. 181, 215.

21 Legg (2012), p. 195.

22 See, especially, Alexy (2009).

23 Howell (2006), p. 729. On the ECtHR's approach to proportionality, see, further, Brems and Lavrysen (2015), p. 166; Mowbray (2010), p. 292. On the approach of investment treaty tribunals, see Stone Sweet and Grisel (2017), p. 247; Henckels (2015); Leonhardsen (2012), p. 124.

24 Stone Sweet and Mathews (2008), p. 95; Henckels (2015); Rivers (2014), p. 413.

25 Webber (2010), p. 191.

26 Young (2014), p. 390; Kratochvil (2011), pp. 326–7.

27 See, generally, Viñuales (2017).

28 See, for example, *Pope & Talbot, Interim Award on Merits, 26-Jun-2000 (UNCITRAL)*, para. 99; *Glamis, Award, 8-Jun-2009 (UNCITRAL)*, para. 354; *Philip Morris (Uruguay), Award, 8-Jul-2016 (ICSID)*, paras 287–91, 305–6. 'Police powers' describes a narrow category of measures pursuing particular public purposes (including health, welfare, and taxation measures) that are bona fide, non-discriminatory, and enacted in accordance with due process: Re (1951), p. 328; Newcombe (2005), p. 24; Herz (1941), p. 252. See, further, for discussion of how deference might feature in a police powers analysis Shirlow (2014b); Shirlow (2014c).

A public purpose might also provide a justification or excuse for conduct that would otherwise be deemed discriminatory. The ECtHR has held, for example, that a measure will not violate P1-1 in conjunction with Article 14 of the ECHR[29] if different treatment pursues a legitimate aim in a proportionate manner. [30] Investment treaty tribunals have similarly deemed differential treatment to be non-discriminatory where it is justified by a public purpose.[31] Some commentators further suggest that a 'right to regulate' operates as an exception or excuse, 'permitting the host state to regulate in derogation of international commitments'.[32] In the reviewed cases, however, such 'right to regulate' was instead referred to exclusively as a factor relevant to the application of balancing tests,[33] or otherwise to describe State powers that were unbound by international obligations.[34] Public purposes also gain relevance through treaty carve-outs or defences. Some treaties exclude State responsibility, for example, where a State acts to protect public order or its essential security interests.[35] Customary international law, too, recognises justifications and exceptions entailing the assessment of public purposes. This includes the defence of necessity, by which a State may be able to avoid international responsibility if its conduct was taken in response to a public necessity meeting particular criteria.[36]

29 European Convention on Human Rights and Fundamental Freedoms (1950/1953) ETS 5, art 14 ('The enjoyment of the rights and freedoms set forth in this Convention shall be secured without discrimination on any ground').

30 See, for example, *Marckx, Judgment, 13-Jun-1979 (ECtHR)*, para. 65; *Chassagnou, Judgment, 29-Apr-1999 (ECtHR-GC)*, para. 92; *Stec, Judgment, 12-Apr-2006 (ECtHR-GC)*, paras 57–66; *Andrejeva, Judgment, 18-Feb-2009 (ECtHR-GC)*, paras 81–9; *Guberina, Judgment, 22-Mar-2016 (ECtHR)*, paras 69–97.

31 See, for example, *SD Myers, Partial Award, 13-Nov-2000 (UNCITRAL)*, paras 161–95, 246–50; *Unglaube, Award, 16-May-2012 (ICSID)*, para. 262. See, further, Ortino (2005); Klager (2010), p. 440.

32 Titi (2014), p. 18.

33 See, for example, *ELSI, Judgment, 20-Jul-1989 (ICJ)*, para. 74; *Saluka, Partial Award, 17-Mar-2006 (UNCITRAL)*, paras 305–7; *Parkerings-Compagniet, Award, 11-Sept-2007 (ICSID)*, paras 332–8; *BG, Final Award, 24-Dec-2007 (UNCITRAL)*, paras 153, 298. See, similarly: Korzun (2017), p. 374; Olynyk (2012), pp. 265–6; Freeman (2003), p. 209.

34 See, for example, *Serbian Loans, Judgment, 12-Jul-1929 (PCIJ-A20)*, p. 44; *Oscar Chinn, Judgment, 12-Dec-1934 (PCIJ-A/B63)*, pp. 78–86; *Stran, Judgment, 9-Dec-1994 (ECtHR)*, para. 72.

35 See, for example, *Oil Platforms, Merits Judgment, 6-Nov-2003 (ICJ)*, paras 40–78; *Patrick Mitchell, Annulment Decision, 1-Nov-2006 (ICSID)*, paras 51–7. See, generally, Stone Sweet and Grisel (2017), p. 214; Burke-White and von Staden (2008); Moon (2012).

36 *Oscar Chinn (Dissent/SO-Anzilotti), 12-Dec-1934 (PCIJ-A/B63)*, pp. 112–13; *Norwegian Loans (Dissent/SO-Read), 6-Jul-1957 (ICJ)*, pp. 84, 89–90; *Bernhard von Pezold, Award, 28-Jul-2015 (ICSID)*, paras 642–5; *Total, Annulment Decision, 1-Feb-2016 (ICSID)*, paras 238–9. See, generally, Viñuales (2008), p. 99; Desierto (2012).

The right to regulate activities in a given territory or over a given subject matter is typically considered to be 'precisely the function of domestic legislatures' and a vital attribute of State sovereignty.[37] Adjudicative consideration of measures pursuing public purposes will therefore frequently raise issues of deference.[38] Adjudicative deference may be relevant to both the identification of 'public purposes', and the analysis of whether particular measures are connected to those purposes.

Deference may be relevant to an adjudicator's analysis of the types of 'public purposes' that may be invoked by a State to justify interferences with private property. Numerous international private property obligations require an assessment of whether a State's measure pursues a 'public purpose'. A State could conceivably be given complete discretion in determining which aims will constitute legally relevant 'public purposes'.[39] Alternatively, an adjudicator might exercise restraint in analysing State claims to be acting in the public interest. It might decide, for example, that a multitude of permissible aims fall within the notion of 'public purpose', that States are better placed to identify them, and thus not intervene unless that choice appears to be manifestly unreasonable, abusive, or arbitrary. The adjudicator could otherwise refer to second-order reasons (for example, relative expertise or legitimacy) to alter the burden required for the State to establish that it acted for a public purpose. It could require, for example, proof of a 'compelling', as opposed to merely an 'important', objective.[40]

A second question of deference arises in setting and assessing the requisite nexus between a public purpose and the measure adopted by the State.[41] The requisite nexus will rarely be set with specificity by the applicable obligation. Even where the applicable obligation specifies the required nexus, the adjudicator may nevertheless enjoy some discretion in interpreting the precise connection required. An adjudicator might therefore identify the nexus required by reference to second-order reasons, including because it perceives itself to be ill equipped to assess public purposes due to its relative lack of expertise or legitimacy.[42] An adjudicator assessing the existence of a 'reasonable' connection between an aim and a measure might, for example, require merely a 'rational connection' between the measure and the aim, or instead a 'strict connection'

37 Banks (1999), p. 506.

38 On public 'interests' and 'purposes', see, further, Friedman (1953), p. 47; Martinez-Fraga and Reetz (2015).

39 Stone Sweet and Grisel (2014), p. 247.

40 Gerards (2004), p. 147.

41 See, further, Mitchell et al. (2018); Young (2014), p. 378; Schauer (1977), p. 26; Brems and Lavrysen (2015), p. 140.

42 Cottier et al. (2017), pp. 666–7.

such that only a 'narrowly tailored measure' will satisfy the burden.[43] Alternatively, the adjudicator could adopt an approach whereby the '[s]uitability or fitness of a measure will largely be taken for granted' and not examined.[44]

4.1.3 *Decisions about, or Applying, Domestic Law*

The application and interpretation of domestic law may also prompt an international adjudicator to confront issues of deference. States may, for example, appoint administrators, prosecutors, or political commissions to investigate the legality of a property interest or of the State measure affecting it.[45] States might also make decisions under domestic law concerning the ownership of property or the nationality of a property holder.[46] Where domestic law is relevant to an issue the international adjudicator is empowered to determine, it will need to decide whether a domestic decision-maker is better placed to interpret what domestic law requires. An adjudicator could itself interpret domestic law and in so doing expressly or impliedly reject the relevance of existing domestic interpretations.[47] Alternatively, it could adopt as dispositive the interpretations of domestic decision-makers in the State whose law is at issue.[48] It could instead treat domestic interpretations as merely one source among others relevant to the interpretation of domestic law. Differently still, the adjudicator could stay its proceedings to allow a domestic decision-maker to determine the proper interpretation or application of domestic law prior to the international adjudicator reaching a view on this issue.

Whether an international adjudicator confronts these issues of deference is heavily dependent on the role it gives to domestic law.[49] The empirical

43 Gerards (2004), p. 147; Çoban (2004), p. 203; Stone Sweet and Grisel (2014), p. 247; Young (2014), p. 378.

44 Cottier et al. (2017), pp. 666.

45 See, for example, *Fraport, Award, 16-Aug-2007 (ICSID)*, paras 390–1; *Metal-Tech, Award, 4-Oct-2013 (ICSID)*, paras 76–9; *Cacan, Judgment, 26-Oct-2004 (ECtHR)*, paras 63–5; *Luigiterzo Bosca, Award, 17-May-2013 (UNCITRAL)*, paras 146–7; *Anglo-Iranian Oil (Dissent/SO-Levi Carneiro), 22-Jul-1952 (ICJ)*, p. 165.

46 See, for example, *Certain German Interests, Merits Judgment, 25-May-1926 (PCIJ-A7)*, pp. 72–3; *Waguih Siag, Decision on Jurisdiction, 11-Apr-2007 (ICSID)*, paras 144, 152–3, 198–201; *Soufraki, Annulment Decision, 5-Jun-2007 (ICSID)*, paras 28, 55–78. See, generally, Watts (1996), p. 424; Sloane (2009a).

47 d'Aspremont (2012); Jenks (1938), p. 92; Hepburn (2017), p. 109; Leigh (1971), p. 464.

48 Hepburn (2017), p. 109; Lourie (2015), p. 516; Watts (1996), p. 425.

49 This differs from analysis of which State's domestic law is applicable to a particular question. On this issue (which lies outside the scope of the present work) see: Hayward (2017); Kjos (2013), p. 89; Schreuer (1996), p. 102.

study confirmed that international adjudicators examine domestic law from two key standpoints.[50] First, they may consider whether the factual situation created by a domestic law is consistent with international law.[51] To do so, the international adjudicator treats domestic law as fact. If a State were alleged to have implemented discriminatory legislation, for example, an international adjudicator would interpret domestic law or assesses how it was applied to determine whether it is discriminatory, but would not apply it *as law*.[52] Alternatively, adjudicators may apply domestic law as a law governing certain facts. Domestic law was, for example, applied to identify 'property', and to analyse its scope and validity.[53] Domestic law was also in many cases determinative of a property holder's nationality[54] and legal personality.[55] It was also invoked to identify 'state organs' for the analysis of attribution;[56] to assess the availability of local remedies;[57] to identify applicable interest rates;[58] and to analyse whether an impugned measure was 'in accordance'

[50] For further discussion of these two approaches to municipal law see, generally, Oppenheim et al. (1996), p. 83; Steiner (1936), p. 436; Tomka et al. (2015), p. 37; Hepburn (2016), p. 366; Danilowicz (1983), p. 162; Peat (2013), p. 4; O'Connell (1960), p. 442; Kjos (2013), p. 254; Ferrari-Bravo (1983), p. 719; Sasson (2010), p. 68; Kanto (2017), p. 232; Rogge (1993), pp. 680–1.

[51] See, especially, *International Thunderbird, Award, 26-Jan-2006 (UNCITRAL)*, para. 127. See, also, *Petrobart, Award, 29-Mar-2005 (SCC)*, p. 23; *RosInvest, Final Award, 12-Sept-2010 (SCC)*, para. 249; *Alps Finance, Award, 5-Mar-2011 (UNCITRAL)*, para. 197 (iii); *Binder, Final Award, 15-Jul-2011 (UNCITRAL)*, para. 391.

[52] Kjos (2013), pp. 254–5; Hepburn (2016), p. 366; Jenks (1964), p. 558.

[53] See, for example, *Panevezys-Saldutiskis, Preliminary Objections Judgment, 28-Feb-1939 (PCIJ-A/B76)*, pp. 7–10; *Pressos, Judgment, 20-Nov-1995 (ECtHR)*, p. 31; *Mavrommatis, Judgment, 26-Mar-1925 (PCIJ-A5)*, pp. 29–30; *Lighthouses between France and Greece, Judgment, 17-Mar-1934 (PCIJ-A/B62)*, pp. 5, 13, 18–20, 24; *Diallo, Preliminary Objections Judgment, 24-May-2007 (ICJ)*, paras 53, 155. On the ECtHR's 'autonomous' concept of 'possessions' (and its linkage to domestic law) see, further, Frowein (1993), p. 517; Bernhardt (1993); Schabas (2015), p. 970. See, for example, *Anheuser-Busch, Judgment, 11-Jan-2007 (ECtHR-GC)*, para. 65.

[54] See, for example, *Nottebohm, Judgment, 6-Apr-1955 (ICJ)*, pp. 20–1; *Feldman, Interim Decision on Preliminary Issues, 6-Dec-2000 (ICSID-AF)*, para. 31; *Olguín, Award, 26-Jul-2001 (ICSID)*, paras 61–2.

[55] *Peter Pázmány, Judgment, 15-Dec-1933 (PCIJ-A/B61)*, pp. 228–36; *LESI-DIPENTA, Award, 10-Jan-2005 (ICSID)*, para. 39; *Impregilo (Pakistan), Decision on Jurisdiction, 22-Apr-2005 (ICSID)*, paras 119–20, 134–6.

[56] See, for example, *Eureko, Partial Award, 19-Aug-2005 (UNCITRAL)*, para. 127; *F-W Oil, Award, 5-Mar-2006 (ICSID)*, paras 200–3; *Paushok, Award on Jurisdiction and Liability, 28-Apr-2011 (UNCITRAL)*, paras 574–86; *Ulysseas, Final Award, 12-Jun-2012 (UNCITRAL)*, paras 126, 134.

[57] See, for example, *Panevezys-Saldutiskis, Preliminary Objections Judgment, 28-Feb-1939 (PCIJ-A/B76)*, p. 19. See, further, d'Aspremont (2012).

[58] See, for example: *Gaygusuz, Judgment, 16-Sept-1996 (ECtHR)*, para. 71; *Akdivar, Judgment, 16-Sept-1996 (ECtHR-GC)*, para. 113; *SwemBalt, Award, 23-Oct-2000 (UNCITRAL)*, para. 46. Cf. *Wena Hotels, Annulment Decision, 5-Feb-2002 (ICSID)*, para. 52.

with law.[59] Domestic law was also frequently applied by investment treaty tribunals to determine if an investor held rights protected under an umbrella clause.[60] The empirical study also revealed matters in respect of which adjudicators tended to reject a role for domestic law. This included analysis of the rules applicable to analysing compensation and periods of limitation.[61]

Domestic law thus does not function *only* as fact *or* law in private property claims. Instead, the role of domestic law depends on the issues presented for determination and the applicable procedural and jurisdictional rules. Recent treaty practice categorically relegating domestic law to the status of fact is therefore questionable.[62] In fact, relative to other international disputes, private property claims are particularly likely to require the application of domestic law *as law*.[63] This is because private property is 'anchored in municipal law'.[64] Each State enjoys, as an incident of its sovereignty, the 'right to regulate matters pertaining to the ownership of property . . . within its territory'.[65] International rules of private property often also rely on the application of domestic law either expressly or by necessary implication. Treaties protecting private property very frequently, for instance, refer to 'legal concept[s] or situation[s] which need to be specified . . . with reference to a particular system of municipal law'.[66] Domestic law may also be applied because international law lacks its own rules to determine an issue, or because

59 See, for example, *Iatridis, Judgment, 25-Mar-1999 (ECtHR-GC)*, para. 58; *Malama, Judgment, 1-Mar-2001 (ECtHR)*, paras 43–4; *Silickiene, Judgment, 10-Apr-2012 (ECtHR)*, para. 64; *Sedelmayer, Award, 7-Jul-1998 (SCC)*, p. 73.

60 See, for example, *SGS (Pakistan), Decision on Jurisdiction, 6-Aug-2003 (ICSID)*; *SGS (Philippines), Decision on Jurisdiction, 29-Jan-2004 (ICSID)*, para. 115; *Noble Ventures, Award, 12-Oct-2005 (ICSID)*, para. 54; *Continental, Award, 5-Sept-2008 (ICSID)*, para. 298.

61 See, for rejections of a role for domestic law in assessing reparation: *Factory at Chorzów, Merits Judgment, 13-Sept-1928 (PCIJ-A17)*, para. 28; Diallo *(Dissent/SO-Cançado Trindade), 30-Nov-2010 (ICJ)*, para. 212; *Occidental, Final Award, 1-Jul-2004 (LCIA)*, para. 616; *Venezuela Holdings, Award, 9-Oct-2014 (ICSID)*, para. 399. Cf. the respondent's submission in *Nottebohm, Judgment, 6-Apr-1955 (ICJ)*, p. 11. On the role of domestic law in analysing limitation periods, see *Maffezini, Award, 13-Nov-2000 (ICSID)*, paras 92–3; *William Nagel, Final Award, 9-Sept-2003 (SCC)*, para. 334; *Luigiterzo Bosca, Award, 17-May-2013 (UNCITRAL)*, para. 120. On the 'internationalisation' of the sources of law in international private property claims see, generally Kulick (2010), pp. 182, 191–2; Schreuer (1996), p. 99; Dumberry and Stone (2014), p. 477.

62 See, for example, Comprehensive Economic and Trade Agreement between Canada and the European Union (2016/2017) art 8.31(2). See, further, European Commission (2015), pp. 10–11; American Bar Association (2016), p. 63.

63 See, similarly, Crawford (2005), p. 89; Emberland (2006), p. 93.

64 De Dycker (2010), p. 488.

65 Sprankling (2013), p. 467, quoting Hyde (1947).

66 Ferrari-Bravo (1983), p. 719.

domestic law has a closer connection than international law to the issues in dispute.[67]

Deciding whether domestic law operates as fact or law has important implications in individual claims. It informs what substantive law will be applied by the adjudicator, and may also impact the scope of issues subject to appeal or annulment.[68] The role played by domestic law also has broader impacts. The application of domestic law *as law* has, for instance, led some commentators to doubt whether certain courts or tribunals are 'international' at all.[69] The distinction may also reveal underlying theoretical paradigms. An adjudicator adopting a dualist approach is, for example, particularly likely to characterise domestic law as fact.[70] Whether domestic law is treated as fact or law also has significant implications for the analysis of deference. As a fact, domestic law is treated as empirically ascertainable, with an adjudicator potentially less likely to evaluate it or to reinterpret what it requires.[71] The treatment of domestic law as fact or law might also influence an adjudicator's appraisal of the relevant second-order reasons for deference, including their relative competence/expertise or legitimacy vis-à-vis a domestic actor to interpret what domestic law requires. Statements as to whether domestic law is fact or law may also be strategic. Douglas, for example, suggests that an adjudicator might expressly characterise domestic law as a fact, even if applying it as law, 'to avoid the unmistakable impression that it was usurping the function of the [domestic] courts'.[72] Whether or not domestic law is applied as fact or law,

67 See, further, Douglas (2003), p. 197; Sasson (2010), p. 74; Jenks (1938), p. 88; Emberland (2004), p. 263; Sprankling (2014), p. 34; Higgins (1982), p. 331; Schreuer (1996), p. 89; Grisel (2014b), pp. 216–17; Kulick (2010), p. 172; Kjos (2013), p. 258.

68 A failure to apply the proper 'law' may constitute grounds for annulment of ICSID awards. See, further, Hepburn (2017), p. 108. Annulment or appeal may also be available for 'manifest errors in the appreciation of the facts, including the appreciation of relevant domestic law': Comprehensive Economic and Trade Agreement between Canada and the European Union (2016/2017) art 8.28. On the difference between annulment and appeal see, further, Caron (1992).

69 Kaushal (2009), p. 515; Douglas (2003), pp. 152–3; Alvik (2010), p. 91; Hernández (2014), p. 66.

70 By characterising domestic law as a 'fact', the adjudicator indicates that domestic rules are being treated as non-law within the international system. A *renvoi* method may also reflect dualism, indicating a view that international law conditions the 'validity and operation' of domestic norms within the international sphere. See, generally, Crawford (2002), p. 23; Danilowicz (1983), pp. 153–4; Crawford and Brownlie (2012), p. 51; Oppenheim et al. (1996), p. 125; Tomka et al. (2015), p. 36; Nollkaemper (2011), p. 244; Crawford (2014), para. 272. On monist, dualist, and pluralist approaches, see, further, Chapter 9.

71 Mosk (2003), p. 31; Jennings (1998), p. 6; de Brabandere (2015), p. 102; Jenks (1964), p. 558. Some domestic courts take a similar approach to interpret foreign law. See, further, Ruse-Khan (2013), pp. 335–7.

72 Douglas (2009), p. 70.

however, a question of deference will arise: adjudicators will need to decide whether to defer to domestic interpretations of domestic law or reach their own interpretations. The extent to which they do so is considered in the subsequent chapters.

4.2 A TAXONOMY OF DEFERENCE: DEFERENCE AND STRUCTURES OF AUTHORITY IN INTERNATIONAL ADJUDICATION

Identifying the range of domestic decisions referred to in international adjudication supports a comprehensive analysis of how international adjudicators use deference to accord weight to those decisions. The references to domestic decisions and the possibility of domestic decisions canvassed in Section 4.1 were thus analysed systematically to identify how international adjudicators distributed authority between themselves and domestic decision-makers to determine the matters at issue. This analysis of references to domestic decision-making in the reviewed cases indicated that international adjudicators use a wide variety of devices to attribute and regulate conflicting claims to decision-making authority. Adjudicators invoked several devices which, when founded upon particular second-order reasons, may designate deferential reasoning. Such reasoning devices have been referred to variously in the literature as devices of 'deference', 'subsidiarity', or 'restraint', and as conflict-, jurisdiction- or interface-mediating norms.[73] These are arrayed in no particular order in Figure 4.1.

Being arranged by device, Figure 4.1 does not reveal the relationships between these various modes of reasoning or indicate how they achieve deference. As noted in Part I, these devices have typically been examined separately, and largely from doctrinal perspectives. Their connections have thus been underexplored. While doctrinally distinct, the devices arrayed in Figure 4.1 are conceptually and functionally linked because they all operate to determine the extent to which decisions adopted in domestic systems will have effects in international adjudication. They may each also operate based on second-, rather than first-, order reasons. Collectively, they signify the 'openness and closure, friendliness or hostility'[74] of international adjudicators towards domestic decisions and decision-makers. This section introduces these devices and highlights the connections between them. It groups these devices according to their function, rather than their linguistic or doctrinal designation.

[73] See, especially, Schill (2012); Henckels (2015); Burke-White and von Staden (2008); Krisch (2010), p. 286; Young (2005), p. 105; Shany (2006).

[74] Krisch (2010), pp. 286.

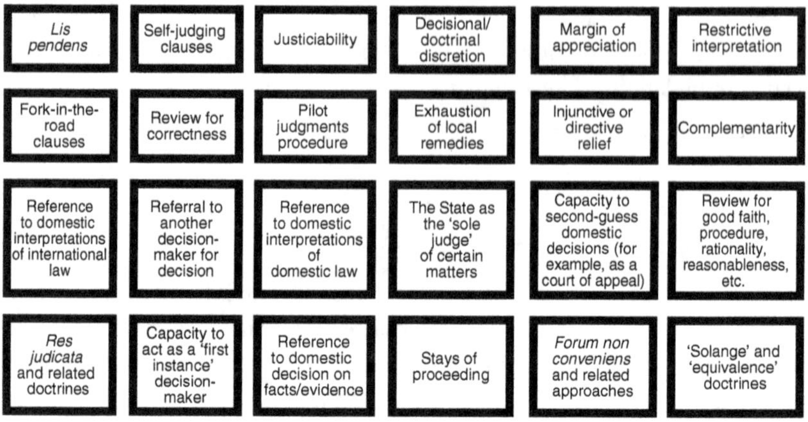

FIGURE 4.1 Array of devices used by international adjudicators to analyse domestic decision-making

The devices may be organised functionally according to the differing impacts they have on the relationship between two decision-makers. Dyzenhaus in his analysis of domestic deference identified two such relationships, distinguishing between 'deference as submission' and 'deference as respect'.[75] In the first form, deference operates on the basis of exclusionary second-order reasons.[76] A decision of another decision-maker takes conclusive effect and is dispositive of the question before the second decision-maker. The second decision-maker 'submits' to the decision of the first decision-maker. The resulting relationship is one in which the will of the first decision-maker controls that of the second. In the latter form, deference is more searching. Deference as respect 'requires not submission but a respectful attention to the reasons offered or which could be offered in support of a decision'.[77] The relationship resulting from this form of deference is one of greater equality and autonomy than that achieved by deference as

[75] Dyzenhaus (1997), p. 286. I use these labels in what follows in a slightly different way to the use Dyzenhaus makes of them. Dyzenhaus' mode of 'submission', in particular, differs from that developed in the following pages. For Dyzenhaus, the mode of submission refers to judges 'submit[ting] to the intention of the legislature': p. 286. As explored in Chapter 9, this model of deference pertains in a particular setting of domestic (administrative) review not necessarily transposable to the international setting. For the present chapter, Dyzenhaus' model of submission is extrapolated to refer to a relationship of submission between an adjudicator and another decision-maker (here, the State). The modes of deference as 'submission' and 'respect' are also suggested by the dictionary definition of 'deference'. On which see, further, Allars (1994), p. 164.

[76] On exclusionary and non-exclusionary second-order reasons, see Chapter 1.

[77] Dyzenhaus (1997), p. 286. See, similarly, de Ville (2006), p. 13.

submission. It also operates on the basis of a different structure of authority. Rather than being exclusionary, second-order reasons in a mode of respect are treated as non-exclusionary. As discussed in Chapter 1, this means that they do not preclude an adjudicator's own analysis of relevant first-order reasons. The adjudicator instead balances first- along with second-order reasons to render its decision.

This functional approach is particularly apt for an inductive categorisation of the approaches used by different adjudicators applying different legal tests, in different regimes, and over different time periods. It focuses on how deference devices operate conceptually, rather than how they are labelled. The approach therefore respects the multifaceted nature of deference in practice. It offers a common framework for conceptualising deference while accommodating the possibility that particular doctrines, devices, or labels may not be present in all regimes or – if they are present – may diverge in the approach to deference they designate. It offers a means of analysing the concept of deference without collapsing the differences between its various manifestations.

Applying this approach to categorisation, it may be observed that the application of some of the devices identified in Figure 4.1 result in relationships between domestic and international decision-makers akin to the modes of 'submission' and 'respect' identified by Dyzenhaus. However, some of the devices signify approaches to deference resulting in different relationships between domestic and international decision-makers. In fact, five additional 'modes' of deference can be identified in the analysed decisions. These relationships are introduced in the following chapters, which examine the devices used by international adjudicators to create relationships with domestic decision-makers of 'submission', 'deferral', 'abstention', 'restraint', 'reference', 'respect', and 'control/dismissal'. The seemingly disparate devices of deference identified in Figure 4.1 can thus be connected functionally and conceptually, as represented in the taxonomy in Figure 4.2. As Figure 4.2 highlights, the application of each mode of deference can be explained conceptually according to how an international adjudicator has structured the recognition of decision-making authority to balance its own authority with that of the relevant domestic decision-maker.

Figure 4.2 indicates how these approaches to deference may be distinguished based on the structure of second-order reasons in the reasoning process. As Chapter 1 explained, second-order reasons can be both exclusionary (akin to an order) and non-exclusionary (akin to a request) of first-order reasons. The modes of deference discussed in this part exhibit three distinct ways of structuring the interaction between first-order and second-order

Deference as Submission	Deference as Deferral	Deference as Abstention	Deference as Restraint	Deference as Reference	Deference as Respect	Deference as Control/ Dismissal
Conclusive domestic authority	**Suspensive authority**		**Concurrent authority**			**Conclusive international authority**

FIGURE 4.2 Array of modes of deference and types of authority

reasons for decision. In the modes of submission and control/ dismissal, second-order reasons *replace* one decision-maker's analysis of the first-order reasons for decision with another decision-maker's analysis of those reasons. This conclusive view of authority means that one decision-maker controls the reasoning process in a manner akin to having issued an order to the other decision-maker to decide in a particular way. In the modes of deferral and abstention, by contrast, second-order reasons *cut off* and so suspend the international adjudicator's analysis of first-order reasons for decision. Deference in the modes of restraint, reference, and respect instead operates in a manner more akin to a request. In these modes, the international adjudicator's judgment is not pre-empted. Instead, the adjudicator balances its own authority with that of the domestic decision-maker. Domestic authority becomes a reference point and reason for decision that is either balanced alongside the adjudicator's own analysis of first-order reasons, or used to inform the adjudicator's selection of first-order reasons for decision.

These modes of deference and the structures of authority underpinning them are introduced in more detail in the following chapters. The mode of submission is the most deferential of the seven approaches. It results in a relationship of submission from the international adjudicator to domestic decision-makers. Underlying this mode of deference is an approach to analysing domestic decision-making authority that treats it as conclusive. Such deference is founded on exclusionary second-order reasons. A domestic decision is treated as decisive and displaces international adjudicative decision-making authority entirely. Similarly structured, but achieving a different outcome, the mode of control/dismissal also introduced in Chapter 5 indicates a conclusive view of authority in favour of the international adjudicator. The international adjudicator's own authority displaces that of the domestic decision-maker. By contrast, the modes of deferral and abstention introduced in Chapter 6 conceptualise domestic decision-making authority as suspensive. In these modes, second-order reasons prevent the exercise of international decision-making authority (even if only temporarily). The modes of restraint, reference and respect discussed in Chapter 7 indicate a view that international and domestic decision-making authority operate concurrently. According to this view, domestic decision-making authority complements or supplements, rather than displaces or precludes, the exercise of international decision-making authority. Second-order reasons are treated in these 'concurrent' forms of authority as non-exclusionary. While ultimately the application of any of these modes of deference might result in a similar outcome (deference to a domestic decision), their application reflects differing perspectives on the role of domestic decisions in international adjudication and, more fundamentally, differing approaches to structuring authority.

The conceptual taxonomy thus organises deference according to the types of relationship it creates between domestic decision-makers and international adjudicators, and the structures of authority that underpin each such relationship. Some of the modes accord decision-makers a form of supremacy vis-à-vis other decision-makers (submission and control/dismissal); others conceptualise authority horizontally and accord decision-makers certain exclusive competencies, even if only for a limited time (deferral and abstention); while others recognise concurrent and overlapping competencies (restraint, reference, and respect). Each mode thus reflects a different view as to the structural relationship between domestic and international decision-making authority. These different structures imply differing approaches to managing conflicting claims to authority, and to distributing decision-making power within international adjudication. An overview of such devices and where they fit in the taxonomy is presented in Figure 4.3. The figure builds on Figures 4.1 and 4.2 to organise individual approaches to deference according to the impact they have on the relationship between domestic and international decision-makers, and the structures of authority that underlie them. The following chapters develop this conceptual framework in order to shed light on the range of approaches adopted by international adjudicators towards deference in international private property cases.

The structure of authority underlying each mode of deference, in turn, affects its degree. As observed in Chapter 1, the degree of deference will depend on the structural relationship between first- and second-order reasons. In many of the modes of deference, questions as to degree will simply not arise. Where second-order reasons are treated as exclusionary and akin to an order, deference takes a categorical, 'all or nothing', structure (submission, deferral, abstention, and control/dismissal). In these modes, domestic decisions are treated either as conclusive, preclusive or as irrelevant. Questions of degree will only be relevant in the middle of the taxonomy, in modes that treat second-order reasons for deference as non-exclusionary and akin to a request (restraint, reference, respect). In these modes, second-order reasons either inform the interpretation of first-order reasons

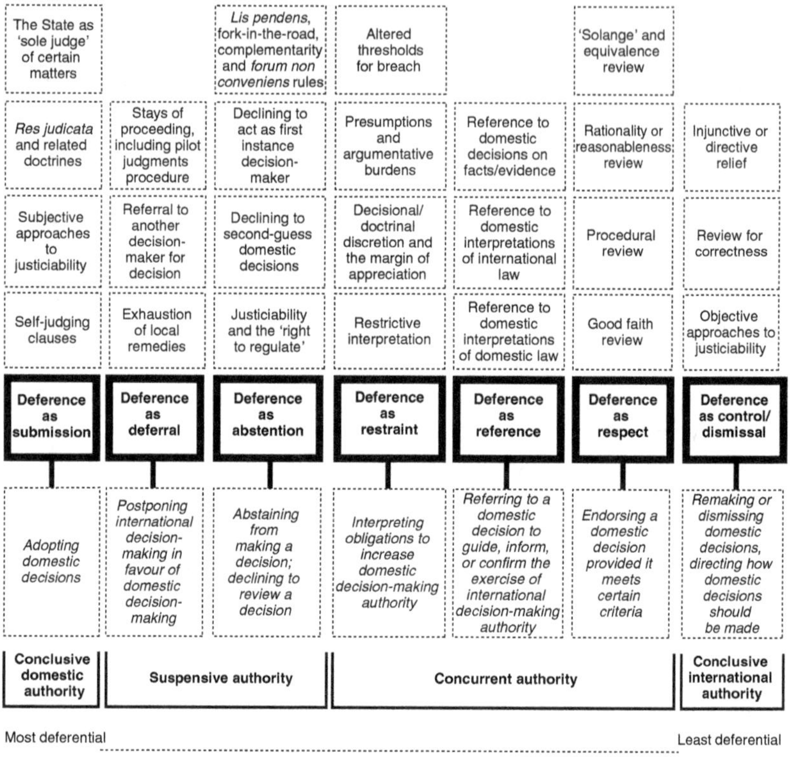

FIGURE 4.3 Modes of deference and illustrative devices

or otherwise are balanced alongside them in making a decision. This means that the first set of approaches result in more binary choices (defer/not), whereas the latter result in decisions of degree (more/less deference).

This relationship between degrees of deference and the structure of second-order reasons has been underexplored in existing literature. The taxonomy illuminates the distinction between categorical and conditional approaches to deference and permits analysis of the implications of this distinction. As will be explored in more detail in Part III, categorical and conditional approaches to deference result in fundamentally different methods of settling conflicting claims to authority. Categorical approaches prompt the use of principles of trumping and non-engagement to manage conflicting claims to authority. Conditional approaches by contrast prompt attempts to balance and coordinate domestic and international claims of authority. Different modes of deference thus reflect differing responses to conflict, moving from suspension, deferral, or abdication of authority, to coordination and cooperation.

The modes of deference further differ in their focus on the qualities of decisions (restraint, reference, respect) or their origin, structure, or form (submission, deferral, abstention). As adjudicators move through the taxonomy, the relevance of a decision's origin and context changes. At the far left of the taxonomy, subject matter and source take priority.[78] Moving into the centre, however, the adjudicator takes a more contextual approach, such that a decision's subject matter or source will typically not be dispositive of whether it will attract deference. Instead, deference is accorded only insofar as any superior qualities of a domestic decision-maker have been deployed in the making of a particular decision.[79] As foreshadowed in Chapter 1, such modes of deference therefore reflect differing conceptions as to the sources of a domestic actor's empirical and normative epistemic authority. Whereas some approaches to deference favour institutional expertise or source-based or procedural legitimacy, for example, others impose more exacting requirements. This may require, for example, substantive legitimacy or evidence of an application of personal expertise and competence in the making of a decision. The taxonomy reflects these shifting focal points, reflecting a distinction between approaches to deference focusing on 'the formal appreciation of a [decision's] source' to those engaging with 'a more substantive evaluation of its content and context'.[80]

These differences between the modes of deference mean that the taxonomy tracks fundamentally different cultures of review. Whereas deference as submission and deferral reflect a 'culture of authority' that focuses on the identity of the domestic decision-maker, deference as reference and respect feature as part of a 'culture of justification'.[81] As deference moves into the modes of reference and respect, the character of international review changes. In these modes, an international adjudicator is more likely to require that domestic decisions be 'objectively justifiable' or 'supported by rational and cogent argument' to attract deference.[82] In the mode of respect, adjudication incentivises domestic decision-makers to exercise or structure authority in particular ways.[83] This contrasts with other modes of deference in which the domestic decision-maker may merely rely on 'their democratic credentials or superior constitutional status to justify their actions'.[84] The taxonomy also identifies

78 On such 'spatial' approaches see, further, Young (2009), pp. 564–7, 570; Cohen-Eliya and Porat (2011).

79 Young (2009), pp. 564–5, 570.

80 Krisch (2010), p. 294.

81 Mureinik (1994), p. 32.

82 Raine (2013), p. 82.

83 Harowitz (2008), p. 1072; Cohen-Eliya and Porat (2011).

84 Raine (2013), p. 82.

a further 'culture' in international review: a culture of 'control', or even 'distrust'. This culture applies in the mode of control/dismissal. It reverses the hierarchy between international and domestic decision-makers applicable in the mode of submission at the opposite end of the taxonomy, asserting the supremacy of international – as opposed to domestic – decision-making authority.

5

Conclusive Decision-Making Authority: Deference as Submission or Control

As noted in Chapter 1, deference may operate akin to an order, such that the second-order reasons for recognising a State's authority effectively shut off the adjudicator's exercise of its own decision-making authority. This is Raz's understanding of the impact of recognising another actor's authority; the recognition of authority creates in effect a *duty* to follow the authority's decision.[1] Two modes of deference reflect this understanding of authority. In a 'deference as submission' mode, a domestic decision becomes dispositive of the outcome of an international adjudicator's enquiry on the issue to which deference relates. This mode of deference is introduced in Section 5.1. At the other end of the deference spectrum, a 'deference as control' mode also reflects this approach to authority albeit in reverse. In this latter mode, the international adjudicator's authority is treated as dispositive, precluding any reference to second-order reasons for deference to a domestic decision-maker's authority. This mode of deference is introduced in Section 5.2. Although they sit at opposite ends of the deference spectrum, both modes of deference are considered together in this chapter due to the underlying structure of conclusive authority that informs their operation.

5.1 DEFERENCE AS SUBMISSION

In the mode of deference as submission, the international adjudicator limits itself to adopting and endorsing a domestic decision as authoritative without reopening or examining the basis for that decision. The international adjudicator thus does not itself render an independent decision on the matter, instead 'surrender[ing] a slice of its own authority' to the

[1] Raz (1986). See, also, Grant (2017), p. 523.

domestic decision-maker.[2] Deference as submission provides a significant role for domestic decisions in international adjudication. This mode of deference manifests through the application of certain justiciability doctrines[3] and self-judging clauses,[4] in the analysis of State claims to be acting for public purposes, in the interpretation of domestic law, and through recourse to doctrines such as *res judicata* and issue estoppel.[5] The application of a mode of submission in these contexts is examined in the subsequent subsections.

5.1.1 *Subjective Approaches to Justiciability, Self-Judging Clauses, and Related Approaches*

Justiciability and like doctrines may prompt an adjudicator to determine that a domestic actor is a more appropriate decision-maker on a particular matter than the international adjudicator. An international adjudicator may exhibit deference as submission by restricting itself to merely registering the State's decision on the matter said to be non-justiciable without itself testing that claim.[6] As Judge Lauterpacht explained in *Certain Norwegian Loans*, claiming that an adjudicator should adopt a submission mode to analyse a claim of non-justiciability posits that the Court:

> must accept that view not because it agrees with it, but because it is the view of the [State]. Its accuracy is irrelevant.... [It] is quite peremptory, fully effective to the point of being automatic, and is not subject to review by the Court.[7]

As noted in Chapter 1, the treatment of State claims that certain matters are non-justiciable as dispositive may not in all cases reflect deference. It may, for example, simply stem from the terms of a treaty: such matters may fall outside of the adjudicator's jurisdictional competence such that the adjudicator has no choice but to accede to the State's views on those matters.[8] When grappling with an allegedly non-justiciable matter, an adjudicator exhibits deference

2 Little (2009), p. 992.

3 For a doctrinal and historical analysis of such doctrines see, especially, Lauterpacht (1933); Brownlie (1967).

4 For a comprehensive discussion of such clauses see, especially, Schill and Briese (2009); Gibson (2015).

5 For doctrinal examination see, further, Ghosh (2015); Lowe (1996); Magnaye and Reinisch (2016).

6 Justiciability might also reflect deference as 'deferral' or 'abstention'. See Chapter 6.

7 *Norwegian Loans (Dissent/SO-Lauterpacht), 6-Jul-1957 (ICJ)*, pp. 42–3.

8 Nonetheless, even where a treaty classifies certain disputes as non-justiciable, the international adjudicator retains considerable discretion in deciding whether to use second-order reasons to give some weight to State views about whether a given matter is non-justiciable.

only insofar as it submits to the State's assessment of justiciability by reference to second-order reasons. The adjudicator might, for instance, consider the State to be better placed to identify what constitutes a 'political question' or a matter falling within its reserved domain.[9] Lammasch argued to this effect that '[t]he vital interests and the honour of a State are matters so individual, and so dependent on subjective valuation' that only the State is competent to identify them.[10] An adjudicator will thus exhibit deference as submission to the extent that it uses second-order reasons to adopt a State's view on a non-justiciable matter without reopening or examining the basis on which the State has reached that view.

Of the four adjudicative bodies under review, the PCIJ and ICJ most frequently encountered State requests for deference as submission to justiciability determinations. In *Certain Norwegian Loans*, for example, the responding State (Norway) had, throughout its diplomatic negotiations with the applicant (France), maintained that the claims of French bondholders 'were within the jurisdiction of the Norwegian courts, that the latter were competent to deal with them, and that these claims involved solely the interpretation and application of Norwegian law'.[11] When France submitted the claim to the PCIJ, Norway contended on these grounds that the matters raised were matters essentially within its national jurisdiction. It contended that it alone was competent to make this determination, and submitted that due to the presence of self-judging language in the French optional clause declaration the PCIJ could not review its determination to this effect.[12] The PCIJ noted that the validity of this self-judging reservation had 'not been questioned by the Parties', and held on this basis that it was not 'called upon to enter into an examination of the reservation'.[13] In subsequent proceedings, however, the validity of such self-judging reservations was expressly put at issue by applicant States. In response, adjudicators in both Courts rejected the appropriateness of submitting to State determinations that matters were within their reserved domain. This was largely due to a view that both Courts' powers of competence-competence empowered them to determine all aspects of their own jurisdiction.[14] They thus rejected any scope for a mode of submission, even

9 See, for claims to this effect, Mulhern (1988), p. 99; Fredman (2006), p. 55; Bodie (1995); Wellens (1996), p. 220.

10 Quoted in Lauterpacht (1933), p. 199.

11 *Norwegian Loans, Judgment, 6-Jul-1957 (ICJ)*, p. 20.

12 Ibid, p. 21.

13 Ibid, p. 26.

14 *Norwegian Loans (Dissent/SO-Guerrero), 6-Jul-1957 (ICJ)*, pp. 68–9. See, similarly, *Norwegian Loans (Dissent/SO-Lauterpacht), 6-Jul-1957 (ICJ)*, pp. 34, 43–4; *Interhandel (Dissent/SO-*

where founded on express treaty clauses, instead emphasising their own authority to determine whether disputes raised 'political' matters, or matters within the reserved domain.[15]

Treaties may also incorporate self-judging clauses that operate in a manner akin to justiciability doctrines. This may include, for example, clauses specifying that States hold power to judge for themselves matters related to national security, or particular public purposes.[16] Empirical studies indicate that self-judging clauses in some areas of international law are on the rise. A 2016 study of investment treaties, for example, identified an increase in self-judging essential security interests clauses from 'negligible' numbers in 2000 to inclusion in over 60 per cent of the treaties concluded in 2015.[17] Self-judging clauses may prompt deference as submission where an adjudicator – due to the perceived greater authority of a State – adopts the State's determination on a matter deemed to be self-judging.[18] Some such clauses specifically require this approach, stipulating that 'if a Party invokes [the clause] . . . the tribunal or panel hearing the matter shall find that the exception applies'.[19] Interpreting a self-judging clause through a deference as submission lens renders the matters covered by the clause effectively non-justiciable, precluding even good faith review.[20]

Self-judging language in a treaty will, however, not always necessarily be dispositive of whether an international adjudicator should defer to the State's own decision about the matter at issue. Under P1-1 of the ECHR, for example, each State retains the right 'to enforce such laws as it deems necessary to control the use of property in accordance with the general interest'.[21] Early ECtHR decisions adopted a mode of submission to analyse State assessments

Klaestad), 24-Oct-1957 (ICJ), pp. 77, 116; *Interhandel (Dissent/SO-Lauterpacht), 24-Oct-1957 (ICJ)*, pp. 101–2; *Interhandel (Dissent/SO-Armand-Ugon), 21-Mar-1959 (ICJ)*, pp. 92–4; *Interhandel (Dissent/SO-Spender), 21-Mar-1959 (ICJ)*, p. 56; *Interhandel (Dissent/SO-Lauterpacht), 21-Mar-1959 (ICJ)*, pp. 103–4; *Interhandel (Dissent/SO-Klaestad), 21-Mar-1959 (ICJ)*, p. 76. See, similarly, *CEMEX, Decision on Jurisdiction, 30-Dec-2010 (ICSID)*, para. 70 (the tribunal is not bound by 'a sovereign State's interpretation of its own unilateral consent').

15 See, further, Arndt (1959), p. 17; Rosenne (1995), pp. 91–2; Christol (1959), p. 385; Bodie (1995); Burke-White and von Staden (2008), p. 377; Reinisch (2011), p. 141.

16 See, further, on self-judging clauses, Schill and Briese (2009), p. 81; Viñuales (2017); Gibson (2015).

17 Sauvant et al. (2016), p. 1.

18 See, further, Desierto (2012), p. 139; Bücheler (2015), p. 222; Schill and Briese (2009), p. 66; Sornarajah (2011), p. 229; Titi (2014), pp. 195–7; Reinisch (2011), p. 143.

19 Free Trade Agreement between the United States and Peru (2006/2009) art 2.2. See, also, Roberts and Braddock (2016).

20 Vandevelde (2013), p. 451; Desierto (2012), p. xiv.

21 Protocol 1 to the European Convention for the Protection of Human Rights and Fundamental Freedoms (1952/1954) ETS 9.

that controls on property were 'necessary' under the second paragraph of P1-1.[22] In *Handyside*, for example, the ECtHR held that P1-1 'sets the Contracting States up as sole judges of the "necessity" for an interference'.[23] However, three years later, in *Sporrong*, the Court held that a proportionality test should be applied to determine the necessity of an interference, removing the matter from the State's exclusive authority and subjecting it to international review.[24] This demonstrates the malleable nature of approaches to deference, even in the application of the same clause over time.

States have similarly contended that defences and exceptions, particularly relating to necessity or essential security interests, should be treated as self-judging. In *CMS Gas*, for example, Argentina contended that self-judging language in an essential security interests clause meant that:

> the State adopting the measures in question is the sole arbiter of the scope and application of that rule, or whether the invocation of necessity, emergency or other essential security interests is subject to some form of judicial review.[25]

Such requests for submission have, again, been squarely rejected by most adjudicators. In *Oil Platforms*, for example, the ICJ rejected that it should submit to the State's judgment that measures were necessary to protect its essential security interests. It instead held that 'whether a given measure is "necessary" is "not purely a question for the subjective judgment of the party" . . . and may thus be assessed by the Court'.[26] Numerous other decisions can be quoted to the same effect.[27]

5.1.2 *The State as 'Sole Judge'*

Adjudicators may adopt a mode of submission even in the absence of a self-judging clause. An adjudicator might, for instance, recognise that a State is the

22 See, generally, Frowein (1993), p. 525; Allen (2010), p. 1065; López Escarcena (2014), p. 64; Greer (2000), p. 12.

23 *Handyside, Judgment, 7-Dec-1976 (ECtHR)*, para. 62. See, also, *Marckx, Judgment, 13-Jun-1979 (ECtHR)*, para. 64.

24 *Sporrong, Judgment, 23-Sept-1982 (ECtHR)*, para. 69. See, further, Arai-Takahashi (2002), p. 151; López Escarcena (2014), p. 63; Frigo (2000), p. 54; Rook (2001), p. 86; Çoban (2004), p. 183.

25 CMS Gas, Award, 12 May 2005 (ICSID), paras 366–7.

26 *Oil Platforms, Merits Judgment, 6-Nov-2003 (ICJ)*, para. 43.

27 See, for example, *Oil Platforms (Dissent/SO-Rigaux), 6-Nov-2003 (ICJ)*, paras 15–16; *CMS Gas, Award, 12-May-2005 (ICSID)*, para. 370; *Enron, Award, 22-May-2007 (ICSID)*, paras 332, 335–8 (essential security interests); *Fireman's Fund, Award, 17-Jul-2006 (ICSID-AF)*, para. 167 (prudential measures); *Bernardus Henricus Funnekotter, Award, 22-Apr-2009 (ICSID)*, para. 105 (necessity).

'sole judge' of particular matters due to its greater legitimacy or expertise/competence vis-à-vis the adjudicator. In *Oscar Chinn*, for example, the PCIJ adopted a deference as submission mode to analyse a State's claim to have acted for a public purpose.[28] The responding State had in that case contended that the impugned measure was adopted to respond to a general economic depression, and was necessary to avert 'the danger which threatened to involve the whole colony in a common disaster'.[29] The Court accepted that the responding State 'was the sole judge of this critical situation and of the remedies that it called for'.[30] Allowing the State to be the 'sole judge' of a given issue indicates that the adjudicator has treated the second-order reasons for deference as exclusionary in structure, thus adopting a mode of deference as submission.

Submission to a State's decision might follow, for example, from a perception that the State has greater normative epistemic authority (legitimacy) to determine certain matters. Many commentators endorse for this reason a submission mode for analysing whether a State has acted out of necessity or for a 'public purpose'.[31] In 1941, for example, Herz argued that international law did not itself define what constitutes a 'public purpose', such that States should be the sole judge of whether an expropriation was motivated by such purpose.[32] McHarg similarly argues, for example, that 'only the public itself is competent to determine what its goals should be'.[33]

A submission mode would prompt the adjudicator in such circumstances to endorse without reviewing the State's claim to have acted for a public purpose out of deference to its superior authority to identify public purposes or craft measures to achieve public goals. Such deference might be afforded on similar grounds to national authorities interpreting and applying national law. Judge Klaestad in *Nottebohm*, for example, argued in favour of submission to a State's interpretation of its nationality law. He reasoned that:

28 *Oscar Chinn, Judgment, 12-Dec-1934 (PCIJ-A/B63)*. See, further, discussion of this case in Christie (1962), p. 322; Steiner (1936), p. 430; Elias (1983), pp. 308–10.

29 *Oscar Chinn, Judgment, 12-Dec-1934 (PCIJ-A/B63)*, pp. 78–9.

30 Ibid, pp. 78–9. Ultimately, the PCIJ held that Belgium's power to respond to such circumstances remained 'subject of course to its duty of respecting its international obligations'. See, further, *Oscar Chinn (Dissent/SO-Anzilotti), 12-Dec-1934 (PCIJ-A/B63)*, para. 6.

31 See, especially, Akinsanya (1980), p. 3; Harding (1962), p. 53; Sohn and Baxter (1961), p. 555; White (1961), p. 146; Friedman (1953), p. 141; Lauterpacht (1962), pp. 30–1; Arangio-Ruiz (1996), p. 463. Cf. *ADC, Award, 2-Oct-2006 (ICSID)*, para. 432 (a 'public purpose' requirement 'would be rendered meaningless', '[i]f mere reference to "public interest" can magically put such interest into existence'). See, similarly, *Patrick Mitchell, Award, 9-Feb-2004 (ICSID)*, para. 74; *Bernhard von Pezold, Award, 28-Jul-2015 (ICSID)*, para. 464.

32 Herz (1941), p. 253.

33 McHarg (1999), p. 678. See, also, Herz (1941), p. 248; Bring (1980), p. 107.

> it would not be in conformity with the function for which the Court is established if it proceeded to examine and decide whether the competent authorities of Liechtenstein have applied the various provisions of their Nationality Law of 1934 in a correct manner. The Court is not deemed to know the national law of the different States. It would hardly be possible for it to place its own construction upon the provisions of the Liechtenstein Nationality Law and to disregard the interpretation and application made by the competent local authorities. By so doing, the Court would substitute itself for these local authorities and pronounce upon matters which have no bearing on international law, and which therefore are solely within the competence of these authorities.[34]

Deference as submission might alternatively be prompted by considerations of empirical epistemic authority (expertise/competence), it being thought that a State organ, rather than the international adjudicator, is 'best qualified to appreciate the necessities of a particular situation'.[35] The PCIJ in *Lighthouses between France and Greece* accepted this justification for submission when analysing whether concessionary contracts had been validly authorised by a domestic provisional decree law.[36] Under the Ottoman constitution, the issue of decree laws was restricted to cases of 'urgent necessity'. Greece contended that a decree law authorising certain concession contracts had not been required to respond to such a necessity. The Court held that the identification of an 'urgent necessity' was:

> a question of appreciating political considerations and conditions of fact, a task which the Government, as the body possessing the requisite knowledge of the political situation, is alone qualified to undertake. It follows from the foregoing that the Ottoman Government, in the first instance, and, subsequently, the Turkish Parliament, were alone qualified to decide whether a given decree law should, or should not, be issued ... The Decree Law ... must, therefore, be accepted as having been regularly issued.[37]

Judge Levi Carneiro in *Anglo-Iranian Oil* similarly opined that the determination of whether an expropriation was for a public purpose was 'generally regarded as a political question outside the scope of judicial appraisal'.[38] Deference as submission may thus result from a view that a certain matter – albeit within the jurisdiction of the international court or tribunal – nonetheless falls substantively 'outside the law',[39] such that States should be left to determine

34 *Nottebohm (Dissent/SO-Klaestad), 6-Apr-1955 (ICJ)*, pp. 28–9.

35 Crawford and Brownlie (2012), p. 666.

36 *Lighthouses between France and Greece, Judgment, 17-Mar-1934 (PCIJ-A/B62)*, p. 21.

37 Ibid, pp. 22–3.

38 *Anglo-Iranian Oil (Dissent/SO-Levi Carneiro), 22-Jul-1952 (ICJ)*, p. 159.

39 Reinisch (2011), p. 140.

that matter through their own policy judgments. This may be on the basis that such matters are better left to (more legitimate) decision-makers within States, or because such matters are 'analytically unsuited to adjudication' at the international level such that they should be left to better equipped (more expert) domestic decision-makers.[40]

5.1.3 Res Judicata *and Related Approaches*

International adjudicators may also accord deference as submission by treating domestic judicial decisions as dispositive. Doctrines like *res judicata* or issue estoppel prompt adjudicators to treat certain decisions rendered by earlier adjudicators as dispositive of either an entire claim or an aspect of it.[41] Such doctrines typically operate on the basis of a 'triple identity test', requiring an identity between the first and second suits as to (i) the parties (*persona*), (ii) the object of the dispute or its subject matter (*petitum*); and (iii) the cause of action or legal rights claimed (*causa petendi*).[42] This renders such doctrines particularly unlikely to apply in international adjudication in favour of domestic judicial decisions. For international courts or tribunals empowered to adjudicate only State–State claims, domestic judicial decisions will rarely satisfy the requirement of identity of parties.[43] Individual–State claims are also likely to be based on different causes of action to domestic judicial proceedings, even if the parties and object of the dispute are identical.[44] This has prompted some adjudicators to relax these requirements.[45] Others, by contrast, reject that

40 Galligan (1986), p. 241.

41 On the distinction between these doctrines, see Lowe (1996), p. 42. Their impact is similar insofar as they result in a domestic decision or an aspect of a domestic decision taking dispositive effect in the international adjudication. *Apotex, Award, 25-Aug-2014 (UNCITRAL)*, paras 7.17–7.18. For doctrinal accounts of these devices, see El Hayek and Gilles (2014), p. 589; Ghosh (2015); Lowe (1996); Amaza (2012); Magnaye and Reinisch (2016), p. 275.

42 See, for example, *Gavazzi, Decision on Jurisdiction, Admissibility and Liability, 21-Apr-2015 (ICSID)*, para. 166.

43 See, for example, *Peter Pázmány, Judgment, 15-Dec-1933 (PCIJ-A/B61)* (distinguishing a dispute between the individual and a State from a State–State dispute in the form of a diplomatic protection claim).

44 Numerous investment treaty arbitration decisions have rejected for this reason the application of *res judicata* to domestic court decisions. See, for example, *Inceysa, Award, 2-Aug-2006 (ICSID)*, paras 214–18; *Fraport, Award, 16-Aug-2007 (ICSID)*, para. 390; *EURAM, Award on Jurisdiction, 22-Oct-2012 (PCA/UNCITRAL)*, para. 394; *TECO, Award, 19-Dec-2013 (ICSID)*, paras 516–18.

45 See, especially, *Libananco, Award, 2-Sept-2011 (ICSID)*, para. 548. This is particularly the case where the adjudicator applies a doctrine of issue estoppel rather than *res judicata*: *Apotex, Award, 25-Aug-2014 (UNCITRAL)*, paras 7.15–7.16.

a domestic judicial decision should ever be given *res judicata* effect in international adjudication, even if the triple identity test were satisfied.[46]

Even if such doctrines are deemed inapplicable, however, an international adjudicator might nevertheless act analogously by treating itself as bound by domestic judicial decisions. Vattel was an early proponent of the view that domestic judicial decisions should be analysed through an approach resembling a submission mode. Linking such deference to sovereignty, Vattel opined that:

> to inquire into the justice of a definitive sentence is an attack upon the jurisdiction of the court which passed it . . . The principle may be accepted without any reference to the merits of the particular case which turned on the facts involved.[47]

Such deference is based on assessments of the relative authority of domestic courts vis-à-vis the international adjudicator. The international adjudicator might consider, for example, that a domestic court is better placed to interpret and apply domestic law. As such, it might adopt without reviewing domestic judicial decisions on matters of domestic law relevant to the international claim. This might include, for example, domestic decisions concerning the ownership or scope of property subject to an international claim.[48] The UNCITRAL[49] tribunal in *Invesmart*, for instance, noted that it had 'no basis for considering' share purchase agreements to be void in light of domestic judicial decisions upholding their validity.[50] As such, it noted that it:

> assumes the validity of the share purchase agreements unless and until it is established that another court or tribunal with authority has determined that the share purchase agreements are void as a matter of Czech law.[51]

In other cases, international adjudicators have treated domestic judicial findings of domestic legality or constitutionality as sufficient grounds to conclude that a measure was 'in accordance with law' or not 'arbitrary'.[52] The ECtHR,

46 *Urbaser, Decision on Jurisdiction, 19-Dec-2012 (ICSID)*, para. 191.

47 Translation from Sherwood Dunn (1932), p. 56.

48 *Papamichalopoulos, Judgment, 24-Jun-1993 (ECtHR)*, paras 38–9; *Brumarescu, Judgment, 28-Oct-1999 (ECtHR-GC)*, paras 67, 80; *Anheuser-Busch, Judgment, 11-Jan-2007 (ECtHR-GC)*, para. 65.

49 A tribunal constituted under the United Nations Commission on International Trade Law ('UNCITRAL') Arbitration Rules.

50 *Invesmart, Award, 26-Jun-2009 (UNCITRAL)*, para. 190.

51 Ibid, para. 193.

52 *Former King of Greece, Judgment, 23-Nov-2000 (ECtHR-GC)*, paras 81–2; *R&L, Judgment, 3-Jul-2014 (ECtHR)*, paras 115–26; *Uniya, Judgment, 19-Jun-2014 (ECtHR)*, para. 306; *Mago, Judgment, 3-May-2012 (ECtHR)*, para. 97; *Arsovski, Judgment, 15-Jan-2013 (ECtHR)*, paras

for example, observed in *Former King of Greece* that 'it is in the first place for the domestic authorities, notably the courts, to interpret and apply the domestic law and to decide on issues of constitutionality'.[53] An international adjudicator might similarly consider a domestic court to be better able to analyse facts or evidence relevant to the international claim.[54] In *Rompetrol*, for example, an ICSID tribunal assessing alleged interference with an investment through wiretapping deemed 'authoritative' and conclusive domestic judicial findings that: (i) 'national security was not the real motive for the interception but only a convenient device'; and (ii) 'Rompetrol had not substantiated its claim of interference with its own business operations'.[55]

The likelihood of international adjudicators submitting to domestic judicial decisions is linked closely to their analysis of applicable law.[56] In *Maffezini*, for example, an ICSID tribunal rejected that a domestic judicial determination as to the status of an entity should bind its analysis of attribution, holding that:

> while it is to be given considerable weight, [it] is not necessarily binding on an international arbitral tribunal. Whether an entity is to be regarded as an organ of the State and whether this might ultimately engage its responsibility, is a question of fact and law to be determined under the applicable principles of international law.[57]

The ICSID *PNG Sustainable Development* tribunal likewise rejected that a domestic judicial finding of non-urgency for the grant of provisional measures under domestic law could be dispositive of the tribunal's analysis of 'urgency' for the purposes of ordering provisional measures under international law.[58] The SCC *Petrobart* tribunal similarly rejected that domestic judicial decisions could bind its consideration of alleged treaty breaches,

50–1. Cf: *Ahmonseto, Award, 18-Jun-2007 (ICSID)*, para. 256; *ELSI, Judgment, 20-Jul-1989 (ICJ)*, para. 73.

53 *Former King of Greece, Judgment, 23-Nov-2000 (ECtHR-GC)*, para. 82; *R&L, Judgment, 3-Jul-2014 (ECtHR)*, para. 115.

54 See, to this effect, Foster (2011), p. 262; Butler (2013), p. 622; Kurtz (2015), p. 292; Graham (1970), p. 293. Cf. *Factory at Chorzów, Merits Judgment, 13-Sept-1928 (PCIJ-A17)*, para. 84; *Adel Hamadi, Award, 3-Nov-2015 (ICSID)*, para. 358.

55 *Rompetrol, Award, 6-May-2013 (ICSID)*, paras 256–61.

56 See, for example, *Mobil, Decision on Liability and Quantum, 22-May-2012 (ICSID-AF)*, para. 167 (a domestic judicial decision was 'dispositive' of domestic law issues, but only 'relevant' to analysis of matters of international law). See, similarly, *GAMI, Final Award, 15-Nov-2004 (UNCITRAL)*, para. 41.

57 *Maffezini, Decision on Jurisdiction, 25-Jan-2000 (ICSID)*, para. 82.

58 *PNG Sustainable Development, Provisional Measures Decision, 21-Jan-2015 (ICSID)*, para. 168.

because the relevant domestic proceedings 'concerned exclusively the interpretation and application of Kyrgyz domestic law and . . . the Treaty was not in issue in that case'.[59] The likelihood of deference as submission thus depends on the nature of the questions at issue, the law applicable to determining them, and an assessment as to the relative authority of the available decision-makers in relation to those questions.[60] For questions of international law, it may also depend on whether the domestic decision was reached through application of international, rather than domestic, law.

5.2 DEFERENCE AS CONTROL/DISMISSAL

At the opposite end of the spectrum, another mode of deference that discloses a conclusive view of decision-making authority is the mode of deference as control/dismissal (referred to as 'deference as control' throughout this section). In the mode of deference as control, the international adjudicator adopts a view of authority according to which its own authority displaces that of a domestic decision-maker. In this mode, the adjudicator declines to accord a domestic decision-maker *any* deference. It instead uses second-order reasons either to expressly replace domestic decisions with its own (control) or to otherwise reject their relevance entirely (dismissal). Such adjudicators do not defer to domestic decision-making authority and instead treat their own authority as controlling. Several approaches adopt this reasoning structure, and are considered in turn in the following subsections.

5.2.1 *Objective Approaches to Justiciability*

Adjudicators exhibit deference as control where they reject a role for justiciability doctrines, instead endorsing the view that '[t]here are *no* matters at all' which a State will be more competent or authorised than an international adjudicator to assess.[61] For the adjudicator adopting this view, the only question would be whether it has jurisdiction or rules available to determine the matters raised.[62] Adjudicators also operate in a control mode by adopting objective approaches to defining what will constitute a non-justiciable

[59] *Petrobart, Award, 29-Mar-2005 (SCC)*, p. 64.

[60] See, for example, *Helnan, Award, 3-Jul-2008 (ICSID)*, paras 125–31; *Mobil, Decision on Liability and Quantum, 22-May-2012 (ICSID-AF)*, paras 353–6; *TECO, Award, 19-Dec-2013 (ICSID)*, paras 474–5, 560; *Vigotop, Award, 1-Oct-2014 (ICSID)*, para. 509; *Dunkeld, Award, 28-Jun-2016 (PCA/UNCITRAL)*, paras 219–24; *CCL, Jurisdictional Award, 1-Jan-2003 (SCC)*, pp. 126, 134; *CCL, Final and Supplemental Award, 1-Jan-2004 (SCC)*, p. 161.

[61] Kunz (1960), p. 546. See, similarly, Brierly (1925), pp. 13–14; Schweigman (2001), p. 264.

[62] Brownlie (1963), p. 286; Kolb (2013), pp. 334–8; Wellens (1996), p. 29; Arndt (1959), p. 12; Christol (1959), p. 384.

matter.[63] Such adjudicators themselves make 'political judgments', including by defining the very nature of 'public purposes' and 'political questions'.[64] Such adjudicators consider themselves equally, or more, suited than the State to identify what such matters are and whether they are present on the facts.[65] By controlling the definition and identification of such matters, the international adjudicator asserts its 'supremacy' on these points, taking them outside the State's unilateral control.[66]

5.2.2 *Correctness Review*

An adjudicator may also adopt a mode of control by reviewing domestic decisions for *correctness*. Arbitrator Torres Bernardez in *Ambiente Ufficio*, for example, adopted this view when he stated that 'an international tribunal is fully empowered to make its own nationality determinations, even if its decision contradicts official government documents'.[67] Adjudicators also exhibit the mode of control where they hold there to be one way to address a situation, and assert their authority to identify it and to assess whether the State's decision conforms to it. Care must be taken in equating this form of review with *de novo* review.[68] In some circumstances a *de novo* assessment may be required because 'there are simply no existing findings' on certain questions.[69] An international adjudicator exercising *de novo* review will only operate in the mode of deference as control if it rejects any relevance for domestic decision-making authority in principle. The adjudicator might, for example, decline to defer to existing domestic interpretations of domestic law and instead offer its own interpretation based on a 'reasonable construction' of statutory text.[70] An adjudicator thus indicates a deference as control mode of

63 Christol (1959), p. 380; Lauterpacht (1928); Sucker (2014), p. 15.

64 Seidman (2004), p. 462.

65 Garner (1929), p. 598; Weiner (2003), pp. 171–4; Herz (1941), p. 251; Kratochwil (1982), p. 2; Martinez-Fraga and Reetz (2015), p. 351; Rivers (2014), p. 415.

66 Arndt (1959), p. 18.

67 *Ambiente Ufficio, Dissent/SO (Torres Bernardez), 2-May-2013 (ICSID), para.* 138. Cf. *Cargill, Award, 18-Sept-2009 (ICSID-AF)*, para. 292 (international law is not breached merely because 'a domestic agency or legislature incorrectly weighed the various factors ... or applied social or economic reasoning in a manner that the tribunal criticizes'); *Lemire, Decision on Jurisdiction and Liability, 14-Jan-2010 (ICSID)*, para. 283 (international law is not breached merely because the decision 'is different from the one the arbitrators would have made if they were the regulators'). See, further, Çali (2016), p. 139; Blades (2006), pp. 32–3; Douglas (2014b), p. 870.

68 Cf. Vadi (2018), p. 193.

69 Ortino (2014), p. 25.

70 Jenks (1964), p. 598.

review where – in spite of there being a pre-existing domestic decision on a given matter, or the possibility of such a decision – it undertakes 'an independent examination'[71] to consider the issues anew and without any reference to the decision-making authority of domestic actors.

A choice of control is particularly likely to arise in the analysis of necessity under customary international law. To invoke necessity, a State must establish that its conduct was the 'only way' to respond to circumstances of necessity.[72] This requirement can be interpreted in a range of ways, each implying a different level of control on State authority to respond to crises.[73] As the *Enron* Annulment Committee asked:

> Does the Tribunal determine this at the date of its award, when the Tribunal may have the benefit of knowledge and hindsight that was not available to the State at the time that it adopted the measure in question? Or does the Tribunal determine whether, on the basis of information reasonably available at the time that the measure was adopted, a reasonable and appropriately qualified decision maker would have concluded that there was a relevant alternative open to the State? Or does customary international law recognise that reasonable minds might differ in relation to such a question, and give a 'margin of appreciation' to the State in question?[74]

An adjudicator adopting a mode of control would interpret such requirement as permitting it to assess whether a measure was 'indispensable' or the 'least restrictive' means of protecting the State.[75] Such an adjudicator would in effect impose a test that is 'strict and objective, leaving no room for any "measure of discretion"'.[76] This approach contrasts with approaches under other modes of deference, considered in the next chapters. It contrasts, for instance, with the approach that would be taken in the mode of respect, according to which the measure adopted by the State might be assessed only on the grounds of reasonableness. It contrasts, also, with the mode of restraint,

[71] Oesch (2003), p. 638.

[72] See, for example, *Oscar Chinn (Dissent/SO-Anzilotti), 12-Dec-1934 (PCIJ-A/B63)*, para. 113; *CMS Gas, Award, 12-May-2005 (ICSID)*, paras 323–4. See, further, Crawford (2005).

[73] Compare, for example, *Enron, Award, 22-May-2007 (ICSID)*, para. 309; *Enron, Annulment Decision, 30-Jul-2010 (ICSID)*, para. 377; *James, Judgment, 21-Feb-1986 (ECtHR)*, para. 51. See, further, Allen (2005a), pp. 135–6.

[74] *Enron, Annulment Decision, 30-Jul-2010 (ICSID)*, paras 369–72.

[75] See, for example, *Gasus (Dissent/SO-Foighel, Russo and Jungwiert), 23-Feb-1995 (ECtHR)*, para. 4.

[76] *Oil Platforms, Merits Judgment, 6-Nov-2003 (ICJ)*, p. 39. See, similarly, *Oil Platforms (Dissent/SO-Simma), 6-Nov-2003 (ICJ)*, para. 11; *Oil Platforms (Dissent/SO-Higgins), 12-Dec-1996 (ICJ)*, para. 48.

according to which a measure might only be reviewed if it were shown to be 'manifestly' disproportionate or unnecessary.[77]

5.2.3 *Awards of Injunctive Relief*

Awards of injunctive relief may also indicate that an adjudicator is operating in a control mode. Assuming the adjudicator is empowered to issue such relief,[78] its exercise of that power may be influenced by second-order reasons for deference. It may, for instance, adopt deference in the mode of abstention[79] by declining to grant injunctive relief because it would constitute 'an intolerable interference in the internal sovereignty of a State'.[80] Such an adjudicator could otherwise limit itself to declaring a breach of international law, leaving the State with 'the choice of the means' to comply with that judgment.[81] Where an adjudicator orders injunctive relief, it enters a mode of control because it uses its own authority to direct the domestic decision-maker to exercise its authority in a particular way.[82]

Not all injunctive relief will control domestic decision-making authority in this manner. Some adjudicators, for example, order disputing parties to refrain from resorting to domestic processes in respect of issues subject to the international claim. This includes orders for parties to suspend or withdraw pending domestic proceedings,[83] or to refrain from enforcing domestic judgments.[84] Such orders do not themselves constitute a control of domestic decision-making authority. They instead bind the disputing parties on the basis of their agreement to subject themselves to the decisions of the adjudicator. Second-order reasons may nonetheless

77 Çoban (2004), p. 207.

78 On the power to award such relief see, further, Schreuer et al. (2009), pp. 1137–8; Sabahi (2011); Higgins (1982), pp. 338–9; Barkhuysen and van Emmerik (2009), p. 439; Dzehtsiarou and Greene (2011), p. 1709.

79 See Chapter 6.

80 *Libyan American Oil Co., Award (1981) 20 International Legal Materials 1*, p. 125. See, to similar effect, Higgins (1982), pp. 3389.

81 Shany (2005), p. 917. See, similarly, Kanetake (2016b), pp. 277–8; Kawano (2014), p. 136; Kratochvil (2011), pp. 333–4. See, also: Çali (2018), pp. 220–21 (discussing the initially 'deferential' approach of the ECtHR to remedies, with the Court 'indicating a clear preference for declaratory judgments', but 'adopting a more subtle and selective intrusiveness over time').

82 See, similarly, Niedlispacher (2018), p. 1.

83 *Tokios Tokelés v. Ukraine, Provisional Measures Order, 1-Jul-2003 (ICSID)*, paras 1, 3, 7; *Plama, Provisional Measures Order, 6-Sept-2005 (ICSID)*, para. 44.

84 See, for example, *Chevron, Order on Interim Measures, 9-Feb-2011 (PCA/UNCITRAL)*; *Merck, Decision on Interim Measures, 7-Mar-2016 (PCA/UNCITRAL)*.

prompt the framing of such injunctive relief. As the *Plama* ICSID tribunal noted:

> The Tribunal is reluctant to recommend to a State that it order its courts to deny third parties the right to pursue their judicial remedies and is not satisfied that if it did so in this case, Respondent would have the power to impose its will on an independent judiciary.[85]

Many adjudicators thus decline to issue injunctive relief binding the State's general regulatory powers or judiciary.[86] It is interesting to note, however, that adjudicators are comparably more willing to issue injunctive relief impacting executive or administrative processes. In *Quiborax*, for example, the ICSID tribunal ordered the respondent to 'take all appropriate measures to suspend … criminal proceedings directly related to the present arbitration until this arbitration is completed'.[87] In doing so, it 'insist[ed] that it does not question the sovereign right of a State to conduct criminal cases'.[88] Injunctive relief might thus be used as a means of preventing States from enforcing tax laws,[89] or pursuing prosecutorial[90] or extradition proceedings.[91] International adjudicators might also grant final restitutionary relief requiring legislative amendments[92] or the return of property.[93] International adjudicators exhibit

[85] *Plama, Provisional Measures Order, 6-Sept-2005 (ICSID)*, para. 43. See, similarly, *Valeri Belokon, Award, 24-Oct-2014 (UNCITRAL)*, paras 267–75; *Merck, Decision on Interim Measures, 7-Mar-2016 (PCA/UNCITRAL)*, paras 72–3.

[86] *Millicom, Provisional Measures Decision, 9-Dec-2009 (ICSID)*, para. 49 (the tribunal holding that it had 'no power to command' the domestic court to suspend proceedings, instead ordering the respondent to request the court for such suspension).

[87] *Quiborax, Provisional Measures Decision, 26-Feb-2010 (ICSID)*.

[88] Ibid, paras 164–5.

[89] See, for example, *Gabriel Resources, Emergency Provisional Measures Decision, 21-Oct-2016 (ICSID)*, paras 36–42 (denying the request, in order to respect 'the right of the State to enforce its domestic laws'). See, also, *Enron, First Decision on Jurisdiction, 14-Jan-2004 (ICSID)*, paras 76–9.

[90] *Libananco, Decision on Preliminary Issues, 23-Jun-2008 (ICSID)*, para. 79; *Lao Holdings, Ruling on Motion to Amend Provisional Measures Order, 30-May-2014 (ICSID-AF)*, paras 73–4.

[91] *Hydro, Provisional Measures Order, 3-Mar-2016 (ICSID)*, para. 3.20; *Hydro, Order on Provisional Measures Modification, 1-Sept-2016 (ICSID)*, para. 4.16.

[92] *LG&E, Award, 25-Jul-2007 (ICSID)*, para. 87 (an order of restitution requiring the annulment of legislation would be an 'undue interference with [the respondent's] sovereignty'). See, also, the ECtHR's pilot judgments and Article 46 procedures: *Fabris (Dissent/SO-Popović and Gyulumyan), 7-Feb-2013 (ECtHR-GC)*; *Alisic, Dissent/SO (Nußberger and Popović), 16-Jul -2014 (ECtHR-GC)*. See, further, Croquet (2010), p. 363; Helfer (2008), pp. 146–8; Jackson (2006), p. 762; Çali (2018), p. 223.

[93] *Bernhard von Pezold, Award, 28-Jul-2015 (ICSID)*, paras 681–743 (requiring the reissuance of title to property 'does not involve any … attack on Zimbabwe's sovereignty'). Cf. *Occidental, Provisional Measures Decision, 17-Aug-2007 (ICSID)*, para. 84 ('To impose on a sovereign

differing degrees of willingness to impose such controls on domestic actors, including by reference to whether they wield judicial, legislative, executive, or administrative decision-making authority. This is returned to in Chapter 8.

5.3 CONCLUSIONS

The approaches to deference considered in this chapter are based on conclusive views of decision-making authority. International adjudicators adopting a mode of submission exhibit a view of international adjudication as in some respect *subordinate* to domestic processes. In the mode of deference as submission, second-order reasons are treated as exclusionary. The recognition of domestic decision-making authority operates akin to an order, leaving no scope for the exercise of international decision-making authority by reference to available first-order reasons for decision. By contrast, in the mode of control, international adjudication is viewed to be *superior* to domestic processes such that international adjudication *replaces* domestic decision-making. The adjudicator approaches the issues for decision on the basis of 'traditional legal methods of persuasiveness',[94] and does not accord special status to decisions already made – or which could be made – by domestic decision-makers. Such a mode gives second-order reasons for deference no role in the adjudicative decision-making process. While they sit at opposite ends of the deference taxonomy introduced in Chapter 4, devices achieving submission and control nonetheless share a categorical application and are based on a similar conceptual structuring of the interface between domestic and international decision-making authority. They preclude independent international or domestic decision-making on certain issues, at least in part,[95] because those issues are considered better suited for determination at the domestic or international level.

State reinstatement of a foreign investor in its concession ... would constitute a reparation disproportional to its interference with the sovereignty of the State when compared to monetary compensation').

94 d'Aspremont and Mbengue (2014), p. 252; Cunliffe and Reeve (1999), p. 462; Fukunaga (2012), p. 570.

95 They may also reflect other values, such as finality and efficiency.

6

Suspensive Decision-Making Authority: Deference as Deferral and Abstention

Rather than treating second-order reasons for deference as conclusive, an adjudicator could instead treat them as suspensive. Adjudicators adopt a suspensive view of domestic authority in the modes of deferral and abstention. Adjudicators adopting this view of authority refer to second-order reasons for deference to justify not engaging with certain matters for a period of time (deferral) or at all (abstention). In both modes, domestic decisions are not endorsed. The international adjudicator instead declines to exercise its own decision-making authority in favour of the exercise of domestic decision-making authority. This is a form of 'passive' judicial participation.[1] In these modes, deference is displayed by the adjudicator refraining from exercising its decision-making authority in preference to the decision-making authority of a domestic actor. The adjudicator does this by declining to determine a dispute, or a particular matter in dispute, either at all (abstention), or otherwise until a domestic decision-maker has had an opportunity to make a decision relevant to the case (deferral).

In the modes of deferral and abstention, adjudicators conceptualise domestic and international decision-makers as operating in distinct spheres, offering *alternative* decision-making processes. The second-order reasons underlying the modes of deferral and abstention are, like those underlying the modes of submission and control/dismissal, exclusionary in structure. They operate in the manner of an order rather than a request. Rather than replacing the adjudicator's analysis of the first-order reasons for decision with a domestic actor's conclusion on those reasons, however, they foreclose the adjudicator's analysis of first-order reasons entirely. They prompt the international adjudicator, on recognising the presence of instrumental, prudential or non-instrumental reasons for deference, to decline to exercise its own decision-making authority in favour of a domestic actor. While they share

[1] Heise (2000); Bickel (1962).

a categorical structure, the second-order reasons in these modes of deference nonetheless differ in impact from those underlying the modes of submission and control/dismissal. The international adjudicator treats domestic authority as suspensive and so does not *adopt* domestic decisions as *conclusive* (as in the mode of submission) or *irrelevant* (as in the mode of control/dismissal). It instead *suspends* the exercise of its own decision-making authority, neither adopting nor rejecting domestic decisions. Doing so, it recognises domestic decision-making authority by deferring the exercise of its own authority or abstaining from exercising it entirely.

6.1 DEFERENCE AS DEFERRAL

Deference as deferral may arise where a domestic decision-maker is yet to make a decision when a matter comes before an international adjudicator. In such circumstances, the international adjudicator could defer to the authority of a domestic decision-maker by allowing it to make a decision prior to the international adjudicator considering the matter itself. Deference as deferral accords *temporal* rather than *ultimate* authority. As such, international adjudicators exhibiting deferral will later confront a further choice between modes of deference.[2] This might lead some readers to dispute that deferral is a mode of deference at all. Deferral nonetheless can operate to recognise domestic decision-making authority in a manner akin to the other forms of deference addressed in this book. Deference as deferral might operate on the basis of non-instrumental second-order reasons, including respect for State sovereignty.[3] It might, alternatively, reflect instrumental or prudential second-order reasons for deference. Deferral might, for example, be favoured by international adjudicators seeking to benefit from clarifications of fact or law by domestic decision-makers.[4] Deferral in such circumstances permits the international adjudicator to postpone its decision-making process in order to benefit from any superior competence or legitimacy that a domestic decision-maker might bring to bear on the matters presented for international determination. Deferral might otherwise be used prudentially to avoid the impression that the adjudicator is usurping domestic authority on a matter that should, in principle, be decided first by a domestic actor.

[2] See, especially, Schill (2012), p. 19; Nollkaemper (2011), p. 253.

[3] D'Ascoli and Scherr (2007). See, further, Adede (1977b); Peters (1997), p. 242.

[4] Coe Jr (2003), p. 1418; Bjorklund (2004), p. 258; International Law Association (2006), p. 361; Adler (1990), p. 641; Blades (2006), p. 123.

Decisions about deferral therefore frequently follow adjudicative analyses of the same second-order reasons relevant to deference under the other modes introduced in this part. Only the *impact* of recognising those second-order reasons differs. Whereas in other modes of deference the recognition of a domestic actor's superior authority *excludes* or *informs* the adjudicator's analysis of the first-order reasons for decision, in the modes of deference addressed in this chapter such second-order reasons *suspend* such analysis. Deferral, of course, only suspends the adjudicator's analysis of the first-order reasons for decision for a period of time. I have included it in this chapter due to the structural relationship between the first- and second-order reasons for decision applicable in this and the mode of deference as abstention. I have placed it on the more deferential end of the taxonomy for more practical reasons. Where an adjudicator operates in a deferral mode, there is good reason to expect that the resulting domestic decisions will attain some degree of ultimate authority from a practical standpoint. Rejecting any relevance for resulting domestic decisions would mean that the initial deferral is merely an inefficient hurdle for the applicant serving no real purpose other than delaying the claim.[5] At the same time, however, complete deference to the domestic decision 'would lead to the paradoxical situation in which the application would be admissible for having satisfied [a deferral requirement] but at the same time rejected *ipso jure* as unfounded'.[6] Deference as deferral is thus placed in the taxonomy next to the mode of submission because it makes it more likely that a domestic decision will be given some weight by an international adjudicator. This is because it increases the chances that, on any resumption of a claim following the deferral, the international adjudicator has available, and is therefore likely to accord at least some weight to, a domestic decision.[7]

Deference as deferral may be exhibited by a range of more specific reasoning devices and approaches that are introduced in the following subsections.

5 See, however, *Plama, Decision on Jurisdiction, 8-Feb-2005 (ICSID)*, para. 224 (requirement of recourse to local remedies 'nonsensical from a practical point of view').

6 Costa (2011), p. 182. See, similarly, Wehland (2019). See, for example, *Urbaser, Decision on Jurisdiction, 19-Dec-2012 (ICSID)*, para. 191; *Azinian, Final Award, 1-Nov-1999 (ICSID-AF)*, para. 86 (if the domestic decision were subsequently binding, it would discourage resort to local remedies). See, similarly, Sherwood Dunn (1932), p. 51. Cf. *Philip Morris (Uruguay), Decision on Jurisdiction, 2-Jul-2013 (ICSID)*, paras 146, 231 (a decision rendered under a recourse to local remedies requirement 'whether favourable or not … would appear to preclude resort to arbitration'); *HOCHTIEF (Dissent/SO-Thomas), 7-Oct-2011 (ICSID)*, para. 9 (domestic judicial decisions 'alter the scope of a subsequent international proceeding through the expansion or reduction of the international claim').

7 See, especially, Schill (2012), p. 19 ('a more deferential standard' can be applied 'because the conduct under review has already been reviewed by another independent instance').

These include requirements to exhaust or have recourse to local remedies, stays of proceedings in favour of domestic decision-making processes, and the referral of specific issues for determination by domestic decision-makers.

6.1.1 *Requirements to Exhaust or Have Recourse to Local Remedies*

Treaty-based[8] and customary[9] rules requiring the exhaustion of local remedies ('ELR') bar the international adjudication of claims until a respondent State's courts have had an opportunity to adjudicate the dispute.[10] Related rules require 'recourse to' local remedies, usually for a designated period of time.[11] The application of ELR and recourse rules does not necessarily evidence deferential reasoning.[12] Instead, adjudicators applying such requirements

8 See, for example, European Convention on Human Rights and Fundamental Freedoms (1950/1953) ETS 5, art 26. On the interpretation of Article 26, see, generally, D'Ascoli and Scherr (2007); Bultrini (2010); Schabas (2015). A study of 409 investment treaties concluded between 1990 and 1995 reported only five requiring exhaustion, and twenty-eight requiring recourse to local remedies. The ELR requirement was 'specifically excluded in 20 BITs and implicitly renounced in 345': Peters (1997), pp. 234–6. See, also, Adede (1977b).

9 Adjudicators differ in implying ELR requirements in the absence of a treaty requirement. Compare, for example, *Panevezys-Saldutiskis (Dissent/SO-Van Eysinga), 28-Feb-1939 (PCIJ-A/B76)*, pp. 37–9; *Panevezys-Saldutiskis (Dissent/SO-Hudson), 28-Feb-1939 (PCIJ-A/B76)*, pp. 46–8; *ELSI, Judgment, 20-Jul-1989 (ICJ)*, para. 50; *Loewen, Final Award, 26-Jun-2003 (ICSID-AF)*, paras 160–2; *Mytilineos, Partial Award on Jurisdiction, 8-Sept-2006 (UNCITRAL)*, paras 220–1; *Saar Papier, Award on Jurisdiction, 17-Aug-1994 (UNCITRAL)*, paras 72, 76. See, further, Borchard (1919); Dugard (2005).

10 There is a vast doctrinal literature examining this rule. See, especially, Haesler (1968); Adede (1977b). As noted earlier, these rules accord only temporal, not normative, priority. International adjudication may follow from exhaustion if the impugned conduct remains unremedied: Amerasinghe (2008), p. 97. On the history of the ELR requirement see, further, Shelton (2007).

11 The requirement of recourse to diplomatic negotiations similarly 'suspends' the competence of the international adjudicator: *Mavrommatis, Preliminary Objection Judgment, 30-Aug-1924 (PCIJ-A2)*, p. 15. While conceptually similar to the deferrals discussed in this chapter, such deferrals are excluded from the present study because the deferral is to an *international* (intergovernmental) process: *Panevezys-Saldutiskis (Dissent/SO-Van Eysinga), 28-Feb-1939 (PCIJ-A/B76)*, p. 39.

12 The application of such rules can also give rise to a second layer for deferential reasoning, insofar as their application depends upon a determination that remedies are available in the domestic system. Compare, for example, *Panevezys-Saldutiskis, Preliminary Objections Judgment, 28-Feb-1939 (PCIJ-A/B76)*, p. 19 (whether the Lithuanian courts have jurisdiction is a question 'on which the Lithuanian courts alone can pronounce a final decision'); *Interhandel, Judgment, 21-Mar-1959 (ICJ)*, p. 8 ('Neither is it practicable, before the final decision of the domestic courts, to anticipate what basis they may adopt for their judgment'); *Akdivar, Dissent/SO (Gölcüklü), 16-Sept-1996 (ECtHR-GC)*, para. 9 ('If there is doubt as to the effectiveness of a domestic remedy, the point must be taken before the domestic courts'); *Sargsyan, Judgment, 16-Jun-2015 (ECtHR-GC)*, paras 118–19 ('the Government have not provided a single example of a case in which a person in the applicant's situation had been

may merely be adhering to the limits of their jurisdictional mandates. Deference will therefore not be present in every application of a treaty or customary rule requiring recourse to local remedies. However, in some cases adjudicators interpret and apply, or even derive, ELR and recourse rules by emphasising the deference-achieving qualities of these rules. This reflects that ELR and recourse rules may operate on the basis of instrumental, prudential or non-instrumental second-order reasons for deference. Such applications of ELR and recourse rules achieve deference by informing adjudicative analysis of 'when and in what circumstances the local courts, on the one hand, and international tribunals, on the other, must or may assume jurisdiction over the issue'.[13]

Instrumentally, the application of ELR and recourse requirements increases the chances that disputes brought before international adjudicators will 'already have been discussed extensively on the national level'.[14] They thus allow international adjudicators to benefit from the application of any superior domestic decision-making authority to the range of factual and legal issues the international adjudicator will ultimately have to decide. The application of ELR and recourse rules may thus reflect international adjudicative assessments of the relative competence and legitimacy of domestic decision-makers. Their application may follow, for instance, from a perception that domestic machinery is 'better equipped to determine the existence of an international wrong'[15] or certain matters of fact or law relevant to the international claim.[16] As the ECtHR observed in *Burden*, such rules permit international adjudicators to 'have the benefit of the views of the national courts, as being in direct and continuous contact with the forces of their countries'.[17]

The application of such rules may also reflect certain instrumental goals underpinning the regime in which the adjudicator operates. Such rules provide States, for example, with an opportunity – or even duty – to develop local means of redressing private property disputes.[18] The ICSID *Daimler* tribunal observed to this effect that such requirements provide domestic courts with 'opportunities to gain experience in administering treaty-based

successful before the Azerbaijani courts'). See, also, *Third Report of the Special Rapporteur, Mr. John R. Dugard, (54th session of the ILC (2002))*, para. 25.

13 Fawcett (1954), p. 454.

14 Gerards (2009).

15 International Law Association (2000), pp. 612.

16 See, for example, *Norwegian Loans (Dissent/SO-Read), 6-Jul-1957 (ICJ)*, para. 97. See, further, Dodge (2006), pp. 6–7; Crawford and Brownlie (2012), pp. 612, 711; Young (2005), p. 203.

17 *Burden, Judgment, 29-Apr-2008 (ECtHR-GC)*, para. 42.

18 See, for example, *Akdivar, Dissent/SO (Gotchev), 16-Sept-1996 (ECtHR-GC)*; *Loewen, Final Award, 26-Jun-2003 (ICSID-AF)*, para. 153. See, further, D'Ascoli and Scherr (2007).

investor-State claims'.[19] This policy rationale is reflected in the exceptions to the ELR rule, which will not apply wherever domestic redress is shown to be unavailable or ineffective.[20] Some adjudicators conversely cite instrumental second-order reasons to reject any role for ELR or recourse requirements. This includes, for example, because such requirements merely subject private property claims to the 'hazards of delays and political pressures' in domestic systems.[21]

The application of ELR and recourse rules might also reflect prudential second-order reasons for deference. They may, for example, be invoked in an effort to preserve the effectiveness and legitimacy of international adjudicators, including by avoiding allegations that they are inappropriately 'playing the role of a court of first instance'.[22]As the ECtHR observed in *Sargsyan*:

> The Court . . . cannot, and must not, usurp the role of Contracting States . . . The rule of exhaustion of domestic remedies is therefore an indispensable part of the functioning of this system of protection . . . The Court cannot emphasise enough that it is not a court of first instance; it does not have the capacity, nor is it appropriate to its function as an international court, to adjudicate on large numbers of cases which require the finding of basic facts or the calculation of monetary compensation – both of which should, as a matter of principle and effective practice, be the domain of domestic jurisdiction.[23]

Finally, the application of ELR and recourse rules may follow from non-instrumental second-order reasons for deference. Such rules, for example, may be used by international adjudicators to exhibit respect for State sovereignty, equality, and independence.[24] As the ICSID *Ambiente Ufficio* tribunal observed, such requirements 'serve the purpose of honouring the host State's

[19] Daimler, Award, *22-Aug-2012 (ICSID)*, para. 197.

[20] See, for example, *Urbaser, Decision on Jurisdiction, 19-Dec-2012 (ICSID)*, para. 148; *Mifsud, Decision on Admissibility, 11-Sept-2002 (ECtHR-GC)*, para. 15.

[21] *Gas Natural, Decision on Jurisdiction, 17-Jun-2005 (ICSID)*, para. 29. See, similarly, *Mytilineos, Partial Award on Jurisdiction, 8-Sept-2006 (UNCITRAL)*, para. 222.

[22] See, for example, *Sargsyan (Dissent/SO-Pinto de Albuquerque), 16-Jun-2015 (ECtHR-GC)*, para. 2 ('the majority imposed their own assessment of domestic law, as if they were sitting as a first-instance court, without giving the domestic courts the opportunity to express their own views on the application of domestic law to a novel legal issue, with possible major systemic legal consequences'). *Michael (Dissent/SO-Karakaş), 27-Jan-2009 (ECtHR)*.

[23] *Sargsyan, Judgment, 16-Jun-2015 (ECtHR-GC)*, para. 115.

[24] See, for example, *Interhandel (Dissent/SO-Córdova), 21-Mar-1959 (ICJ)*, p. 45 ('respect for the sovereignty of States is brought about by giving priority to the jurisdiction of the local courts'). See, further, Jimenez de Arechaga (1978), p. 292; Borchard (1919), p. 817; Haesler (1968), p. 113; Peters (1997), p. 243; Garrity-Rokous and Brescia (1993), p. 592.

sovereignty by providing the latter the opportunity to settle a dispute in its own fora before moving on to the international level'.[25] The application of such rules may also reflect an adjudicator's acknowledgement that a State has in place domestic measures of redress that are effective for resolving certain issues.[26] ELR and recourse rules also reflect principles of subsidiarity and complementarity.[27] They offer a means of keeping 'domestic claims in domestic courts'.[28]

6.1.2 *Stays of Proceeding*

An international adjudicator may also exhibit deference as deferral by staying its proceedings in deference to a domestic proceeding.[29] Stays of proceeding recognise domestic decision-making authority by providing domestic processes a first opportunity to determine a dispute.[30] Stays of proceeding may be based on instrumental second-order reasons for deference, including recognition of a domestic decision-maker's greater competence or expertise to make certain decisions. An international adjudicator might, for example, stay its proceedings in order to have the benefit of domestic decisions concerning the dispute. The PCIJ in *Prince von Pless* noted to this effect that:

> it will certainly be an advantage to the Court, as regards the points which have to be established in the case, to be acquainted with the final decisions of the Supreme Polish Administrative Tribunal upon the appeals brought by the

25 *Ambiente Ufficio, Decision on Jurisdiction and Admissibility, 8-Feb-2013 (ICSID)*, para. 602.

26 See, for example, *Barcelona Traction (Dissent/SO-Tanaka), 5-Feb-1970 (ICJ)*, p. 143; *Akdivar, Judgment, 16-Sept-1996 (ECtHR-GC)*, para. 65; *Kozacioglu, Judgment, 19-Feb-2009 (ECtHR-GC)*, para. 36; *R&L, Judgment, 3-Jul-2014 (ECtHR)*, para. 60. See, further, Jimenez de Arechaga (1965), p. 77; Borchard (1919), p. 817; Amerasinghe (2008), p. 142; Haesler (1968), p. 60.

27 Romano (2013), p. 563.

28 Blades (2006), p. 111. See, for example, *Akdivar, Judgment, 16-Sept-1996 (ECtHR-GC)*, para. 65; *Azinas, Judgment, 28-Apr-2004 (ECtHR-GC)*, para. 38; *Akdivar, Dissent/SO (Gölcüklü), 16-Sept-1996 (ECtHR-GC)*, para. 3; *Alexandrou, Dissent/SO (Karakaş), 20-Jan-2009 (ECtHR)*. See, similarly, Lourie (2015), p. 523; Iluyomade (1977), p. 84; Borchard (1919), pp. 817–18; Amerasinghe (2008), p. 143; Jenks (1964), p. 537; Dodge (2006), pp. 6–7; Huiping (2008), p. 470; European Commission (2015), p. 10. Cf. rejection of such requirements on the basis that international adjudication 'is not intended to be a subsidiary system [but] . . . rather is set up as an alternative to the host State's remedies': *Arif, Award, 8-Apr-2013 (ICSID)*, para. 345.

29 See, for example: *Soufraki (Dissent/SO-Nabulsi), 27-Mar-2007 (ICSID)*, paras 59–60 (the proceedings should have been stayed to allow a domestic court to assess challenges to nationality certificates).

30 See, generally, Brownlie (1967), p. 124; Shany (2007), p. 128; Young (2005); Peters and Schaffer (2013); Wilson (1977). This may include the entirety of the claim, or aspects of it.

> Prince von Pless and now pending before that Tribunal … the Court must therefore arrange its procedure so as to ensure that this will be possible.[31]

Stays of proceeding may similarly be prompted by prudential second-order reasons. The ECtHR, for example, uses stays to address the growing caseload of the Court. This caseload has widely been perceived to have diminished positive perceptions of the Court's decision-making competence and legitimacy.[32] In response, the Court has developed a 'pilot judgment' procedure[33] to permit the adjournment of certain cases for a period of time, as a 'means of encouraging the national authorities to take the necessary steps' to comply with ECtHR decisions that have implications for 'a large number of applications concerning the same problem'.[34] This procedure is informed in part by prudential assessments as to the value of deference. By recognising the decision-making authority of domestic actors, the ECtHR seeks to bolster perceptions of its own authority.[35] The Court has continued to elaborate on the function and operation of the pilot judgments procedure since it was first used in *Broniowski* in 2004. In *Burmych*, for example, the Court took the view that while it could *indicate* what steps authorities ought to take to rectify an alleged wide-scale breach of the Convention, it should not *supervise* the State's compliance with such recommendations.[36] In the case at issue, this was for the reason that such supervision would put the Court:

> [at] risk of operating as part of the Ukrainian legal enforcement system and substituting itself for the Ukrainian authorities … That task is not compatible with the subsidiary role which the Court is supposed to play in relation to the High Contracting Parties … and runs directly counter to the logic of the pilot-judgment procedure developed by the Court. … [T]he Court does not have the capacity, nor is it appropriate to its function to adjudicate on large numbers of repetitive cases which require the finding of basic facts or the calculation of monetary compensation – both of which should, as a matter of principle and effective practice, be the domain of domestic jurisdictions.[37]

31 *Prince Von Pless, Interim Measures Order, 4-Feb-1933 (PCIJ-A/B52)*, para. 26 (the dispute was subsequently settled).

32 See, especially, the detailed analysis of such pressures on the Court in Christoffersen and Madsen (2011).

33 *Broniowski, Judgment, 22-Jun-2004 (ECtHR-GC); Broniowski, Judgment (Friendly Settlement), 28-Sept-2005 (ECtHR-GC)*, para. 35. See, similarly, *Hutten-Czapska (Dissent/SO-Zagrebelsky), 19-Jun-2006 (ECtHR-GC)*.

34 Registrar of the European Court of Human Rights (2009), p. 2. See, for example, use of the procedure in *Lavrov, Judgment, 17-Jan-2012 (ECtHR)*, paras 4–5; *Alisic, Judgment, 16-Jul-2014 (ECtHR-GC)*.

35 Jackson (2006), p. 762.

36 *Burmych* v. *Ukraine, GC Judgment (Striking Out), 12 October 2017*.

37 Ibid, paras 155, 159.

The pilot judgment procedure thus *suspends* the Court's exercise of authority, pending the State's resolution of issues highlighted in the Court's decision. Over time, the procedure has become less passive, with the Court issuing more detailed recommendations to States benefitting from such stays.[38]

The principle of 'comity' might also prompt a stay of proceedings. This would reflect a perception that a 'second authority should act, where possible, with respect for the legitimate authority of the first'.[39] In *British Caribbean Bank*, for example, the respondent requested the UNCITRAL tribunal 'to defer to the Belize courts insofar as the issue [to be determined by them] would be dispositive in these proceedings'.[40] The tribunal accepted that 'municipal judicial proceedings may sometimes need to be taken into account in the exercise of international comity'.[41] The tribunal distinguished, however, between situations in which a domestic body had 'exclusive jurisdiction' over matters relevant to the dispute, and those in which 'a party merely argues that another forum would be preferable or should be allowed to pronounce first on the issues in dispute'.[42] In the latter situation, the tribunal cautioned that 'an arbitral tribunal may well be advised to approach the request for a stay sceptically and not lightly to withhold the judgment called for by the Treaty'.[43] It ultimately declined to grant the requested stay, holding that analysis of the alleged treaty breach 'does not depend upon any decision by the courts of Belize'.[44] In so holding, it emphasised its view that it was not 'in any way trespassing on the jurisdiction of the Belizean Judiciary or their prerogative to evaluate the same facts by reference to the Constitution of Belize'.[45] Other adjudicators have similarly rejected such suspensions of their own authority in favour of domestic processes, citing a range of reasons to justify their approach. Such adjudicators have rejected requests to defer to domestic proceedings, inter alia, because they: were 'uncertain in time',[46] concerned matters distinct from those at issue in the international claim;[47] raised little risk of

38 On similar techniques in domestic settings, see Katyal (1998); Krotoszynski Jr (1998).

39 Endicott (2015), p. 3.

40 *British Caribbean Bank, Award, 19-Dec-2014 (PCA/UNCITRAL)*, para. 181.

41 Ibid, para. 187.

42 Ibid, para. 188.

43 Ibid, para. 188.

44 Ibid, para. 189. The tribunal considered that any possible double recovery was a 'practical' issue to be addressed at the quantum phase: paras 190, 213–15.

45 Ibid, para. 189.

46 *CME, Final Award, 14-Mar-2003 (UNCITRAL), para.* 58; Jan de *Nul, Award, 6-Nov-2008 (ICSID)*, paras 260–1. Cf. *Unglaube, Award, 16-May-2012 (ICSID)*, para. 296 (finding that domestic petitions 'can be and should be processed promptly and in good faith').

47 See, for example, *Bayindir, Decision on Jurisdiction, 14-Nov-2005 (ICSID)*, paras 270–3; *William Nagel, Final Award, 9-Sept-2003 (SCC)*, para. 285.

irremediable double recovery;[48] or would not be determined by decision-makers sufficiently 'detached' from the dispute.[49]

As the *British Caribbean Bank* tribunal indicated, international adjudicators may elect to defer their proceedings in deference to fora with exclusive jurisdiction over aspects of the dispute. This is particularly likely where a contract with an exclusive choice-of-forum provision is implicated in the international private property claim.[50] While domestic fora may benefit from such a stay of proceedings, the international adjudicator is not deferring *to* the domestic court in such situations. Rather, any stay results from the adjudicator's respect for principles of party autonomy and *pacta sunt servanda*. The adjudicator by staying the proceedings does not express confidence in the State's greater expertise or legitimacy, but instead seeks to respect the contours of the bargain struck by the disputing parties concerning the proper fora for settlement of their dispute. Such deferrals to contractually selected fora have thus not been included as instances of deference as deferral for this book.[51]

6.1.3 *Referring Matters for Domestic Determination*

An international adjudicator may also exhibit deference as deferral by referring certain questions to domestic processes for determination.[52] In several of the reviewed cases, international adjudicators were asked by disputing parties to refer matters back to the domestic level for determination.[53] The *Yukos* UNCITRAL tribunal, for instance, declined one such request,

48 *Plama, Decision on Jurisdiction, 8-Feb-2005 (ICSID)*, paras 180–1.

49 *Anglo-Iranian Oil (Dissent/SO-Levi Carneiro), 22-Jul-1952 (ICJ)*, p. 165.

50 See, for example, *SGS (Paraguay), Decision on Jurisdiction, 12-Feb-2010 (ICSID)*, paras 155–75.

51 The analysis captures, however, adjudicative deference in subsequent international proceedings concerning the contractual proceedings (as, for example, in some cases of alleged denial of justice).

52 Procedures exist to allow domestic courts to refer matters to some international adjudicators. See, further, von Papp (2013); Helfer and Alter (2009). One investment tribunal was requested to 'ask a national court to make a referral to the ECJ in order to decide all questions relating to the application of the Dutch-Slovak BIT in the present dispute' but declined to do so having 'encountered no difficulty in deciding the issues raised by the Parties': *Jan Oostergetel, Decision on Jurisdiction, 30-Apr-2010 (UNCITRAL)*, para. 105.

53 See, for example, *European Media Ventures, Partial Award on Liability, 8-Jul-2009 (UNCITRAL)*, para. 39 (domestic 'franking' of a right *in personam* for it to be recognised as a protectable investment); *CMS Gas, Award, 12-May-2005 (ICSID)*, paras 214–25, 241–6 (whether to 'remand' to a domestic authority the determination of compensation for contractual breach); *Norwegian Loans (Dissent/SO-Basdevant), 6-Jul-1957 (ICJ)*, p. 78 (rejecting referral of questions concerning domestic law 'to the consideration and decision of any particular national tribunal').

rejecting that domestic authorities had 'particular expertise' to determine whether a tax measure 'is in reality implemented for improper reasons'.[54] Where granted, such referrals would reflect deference as deferral insofar as they recognise that domestic decision-makers have greater legitimacy or competence to determine aspects of the dispute raised for international decision.[55] A referral could, for instance, recognise the domestic decision-maker's greater competence and thus function in a manner akin to procedures allowing for the referral of questions to experts.[56]

6.2 DEFERENCE AS ABSTENTION

'Deference as abstention' occurs where an adjudicator abstains from exercising its decision-making authority in favour of State decision-making on particular issues. The adjudicator thereby recognises a zone of exclusive domestic decision-making authority, declining to exercise its own decision-making authority so that the State's decisions on certain topics stand unchallenged (but also unendorsed). Adjudicators adopt a range of reasoning techniques that may indicate that they are operating in an abstention mode. These include certain approaches to applying justiciability doctrines, recognition of a domestic 'right to regulate', and situations in which adjudicators decline to 'second-guess' State decisions or act as a 'first-instance' decision-maker. Deference as abstention may also be achieved through the application of *lis pendens*, fork-in-the-road, complementarity, and *forum non conveniens* rules. All such approaches exhibit a view of domestic decision-making authority as suspensive. They differ from the mode of deferral insofar as international decision-making is suspended in favour of domestic decision-making authority indefinitely rather than for a specified period of time. Deference as abstention does not serve to improve the adjudicator's own decision-making by allowing it

[54] *Yukos, Final Award, 18 July 2014 (PCA/UNCITRAL)*, para. 1435. The applicable treaty required tribunals to 'make a referral to the relevant Competent Tax Authorities' wherever an investor alleged expropriation by taxation. The 'Authority' was 'the competent authority pursuant to a double taxation agreement' or 'the minister or ministry responsible for taxes': Energy Charter Treaty (1994/1998) 2080 UNTS 95, art 21.

[55] See, similarly, on a referral mechanism for matters of domestic law Jenks (1938), pp. 92, 101; Jenks (1964), p. 601; Schill (2016); Ewing-Chow (2001), p. 763.

[56] On which see, for example, *Oscar Chinn (Dissent/SO-Hurst), 12-Dec-1934 (PCIJ-A/B63)*, pp. 120–1; *Oscar Chinn (Dissent/SO-Anzilotti), 12-Dec-1934 (PCIJ-A/B63)*, pp. 112–13; *Panevezys-Saldutiskis (Dissent/SO-Van Eysinga), 28-Feb-1939 (PCIJ-A/B76)*, p. 146; *Interhandel, Judgment, 21-Mar-1959 (ICJ)*, p. 9; *Loizidou (Dissent/SO-Petiti), 18-Dec-1996 (ECtHR-GC)*; *Chiragov (Dissent/SO-Pinto De Albuquerque), 16-Jun-2015 (ECtHR-GC)*, para. 37. On the use of experts by international adjudicators, see, further, Teitelbaum (2007), p. 122; Jennings (1998), p. 17; Rogge (1993), p. 677; Simma (2012), pp. 231–2.

to benefit from a decision reflecting a domestic actor's superior expertise. Deference as abstention therefore does not 'serve' the adjudicator by allowing it to make a better decision. Instead, when adopting these approaches, adjudicators do not reach a decision on the matter in issue at all. These approaches to deference are therefore particularly likely to be informed by assessments of comparative normative epistemic authority (legitimacy) or by the prudential and/or non-instrumental analyses of authority introduced in Chapter 1. By leaving a matter entirely within the discretion of a superior domestic authority, the adjudicator bolsters its own power and legitimacy.

6.2.1 *Justiciability and the 'Right to Regulate'*

Justiciability doctrines demarcate zones of domestic and international decision-making authority. As explored in Chapter 1, justiciability doctrines may reflect deferential reasoning if an adjudicator invokes justiciability to hold that certain matters – while within its jurisdiction – are non-justiciable because they are more appropriately determined by domestic decision-makers. An adjudicator might, for example, determine that certain matters fall within a State's 'right to regulate' and, on identifying their presence, terminate its enquiry without engaging further with the merits of State decisions on those matters. Alternatively, an adjudicator might decline to review matters it considers to be 'political' or matters falling within the 'domestic jurisdiction' of States, on the basis that such matters are inappropriate for adjudicative settlement or settlement at the international level.[57] For these subjects, the adjudicator exhibits deference as abstention if it: (i) upholds its jurisdiction to determine these matters, but (ii) expresses the view that such matters are better determined by a domestic decision-maker due to instrumental, prudential, or non-instrumental second-order reasons.[58] The adjudicator might, for example, abstain from making a decision on a matter in respect of which it considers a State to hold greater competence or legitimacy. Where an adjudicator abstains from deciding a 'political question', for instance, it is effectively signalling that this 'is an issue that should be authoritatively decided by

[57] See, further, Arangio-Ruiz (1996), p. 440; Arangio-Ruiz (1990), pp. 456–7.

[58] See, similarly, Ehlermann and Lockhart (2004), p. 493; Higgins (1968), p. 74; Arndt (1959), p. 11; Briggs (1960), p. 27; Lauterpacht (1933), pp. 6–7. Cf. where an adjudicator indicates it is 'not its role' to determine a question due to a lack of jurisdiction: *Ulysseas, Final Award, 12-Jun-2012 (UNCITRAL)*, para. 321, or because the claim is not supported by sufficient evidence: *Swisslion, Award, 6-Jul-2012 (ICSID)*, para. 308.

a different institution', such that 'the legislature or executive have the authority to resolve that particular issue'.[59]

Adjudicators might also exhibit deference as abstention by referring to second-order reasons to interpret the scope of jurisdictional clauses designating certain matters as non-justiciable. Some jurisdictional clauses, for instance, excise 'political' disputes and matters within a State's domestic jurisdiction from the scope of international dispute settlement.[60] Such clauses may be drafted based on policy considerations similar to those informing deference as abstention.[61] The Calvo Clause, for example, bars jurisdiction over certain disputes on the basis that they:

> affect the deeply-lying, almost personal, national sentiment, of which no third state can be a judge, each nation being the sole judge of its own dignity and of the rights which guarantee that dignity.[62]

The application of Calvo Clauses, along with like jurisdictional provisions, does not by itself, however, indicate deferential reasoning. Such clauses dictate the ambit of an international adjudicator's jurisdiction over a dispute. Where they apply, the international adjudicator has no jurisdiction and the issue of deference does not arise. Adjudicators retain, however, considerable discretion in identifying those subjects that are non-justiciable under such clauses.[63] Commentators, for example, have long lamented the difficulty associated with identifying 'political' matters, or matters falling within the 'reserved domain'.[64] As such, the class of matters that may be within the jurisdiction of an international adjudicator, but that could nevertheless be found to be non-justiciable, is not fixed.[65] It may, instead, evolve over time or shift depending on the views of

59 Young (2017), p. 129.

60 On 'domestic jurisdiction', see Covenant of the League of Nations (1919/1920) art 15(8); Charter of the United Nations (1945) 1 UNTS XVI art 2(7). On the differences between these provisions, see Arangio-Ruiz (1990), para. 26; Rosenne (1997), p. 780. For discussion of domestic jurisdiction reservations in optional clause declarations, see Owen (1968), p. 723; Peaslee (1931), p. 55; Coquiz (1977), p. 162. On 'political' disputes, see Statute of the Permanent Court of International Justice (1920) art 36; Statute of the International Court of Justice (1945) art 36; Convention on the Settlement of Investment Disputes between States and Nationals of Other States (1965/1966) 575 UNTS 159, art 25.

61 On the development of these jurisdictional limits see, generally, Lauterpacht (1933), p. 388; de Visscher (1956); Kwiecien (2004); Christol (1959), pp. 379–80; Briggs (1960), p. 27; Rosenne (1997), p. 185.

62 Calvo, quoted in Lauterpacht (1933), p. 12.

63 de Ville (2004), p. 597.

64 See, especially, Jennings (1998), pp. 49, 55; Gilmore (1945), p. 1060; Hernández (2014), pp. 73–4; Brown (1924), p. 274; Lauterpacht (1928), p. 279; Higgins (1968), pp. 65–6; Lauterpacht (1933), pp. 8, 19; Kelsen (1943), p. 401; Kolb (2013), p. 326; Steiner (1936), p. 419.

65 See, further, Crawford (2014), pp. 74–5; Arangio-Ruiz (1990), para. 39; Schrijver (2000), p. 75.

an individual decision-maker. Categories of non-justiciable matters are therefore 'essentially fluid, dependent … upon the eminently variable relations existing at any given moment' between the authority of the State and that of the adjudicator.[66] Both the interpretation and application of non-justiciability clauses may thus be based on international adjudicative appraisals of relative international and domestic authority over particular subject matters.

Some States have contended that particular categories of domestic decisions are inherently not justiciable before international adjudicators. In *Loewen*, for example, the respondent argued that a principle akin to the 'act of state' doctrine meant that judicial decisions should be treated as immune from international review.[67] The argument was rejected by the ICSID Additional Facility tribunal, which held that such a principle had not 'been adopted by sufficient countries to be considered as a rule of international law'.[68] The respondent in *Pope & Talbot* raised a similar argument in respect of measures 'in the form of regulations'.[69] There, an UNCITRAL tribunal similarly rejected the submission, holding that:

> much creeping expropriation can be conducted by regulation, and a blanket exception for regulatory measures would create a gaping loophole in international protections against expropriation.[70]

States have requested, with varying success, that international adjudicators decline to review domestic decisions concerning sovereign debt restructuring[71] and currency devaluation;[72] the conduct of banking regulators during a financial crisis;[73] legislative acts;[74] taxation measures;[75] judicial decisions;[76] measures

66 de Visscher (1968), p. 371.

67 *Loewen, Award on Jurisdiction, 5-Jan-2001 (ICSID-AF)*, para. 57.

68 Ibid, para. 57. See, similarly, although on different grounds, *RosInvest, Final Award, 12-Sept-2010 (SCC)*, para. 274 (the treaty not drawing a 'distinction between different organs of the state' for liability).

69 *Pope & Talbot, Interim Award on Merits, 26-Jun-2000 (UNCITRAL)*, para. 99.

70 Ibid, para. 99.

71 *Abaclat, Decision on Jurisdiction and Admissibility, 4-Aug-2011 (ICSID)*, paras 548–50; *Alemanni, Decision on Jurisdiction, 17-Nov-2014 (ICSID)*, paras 318–20.

72 *El Paso, Award, 31-Oct-2011 (ICSID)*, para. 222; *National Grid, Award, 3-Nov-2008 (UNCITRAL)*, para. 96.

73 *Renée Rose, Award, 26-Feb-2014 (ICSID)*, paras 156–8.

74 *Achmea (No. 2), Award on Jurisdiction, 20-May-2014 (UNCITRAL)*, para. 251 (declining to 'intervene in the democratic process of a sovereign State … The design and implementation of its public healthcare policy is for the State alone to assess'). See, also, *Paushok, Award on Jurisdiction and Liability, 28-Apr-2011 (UNCITRAL)*, para. 298; *Lemire, Decision on Jurisdiction and Liability, 14-Jan-2010 (ICSID)*, paras 240–1, 315.

75 *Feldman, Award, 16-Dec-2002 (ICSID-AF)*, paras 112–16; *Renta4, Award on Preliminary Objections, 20-Mar-2009 (SCC)*, para. 179.

76 *Arif, Award, 8-Apr-2013 (ICSID)*, paras 431, 439–43.

related to environmental regulation;[77] prosecutorial decisions;[78] and the conduct of security operations.[79] Adjudicators exhibit deference as abstention wherever they invoke second-order reasons to justify declining to review State decision-making on these topics. They may, for example, decline to engage with such subjects due to a perception that they would be better determined by States.

The non-justiciability of matters within the 'reserved domain' represents one such abstention doctrine. The identification of matters falling within the 'reserved domain' may rely on second-order reasons indicating deference. Some international adjudicators, for example, have held that – if a matter raises an issue of international law – it no longer falls within the State's domestic jurisdiction.[80] Reliance on such criteria may indicate a view that any matter raising an issue of international law should not be treated as immune from review, because the international adjudicator is equally or more competent than the State to determine that matter. As Judge Levi Carneiro in *Anglo-Iranian Oil* explained, the application of such criteria meant that historically the 'reserved domain covered a very wide field', which subsequently narrowed as a result of 'the total or partial internationalization' of matters previously only subject to domestic regulation.[81]

International adjudicators, for example, historically abstained from reviewing domestic grants of nationality because they fell within the State's 'reserved domain' and were unsuited to international review.[82] Contemporary adjudicators have, by contrast, shown greater willingness to review domestic grants of nationality, basing their claims to competence and/or legitimacy in doing so on, inter alia, the modern development of international rules on nationality. Similar criteria have been applied by some international adjudicators to identify matters that fall within a State's margin of appreciation ('MoA'), and

77 *Bilcon, Award on Jurisdiction and Liability, 17-Mar-2015 (PCA/UNCITRAL)*, paras 595–7.

78 *Rompetrol, Award, 6-May-2013 (ICSID)*, para. 152.

79 *Asian Agricultural Products (Dissent/SO-Asante), 27-Jun-1990 (ICSID)* ('the timing and modalities of the security operation must surely fall within [the State's] exclusive discretion . . . the Tribunal should be slow to second-guess the tactics and strategies of military commanders on the ground').

80 See, for example, *Interhandel, Judgment, 21-Mar-1959 (ICJ)*, pp. 24–5; *Norwegian Loans (Dissent/SO-Lauterpacht), 6-Jul-1957 (ICJ)*, p. 42; *Anglo-Iranian Oil, Provisional Measures Order, 5-Jul-1951 (ICJ)*, pp. 92–3; *Norwegian Loans (Dissent/SO-Read), 6-Jul-1957 (ICJ)*, pp. 87–8, 92. See, further: Casas (2016), pp. 69–70; Lourie (2015), p. 516; Amerasinghe (2008), p. 92; Brownlie (1963), p. 284; Steiner (1936), p. 420; Jacoby (1936), p. 244.

81 *Anglo-Iranian Oil (Dissent/SO-Levi Carneiro), 22-Jul-1952 (ICJ)*, p. 127.

82 See, further, Koessler (1947), p. 537; Borchard (1919), p. 7; Lourie (2015), p. 516; Jenks (1964), p. 603; Nollkaemper (2011), p. 246; Sik (1982), p. 101; Brownlie (1963), p. 286; Watts (1996), p. 434; Lauterpacht (1928), p. 281.

which are thus outside the scope of international review. The ECtHR in *Grant*, for example, held that a transsexual's eligibility for a pension fell – at least in 1997 – 'within the Government's margin of appreciation' and therefore outside the scope of review under P1-1.[83] It indicated, however, that developments in European and international consensus concerning the treatment of transsexuals could, in the future, mean that 'the respondent Government could no longer claim that the matter fell within their margin of appreciation'.[84]

International adjudicators may also abstain from determining matters of domestic law out of deference to domestic authorities, particularly domestic courts.[85] This may include declining to determine the extent or existence of proprietary rights under domestic law[86] or the legality of State conduct.[87] International adjudicators have also declined to decide how particular domestic laws should be interpreted,[88] or to rule on matters of domestic constitutional law.[89] Such adjudicators justify abstention on the basis that international adjudication is not an 'appropriate forum' to decide 'contentious' or 'technical'

83 *Grant, Judgment, 23-May-2006 (ECtHR)*, para. 51.

84 Ibid, para. 39.

85 Cf. *Certain German Interests, Merits Judgment, 25-May-1926 (PCIJ-A7)*, pp. 19, 42; *Serbian Loans, Judgment, 12-Jul-1929 (PCIJ-A20)*, pp. 18–19; *EnCana (Dissent/SO-Grigera Naon), 30-Dec-2005 (UNCITRAL)*, paras 10–13.

86 *Occidental (Dissent/SO-Stern), 5-Oct-2012 (ICSID)*, paras 41–4, 53–5, 112–24 (the contract, 'having not been invalidated' by a domestic court, 'should have been considered as still in force and binding'); *Katoulis, Judgment, 8-Jul-2004 (ECtHR)*, paras 31–2 ('it is not for the Court to settle the issue of ownership of the disputed land').

87 See, for example, *International Bank for Commerce and Development, Judgment, 2-Jun-2016 (ECtHR)*, para. 108 ('the Court expresses no view on whether the [Bulgarian National Bank's] decision to revoke the bank's licence was correct in terms of Bulgarian law. The Court's power to review compliance with national law is limited and it is not its task to make such assessments in the place of the national authorities'); *Rompetrol, Award, 6-May-2013 (ICSID)*, para. 174 ('the Tribunal is not called upon to act as Romanian judge of final instance, either to pronounce on the rightness or wrongness of the pending criminal charges or to substitute a view of its own for the decisions of the competent Romanian instances on individual steps in the prosecutions or preliminary investigations, or on any other internal process'). Cf. situations in which a treaty prompts such analysis, including by requiring that State conduct be 'in accordance' with domestic law: *Diallo, Merits Judgment, 30-Nov-2010 (ICJ)*, paras 69–79.

88 See, for example, *AES (Kazakhstan), Award, 1-Nov-2013 (ICSID)*, paras 306–7, 318–29 ('It is not the role of the Arbitral Tribunal to re-assess whether these bodies were mistaken in their understanding of their country's own legislation'). See, similarly, *Petrobart, Award, 29-Mar -2005 (SCC)*, p. 84; *Maria Atansaiu, Judgment, 12-Oct-2010 (ECtHR)*, paras 138–9; *Kulkov, Judgment, 8-Jan-2009 (ECtHR)*, para. 27; *Arif, Award, 8-Apr-2013 (ICSID)*, para. 441; *International Thunderbird, Award, 26-Jan-2006 (UNCITRAL)*, para. 160.

89 *Hutten-Czapska (Dissent/SO-Zupančič), 19-Jun-2006 (ECtHR-GC)* ('an international judicial body does not know how to, and thus does not want to, enter into the details of national legislative happenings. This is the role rightly reserved for national constitutional courts'). Cf. *Bilcon, Award on Jurisdiction and Liability, 17-Mar-2015 (PCA/UNCITRAL)*, para. 526 (indicating willingness to rely on an alleged inconsistency of a measure with constitutional law as

questions of domestic law.[90] They instead consider it to be 'primarily for the national authorities, notably the courts, to resolve problems of interpretation of domestic legislation'.[91] The UNCITRAL tribunal in *Grand River*, for example, observed that '[b]oth parties apparently would have the Tribunal resolve [a] highly contested question of U.S. domestic law'.[92] Declining to do so, the tribunal noted that it was:

> loath to purport to address these delicate and complex questions of U.S. constitutional and Indian law ... These issues of national law belong in national courts, not in an international tribunal.[93]

International adjudicators have on similar grounds abstained from analysing whether State conduct was motivated by a 'public purpose'. In *Paushok*, for example, an UNCITRAL tribunal declined to decide whether a State had acted for a 'public purpose', noting that:

> The definition of public interest is one that varies considerably from one State to another and it is a subject of significant public debate within each State ... This is more a subject for political debate than arbitral decisions.[94]

Thus, even if an adjudicator considers a dispute to be 'legal', and therefore justiciable, it may abstain from determining specific individual issues implicated in the dispute that are themselves perceived to raise political matters. States have similarly argued – albeit with limited success – that the identification of a situation of 'necessity' involves political, and therefore non-justiciable, elements.[95]

a basis for decision, but finding constitutional practice not 'sufficiently clear' to sustain the argument).

90 See, for example, *Barcelona Traction (Dissent/SO-Tanaka), 5-Feb-1970 (ICJ)*, pp. 156–8 ('If an international tribunal were to take up these issues and examine the regularity of the decisions of municipal courts, the international tribunal would turn out to be a "cour de cassation" ... An international tribunal, on the contrary, belongs to quite a different order'). See, similarly, *Yukos, Final Award, 18 July 2014 (PCA/UNCITRAL)*, para. 499; *Saluka, Partial Award, 17-Mar -2006 (UNCITRAL)*, paras 433, 442–4.

91 *Sovtransavto, Judgment, 25-Jul-2002 (ECtHR)*, para. 95. See, further, Hilson (2013), p. 284.

92 *Grand River, Final Award, 12-Jan-2011 (UNCITRAL)*, para. 139.

93 Ibid, para. 234.

94 *Paushok, Award on Jurisdiction and Liability, 28-Apr-2011 (UNCITRAL)*, paras 328, 337; See, similarly, *Guaracachi, Award, 31-Jan-2014 (PCA/UNCITRAL)*, para. 437; *Serbian Loans (Dissent/SO-Novacovitch), 12-Jul-1929 (PCIJ-A20)*, p. 81; *Parkerings-Compagniet, Award, 11-Sept-2007 (ICSID)*, para. 411.

95 See, however, *Serbian Loans (Dissent/SO-Novacovitch), 12-Jul-1929 (PCIJ-A20)*, p. 81. See, generally, Reinisch (2011), pp. 139–40.

International adjudicators may also decline to determine 'political' disputes for reasons of deference.[96] Judge Jambrek in *Loizidou*, for example, opined that the ECtHR should only decide 'monocentric' disputes which were 'not overly … political'.[97] This was because courts play 'a different role' than legislatures and executive bodies, being 'ill-equipped to deal with large-scale and complex issues which as a rule call for normative action and legal reform'.[98] Other adjudicators hold political disputes to be internationally non-justiciable on more prudential grounds, including because local politics 'do not need a solution at European level',[99] or because the adjudication of political disputes risks creating the impression that the international adjudicator is 'a player with its own political views'.[100] The instrumental, prudential, and non-instrumental reasons canvassed in Chapter 1 may thus each prompt reasoning reflecting the mode of abstention.[101] Instead of adopting domestic decisions on these matters in place of their own (as they would in the mode of submission), adjudicators in the mode of abstention excise these matters from the scope of their review. They thereby decline to endorse or second-guess decisions on those matters that have been made – or could be made – by domestic actors. While, in effect, this may achieve a result similar to the submission mode, the work being done by second-order reasons in the reasoning process is different. In the mode of submission, the State's analysis of the first-order reasons will be followed (akin to an order to accept a particular course of conduct). In the mode of abstention, the State's analysis of the first-order reasons forecloses the adjudicator's analysis of those first-order reasons, prompting it to instead either abstain from making a decision or from basing that decision on different first-order reasons (akin to an order to refrain from considering a particular course of conduct).

6.2.2 *Declining to 'Second-Guess' or 'Review' State Decisions*

An international adjudicator may also accord deference as abstention by indicating that it will not 'second-guess' particular domestic decisions. It could, for

96 See, especially, *Loizidou (Dissent/SO-Gölcüklü), 18-Dec-1996 (ECtHR-GC)*, para. 1; *Cyprus v. Turkey (Dissent/SO-Fuad), 10-May-2001 (ECtHR-GC)*, paras 6–7; *Chiragov (Dissent/SO-Ziemele), 16-Jun-2015 (ECtHR-GC)*, para. 1. See, generally, Hudson (1945), p. 10; Jennings (1998), p. 48.

97 *Loizidou (Dissent/SO-Jambrek), 18-Dec-1996 (ECtHR-GC)*, para. 7.

98 Ibid, para. 7. See, similarly, *Continental, Decision on Jurisdiction, 22-Feb-2006 (ICSID)*, para. 66; *Telefónica, Decision on Jurisdiction, 25-May-2006 (ICSID)*, para. 59.

99 *Herrmann (Dissent/SO-Thór Björgvinsson, Vučinić and Nussberger), 26-Jun-2012 (ECtHR-GC)*.

100 Chiragov *(Dissent/SO-Pinto De Albuquerque), 16-Jun-2015 (ECtHR-GC)*, para. 11.

101 The justifications for deference cited by adjudicators are further discussed in Chapter 8.

example, hold that it is not its role to conduct *in abstracto* review of domestic legislation[102] or policy.[103] The *Enron* ICSID tribunal stated to this effect that it:

> will not sit in judgement over the general tax policies pursued by the Argentine Republic or the Provinces ... This is a matter exclusively appurtenant to the sovereignty of the Argentine Republic.[104]

Adjudicators may, on similar grounds, decline to 'second-guess' certain administrative decisions or the factual basis for such decisions. The *Enkev* UNCITRAL tribunal, for instance, observed that:

> this Tribunal is not an appellate court inserted into the Polish legal system. Nor is it entrusted by the Parties with the general task of judicially reviewing the legality or reasonableness of administrative acts by Polish state entities under Polish law. ... In particular, it cannot act as the ultimate town planner for the City of Lodz. It is certain that this Tribunal is no more fitted to decide issues of town planning in the City of Lodz than its town planners are fitted to apply and interpret the Treaty as an international arbitration tribunal: each has different roles.[105]

An international adjudicator may thus decline to review domestic legislation or policy 'as such', including its correctness as a matter of economics, politics, or domestic law.[106] Such adjudicators might instead restrict their analysis to consider only whether 'the application of specific measures or policies to the facts of each individual case' has breached relevant obligations of international law.[107] The adjudicator thereby abstains from interfering with the

102 See, for example, *Merrill & Ring, Award, 31-Mar-2010 (UNCITRAL)*, para. 218 ('the Tribunal's task is ... not to pass judgment on the legitimacy of the legislation or the regulations in force'). See, similarly, *James, Judgment, 21-Feb-1986 (ECtHR)*, para. 36; *Hakansson, Judgment, 21-Feb-1990 (ECtHR)*, paras 46, 52–3; *Holy Monasteries, Judgment, 9-Dec-1994 (ECtHR)*, para. 55; *Paulik, Judgment, 10-Oct-2006 (ECtHR)*, para. 66; *Renée Rose, Award, 26-Feb-2014 (ICSID)*, paras 161–2; *Spacek, Judgment, 9-Nov-1999 (ECtHR)*, para. 57.

103 See, for example, *CMS Gas, Decision on Jurisdiction, 17-Jul-2003 (ICSID)*, paras 25–33 ('ICSID tribunals cannot pass judgment on whether [State] policies are right or wrong'). See, similarly, *LG&E, Decision on Jurisdiction, 30-Apr-2004 (ICSID)*, para. 67; *El Paso, Decision on Jurisdiction, 27-Apr-2006 (ICSID)*, paras 97–9; *Saluka, Partial Award, 17-Mar-2006 (UNCITRAL)*, para. 337.

104 *Enron, First Decision on Jurisdiction, 14-Jan-2004 (ICSID)*, para. 29.

105 *Enkev, First Partial Award, 29-Apr-2014 (PCA/UNCITRAL)*, para. 327.

106 See, for example, *Continental, Decision on Jurisdiction, 22-Feb-2006 (ICSID)*, para. 74; *BG, Final Award, 24-Dec-2007 (UNCITRAL)*, paras 153, 344; *Telefónica, Decision on Jurisdiction, 25-May-2006 (ICSID)*, para. 67; *Total, Decision on Jurisdiction, 25-Aug-2006 (ICSID)*, para. 58; *Rusoro, Award, 22-Aug-2016 (ICSID-AF)*, para. 385; *Paushok, Award on Jurisdiction and Liability, 28-Apr-2011 (UNCITRAL)*, para. 299.

107 *Lee, Judgment, 18-Jan-2001 (ECtHR-GC)*, para. 79. See, similarly, *Perdigao, Judgment, 16-Nov-2010 (ECtHR-GC)*, paras 70–1; *LG&E, Decision on Jurisdiction, 30-Apr-2004 (ICSID)*, para.

freedom of States 'to adopt the policies that they choose', instead focusing on 'the manner in which policies may be changed and implemented, not the policies themselves'.[108]

International adjudicators may also defer to domestic courts by emphasising that they do not operate as courts of 'appeal' or 'fourth instance'.[109] An international adjudicator might thus exhibit deference as abstention by declining 'to correct or cure an error in law' allegedly made by a State's judiciary 'as an appeal court would do'.[110] The international adjudicator may similarly decline to re-examine domestic judicial determinations concerning facts relevant to the international claim.

Various second-order reasons might prompt such deference. International adjudicators might, for example, abstain from second-guessing domestic decisions made by actors with greater normative epistemic authority (legitimacy) than the international adjudicator. In *Perenco*, for example, the ICSID tribunal held that it:

> must recognise the allocation of competencies between adjudicatory bodies at the national and international levels. An international tribunal cannot second-guess the court's interpretation and application of local law.[111]

Abstention may alternatively flow from an assessment that domestic decision-makers are better able to make certain decisions due to the expertise or competence generated by their institutional features.[112] Adjudicative abstention from determining issues subject to a contractual choice of forum is again excluded from this analysis where such abstention functions by reference to party autonomy rather than second-order reasons related to the qualities of domestic decision-making authorities.

67; *National Grid, Decision on Jurisdiction, 20-Jun-2006 (UNCITRAL)*, paras 136–8; *Enron, Award, 22-May-2007 (ICSID)*, paras 104, 144, 339–40.

108 *Achmea, Award, 7-Dec-2012 (PCA/UNCITRAL)*, para. 294.

109 See, for example, *Anatolie, Award, 19-Dec-2013 (SCC)*, paras 1223–4 ('The Tribunal . . . is not a court of appeal for decisions of Kazakh courts'). See, similarly, *Middle East Cement, Award, 12-Apr-2002 (ICSID)*, paras 159–61; *Loewen, Final Award, 26-Jun-2003 (ICSID-AF)*, paras 51, 242. See, further, Çali (2016), p. 140; Arangio-Ruiz (1996), pp. 456–7. Some international adjudicators indicate that they will not act as an appellate court, but nevertheless do review domestic decisions. These cases are discussed in subsequent chapters.

110 *Alps Finance, Award, 5-Mar-2011 (UNCITRAL)*, paras 249–50. See, similarly, *Bolotiny, Judgment, 16-Jul-2015 (ECtHR)*, para. 35; *Jan de Nul, Award, 6-Nov-2008 (ICSID)*, paras 209–11, 254.

111 *Perenco, Decision on Jurisdiction and Liability, 12-Sept-2014 (ICSID)*, para. 583.

112 *Holy Monasteries, Judgment, 9-Dec-1994 (ECtHR)*, paras 59–60 (it was not 'feasible' for the Court to 'determine for itself' the ownership of land); See, further, Pinto (2008), p. 258; Arai (1998), p. 58; Crawford and Brownlie (2012), p. 53.

6.2.3 *Declining to Act as a 'First Instance' Decision-Maker*

International adjudicators may also abstain from determining matters that could have been – but were not – submitted to domestic organs for determination.[113] In such situations, international adjudicators adopting a mode of abstention might excise matters that have not been the subject of a prior domestic process from the scope of their review. This contrasts with the approach adopted in a deferral mode, in which the adjudicator refers such questions back for determination by domestic decision-makers. In both modes, the recognition of domestic decision-making authority prompts the international adjudicator to suspend the exercise of its own authority on certain matters (or even on the dispute as a whole). Such abstention may articulate an adjudicator's view that international adjudication is not intended for the review of 'mere administrative fault[s]' yet to be considered within the domestic system.[114] The denial of justice obligation, for instance, has been frequently interpreted by adjudicators to embed a substantive ELR (finality) requirement. The imposition of such requirements may be prompted by considerations of deference insofar as they recognise autonomy for the State to determine how to comply with its obligations under international law. As Judge Morelli explained in *Barcelona Traction*, for example, international law obligations may:

> require from the States to which they are directed a particular final result in respect of the treatment of foreign nationals, leaving the State which is under the obligation free as regards the means to be used. Consequently, ... the existence of an internationally unlawful act and of the international responsibility of the State cannot be asserted so long as the foreign national has a possibility of securing, through the means provided by the municipal legal system, the result required by the international rule.[115]

The adoption of a deference as abstention mode provides adjudicators in such a situation the capacity to abstain from exercising their international review function, to favour instead domestic decision-making authority on the relevant issue. International adjudicators may similarly decline to make determinations of

[113] *Bilcon (Dissent/SO-McRae), 17-Mar-2015 (PCA/UNCITRAL)*, paras 36–51 (the claimants had a remedy under domestic law but failed to use it; allowing them to bring an international claim for the domestic law complaint in such circumstances 'is a significant intrusion into domestic jurisdiction'). Cf. *Certain German Interests, Merits Judgment, 25-May-1926 (PCIJ-A7)*, pp. 25–6 ('the right of complaint granted by Poland to the owners is a matter of domestic concern which cannot be used in argument against Germany').

[114] *Tenaris, Award, 29-Jan-2016 (ICSID)*, paras 481, 491–2.

[115] *Barcelona Traction (Dissent/SO-Morelli), 24-Jul-1964 (ICJ)*, p. 114.

fact or law that they consider would be better made domestically. The *Saluka* UNCITRAL tribunal, for example, held that '[i]t cannot be for this Tribunal to question the validity [of a domestic transfer] agreement as long as it has not been invalidated by a competent court or tribunal'.[116]

6.2.4 Lis Pendens, *Fork-in-the-Road, Complementarity, and* Forum Non Conveniens *Rules*

Lis pendens and 'fork-in-the-road' rules may also prompt international adjudicators to abstain from exercising jurisdiction over claims concerning subject matter that has already been placed for decision before a domestic court.[117] Complementarity doctrines may similarly prompt abstention where a domestic court is shown to be willing and able to provide a forum for the settlement of the dispute.[118] *Forum non conveniens* rules may also be used to identify an appropriate decision-maker where two adjudicative decision-makers have been entrusted with overlapping jurisdiction to determine a given dispute.[119] Such rules reflect various functions, including to promote efficiency, to pre-empt the need for application of *res judicata*, and to 'promote comity between courts'.[120] Such rules reflect deference wherever they are applied as a means of recognising a State's relative authority vis-à-vis the international adjudicator. International adjudicators differ in their propensity to use these doctrines to exhibit deference. The doctrinal requirements associated with each of these rules may, in particular, limit the situations in which they can be used to achieve deference. *Lis pendens* and fork-in-the-road rules, for example, typically only apply to proceedings satisfying a triple identity test.[121] Such tests are particularly unlikely to be satisfied where applied to domestic and international

116 *Saluka, Partial Award, 17-Mar-2006 (UNCITRAL)*, para. 456. See, similarly, *Generation Ukraine, Award, 16-Sept-2003 (ICSID)*, para. 9.3; *Vestey, Award, 15-Apr-2016 (ICSID)*, paras 262, 272; *Alpha Projektholding, Award, 8-Nov-2010 (ICSID)*, para. 295.

117 For doctrinal accounts of these concepts see, especially, Magnaye and Reinisch (2016), p. 269; Pauwelyn and Salles (2009), p. 106; Amaza (2012), p. 156; Oellers-Frahm (2001), p. 77.

118 See, especially, von Staden (2016b); Burke-White (2008b).

119 See, especially, Pauwelyn and Salles (2009), p. 106; Van Harten (2014), pp. 15–16; Bjorklund (2007), p. 244.

120 McLachlan (2009), p. 215. See, for example, *Pantechniki, Award, 30-Jul-2009 (ICSID)*, para. 64 (party autonomy); *International Thunderbird, Award, 26-Jan-2006 (UNCITRAL)*, para. 118 (preventing conflicting outcomes, double recovery, and/or uncertainty); *H&H Enterprises, Decision on Jurisdiction, 5-Jun-2012 (ICSID)*, para. 366 (preserving finality). See, further, Bjorklund (2007), p. 297; Amaza (2012), pp. 156–8; Oellers-Frahm (2001), p. 77; Schultz and Ridi (2017).

121 See, for example, *Genin, Award, 25-Jun-2001 (ICSID)*, para. 330; Occidental, Final *Award, 1-Jul-2004 (LCIA)*, para. 52. See, further, Amaza (2012), p. 157; El Hayek and Gilles (2014), p. 589; Pauwelyn and Salles (2009), p. 110.

proceedings.[122] The *Lauder* UNCITRAL tribunal, for example, opined that domestic proceedings 'in no way affect the Arbitral Tribunal's authority and effectiveness', because 'all the other court and arbitration proceedings involve different parties and different causes of action'.[123] This has prompted some adjudicators to relax the requirements to ensure that such rules are not deprived of 'all or most of [their] practical effect'.[124]

Adjudicators may accord varying roles to second-order reasons for deference in their analysis of how such rules will be applied. The ICSID tribunal in *BP*, for example, justified recourse to a strict triple identity test in applying a fork-in-the-road clause on the basis that 'tribunals do not assume lightly that choices of forum have been made by claimant parties in favour of the host State's judicial system'.[125] Other tribunals have, by contrast, favoured strict triple identity tests to avoid creating a 'chilling effect on the submission of disputes by investors to domestic fora . . . when the issues at stake are clearly within the domain of local law'.[126] The *Khan* UNCITRAL tribunal reasoned to this effect that a relaxed test:

> may cause claims being brought to international arbitration before they are ripe on the merits, simply because the investor is afraid that by submitting the existing dispute to local courts or tribunals, it will forgo its right to later make any claims related to the same investment before an international arbitral tribunal.[127]

Adopting a differing perspective, other international adjudicators hold that international proceedings are exclusive of any other remedy. This perspective entails a reverse abstention requirement in favour of international proceedings. The *Lanco* tribunal, for example, held that the exclusivity of ICSID proceedings entailed 'a rule of judicial abstention of local courts' such that, 'once valid consent to ICSID arbitration is established, any other forum called on to decide the issue should decline jurisdiction'.[128]

[122] See, for example, *Certain German Interests, Preliminary Objections Judgment, 25-Aug-1925 (PCIJ-A6)*, pp. 19–20; *Genin, Award, 25-Jun-2001 (ICSID)*, para. 332; *CMS Gas, Decision on Jurisdiction, 17-Jul-2003 (ICSID)*, para. 80; *Occidental, Final Award, 1-Jul-2004 (LCIA)*, para. 50; *BP, Decision on Jurisdiction, 27-Jul-2006 (ICSID)*, paras 155–7.

[123] *Lauder, Final Award, 3-Sept-2001 (UNCITRAL)*, paras 171–4.

[124] *Chevron, Third Interim Award, 27-Feb-2012 (PCA/UNCITRAL)*, para. 4.76. See, also, *Pantechniki, Award, 30-Jul-2009 (ICSID)*, paras 61–4; *Khan, Decision on Jurisdiction, 25-Jul-2012 (PCA/UNCITRAL)*, para. 392; *H&H Enterprises, Decision on Jurisdiction, 5-Jun-2012 (ICSID)*, paras 366–8.

[125] *BP, Decision on Jurisdiction, 27-Jul-2006 (ICSID)*, paras 155–7.

[126] *Khan, Decision on Jurisdiction, 25-Jul-2012 (PCA/UNCITRAL)*, para. 391.

[127] Ibid, para. 391. See, also, *Yuri Bogdanov, Final Award, 16-Apr-2013 (SCC)*, paras 171–5.

[128] *Lanco, Decision on Jurisdiction, 8-Dec-1998 (ICSID)*, para. 40. See, similarly, *CMS Gas, Decision on Jurisdiction, 17-Jul-2003 (ICSID)*, para. 72.

6.3 CONCLUSIONS

The modes of deferral and abstention both treat the second-order reasons for deference as suspensive of international decision-making authority. An adjudicator might adopt such a view of authority, for instance, by declining to determine whether domestic legislation is constitutional, instead, considering it to be for more legitimate or expert domestic actors to make such determinations. The implications for an individual case of applying a mode of deference reflecting a suspensive view of authority may be equivalent to treating domestic authority as conclusive. Nevertheless, the view of authority underlying suspensive modes of deference differs in structure to the view of authority underlying the mode of submission. In suspensive modes, second-order reasons prompt the use by the adjudicator of principles of non-engagement, rather than trumping, to resolve conflicting claims to authority. This follows the view that an international adjudicator should not engage with certain matters. Suspensive modes of deference thus do not recognise for domestic decision-makers the right to take decisions that other actors must endorse (as in the mode of submission). They instead recognise a zone of autonomous domestic decision-making authority in respect of which international adjudicators will not intervene either for a period of time or at all.

7

Concurrent Decision-Making Authority: Deference as Restraint, Reference, and Respect

A third set of approaches to deference disclose a concurrent view of authority. In the modes of 'restraint', 'reference', and 'respect', authority provides *non-exclusionary* second-order reasons for action. This distinguishes these modes of deference from those exhibiting conclusive or suspensive views of authority, according to which second-order reasons are treated as *exclusionary*. Under a concurrent view of authority, second-order reasons for recognising domestic decision-making authority are treated akin to a request, rather than an order. This means that in these modes, second-order reasons for reaching a particular decision are balanced alongside or inform the adjudicator's analysis of the first-order reasons for decision, rather than displacing them. Adopting this structure of authority, the adjudicator is able to assert its own decision-making authority, whilst also acknowledging the decision-making authority of other actors. This chapter examines three modes of deference that reflect this understanding of the interface between domestic and international decision-making authority: the modes of deference as restraint (Section 7.1), deference as reference (Section 7.2), and deference as respect (Section 7.3). Each of these approaches to deference differs from those considered in Chapters 5 and 6, because in each the adjudicator engages (even if only in a limited way) with the available first-order reasons for decision despite having recognised second-order reasons to defer to a domestic actor's decision-making authority.

7.1 DEFERENCE AS RESTRAINT

In a mode of 'deference as restraint', an international adjudicator interprets or applies international obligations by reference to second-order reasons to increase a domestic decision-maker's area of discretion. Second-order reasons are thus invoked to interpret or 'reweight' the first-order reasons for decision.[1] Young explains this potential relationship between deference and the interpretation of international obligations as follows:

> Less deference is paid when the court provides a very specific and detailed account of the scope of a Convention right, essentially providing fewer opportunities for a restriction on this right. More deference is paid when the court defines the right in a looser manner, such that there is a wider range of options of restricting the right in order to achieve a particular policy objective. This is often referred to as granting a greater discretionary area of judgment to the legislature. It gives more weight to the opinion of the legislature by providing a greater range of options for the legislature in which it can act to achieve its policy objectives without harming human rights.[2]

Devices operating in this category make it more likely that a domestic decision-maker will have some 'room to manoeuvre' or authority to make a decision lying outside the control of the international adjudicator.[3] This mode of deference typically functions not by reference to specific domestic decisions, but rather by reference to domestic decision-making authority in the abstract. Several devices may indicate this mode of deference, each of which is introduced and examined in this section.

Prior to considering these examples of deference as restraint, a clarification is in order. As Chapter 1 noted, some scholars argue that this form of reasoning does not reflect deference. Narrow interpretations of international obligations do not, of course, in all instances indicate deferential reasoning. They may instead merely indicate that views differ as to the content of the first-order reasons to be applied to determine whether a particular obligation has been breached. 'Restraint' may thus simply reveal that one adjudicator is reasoning on the basis of different first-order reasons to those that might be adopted by a different adjudicator. As argued in Chapter 1, however, it is incorrect to hold that restraint *can never* indicate deference. A narrow interpretation of an international obligation may be informed by second-order reasons. An adjudicator might, for example, interpret an obligation narrowly not because this is its view of the applicable law (and thus its identification of the relevant first-order reasons for decision), but instead because it wishes to recognise and exhibit respect for domestic decision-making authority. Such an adjudicator exhibits deference because it relies on second-order reasons to interpret the

1 Perry (1989), p. 944.
2 Young (2017), p. 228.
3 See, generally, El Boudouhi (2015); Hovius (1985); Brown (2002), p. 462; Sayeed (2005), p. 111; Pandya and Moody (2010), p. 96; Greer (2010), p. 6.

requirements of an obligation narrowly so as to accommodate domestic authority. Restrained reasoning does not treat domestic authority as conclusive or suspensive, but instead as concurrent to international decision-making authority. Such interpretations perform an important conflict-regulating function.[4] In this mode, international adjudicators anticipate and resolve conflicts between international and domestic decisions prior to their materialisation. They do so by negotiating the zones of overlap in order to limit and minimise potential conflict. Approaches reflecting this mode of deference are introduced in the following subsections.

7.1.1 *Restrictive Interpretation*

An international adjudicator may exercise restraint by adopting a '*state sovereignty conscious* method of treaty interpretation'.[5] Such an adjudicator exhibits its deference insofar as it adopts a restrictive reading of an obligation so as to respect a State's authority. One well-known example of this form of deference is the principle of restrictive interpretation (*in dubio mitius*).[6] According to this principle, in the event that two interpretations are possible, the international adjudicator should adopt the one less restrictive of the State's freedom of action.[7] For earlier writers, the principle of restrictive interpretation applied such that clauses 'odious' to international values were interpreted restrictively.[8] The principle later came, however, to be linked to sovereignty and the interpretation of jurisdictional provisions.[9] As Ajevski explains: '[I]f a provision is unclear then the default assumption is that states are jealous of their sovereignty and would want to constrict their freedom of action to the least possible extent.'[10] Adopting this view, Judge Altamira argued in *Oscar Chinn* that international obligations 'cannot have so absolute a meaning as to render it impossible for the governments bound by the Convention to carry out any act or measure of a commercial nature in their own territory within the sphere of their own sovereignty'.[11] The principle of restrictive interpretation

4 International Law Commission (2006), p. 412.
5 Oesch (2003), p. 644.
6 See, generally, Kolb (2015), pp. 29–30; Crema (2010); Lauterpacht (1949), pp. 57–8.
7 See, generally, Lauterpacht (2010); Schreuer et al. (2009), para. 378; van Aaken (2008), p. 11.
8 Lauterpacht (1949), p. 65; Crema (2010), p. 683.
9 See, further, Orakhelashvili (2003); Lauterpacht (1949), p. 65; Kolb (2015), pp. 29–30; Hyde (1930), p. 18.
10 Ajevski (2014), p. 8.
11 *Oscar Chinn (Dissent/SO-Altamira), 12-Dec-1934 (PCIJ-A/B63)*, p. 92. See, similarly, *Lighthouses in Crete and Samos (Dissent/SO-Selferiades), 8-Oct-1937 (PCIJ-A/B71)*, p. 137.

may thus achieve deference by prompting adjudicators to interpret international obligations to maximise State liberty, independence, and sovereignty.

The principle of restrictive interpretation historically operated as a subsidiary means of interpretation: it applied only if ambiguity remained following the application of primary rules of interpretation.[12] Such primary rules are nowadays encapsulated in the *Vienna Convention on the Law of Treaties* ('VCLT'),[13] which adopts a more neutral approach to interpretation.[14] Neutral interpretation proceeds from a presumption that States intend a treaty 'to be fully effective and its operation unhampered by restrictive rules'.[15] The VCLT has been held by some adjudicators to restrict the capacity for adjudicators to invoke second-order reasons to interpret treaty obligations more restrictively in deference to States.[16] The *Loewen* tribunal, for example, held that the principle of restrictive interpretation had been replaced by the VCLT, as 'the primary guide to the interpretation of the provisions of NAFTA'.[17] It therefore rejected a submission 'that NAFTA is to be understood in accordance with the principle that treaties are to be interpreted in deference to the sovereignty of States'.[18] Adjudicators applying the VCLT typically opt instead for a neutral (even if 'strict') interpretation of treaty provisions.[19] They accord 'deference' to the terms of the treaty, deferring to the State as treaty-maker, rather than regulator.[20]

[12] Lauterpacht (1949), p. 63.

[13] Vienna Convention on the Law of Treaties (1969/1980) 1155 UNTS 331. The Convention's provisions on treaty interpretation are widely considered to reflect customary international law.

[14] See, especially, Lauterpacht (2010), pp. 302–3; Larson and Jenks (1965), p. 411; Larouer (2009), pp. 6–7; Crema (2010), p. 682.

[15] Lauterpacht (1949), p. 61. See, for example, *Anglo-Iranian Oil (Dissent/SO-Read), 22-Jul-1952 (ICJ)*, p. 143.

[16] Some scholars have suggested that modern adjudicators adopt a reverse position, such that 'in case of doubt, the interpretation more favourable to the private party must be preferred': Crema (2010), pp. 691–5; Lauterpacht (1949), pp. 66–7. There were few instances of such a view being adopted in the analysed decisions. See, however, *Desert Line, Award, 6-Feb-2008 (ICSID)*, para. 116; *SGS (Philippines), Decision on Jurisdiction, 29-Jan-2004 (ICSID)*, para. 116; *Diallo (Dissent/SO-Cançado Trindade), 30-Nov-2010 (ICJ)*, para. 85.

[17] *Loewen, Award on Jurisdiction, 5-Jan-2001 (ICSID-AF)*, para. 51.

[18] Ibid, para. 51.

[19] See, for example, *Oil Platforms (Dissent/SO-Higgins), 12-Dec-1996 (ICJ)*, para. 35; *Ethyl, Award on Jurisdiction, 24-Jun-1998 (UNCITRAL)*, para. 55; *Aguas del Tunari, Decision on Jurisdiction, 21-Oct-2005 (ICSID)*, para. 91; *Mesa, Award, 24-Mar-2016 (PCA/UNCITRAL)*, para. 405.

[20] See, for example, *Ambiente Ufficio, Decision on Jurisdiction and Admissibility, 8-Feb-2013 (ICSID)*, para. 392 ('the agreement of the Contracting States of a BIT on the definition of investment is entitled to "great deference"'). See, similarly, *Daimler, Award, 22-Aug-2012 (ICSID)*, para. 146.

Even non-restrictive interpretations may, however, reflect deference to the State's decision-making authority. Arbitrator Weil in *Tokios Tokelés*, for example, noted that:

> ICSID arbitral tribunals have to be particularly cautious when they determine their jurisdiction. An unwarranted extension of the ICSID arbitral jurisdiction would entail an unwarranted encroachment on both the availability of diplomatic protection and the jurisdiction of domestic courts.[21]

Furthermore, as Lauterpacht noted in 1949, 'the theoretical relevance of the rule of restrictive interpretation has helped to keep it alive'.[22] This is particularly evident in party pleadings and dissenting opinions.

7.1.2 *Thresholds for Breach*

Adjudicators may also exhibit deferential reasoning in setting thresholds to designate the point at which State conduct 'rises to the level that is unacceptable from the international perspective'.[23] Thresholds indicating deference as restraint are typically set using quantifiers. Adjudicators may require conduct to be 'sufficiently' serious,[24] for the breach to be 'gross', 'patent', 'glaring', 'blatant' or 'manifest', [25] or for there to be a 'complete' denial of a right.[26] Adjudicators adopting this mode of deference exhibit a form of 'judicial minimalism'.[27] They might decide, for instance, only to find a breach – or to disregard, and not defer to, domestic decisions – in situations in which

21 *Tokios Tokelės (Weil), 29-Apr-2004 (ICSID)*, para. 8. See, similarly, *Suez-Interagua (Dissent/SO-Nikken), 30-Jul-2010 (ICSID)*, para. 31 ('an international obligation that includes the State declining to exercise its regulatory power cannot be presumed, considering ... the high measure of deference that international law generally extends to the right of domestic authorities to regulate matters within their own borders').

22 Lauterpacht (1949), pp. 62–3.

23 *SD Myers, Partial Award, 13-Nov-2000 (UNCITRAL)*.

24 *Merrill & Ring, Award, 31-Mar-2010 (UNCITRAL)*, paras 219, 236.

25 See, for example, *Al-Bahloul, Partial Award on Jurisdiction and Liability, 2-Sept-2009 (SCC)*, paras 221, 247, 253, 284 ('It is not for this Tribunal to rule on the correctness of the court's decision, but merely on whether the decision manifestly misapplied the law'). See, similarly, *Ron Fuchs, Award, 3-Mar-2010 (ICSID)*, para. 441; *Mondev, Award, 11-Oct-2002 (ICSID-AF)*, paras 126–7; *Paushok, Award on Jurisdiction and Liability, 28-Apr-2011 (UNCITRAL)*, paras 625–6. Cf. *CCL, Jurisdictional Award, 1-Jan-2003 (SCC)*, pp. 131, 138–9 (rejecting that principles of comity meant it should only review State acts where they disclosed a 'blatant abuse of power').

26 See, for example, *Merrill & Ring, Award, 31-Mar-2010 (UNCITRAL)*, para. 236; *Ron Fuchs, Award, 3-Mar-2010 (ICSID)*, paras 417–18, 441; *Waste Management (No. 2), Final Award, 30-Apr-2004 (ICSID-AF)*, paras 98–115.

27 Young (2017), p. 150.

domestic officials 'have not merely made a mistake, but have made a very clear one, – so clear that it is not open to rational question'.[28] Reflecting this approach of restraint, the *Anatolie* SCC tribunal stated that:

> finding a breach of the FET standard is actually a very high bar. There is a high measure of deference that international law extends to the right of domestic authorities to regulate matters within their own borders. Only cases of blatant misconduct will support a finding of unfair and inequitable treatment.[29]

The respondent in *Al Warraq* similarly contended that: 'The principle of comity alone requires this Tribunal to assume that the Indonesian Court has acted properly unless the Claimant proves that there has been a glaring disregard of due process by the Court.'[30]As the respondent in *Gemplus* and *Talsud* submitted: 'International tribunals use such qualifiers because they recognize that it is not their role to second-guess the acts of States; accordingly, the high threshold for proving a violation of international law protects the autonomy and judgment of government.'[31]

The use of quantifiers to set thresholds for breach allows international adjudicators to defer to State decisions falling within certain 'boundaries' or a 'margin' of permissible conduct.[32] The *Bilcon* UNCITRAL tribunal, for example, held that its interpretation of the minimum standard of treatment had to 'strike an appropriate balance' between the respective roles of domestic and international decision-makers.[33] It held that breaches of the minimum standard of treatment entailed a 'threshold of seriousness',[34] thus excluding from review '[t]he imprudent exercise of discretion or even outright mistakes', given that '[r]oom must be left for judgment' by the State.[35] It further observed that:

> First, third-party adjudicators must, in applying the international minimum standard, take into account that domestic authorities may have more familiarity with the factual and domestic legal complexities of a situation. Secondly, domestic authorities may also enjoy distinctive kinds of legitimacy, such as being elected or accountable to elected authorities. Thirdly, . . .[t]hird-party

28 Thayer (1893), p. 144.
29 *Anatolie, Award, 19-Dec-2013 (SCC)*, para. 923.
30 *Al Warraq, Final Award, 15-Dec-2014 (UNCITRAL)*, para. 405.
31 *Gemplus/Talsud, Award, 16-Jun-2010 (ICSID-AF)*, para. 6.19.
32 *Mobil, Decision on Liability and Quantum, 22-May-2012 (ICSID-AF)*, para. 153; *GEA, Award, 31-Mar-2011 (ICSID)*, para. 236.
33 *Bilcon, Award on Jurisdiction and Liability, 17-Mar-2015 (PCA/UNCITRAL)*, para. 440.
34 Ibid, para. 440.
35 Ibid, para. 437.

> adjudicators may have their own advantages including independence and detachment from domestic pressures.[36]

Taking these considerations into account, the tribunal held that 'there is indeed a high threshold for Article 1105 [of NAFTA] to apply', with that threshold indicated by 'intensifying adjectives' requiring 'gross', 'manifest' or 'complete' misconduct.[37] Using these quantifiers, the tribunal distinguished breaches of international law from 'mere error[s] in legal or factual analysis', leaving the State decision-making authority for 'interpreting grey areas of the law, weighing contested points of evidence, or exercising scientific judgment'.[38]

By setting high thresholds for breach, international adjudicators use second-order reasons for deference to influence their interpretation of first-order reasons for decision. They refrain from requiring correctness or 'perfection',[39] permitting States some freedom to engage in conduct that is 'merely inconsistent or questionable'[40] or 'merely sub-optimal'.[41] As the *Vannessa Ventures* ICSID Additional Facility tribunal stated, in a restraint mode:

> The question is not whether the host State legal system is performing as efficiently as it ideally could: it is whether it is performing so badly as to violate treaty obligations.[42]

Quantifiers indicate an adjudicator's recognition of a margin for State decision-making free from international review. Wherever an adjudicator emphasises that an obligation entails a high threshold for breach, it thereby reassures the State that it is only reviewing domestic decision-making lightly, or at the margins.

7.1.3 *Decisional Discretion*

Adjudicators may also exhibit deference as restraint by affording States decisional discretion. Decisional discretion typically follows ambiguity or

36 Ibid, para. 439.

37 Ibid, paras 441–4.

38 Ibid, paras 454, 594. See, similarly, *Unglaube, Award, 16-May-2012 (ICSID)*, para. 246.

39 *AES (Hungary), Award, 23-Sept-2010 (ICSID)*, para. 9.3.40.

40 *Cargill, Award, 18-Sept-2009 (ICSID-AF)*, para. 293. See, similarly, *Pope & Talbot, Merits Award, 10-Apr-2001 (UNCITRAL)*, para. 181 ('well beyond . . . glitches and innocent mistakes').

41 *HOCHTIEF, Decision on Liability, 29-Dec-2014 (ICSID)*, para. 282.

42 *Vannessa Ventures, Award, 16-Jan-2013 (ICSID-AF)*, para. 227. See, similarly, *Eastern Sugar, Partial Award, 27-Mar-2007 (SCC)*, para. 272; *Glamis, Award, 8-Jun-2009 (UNCITRAL)*, paras 23, 616–26 ('The idea of deference is found in the modifiers "manifest" and "gross" that make this standard a stringent one; it is found in the idea that a breach requires something greater than mere arbitrariness').

flexibility in the applicable law. The adjudicator might, for instance, recognise that multiple interpretations of an obligation are possible and exercise restraint by invoking second-order reasons to hold that the State – rather than the international adjudicator – has better authority to select between those interpretations.[43] An international adjudicator might decide, for example, that the notions of 'police powers' or 'public policy', encompass 'a panoply of state activity', giving rise to a margin of discretion for the State to determine what they cover.[44] This approach differs from that which would be adopted in an abstention mode. Instead of holding such matters to be exclusively within the purview of State decision-making (and so inappropriate for international adjudicative analysis), the adjudicator operating in a restraint mode asserts some limited authority to review those matters – even if only at the margins.

In recognising decisional discretion, an international adjudicator takes the view that it is not its role to rule on whether the State has selected *the best* or *correct* approach to a given issue. Instead, the adjudicator recognises that States have a 'choice of means' or 'margin of appreciation' to exercise their decision-making authority. As the ECtHR in *Mellacher* held:

> The possible existence of alternative solutions does not in itself render the contested legislation unjustified. Provided that the legislature remains within the bounds of its margin of appreciation, it is not for the Court to say whether the legislation represented the best solution for dealing with the problem or whether the legislative discretion should have been exercised in another way.[45]

Deference through the recognition of decisional discretion may follow from the adjudicator's appraisal of instrumental, prudential or non-instrumental second-order reasons for deference. Decisional discretion may follow, for example, from a view that States are better equipped to make certain decisions and should be given latitude to do so. In *Apotex*, for example, the ICSID Additional Facility tribunal indicated that, when applying a due process obligation, it would exercise restraint in reviewing a State's decision to regulate the importation of certain pharmaceuticals.[46] It emphasised a: 'need for international tribunals to exercise caution in cases involving a state regulator's

43 See, to this effect, Fahner (2013), pp. 432–4; Henckels (2012), p. 245; Griffey (2011); Rivers (2006), pp. 196–8; Glashausser (2005), p. 33; Martinez-Fraga and Reetz (2015), p. 6.

44 Henckels (2012), p. 246. Cf. *Bernhard von Pezold, Award, 28-Jul-2015 (ICSID)*, para. 466 ('the Government has agreed to specific international obligations and there is no "margin of appreciation" qualification within the BITs at issue').

45 *Mellacher, Judgment, 19-Dec-1989 (ECtHR)*, para. 53.

46 *Apotex, Award, 25-Aug-2014 (UNCITRAL)*, paras 9.27–9.40.

exercise of discretion, particularly in sensitive areas involving protection of public health and the well-being of patients'.[47] Without such restraint, the tribunal cautioned that:

> NAFTA tribunals would be required in cases such as the present case, as the Respondent submitted at the Hearing, to 'step into the shoes of [the Food and Drug Administration] and evaluate how [the factors relevant to the FDA's regulatory discretion] were applied to Apotex and other companies.' This Tribunal, by inclination, qualification and training, cannot possibly act as a drug regulator.[48]

Deference as restraint through the recognition of decisional discretion may, alternatively, flow from a view that it 'would be illegitimate' for the international adjudicator to control the State's choices within a zone of permitted conduct, the adjudicator's role being 'to secure legality, not correctness'.[49] Restraint in such circumstances allows international adjudicators to 'avoid too easily engaging in substitutionary *de novo* review of discretionary determinations made by host state authorities'.[50] Interpreting an FET provision, for example, the *Saluka* UNCITRAL tribunal held that:

> Even though Article 3 obviously leaves room for judgment and appreciation by the Tribunal, it does not set out totally subjective standards which would allow the Tribunal to substitute ... its judgment on the choice of solutions for the Czech Republic's ... the 'fair and equitable treatment' standard does not create an 'open-ended mandate to second-guess government decision-making'.[51]

The recognition of decisional discretion may also reflect non-instrumental second-order reasons. It may, for instance, permit adjudicators to exhibit respect for plurality and diversity by leaving States latitude to account for local conditions.[52] In a mode of restraint, the adjudicator regulates such plurality by delineating an 'acceptable range of legislative and regulatory behaviour', only intervening to review domestic decisions where the State oversteps that range.[53]

47 Ibid, para. 9.37.
48 Ibid, para. 9.39.
49 Rivers (2006), pp. 193.
50 Paine (2019), para. 19.
51 *Saluka, Partial Award, 17-Mar-2006 (UNCITRAL)*, para. 284.
52 Nollkaemper (2013b).
53 *AES (Hungary), Award, 23-Sept-2010 (ICSID)*, para. 9.3.73. See, similarly, *Chapman (Dissent/SO-Pastor Ridruejo, Bonello, Tulkens, Strážnická, Lorenzen, Fischbach and Casadevall), 18-Jan-2001 (ECtHR-GC)*, para. 4; *Mellacher, Judgment, 19-Dec-1989 (ECtHR)*, para. 55.

7.1.4 *The Margin of Appreciation (MoA)*

Decisional discretion is closely associated with the margin of appreciation (MoA), which has been defined variously as a 'room for manoeuvre',[54] 'discretion',[55] 'leeway'[56] or 'latitude'[57] afforded to States to fulfil their international obligations. The MoA operates within a restraint mode in two forms, both of which are explored in the following subsections.[58]

7.1.4.1 The 'Structural' Margin of Appreciation

A 'structural' MoA addresses whether the international court or a domestic decision-maker is 'better placed to decide' certain issues.[59] A structural MoA arises where international obligations are worded vaguely or flexibly.[60] It is particularly likely to arise in the application of discretionary or result-oriented obligations, and 'positive' rather than 'negative' obligations. This form of an MoA allows the adjudicator to acknowledge that certain 'norms may be interpreted and applied in different, but still normatively justifiable ways'.[61] In such circumstances of normative leeway, the MoA prompts international adjudicators to 'exercise self-restraint'[62] by recognising that States retain authority 'to prefer one course of action over legitimate alternatives'.[63]

Adjudicators applying a structural MoA delineate 'acceptable boundaries' for State conduct, within which they do not second-guess State decision-making.[64] An adjudicator might thus recognise 'a spectrum of choices available to the national authorities for fulfilling their duty'.[65] The structural MoA operates such that:

54 Greer (2010), p. 5; Yourow (1996), p. 13.
55 Merrills (1988), p. 151.
56 Gross and Ni Aolain (2001), p. 626.
57 Arai-Takahashi (2002), p. 2.
58 This analysis draws on Letsas (2006). The MoA is also closely associated with the burden of proof. A wide MoA may mean, for example, that there will be 'an initial presumption in favor of the defendant state': O'Donnell (1982), p. 475. See, similarly, Gerards (2011), p. 105; Kratochvil (2011), p. 350. Presumptions and argumentative burdens are considered in Section 7.1.5.
59 Letsas (2006), p. 709.
60 See, generally, Letsas (2007), pp. 90–8; Rivers (2006), pp. 177, 191–3; Shany (2005), p. 932.
61 von Staden (2016a), p. 1115.
62 Hovius (1985), p. 254.
63 Fahner (2013), p. 431. See, for example, *Broniowski, Judgment, 22-Jun-2004 (ECtHR-GC)*, para. 144; *Alisic, Judgment, 16-Jul-2014 (ECtHR-GC)*, para. 101.
64 von Staden (2016a), p. 1115.
65 Mahoney (1990), p. 78.

> Any choice made within this spectrum, even if it does not correspond to the choice that judges think would have been the best in the circumstances, will not be contrary to the [State's international obligation]. A violation will only be held to have occurred if the national authorities have strayed outside the range of permissible options, that is outside their 'margin of appreciation'.[66]

A structural MoA recognises the State's decisional discretion, assisting 'to identify the point when an interference amounts to a violation'.[67] The width of a structural MoA will determine the 'the limits or intensity' of the adjudicator's review of State conduct, determining when the adjudicator may substitute its own preferences for those of the State.[68]

Some scholars suggest that international adjudicators are precluded from affording a structural MoA to States because the VCLT method of interpretation 'leads to a single, consistent interpretation of a treaty provision'.[69] They argue that it is the international adjudicator, and not the State, that has 'ultimate responsibility' for determining the meaning of international obligations.[70] On this view, States would have no structural MoA to interpret what international law requires. This view, however, denies the potential indeterminacy of international law and/or the reality of its application to contestable issues. The propensity of an adjudicator to deploy MoA reasoning instead indicates its 'readiness to acknowledge normative ambiguity'.[71] It acknowledges that treaty interpretation depends on 'the identity of the interpreter' and the context of application.[72] This also explains why State consensus may be relevant to assessing how much discretionary leeway States enjoy.[73] State consensus concerning the interpretation of a norm may indicate coalescence around a unitary interpretation. This would shrink the range of options considered legitimate for complying with the norm and hence restrict the discretionary ambit of action available to the State. It also demonstrates the connection between first- and second-order reasons in a deference as restraint mode. In this mode, adjudicators use second-order reasons to allocate interpretive authority to domestic decision-makers, rather than claiming for

66 Ibid, p. 78.
67 Leonhardsen (2013), p. 5.
68 Letsas (2006), pp. 706. See, similarly, Shany (2005), p. 910.
69 Oesch (2003), pp. 642. See, for example: *Pantechniki, Award, 30-Jul-2009 (ICSID)*, para. 76; *Jahn (Dissent/SO-Ress), 30-Jun-2005 (ECtHR-GC)*, paras 3–4.
70 Greer (2004), p. 423.
71 Shany (2005), p. 936.
72 Glashausser (2005), p. 27.
73 On State consensus see, generally, O'Donnell (1982), p. 479; Legg (2012), p. 25; Heringa (1996), p. 110; Benvenisti (1999).

themselves the exclusive authority to interpret what international obligations require.

7.1.4.2 The 'Substantive' Margin of Appreciation

The MoA may also be applied where an international obligation is interpreted to require a balancing of interests. In these circumstances, a 'substantive' MoA attributes 'latitude to the domestic authorities to strike their own balance'.[74] It grants States leeway to resolve 'conflicts between individual rights and national interests or among different moral convictions'.[75] A State may warrant such an MoA because it has 'better access to factual information about the need for such restrictions' or is 'in a better position to evaluate how a certain national measure or decision relates to national constitutional rules and traditions'.[76] The substantive MoA allows the adjudicator, in making for example a proportionality assessment, to place 'its finger on the scale to give governments some evidentiary advantage'.[77] As such: 'The more intense the standard of proportionality becomes, the narrower the margin allowed to national authorities.'[78] Conversely, '[a] wide margin results in a less stringent proportionality test'.[79]

The decision as to *how much* discretion a State enjoys will impact the strictness of international review. If the international adjudicator recognises a high degree of discretion, it is more likely to exercise 'low', 'lenient' or 'light' review of the impugned State conduct.[80] As seen earlier, such review might be achieved by requiring proof that the impugned conduct 'blatantly', 'manifestly' or 'clearly' falls outside the zone of permitted conduct.[81] By contrast, if the international adjudicator holds there to be limited or no discretion, it is likely to conduct a 'stricter' review.[82] The MoA, as with other forms of deference as restraint, therefore tends to be accompanied by quantifying statements. A narrow MoA may require, for example, the State to produce 'very weighty reasons' to justify an interference with private property, such that

74 Bemelmans-Videc (2011), para 25. On the 'substantive' MoA see Letsas (2006), pp. 710–11. See, further, Costa (2011), p. 180; Gerards and Senden (2009), p. 645; Saul (2016).

75 Benvenisti (1999), pp. 843–4.

76 Gerards (2018b), p. 498.

77 Franck (2008), p. 761.

78 Arai-Takahashi (2004), p. 14.

79 Burke-White and von Staden (2008), p. 308.

80 Fahner (2013), p. 437; Mik (2014), p. 305.

81 See, generally, Foster (2011), p. 264; Wouters and Hachez (2009), p. 326; Klager (2010), p. 440.

82 Fahner (2013), p. 437.

a 'careful' or 'close' scrutiny is made of State decisions.[83] By contrast, a wide MoA indicates that the adjudicator will not review a State's decisions unless they appear to be '*manifestly* without reasonable foundation',[84] '*manifestly* erroneous',[85] or '*manifestly* unreasonable or arbitrary'.[86] Such tests equate to 'almost a presumption' in favour of domestic decisions.[87] The ICJ in *Diallo* opined, for example, that:

> [I]t is for each State, in the first instance, to interpret its own domestic law. The Court does not, in principle, have the power to substitute its own interpretation for that of the national authorities, especially when that interpretation is given by the highest national courts ... Exceptionally, where a State puts forward a manifestly incorrect interpretation of its domestic law, particularly for the purpose of gaining an advantage in a pending case, it is for the Court to adopt what it finds to be the proper interpretation.[88]

The width of the MoA is informed by an assessment of the authority of the adjudicator vis-à-vis that of the State. A wide MoA recognises that the State is better placed to make the requisite decisions, such that the adjudicator 'refrain[s] from scrutinising [the State's decision] substantively, or will do so only lightly'.[89]

Second-order reasons may thus be used by adjudicators to identify matters in respect of which a State's choices will be only lightly or instead stringently reviewed.[90] The ECtHR, for example, gives States wide leeway to make decisions on social, political, and economic matters.[91] This means that States typically have broad discretion to determine whether measures respond to a 'public' or 'general' interest as required by P1-1. The Court grants States a wide MoA in making such assessments on the basis of two considerations reflecting instrumental

83 See, for example, *Stec, Judgment, 12-Apr-2006 (ECtHR-GC)*, para. 52.

84 See, for example, ibid, para. 52; *Mellacher, Judgment, 19-Dec-1989 (ECtHR)*, paras 45–7; *Scollo, Judgment, 28-Sept-1995 (ECtHR)*, paras 28–31; *Belane Nagy, Judgment, 13-Dec-2016 (ECtHR-GC)*, para. 113 (emphasis added).

85 Allen (2005a), p. 95.

86 *Vikentijevik, Judgment, 6-Feb-2014 (ECtHR)*, para. 65 (emphasis added). See, further, Gerards (2014); Sales (2006), p. 141.

87 López Escarcena (2014), p. 64.

88 *Diallo, Merits Judgment, 30-Nov-2010 (ICJ)*, para. 70. See, similarly, *Fredin, Judgment, 18-Feb -1991 (ECtHR)*, para. 50; *Stere, Judgment, 23-Feb-2006 (ECtHR)*, para. 46; *Sulejmani, Judgment, 28-Apr-2016 (ECtHR)*, para. 35.

89 von Staden (2016a), p. 1115.

90 Compare, for example, *Barrow, Judgment, 22-Aug-2006 (ECtHR)*, para. 49; *Chabauty, Judgment, 4-Oct-2012 (ECtHR-GC)*, paras 49–56; ibid, para. 467.

91 *Herrmann (Dissent/SO-Pinto De Albuquerque), 26-Jun-2012 (ECtHR-GC)* (protection of the environment); *Almeida, Judgment, 11-Jan-2000 (ECtHR)*, para. 53 ('social and economic policies'); *Gnecchi, Judgment, 15-Nov-2002 (ECtHR)*, para. 23 ('spheres such as housing').

second-order reasons for deference. First, the Court has held that 'because of their direct knowledge of their society and its needs, the national authorities are in principle better placed than the international judge to appreciate what is in the public interest'.[92] Second, the Court has emphasised that 'the decision to enact laws [interfering with] property will commonly involve consideration of political, economic, and social issues on which opinions within a democratic society may reasonably differ widely'.[93] The ambit of action available to States may be further broadened for decisions concerning particular subjects or in certain contexts. The ECtHR in *NKM*, for example, noted that while a 'broad' MoA would be afforded to States for 'matters of general social and economic policy', States would enjoy 'some degree of additional deference and latitude' in relation to the 'tax sphere'.[94] Other adjudicators have held that a State is entitled to additional deference in the context of political or economic regime change.[95]

7.1.5 *Presumptions and Argumentative Burdens*

Authority can be assessed as a matter of assumption, presumption, or proof.[96] An international adjudicator might simply assume that another decision-maker has authority because of its institutional type or because of the system in which it operates.[97] Alternatively, the international adjudicator might adopt a presumption to this effect.[98] The adjudicator might, for example, 'be reluctant to exercise jurisdiction to second-guess a procedure presenting *prima facie* regularity'.[99] Arbitrator Ali Khan in *Deutsche Bank*, for example, opined that a domestic court was entitled to a 'high measure of deference' such that 'there

92 *James, Judgment, 21-Feb-1986 (ECtHR)*, para. 46. See, similarly, *Carson, Judgment, 16-Mar-2010 (ECtHR-GC)*, para. 61; *Andrle, Judgment, 17-Feb-2011 (ECtHR)*, para. 56.

93 *James, Judgment, 21-Feb-1986 (ECtHR)*, para. 46. See, similarly, *Vistins, Judgment, 25-Oct-2012 (ECtHR-GC)*, para. 98; *Malama, Judgment, 1-Mar-2001 (ECtHR)*, para. 46; *Broniowski, Judgment, 22-Jun-2004 (ECtHR-GC)*, para. 149.

94 *NKM, Judgment, 14-May-2013 (ECtHR)*, paras 49–50, 54.

95 *Belane Nagy, Judgment, 13-Dec-2016 (ECtHR-GC)*, para. 114; *Jahn, Judgment, 30-Jun-2005 (ECtHR-GC)*, para. 117; *OKO Pankki, Award, 19-Nov-2007 (ICSID)*, para. 256; *Oxus Gold, Award, 17-Dec-2015 (UNCITRAL)*, para. 793; *Toto, Decision on Jurisdiction, 11-Sept-2009 (ICSID)*, para. 165. Cf. where the State's development status impacts analysis of an individual's legitimate expectations. This does not reflect deference, but instead decision-making by reference to first-order reasons: *Ron Fuchs, Decision on Jurisdiction, 6-Jul-2007 (ICSID)*, paras 99–102; *Mamidoil, Award, 30-Mar-2015 (ICSID)*, paras 624–6.

96 See, especially, Rivers (2014), p. 411; Edwards (2002), p. 880; Foster (2010).

97 See, for example, Raine (2013), p. 93; Føllesdal (2013b), p. 60; Grossman (2009); Gibson et al. (1998), p. 356; Ferrero (1942), p. 89; Thomas (2014), p. 746.

98 Gerards (2011), p. 87; Henckels (2012), p. 245; Foster (2011), p. 260; Raine (2013), p. 93.

99 *Renta4, Award on Preliminary Objections, 20-Mar-2009 (SCC)*, para. 33.

should be a presumption that it has acted in a proper manner'.[100] Presumptions and evidentiary standards can thus be used to restrict the circumstances in which an international court or tribunal will review domestic acts, thereby expanding the decision-making autonomy of particular domestic actors. The *Paushok* UNCITRAL tribunal, for example, adopted 'a presumption of validity in favour of legislative measures adopted by a State', reflecting that it did not seek to 'question in any way the sovereign right of a State to enact whatever tax measures it deems appropriate at any particular time'.[101] Other adjudicators, by contrast, reject that particular measures or decision-makers are entitled to 'special deference' through presumptions of validity.[102]

Second-order reasons may similarly prompt adjudicators to require particularly strong evidence or arguments to depart from, or to review, domestic decisions. The ECtHR in *Roche*, for example, required 'strong reasons' to depart from a domestic court's interpretation of a measure, which it took as its 'starting-point'.[103] Arbitrator Covarrubias Bravo in *Feldman* similarly noted that the review of domestic taxation measures involved 'highly delicate' matters, such that allegations of violation should be 'supported by extremely clear and convincing evidence'.[104] Other adjudicators have emphasised that a finding of denial of justice may require 'evidence of the most convincing nature'.[105]

Adjudicators may also impose heightened argumentative burdens on applicants seeking to restrain the exercise of State decision-making authority. In *Caratube*, for example, an ICSID tribunal was asked to grant provisional measures to restrain a State's criminal proceedings. The tribunal held that 'criminal investigations and measures taken by a state in that context require special considerations',[106] because they reflect 'a most obvious and undisputed part of the sovereign right of a state to implement and enforce its national law on its territory'.[107] As provisional measures would 'encroach on the State's

100 *Deutsche Bank (Dissent/SO-Ali Khan), 23-Oct-2012 (ICSID)*, para. 106.

101 *Paushok, Interim Measures Order, 2-Sept-2008 (UNCITRAL)*, paras 81–2. See, similarly, *El Paso, Award, 31-Oct-2011 (ICSID)*, paras 290–1.

102 *Burlington Resources, Decision on Liability, 14-Dec-2012 (ICSID)*, para. 365.

103 *Roche, Judgment, 19-Oct-2005 (ECtHR-GC)*, paras 122–4.

104 *Feldman (Dissent/SO-Covarrubias Bravo), 3-Dec-2002 (ICSID-AF)*. See, similarly, *Renta4, Award on Preliminary Objections, 20-Mar-2009 (SCC)*, para. 158 (distinguishing the ECtHR's finding of non-violation on the same facts: the ECtHR decision was 'based on a heightened requirement of "incontrovertible and direct proof," given the "wide margin of appreciation" a State enjoys under [P1-1]').

105 *White Industries, Award, 30-Nov-2011 (UNCITRAL)*, para. 10.4.8. See, similarly, the respondent's position in *Railroad Development Corporation, Award, 29-Jun-2012 (ICSID)*, para. 161.

106 *Caratube, Provisional Measures Decision, 31-Jul-2009 (ICSID)*, para. 134.

107 Ibid, para. 135.

sovereignty' over such matters, it held that 'a particularly high threshold must be overcome' before they could be recommended.[108] Such an approach seeks to protect the exercise of a State's authority by ensuring that the State's powers in respect of criminal enforcement activities are not interfered with except in exceptional circumstances. Other adjudicators have instead rejected that 'evidentiary requirements can be heightened purely on the grounds of deference or comity or otherwise'.[109]

Adjudicators have also used presumptions and heightened argumentative burdens to exercise restraint in reviewing State grants of nationality. Such adjudicators presume that State grants of nationality are valid, declining to review the validity of nationality save in 'certain limited circumstances'.[110] As Arbitrator Nabulsi explained in *Soufraki*:

> the concept of 'comity' requires that international tribunals should accord respect to official certificates [of nationality] by treating them as 'prima facie evidence'. Accordingly, these certificates should not be totally discarded, and be replaced . . . by the Tribunal's findings.[111]

Adjudicators may exhibit restraint by requiring, before engaging in a review of nationality, 'strong reasons to doubt the accuracy of the official documents'.[112] They might otherwise delineate bounds within which a State's discretionary decisions on nationality will prevail. They might, for example, accept State decisions on nationality unless it is proved that an individual obtained nationality 'by fraud or material error, in other words in a manner inconsistent with international law'.[113] As the *Micula* ICSID tribunal opined:

> it might be that the Tribunal would not necessarily defer to the views of national authorities at least if there has been fraud or an error . . . This said, it is also clear that the State conferring nationality must be given a 'margin of

[108] Ibid, para. 137.

[109] *Tokios Tokelės, Award, 26-Jul-2007 (ICSID)*, para. 124. Cf. also, cases in which adjudicators heighten the State's argumentative burden: *Chapman (Dissent/SO-Pastor Ridruejo, Bonello, Tulkens, Strážnická, Lorenzen, Fischbach and Casadevall), 18-Jan-2001 (ECtHR-GC)*, para. 3 (requiring 'compelling reasons' to justify measures impacting minorities); *Kulkov, Judgment, 8-Jan-2009 (ECtHR)*, paras 24–33 ('substantial and compelling' reasons required to justify measures departing from the principle of legal certainty).

[110] *Soufraki, Annulment Decision, 5-Jun-2007 (ICSID)*, paras 28, 55. See, similarly, *Micula, Decision on Jurisdiction, 24-Sept-2008 (ICSID)*, para. 87.

[111] *Soufraki (Dissent/SO-Nabulsi), 27-Mar-2007 (ICSID)*, para. 84.

[112] *Soufraki, Annulment Decision, 5-Jun-2007 (ICSID)*, para. 28.

[113] *Micula, Decision on Jurisdiction, 24-Sept-2008 (ICSID)*, para. 91. See, similarly, *Waguih Siag, Award, 1-Jun-2009 (ICSID)*, para. 356; *Nottebohm (Dissent/SO-Guggenheim), 6-Apr-1955 (ICJ)*, paras 1, 4 ('the Court is entitled to ascertain, at least up to a certain point, whether the facts relied upon correspond to the real and effective situation').

> appreciation' in deciding upon the factors that it considers necessary for the granting of nationality ... the question is: under which conditions is it appropriate for the Tribunal to overcome the sovereign decision taken by Sweden? ... [T]he Tribunal would only be inclined to disregard the decision of the Swedish authorities if there was convincing and decisive evidence that Viorel Micula's acquisition of Swedish nationality was fraudulent or at least resulted from a material error.[114]

Such restrained review of grants of nationality contrasts with the approach to review adopted in an abstention mode. As Arbitrator Nabulsi noted in *Soufraki*, a restraint mode recognises that although issues of nationality: '[R]emain within the reserved domain of every state, this principle coexists with the principle that international tribunals are empowered to make their own determinations as to whether a claimant has the nationality of a state.'[115] Instead of declining to review such matters as in an abstention mode, the adjudicator asserts its right to review domestic decisions – albeit on limited grounds.

7.1.6 *Ad Hoc Approaches to Restraint*

Adjudicators may also adopt ad hoc approaches to restraint. One ICSID tribunal, for example, indicated that 'judicial prudence and deference to State functions' informed its decision to record a finding of liability under one obligation instead of another.[116] Adjudicators may also exercise restraint by restricting their review of measures to what was known by States at the time of their adoption, rather than assessing measures with the benefit of hindsight. The *Gemplus/Talsud* ICSID tribunal, for example, held that it would accord the respondent 'deference' by assessing the respondent's conduct with 'a generous measure of appreciation, applied without the benefit of hindsight'.[117] The *Continental* ICSID tribunal similarly held that any assessment of whether a State acted out of necessity 'must contain a significant margin of appreciation for the State applying the particular measure: a time of

114 *Micula, Decision on Jurisdiction, 24-Sept-2008 (ICSID)*, paras 94–5.

115 *Soufraki (Dissent/SO-Nabulsi), 27-Mar-2007 (ICSID)*, para. 17. See, similarly, *Arif, Award, 8-Apr-2013 (ICSID)*, para. 357.

116 *Sempra, Award, 28-Sept-2007 (ICSID)*, para. 301. See, similarly, *SD Myers (Dissent/SO-Schwartz), 12-Nov-2000 (UNCITRAL)*, para. 222 (the tribunal should avoid a finding of expropriation where it would not provide additional relief, because it 'might contribute to public misunderstanding and anxiety about both this decision and the wider implications of the investment chapter of NAFTA').

117 *Gemplus/Talsud, Award, 16-Jun-2010 (ICSID-AF)*, para. 6.26.

grave crisis is not the time for nice judgments, particularly when examined by others with the disadvantage of hindsight'.[118]

7.2 DEFERENCE AS REFERENCE

Another mode of deference indicating a concurrent view of authority is that of 'reference'. Deference as reference comprises a range of techniques by which international adjudicators 'take into account' or give 'respectful consideration' to domestic decisions.[119]

In the mode of deference as reference, domestic decisions act as 'content-laden reference points … that redistribute argumentative burdens'.[120] Their precise role depends on their 'persuasive authority'.[121] They are treated as persuasive not due to their content (first-order reasons), but instead because of content-independent (second-order) reasons.[122] In a reference mode, the adjudicator cites domestic decisions as particularly persuasive sources of information due, for example, to their origin in a domestic system.[123] The *Emmis* ICSID tribunal, for example, noted that in applying domestic law an international adjudicator should 'seek to determine … the manner in which the law would be understood and applied by the municipal courts'.[124] It clarified that:

> This is not to say that decisions of municipal courts arising directly out of the same set of facts will be necessarily dispositive of the question before an international tribunal. The tribunal retains its independent power to judge the probative value of evidence placed before it, including evidence of municipal law. But nevertheless, as Claimants accepted, determinations of municipal courts as to the content of the municipal laws that they are mandated to apply are likely to be of great help to an international tribunal.[125]

118 *Continental, Award, 5-Sept-2008 (ICSID)*, para. 181.

119 Shany (2009b), p. 31; Krisch (2010), pp. 286–7; d'Aspremont and Mbengue (2014), p. 267. Merely *referring* to domestic decisions, without more, does not indicate that a court or tribunal is operating in this mode. So, too, references to domestic decisions to establish customary international law or general principles of law, or as impugned conduct, do not necessarily indicate attribution of authoritative weight (deference).

120 Venzke (2013a), p. 383.

121 See, generally, Flanders (2009); Glenn (1987).

122 Flanders (2009), p. 58; Schauer (2008).

123 See, similarly, Flanders (2009), pp. 56–7; Ramsey (1997), p. 902; Venzke (2013a), p. 398; Schauer (2008).

124 *Emmis, Award, 16-Apr-2014 (ICSID)*, para. 175. See, similarly, *Soufraki, Annulment Decision, 5-Jun-2007 (ICSID)*, paras 96–7, 102; *Brazilian Loans, Judgment, 12-Jul-1929 (PCIJ-A21)*, pp. 122–4.

125 *Emmis, Award, 16-Apr-2014 (ICSID)*, para. 176.

The mode of reference differs from modes of deference indicating a conclusive or suspensive view of authority. An international adjudicator adopting a reference mode exercises greater discretion in defining the impact of a domestic decision-making on its own analysis.[126] In a mode of reference, the relationship between first- and second-order reasons is more flexible to that in conclusive and suspensive approaches to authority. As Perry explains:

> I might take the judgment of the authority into account only to the extent of introducing an element of systematic bias into my practical reasoning; I would treat the case for the conclusion which is favored by the authority as being stronger to some specified degree than it actually appears to me to be. I would thus be deferring to the judgment of the authority only partially, in the sense that I would never permit my own judgment to be preempted completely by that of the authority.[127]

The mode of reference offers international adjudicators a means of signalling openness to domestic decisions without treating such decisions as controlling. Such reasoning exhibits a more flexible understanding of authority. Adopting a reference mode, international adjudicators borrow from, and collaborate with, domestic decision-makers to bolster the legitimacy or correctness of their own decisions.[128]

The mode of deference as reference also differs to the mode of restraint. In a reference mode, the adjudicator does not limit its own authority to support its collaboration with domestic decision-makers. Instead, the adjudicator claims – and exercises – the full extent of its authority. It does so, however, by reference to how domestic decision-makers have (or might have) determined the issues before it had they been left to their own devices. By referring to domestic decisions, the adjudicator 'pays attention to, and gives appropriate weight to, the opinion of the [State]'.[129] As Young notes: 'Such interactions may allow the courts to generate better interpretations of [international] rights, as well as providing additional legitimacy to the conclusions reached by any particular court.'[130]

Deference in the mode of reference may give domestic decisions varying impacts. The international adjudicator could, for example, refer to a domestic

126 See, similarly, Schauer (2008).

127 Perry (1989), p. 932.

128 See, further, on 'cooperative' authority Allison (1994), pp. 380–1; Glenn (1987), p. 264. See, also, *GAMI, Final Award, 15-Nov-2004 (UNCITRAL)*, paras 116–19 ('One might imagine a perfect world in which a national court of last recourse sits down with a NAFTA tribunal incapable of reviewable error to discharge their respective responsibilities').

129 Young (2009), p. 562.

130 Young (2017), p. 264.

decision as a source of useful empirical information;[131] to confirm or support its decision;[132] or as a source of guidance.[133] Domestic decisions may also be used to establish the factual context relevant to the international claim.[134] The *Eureko* UNCITRAL tribunal, for example, observed that 'the events of [a factually relevant] period are thoroughly and accurately traversed by Poland's Supreme Audit Chamber in its Report', from which it then quoted 'without any reservation'.[135] International adjudicators may also refer to domestic decisions establishing certain legal facts, including to determine whether an individual has a possession under domestic law[136] or to interpret a contract.[137] The ECtHR in *Hutten-Czapska*, for example, in holding that domestic measures 'impaired the very essence of the applicant's right':

> point[ed] out that the Constitutional Court, in its judgment of 12 January 2000, came to the same conclusion ... basing its findings on comprehensive

[131] Domestic decisions may, for example, be used to confirm or 'evidence' the State's legislative objectives: *Broniowski, Judgment, 22-Jun-2004 (ECtHR-GC)*, para. 158; *Hutten-Czapska, Judgment, 19-Jun-2006 (ECtHR-GC)*, para. 178.

[132] *Brazilian Loans (Dissent/SO-Pessoa), 12-Jul-1929 (PCIJ-A21)*, p. 147 (interpretation of a contractual clause); *Sporrong, Judgment, 23-Sept-1982 (ECtHR)*, para. 72 (prejudicial effect of a law); *AIG, Award, 7-Oct-2003 (ICSID)*, para. 10.5.2 (whether a taking was 'arbitrary').

[133] *SD Myers, Partial Award, 13-Nov-2000 (UNCITRAL)*, para. 249 (citing domestic judicial decisions that had 'explored the complexity' of making comparisons between individuals in analysis of discrimination); *Feldman, Award, 16-Dec-2002 (ICSID-AF)*, para. 133 (a domestic judicial decision holding that a lack of transparency violates NAFTA while not binding was 'instructive').

[134] *Akdivar, Judgment, 16-Sept-1996 (ECtHR-GC)*, paras 24–5, 78 (noting an absence of 'relevant investigations at the domestic level which could be of assistance in elucidating the events'); *Protsch, Judgment, 15-Nov-1996 (ECtHR)*, paras 45–8 (domestic decisions finding that the applicant did not suffer damage from the measure); *Archer Daniels, Award, 21-Nov-2007 (ICSID-AF)*, paras 146–50 (domestic decisions finding a protectionist intent behind the measure); *ELSI (Dissent/SO-Schwebel), 20-Jul-1989 (ICJ)*, p. 103 (criticising the majority's decision as in 'conflict with the construction of Italian law by Italy's most senior officials' and judicial authorities); *Kotov, Judgment, 3-Apr-2012 (ECtHR-GC)*, para. 116 (finding loss as a result of the measures as 'confirmed by the Russian courts'); *Minnotte, Award, 16-May-2014 (ICSID-AF)*, para. 171 (relying on 'the account ... given in 2002 by the Minister of Health to the Secretary of the Committee of the Council of Ministers').

[135] *Eureko, Partial Award, 19-Aug-2005 (UNCITRAL)*, paras 48, 199.

[136] *Timishev, Judgment, 14-Jun-2007 (ECtHR)*, para. 24 (rejecting the State's submission that the applicant had no entitlement to benefits because 'the domestic courts examined that argument, [and] found that it had no basis in the domestic law'). See, similarly, *Katoulis, Judgment, 8-Jul-2004 (ECtHR)*, paras 31–2; *Invesmart, Award, 26-Jun-2009 (UNCITRAL)*, para. 182.

[137] See, for example, *Nykomb, Award, 16-Dec-2003 (SCC)*, pp. 26–7 (taking 'into regard' that the contractual clauses at issue had been 'deemed by the highest legal authority, the Latvian Supreme Court, to be legally binding contractual obligations under Latvian law'). See, also, *Broniowski, Judgment, 22-Jun-2004 (ECtHR-GC)*, paras 173–5, 184–9.

documentary evidence and an assessment of the general situation throughout Poland.[138]

Adjudicators may also seek guidance from domestic decisions to interpret domestic[139] or even international[140] law. As the PCIJ in *Serbian Loans* observed:

> For the Court itself to undertake its own construction of municipal law, leaving on one side existing judicial decisions . . . would not be in conformity with the task for which the Court has been established and would not be compatible with the principles governing the selection of its members.[141]

The *Occidental* ICSID tribunal similarly noted that: '[T]he decisions adopted thus far by Ecuadorian courts on matters of interpretation of the Ecuadorian Tax Law have been of great help to this Tribunal in its own interpretation of both the Treaty and the relevant provisions of Ecuadorian law.'[142] While it held that such decisions had no 'binding or mandatory force', the tribunal emphasised that they nonetheless 'give useful guidance in understanding Ecuadorian legislation and important related concepts'.[143]

Within the mode of deference as reference there is a 'hierarchy of persuasive authority'.[144] International adjudicators might give differing weight to different types of domestic decision. They might also consider those decisions to have greater, less or equal authority to other sources. The *Plama* ICSID tribunal, for example, referred to expert evidence, academic commentary, the 'experience of the members of the Tribunal in other civil law countries', and domestic judicial decisions as authoritative sources of information about the legality of an investment and the attributability of conduct to the State.[145] Second-order reasons will impact such hierarchies.[146] Domestic

138 *Hutten-Czapska, Judgment, 19-Jun-2006 (ECtHR-GC)*, paras 202–7.

139 *Kotov, Judgment, 3-Apr-2012 (ECtHR-GC)*, paras 122–33; *F-W Oil, Award, 5-Mar-2006 (ICSID)*, paras 152–4, 166–74; *Enron, Award, 22-May-2007 (ICSID)*, paras 218–20, 293; *Gold Reserve, Award, 22-Sept-2014 (ICSID-AF)*, para. 365.

140 *Renta4, Award on Preliminary Objections, 20-Mar-2009 (SCC)*, paras 34–5; *Glamis, Award, 8-Jun-2009 (UNCITRAL)*, paras 332–4.

141 *Serbian Loans, Judgment, 12-Jul-1929 (PCIJ-A20)*, pp. 46–7.

142 *Occidental, Final Award, 1-Jul-2004 (LCIA)*, para. 58.

143 Ibid, para. 137.

144 Flanders (2009), p. 58. See, similarly, Schauer (2008).

145 *Plama, Award, 27-Aug-2008 (ICSID)*, paras 131–6, 253. International adjudicators could otherwise weight such sources equally or more highly than domestic judicial decisions. See, for example, *Metal-Tech, Award, 4-Oct-2013 (ICSID)*, para. 287 (seeking 'guidance from academic writings' to interpret domestic law); *Eureko, Partial Award, 19-Aug-2005 (UNCITRAL)*, para. 121 (examining domestic law 'with the benefit of the exceptional knowledge and insight of its distinguished member who is steeped in Polish law').

146 Flanders (2009), p. 58.

decisions might, for example, be accorded greater authority in adjudicative reasoning than social media posts.[147] This comes down to an analysis of the relative authority of these sources of information. Domestic judicial decisions might, for example, be treated as more authoritative than other types of domestic decision. This is because the 'structural features of court systems . . . make their decisions possibly more compelling, simply as a matter of presentation and argument, to other courts'.[148] Adjudicators may thus treat domestic judicial decisions differently to, for example, domestic political decisions.[149] The *National Grid* UNCITRAL tribunal declined to this effect to refer to the findings of the Overseas Private Investment Corporation because it was 'a decision of an organ of a government, not one arrived at by an independent tribunal after hearing the parties'.[150] These analyses share in common a more flexible approach to authority, according to which the recognition of a domestic actor's decision-making authority influences – but does not displace – the adjudicator's own analysis of the available first-order reasons for decision.

7.3 DEFERENCE AS RESPECT

A final set of approaches indicating a concurrent view of authority can be grouped under the label of 'deference as respect'.[151] This mode is the least deferential to domestic decision-making authority of the three modes of deference reflecting a concurrent view of authority. This is because it operates conditionally. In this mode, deference must be *earned* for each particular decision.[152] Decisions are 'respected' if the international adjudicator feels justified in placing confidence in them, even if the international adjudicator disagrees with them.[153] If the decision is deemed unworthy of respect, the adjudicator will ignore it and reach its own decision by reference to the applicable first-order reasons for decision.[154] The mode of deference as respect is nonetheless more deferential than the mode of control/dismissal considered in Chapter 5. Adjudicators applying the mode of respect focus not on whether a decision is *justified* but instead on whether it is *justifiable*.[155] They

147 Schauer (2008).

148 Flanders (2009), p. 72.

149 Ibid, p. 58.

150 *National Grid, Award, 3-Nov-2008 (UNCITRAL)*, para. 144.

151 This label is borrowed from Dyzenhaus (1997), p. 131, albeit that the elaboration of what it signifies differs somewhat from Dyzenhaus' analysis. See, further, Chapter 4.

152 See, on this approach to deference, Young (2009), pp. 566–70; Nollkaemper (2011), p. 256; D'Alterio (2011), p. 402; Lazarus and Simonsen (2015), p. 5; Cunliffe and Reeve (1999), p. 462.

153 Rivers (2006), pp. 191, 203; Dye (2013), p. 25; Young (2005), p. 116; Raine (2013), p. 85.

154 Young (2009), p. 556.

155 Dyzenhaus (1998), p. 32.

consider 'whether the decision maker has shown it to be defensible'.[156] The adjudicator limits itself to assessing the reasons offered, or which could be offered, in support of the decision, rather than evaluating the merits or correctness of the decision itself.

Adjudicators may select different criteria to identify decisions warranting respect. A decision may be deemed justifiable by reference to the reasoning offered to support it, or the process used to reach it. As examined in the following subsections, adjudicators might, for example, only 'respect' domestic decisions if they were made in *good faith*, through particular *procedures*, or on the basis of *rational* or *reasonable* reasons. The criteria selected to identify decisions worthy of respect disclose the international adjudicator's views on how States should exercise their decision-making authority. An adjudicator influenced by second-order reasons of empirical epistemic authority (expertise/competence) might, for example, value decisions deriving from evidence-based or expert-led decision-making processes. State consensus may also inform whether a decision warrants deference as respect. That States have made similar decisions to the decision in contention may confirm, for example, that it was made in good faith, is reasonable, or is otherwise justifiable.

The grounds for respect may be closely associated with, and influenced by, the content of the law applied by an adjudicator (i.e. the applicable first-order reasons for decision). The applicable law must not, however, be conflated with deference in the mode of respect. 'Reasonableness' and 'rationality', like 'good faith' or 'due process', may themselves form a standalone obligation binding on the State. A treaty may, for example, require that the State not impose 'unreasonable' measures on property owners. Such an obligation may require assessment of the reasonableness of the State's measure.[157] This does not entail, however, that such an obligation will be assessed on a *reasonableness* standard, or that the standard of review of reasonableness is restricted only to this obligation. Instead, an adjudicator might operate in a 'deference as control' mode to analyse the reasonableness of the measure on the basis of a standard of *correctness* or by reference to what the adjudicator itself views to be reasonable. Alternatively, the adjudicator could examine not the substantive reasonableness of the decision but rather the decision-maker's *procedural* reasonableness. Similarly, in applying an obligation of non-arbitrariness, an adjudicator could variously require proof that the State acted in good faith, provided reasons for its decision, used a particular decision-making procedure, or can demonstrate a logical connection between the measure and the aim. Such analyses will reflect

156 Ibid, p. 28.
157 See, for example, Ortino (2017), p. 17; Elliott (2015b), p. 75; Vadi (2018), p. 130.

deference when the grounds for review are influenced by the adjudicator's analysis of second-order reasons for deference. The indicia identified to warrant such deference as respect will likely link closely to the first-order reasons for decision. The indicia used by adjudicators may nevertheless differ '[a]ccording to changes in judicial and social attitudes' as to what the obligation requires and the role accorded to second-order reasons in its interpretation and application.[158]

This approach to deference differs from earlier modes in which second-order reasons are treated as exclusionary (giving rise to a view of authority as conclusive or suspensive). As noted in Chapters 5 and 6, conclusive and suspensive approaches to authority reject any assessment of the merits of a domestic decision, including for whether it is 'reasonable'. This is because, as Grant explains, conclusive and suspensive approaches to authority adopt the view that: '[I]f a legitimate authority's subjects challenged its decisions every time it deviates too much from what is reasonable, the value of legitimate authority would be lost – its decisions would not have pre-emptive force.'[159] The *qualitative* criteria adopted in a mode of respect also differ from the quantitative measures used in a restraint mode. Nevertheless, in both modes, the adjudicator signifies that it will not intervene to second-guess State decision-making *except* in certain circumstances. Those circumstances are sufficient to *defeat* the second-order reasons that would otherwise justify deferring to the domestic decision-maker. The adjudicator only intervenes when the domestic decision-maker:

> acts for a defeated reason, which takes its decision outside the range of reasonable decisions. ... That is, there must be some reason that defeats the legitimacy of the authority, and hence defeats the pre-emptive reason that the court had to refrain from acting on its own judgment of the merits.[160]

In a restraint mode, the adjudicator limits the circumstances in which it will intervene by imposing high thresholds to conclude that an adjudicator has acted for a 'defeated' reason. In a respect mode, the adjudicator only defers to decisions manifesting particular qualities. In the mode of respect, domestic decision-makers earn deference by 'showing their loyalty' to particular standards of decision-making.[161] Such criteria specify the point at which confidence in the decision dissipates, leaving the international adjudicator free to disregard the decision or remake it.[162] Deference as respect is therefore in some ways a more proactive approach to deference than deference as restraint. In

158 Daly (2012), p. 292.
159 Grant (2017), p. 520.
160 Ibid, p. 532–3.
161 Çali (2016), p. 145.
162 Griffey (2011), p. 304.

this mode, authority is derived from indicia of 'good' decision-making and, where such indicia are present, provides reasons for decision that affect the analysis of the first-order reasons for decision.

Criteria for respect may impose differing burdens on decision-making. The role of second-order reasons in a deference as respect mode means that the distinction between first- and second-order reasons will often blur in this mode of reasoning.[163] Particularly at the 'equivalence' end of the deference as respect spectrum (introduced below), the number of defeating reasons to which an adjudicator might have reference may mean that the State is no better off overall than it would have been had the court or tribunal made a decision on the basis of analysing the first-order reasons. The following subsections explore such modes of reasoning, arrayed from most to least deferential.

7.3.1 *Good Faith Review*

An adjudicator may exhibit deference as respect by deferring to domestic decisions reached in good faith. A good faith standard seeks only to identify a minimal justification for the State's decisions and/or to ensure that decisions are not informed by opportunistic or bad faith motives.[164] This is an 'extremely lenient'[165] standard, prompting international adjudicators to defer to State decisions 'except in the most evident cases of abuse'.[166] Adjudicators may use different tests to determine whether a decision has been adopted by a State in 'good faith'. An adjudicator could, for example, defer to State decisions with a 'tenable' basis, or limit itself to assessing whether claimed public purposes have a 'plausible' connection to the measure.[167] The *Frontier Petroleum* UNCITRAL tribunal, for example, indicated that:

> States enjoy a certain margin of appreciation in determining what their own conception of international public policy is. This Tribunal determines that it is sufficient to examine whether the conclusion reached by the Czech courts applied a plausible interpretation ... Put another way, was the decision by the Czech courts reasonably tenable and made in good faith?'[168]

[163] Grant (2017), p. 535.

[164] See, generally, Mamolea (2014), pp. 74, 84; Burke-White and von Staden (2010), p. 313; Schill and Briese (2009), p. 136.

[165] Burke-White and von Staden (2010), p. 312.

[166] López Escarcena (2014), p. 196.

[167] See, to this effect, Martinez-Fraga and Reetz (2015), p. 352; Weiner (2003), pp. 166–7; Higgins (1982), p. 291; Christie (1962), p. 332.

[168] *Frontier Petroleum, Final Award, 12-Nov-2010 (UNCITRAL)*, para. 527.

Testing for plausibility allows the adjudicator to ascertain whether a State's claimed public purpose is 'genuine and not fictitious or imagined'.[169] The threshold of plausibility required of a measure may increase depending on the context, including if a measure has a severe impact on private property.[170] An adjudicator could alternatively operationalise good faith as rationality or non-arbitrariness, deferring only to State decisions shown to have a 'rational basis'.[171] The *Enron* ICSID tribunal, for example, observed that:

> The measures adopted might have been good or bad, a matter which is not for the Tribunal to judge ... but they were not arbitrary in that they were what the Government believed and understood was the best response to the unfolding crisis.[172]

Adjudicators could otherwise require proof that the decision was not informed by 'discriminatory, protectionist or otherwise impermissible objective[s]'.[173] Adjudicators might test good faith, for example, by declining to defer to 'abusive' domestic decisions, including those that target individuals in bad faith, or those made through a misuse of domestic powers.[174]

Many commentators position good faith as the minimum permissible level of scrutiny in international adjudication.[175] Such a view precludes the possibility that an adjudicator would operate in a submission mode even in respect of a self-judging clause.[176] Judge Read in *Certain Norwegian Loans*, for example, considered that a self-judging 'domestic jurisdiction' clause:

> properly construed means that the respondent State, in invoking the reservation, must establish that there is a genuine understanding, i.e. that the circumstances are such that it would be reasonably possible to reach the

169 Cheng (2006), p. 39. See, for examples of adjudicators finding claimed purposes to be 'artificial' and non-genuine, *Jahn (Dissent/SO-Pavlovschi), 30-Jun-2005 (ECtHR-GC)*; *Bernhard von Pezold, Award, 28-Jul-2015 (ICSID)*, paras 498–9, 502.

170 Newcombe (2005), p. 30; Crawford and Brownlie (2012), p. 670.

171 von Staden (2012), p. 1038. Rationality in this context is used as indicia of the State's good faith, so differs from review for rationality in substantive review (see subsection 7.3.3).

172 *Enron, Award, 22-May-2007 (ICSID)*, para. 281. See, similarly, *Sempra, Award, 28-Sept-2007 (ICSID)*, para. 318.

173 Henckels (2014), p. 125. See, for example, *Suez-Interagua, Decision on Liability, 30-Jul-2010 (ICSID)*, para. 217 ('Such actions ... were outside the scope of Santa Fe's legitimate right to regulate and in effect constituted an abuse of regulatory discretion').

174 See, for example, *Link-Trading, Final Award, 18-Apr-2002 (UNCITRAL)*, paras 63–4, 68–71; *CME, Partial Award, 13-Sept-2001 (UNCITRAL)*, para. 603.

175 See, for example, Burke-White and von Staden (2010), p. 311; Titi (2014), p. 201; Schill (2012), p. 595.

176 Leonhardsen (2013), p. 2; Brownlie (1963), p. 293; Sauvant et al. (2016), p. 2; Burke-White and von Staden (2008), p. 377. See, also, *Norwegian Loans (Dissent/SO-Basdevant), 6-Jul-1957 (ICJ)*, p. 73; *Continental, Award, 5-Sept-2008 (ICSID)*, paras 183, 189.

> understanding that the dispute was essentially national ... assuming that such circumstances existed, the conclusion reached by a respondent Government could not be reviewed by the Court.[177]

This position is frequently supported by an argument that all States must perform their international obligations in good faith, such that international adjudicators will always be required to ensure that decisions have been reached in good faith.[178] Such a conclusion, however, rests on an assumption that it is for international adjudicators, rather than for other actors, to assess whether a State has complied with these obligations of good faith. It also risks conflating a State's *obligations* with individual State *decisions*.[179] It may be that a State does not comply with its obligation to act in good faith if its conduct is informed by a set of decisions made in bad faith.[180] However, establishing whether a State has acted in good faith does not necessarily require that the State's decisions be assessed on the basis of a good faith standard of review. They could instead be reviewed *de novo* or, alternatively, entirely in deference to the State's characterisation of its own intent or motives.

7.3.2 *Procedural Review*

An adjudicator might otherwise defer to decisions reached through particular procedures. An adjudicator adopting a procedural mode of review would consider only whether a *proper procedure* was followed in making a decision, to assess whether it is sufficiently justifiable to warrant deference.[181] International adjudicators signal procedural review by deferring to domestic decisions that result from a 'considered' or 'conscious' decision-making process, or that have been formed based on a 'careful evaluation' of relevant materials.[182] This approach to deference reflects a view that the way in which a decision has been reached matters more than the content of the decision itself.[183] Adjudicators may give different weight to the relevance of procedure. The adjudicator might, for example, reject the possibility of affording *any* deference

177 *Norwegian Loans (Dissent/SO-Read), 6-Jul-1957 (ICJ)*, pp. 94–5.

178 Vienna Convention on the Law of Treaties (1969/1980) 1155 UNTS 331, art 26. See, further, Zeitler (2005), p. 722; Franck (1998), p. 32; Shany (2005), p. 910.

179 Mamolea (2014), p. 75 (discussing good faith as an element of lawfulness/ground of review, not as a standard of review).

180 On the obligation of good faith see, especially, Bonnitcha (2014), p. 160.

181 See, generally, Alter (2008b), p. 47; Arnardóttir (2015), p. 5; Henckels (2015), p. 149; Schill and Briese (2009), p. 66; Harbo (2017), p. 32.

182 Kavanagh (2014), p. 444–5; Gerards (2017), p. 128.

183 Grant (2017), p. 516.

to decisions not reached through the identified procedure.[184] Alternatively, procedural shortcomings could prompt more intrusive review, such as a second stage of substantive reasonableness review.[185] Adjudicators might also emphasise *different types* of procedure in their decisions about deference.[186]

Procedural review may indicate that an adjudicator values the normative and/or empirical epistemic authority of certain decision-making structures, or certain non-instrumental values. Deference to decisions reached through a democratic procedure, for example, may indicate that the adjudicator values the fairness of those processes.[187] Alternatively, it may manifest a view that certain procedures will lead to more legitimate decisions than would be reached through an international adjudicative procedure.[188] While an adjudicator might, for instance, decline to review the merits of a decision requiring moral judgment, it may be comparably more comfortable in reviewing the procedure through which that decision was reached.[189] Deference to decisions reached through particular procedures might otherwise indicate a view that some processes are more likely to produce empirically correct outcomes than others.[190] Procedural review allows the adjudicator to check that a decision has been made through an exercise of empirical epistemic authority. As Parker notes:

> If judicial deference to legislative fact-finding is based on competency ... such deference no longer makes sense when the legislature fails to exercise this competency. ... By evaluating the procedures [the legislature] uses to find facts, courts can determine whether [the legislature] has really earned competency-based deference.[191]

Procedural review is less intrusive than substantive review. It allows the adjudicator to review the process by which decisions are made, 'while leaving the content of the decisions entirely to the discretion of the official who has authority'.[192] Procedural review thus reflects institutional separations of power and competence. It allows an adjudicator to respect that other decision-makers may be comparatively better at making decisions of substance, while leveraging the adjudicator's capacity to assess any procedural deficiencies associated with

184 Gerards (2017), p. 145.
185 Brems and Lavrysen (2015), pp. 150–1; Gerards (2017), pp. 144–5; Brems and Gerards (2017), p. 6.
186 Galligan (1986), p. 337.
187 See, further, Pirker (2014), p. 60; Tyler (2006).
188 Saul (2016).
189 Ely (1980), pp. 70–4.
190 Brems (2017), p. 19.
191 Parker (2013), p. 1346.
192 Dyzenhaus (2003), p. 22.

those decisions.[193] Adjudicators may exercise procedural review by adopting a number of focal points. They might focus on the structural qualities or inputs into the decision-making process; the procedural qualities of individual decision-makers; or the procedural qualities of the reasoning process or the way in which a decision is communicated to those it impacts. These are considered in turn.

International adjudicators might recognise the authority of domestic actors by reference to their decision-making procedures. Adjudicators might defer, for instance, to decisions reached through democratic, participatory, or transparent processes, or processes drawing on scientific expertise or evidence.[194] The *Glamis* UNCITRAL tribunal, for instance, emphasised in upholding a State's conduct that the State's decisions had been informed by 'cultural studies and the guidance of professional archaeologists and researchers'.[195] The tribunal opined that, in such circumstances:

> [I]t is not for this Tribunal to assess the veracity of evidentiary support for domestic governmental decisions; the Tribunal may assess only whether there was reasonable evidence, and thus the government's reliance on such was not obviously and actionably misplaced.[196]

To similar effect, Arbitrator Born in *Philip Morris* concluded that a measure had been 'adopted with no meaningful study, discussion, deliberation, or consultation with the industry'.[197] He observed that:

> claims that a governmental action is entitled to deference because of administrative or regulatory expertise are less persuasive where there is no indication that any such expertise was ever relied upon or brought to bear with respect to the challenged measures.[198]

Deferential review may also focus on whether decision-making procedures provide mechanisms for review or other safeguards for individual rights;[199]

193 Brems and Gerards (2017), p. 7; Fredman (2006), p. 62; Daly (2012), p. 3.

194 See, for example, *Lee, Judgment, 18-Jan-2001 (ECtHR-GC)*, paras 94, 121 ('the procedural safeguards available to the individual applicant will be especially material in determining whether the respondent State has, when fixing the regulatory framework, remained within its margin of appreciation'); *Methanex, Final Award, 3-Aug-2005 (UNCITRAL)*, paras 11–12, 54 of Part II, Chapter B (the measure was 'contingent' on a 'scientific study . . . to be followed by public hearings, public testimony and peer review').

195 *Glamis, Award, 8-Jun-2009 (UNCITRAL)*, para. 781.

196 Ibid, para. 786.

197 *Philip Morris (Uruguay) (Dissent/SO-Born), 8-Jul-2016 (ICSID)*, para. 124.

198 Ibid, para. 126.

199 See, for example, *EnCana, Award, 3-Feb-2006 (UNCITRAL)*, para. 194, footnote 138; *Phocas, Judgment, 26-Mar-1996 (ECtHR)*, para. 60; *Pchelintseva, Judgment, 17-Nov-2016 (ECtHR)*, para. 100; *Papachelas, Judgment, 25-Mar-1999 (ECtHR-GC)*, para. 54.

'flexible' procedures to allow reassessment of a decision as circumstances change;[200] and procedures that permit decision-makers 'to take into account the particular circumstances of each case'.[201] The *TECO* ICSID tribunal, for example, being 'mindful of the deference that international tribunals should pay to a sovereign State's regulatory powers',[202] held:

> As a consequence, although the role of an international tribunal is not to second-guess or to review decisions that have been made genuinely and in good faith by a sovereign in the normal exercise of its powers, it is up to an international arbitral tribunal to sanction decisions that amount to an abuse of power, are arbitrary, or are taken in manifest disregard of the applicable legal rules and in breach of due process in regulatory matters.[203]

All of these features of domestic decision-making processes link back to the bases for recognising authority canvassed in Chapter 1. As was noted in that chapter, such procedures may be valued because they lead to empirically better, or more legitimate, decisions. The ECtHR has rejected deference, for example, to domestic decisions reached through procedures inconsistent with the principle of 'good governance'. The Court has stated to this effect that:

> While they have a wide margin of appreciation in assessing the existence of a problem of public concern warranting specific measures and in implementing social and economic policies ... where an issue in the general interest is at stake it is incumbent on the public authorities to act in good time, in an appropriate manner and with utmost consistency.[204]

200 See, for example, *Sporrong, Judgment, 23-Sept-1982 (ECtHR)*, paras 69–72; *Erkner, Judgment, 24-Mar-1987 (ECtHR)*, paras 76–9; *Stummer (Dissent/SO-Tulkens, Kovler, Gyulumyan, Spielmann, Popović, Malinverni and Pardalos), 7-Jul-2011 (ECtHR-GC)*, paras 3, 9–12.

201 *Grigaliuniene, Judgment, 23-Feb-2016 (ECtHR)*, paras 32–6. See, similarly, *Tunaitis, Judgment, 24-Nov-2015 (ECtHR)*, paras 32–43; *Guberina, Judgment, 22-Mar-2016 (ECtHR)*, para. 93. See, also, *Kopecky (Dissent/SO-Strážnická), 28-Sept-2004 (ECtHR-GC)*, para. 7 (rejecting deference to 'a particularly formalistic and strict interpretation' of domestic law).

202 *TECO, Award, 19-Dec-2013 (ICSID)*, para. 490.

203 Ibid, para. 493.

204 *Sierpinski, Judgment, 3-Nov-2009 (ECtHR)*, para. 71. The Court has also emphasised that the principle may protect individuals from arbitrary or unforeseeable decisions: *Immobiliare, Judgment, 28-Jul-1999 (ECtHR-GC)*, para. 52; *Luciano Rossi, Judgment, 15-Nov-2002 (ECtHR)*, para. 25; *Tona, Judgment, 15-Nov-2002 (ECtHR)*, para. 30. The Court has further noted that such analysis may entail ascertaining that the State has in place 'internal procedures which enhance the transparency and clarity of their operations, minimise the risk of mistakes ... and foster legal certainty': *Digryte Klibaviciene, Judgment, 21-Oct-2014 (ECtHR)*, para. 33.

The *Crystallex* ICSID Additional Facility tribunal similarly held that 'deference to the primary decision-makers cannot be unlimited', and is unjustified where a decision-making process suffers from 'serious procedural flaws' raising a risk of resultant 'arbitrary', 'non-transparent', or 'inconsistent' decisions.[205] As the tribunal explained:

> Differently put, while the Tribunal will refrain from making findings as to whether or not the concerns expressed by the Ministry were 'adequately' addressed by the Claimant, or whether the reasons put forward by the Respondent in denying the Permit were substantively valid, the Tribunal will, in its review of the government conduct, assess whether there have been serious procedural flaws which have resulted in the Permit being arbitrarily denied, or in the investor being treated non-transparently or inconsistently throughout the process and thereafter.[206]

International adjudicators might alternatively focus on the qualities of individual decision-makers to analyse whether deference is due to their decisions. They might defer, for instance, to decisions of 'independent' or 'impartial' decision-makers.[207] The *Fraport* Annulment Committee, for example, emphasised the importance of deference to domestic interpretations of municipal law, given that 'the Tribunal had not been chosen for its knowledge of Philippine law'.[208] The Annulment Committee emphasised that such deference did not mean, however, that domestic interpretations would be 'necessarily dispositive'.[209] Instead, it accepted that they 'may need to be scrutinised very carefully by an international tribunal', which 'would need to satisfy itself, *inter alia*, as to the impartiality of the relevant decision-maker'.[210] The *Tatneft* UNCITRAL tribunal similarly adopted the view that 'deference on the part of international tribunals requires the clear perception that domestic courts are independent, competent and above all clear of suspicion of corruption'.[211]

Procedural review could also focus on how a decision was reached and/or communicated. Adjudicators might, for example, defer to decisions for which domestic decision-makers offer reasons (regardless of what those

[205] *Crystallex, Award, 4-Apr-2016 (ICSID-AF)*, paras 583–5.
[206] Ibid, para. 585.
[207] See, further, Nollkaemper (2011), p. 257; Hepburn (2017), p. 128. On the link between independence and legitimacy see, further, Caron (1993), p. 561.
[208] *Fraport, Annulment Decision, 23-Dec-2010 (ICSID)*, paras 117, 236.
[209] Ibid, para. 242.
[210] Ibid, para. 242.
[211] *Tatneft, Merits Award, 29-Jul-2014 (UNCITRAL)*, para. 476. See, also, para. 350: 'Deferential treatment of the role of courts by international tribunals is necessary, above all when their independence is fully established.'

reasons are).[212] The *British Caribbean Bank* UNCITRAL tribunal held, for example, that, although 'a State is entitled to broad latitude to devise its public policy as it sees fit', the requirement that an expropriation be undertaken for a public purpose:

> requires – at least – that the Respondent set out the public purpose for which the expropriation was undertaken and offer a *prima facie* explanation of how the acquisition of the particular property was reasonably related to the fulfilment of that purpose.[213]

An international adjudicator might alternatively limit itself to assessing whether the domestic decision-maker considered other alternative approaches or competing interests.[214] The *Bernhard von Pezold* ICSID tribunal, for example, rejected that the State's conduct was the 'only way' of responding to a necessity situation, finding that '[t]he Respondent has not demonstrated that it carried out a rigorous process of assessing all possible alternatives'.[215] An adjudicator might thus focus on whether a domestic decision-maker at least *attempted* to make a decision that was balanced or proportionate, well-founded, or consistent with international law. An adjudicator might defer to a decision, for example, if in making the decision the State expressly attempted to balance competing interests, regardless of how it ultimately struck that balance.[216] Adjudicators could otherwise require that domestic decision-makers consider certain factors in making their decision, again without seeking to determine how those factors were analysed.[217] The ECtHR's 'responsible courts doctrine', for

[212] See, for example, *Baroul, Judgment, 16-Jul-2009 (ECtHR)*, paras 48–52 ('the domestic courts did not provide any justification whatsoever for such interference'). See, similarly, *National Grid, Award, 3-Nov-2008 (UNCITRAL)*, para. 198; *Kern, Judgment, 24-Feb-2005 (ECtHR)*, para. 67; *Rafig Aliyev, Judgment, 6-Dec-2011 (ECtHR)*, paras 125–7; *Brumarescu, Judgment, 28-Oct-1999 (ECtHR-GC)*, paras 79–80. See, further, Schill and Briese (2009), p. 134; Fredman (2006), p. 62.

[213] *British Caribbean Bank, Award, 19-Dec-2014 (PCA/UNCITRAL)*, paras 236, 241.

[214] See, for example, *Brosset-Triboulet (Dissent/SO-Bratza, Vajić, Björgvinsson and Kalaydjieva), 29-Mar-2010 (ECtHR-GC)*, para. 10 ('measures less radical than demolition of the house do not appear to have been considered by the authorities').

[215] *Bernhard von Pezold, Award, 28-Jul-2015 (ICSID)*, paras 644–5.

[216] See, for example, *Sia Akka-Laa, Judgment, 12-Jul-2016 (ECtHR)*, para. 70; *Skibinscy, Judgment, 14-Nov-2006 (ECtHR)*, para. 90; *Gold Reserve, Award, 22-Sept-2014 (ICSID-AF)*, para. 595. See, further, Arnardóttir (2015), p. 6; Council of Europe (2018), para. 28(c).

[217] See, for example, *Waldemar Nowakowski, Judgment, 24-Jul-2012 (ECtHR)*, paras 50–8 ('the domestic courts failed to take into account the applicant's personal situation and characteristics'). *Silickiene, Judgment, 10-Apr-2012 (ECtHR)*, paras 66–70 ('It must therefore determine whether the Lithuanian courts had regard to the applicant's degree of fault or care or, at least, the relationship between her conduct and the offences which had been committed'); *Arsovski, Judgment, 15-Jan-2013 (ECtHR)*, paras 58–9.

example, prompts deference to domestic judicial decisions in which domestic judges have sought to apply 'the standards developed by the ECtHR appropriately'.[218] Finally, adjudicators might decline to defer to decisions that operate retrospectively, are tainted by delay, or are made in a system lacking procedures for assessing compensation for interferences with private property rights.[219]

7.3.3 *Substantive Review*

Adjudicators may also exhibit deference as respect by deferring to 'rational', 'reasonable', or 'appropriate' exercises of State decision-making authority.[220] An adjudicator could defer to the State's claim to have acted for a public purpose, for example, if it is satisfied that there were 'at least some rational bases' for the measure.[221] Alternatively, the adjudicator could defer to State measures if they are 'rationally and intrinsically',[222] 'reasonably',[223] 'rationally',[224] plausibly,[225] or 'appropriately'[226] connected to a public purpose. All such approaches share in common a disinclination – for reasons of deference – to assess the 'correctness', merits, or efficacy of State decisions.[227] Instead, the adjudicator uses second-order

218 Çali (2016), p. 143.

219 See, for example, *Pressos, Judgment, 20-Nov-1995 (ECtHR)*, paras 38–44; *Inci, Judgment, 14-Jun-2007 (ECtHR)*, paras 26–7.

220 See, further, Clayton and Ghaly (2007), p. 210; Vadi (2015), p. 211; Shany (2005), p. 937.

221 *Feldman, Award, 16-Dec-2002 (ICSID-AF)*, para. 170. See, also, *El Paso, Award, 31-Oct-2011 (ICSID)*, paras 310, 314–15; *Saluka, Partial Award, 17-Mar-2006 (UNCITRAL)*, para. 490; *James, Judgment, 21-Feb-1986 (ECtHR)*, para. 52.

222 *UPS, Merits Award, 24-May-2007 (ICSID-administered/UNCITRAL)*, paras 167–9.

223 See, for example, *Pope & Talbot, Merits Award, 10-Apr-2001 (UNCITRAL)*, paras 78–9; *Mesa, Award, 24-Mar-2016 (PCA/UNCITRAL)*, para. 579.

224 See, for example, *Cargill, Award, 18-Sept-2009 (ICSID-AF)*, para. 203; *Chassagnou (Dissent/SO-Zupančič), 29-Apr-1999 (ECtHR-GC)*; *Valeri Belokon, Award, 24-Oct-2014 (UNCITRAL)*, para. 232 ('States have considerable leeway in their policy actions, especially when faced with emergency situations such as the overthrow of a regime. . . . Although States are often said to enjoy margins of discretion with respect to such matters, the Respondent's actions must still be rationally connected to their objectives').

225 See, for example, *Siemens, Award, 17-Jan-2007 (ICSID)*, para. 273 ('This is a legitimate concern of Argentina and the Tribunal defers to Argentina in the determination of its public interest. However, . . . the Tribunal cannot ignore the context in which Decree 669/01 was issued . . . From this perspective, while the public purpose of the 2000 Emergency Law is evident, its application through Decree 669/01 to the specific case of Siemens' investment and the public purpose of same are questionable').

226 See, for example, *Micula, Final Award, 11-Dec-2013 (ICSID)*, para. 525; *Electrabel, Award, 25-Nov-2015 (ICSID)*, paras 179–80; *AES (Hungary), Award, 23-Sept-2010 (ICSID)*, paras 10.3.7–10.3.36.

227 See, for example, *Vestey, Award, 15-Apr-2016 (ICSID)*, para. 296 ('the objective is not to review the effectiveness of the measures . . . the idea is to determine whether the measure . . . was at

reasons to defer to exercises of domestic decision-making authority that reflect qualities the adjudicator associates with competent or legitimate decision-making such as, for example, rationality or reasonableness.

The substantive criteria used to accord deference as respect may vary depending on the relevant measure and context.[228] The ECtHR has indicated, for example, that it might apply differing modes of substantive review depending on the grounds of justification offered for allegedly discriminatory treatment. Whereas the Court might enquire of differentiation on social and economic grounds whether the distinction is 'rationally related' to the claimed objective, differentiation on the grounds of race and nationality might be required to be 'suitably tailored' to the claimed objective.[229] Such distinctions indicate that certain topics may attract wider regulatory discretion than others. As Judge Kooijmans observed when analysing an essential security interests clause in *Oil Platforms*:

> with regard to the measures taken a stricter test must be used than with regard to the assessment that essential security interests are at risk. There seem to be good reasons for such a distinction with regard to the margin of discretion to be left to governmental authorities. The evaluation of what essential security interests are and whether they are in jeopardy is first and foremost a political question and can hardly be replaced by a judicial assessment. ... And although the choice of means to be taken in order to protect those interests will also be politically motivated, that choice lends itself much more to judicial review and thus to a stricter test, since the means chosen directly affect the interests and rights of others.[230]

Regardless of what level of intensity an adjudicator selects, all such approaches share in common a requirement for State decisions to exhibit certain qualities to attract deference. This differs from the approach that would be adopted in the mode of deference as restraint because it entails a more proactive review by

least capable of furthering that purpose'). *Invesmart, Award, 26-Jun-2009 (UNCITRAL)*, paras 454–63; *Electrabel, Award, 25-Nov-2015 (ICSID)*, para. 219 ('Whether the Tribunal, acting in Hungary's shoes, would have come to a different figure from Hungary is not the right question under the ECT's FET standard. The Tribunal is not a court of appeal. Rather, the question is whether Hungary, at the relevant time, acting in good faith, could have arrived at that figure in a rational manner').

228 See, for example, *Oil Platforms (Dissent/SO-Kooijmans), 6-Nov-2003 (ICJ)*, para. 46 (a State has less 'discretion' to use force than it would if it opted to achieve its aim through 'economic measures').

229 *Chassagnou (Dissent/SO-Zupančič), 29-Apr-1999 (ECtHR-GC)*; *Burden (Dissent/SO-Thór Björgvinsson), 29-Apr-2008 (ECtHR-GC)*. This differs from a restraint mode, because the adjudicators use qualitative criteria to (partially) review the decision.

230 *Oil Platforms (Dissent/SO-Kooijmans), 6-Nov-2003 (ICJ)*, para. 44.

the adjudicator. Instead of starting from an assumption that domestic decisions should be deferred to (unless certain limited circumstances exist) it requires that domestic decisions be *justifiable* by reference to certain substantive criteria in order to attract deference.

Adjudicators may differ in selecting the qualities that will indicate substantively authoritative domestic decision-making. An adjudicator could elect to defer, for instance, only to 'reasonable' State decisions. In analysing the ownership of a consignment of alcohol, for example, the ECtHR in *Uniya* observed that a domestic judicial decision determining ownership 'was based on a reasonable assessment of evidence, so the Court is prepared to defer to the national judge on this point'.[231] Judge Buergenthal in *Oil Platforms* similarly held that in assessing the 'necessity' of measures taken to protect essential security interests, the Court should limit itself to enquiring 'whether, on the facts before it, a party had convincing reasons for believing that the measures were necessary'.[232] He stated:

> while a Government's determination is ultimately subject to review by the Court, it may not substitute its judgment completely for that of the Government which, in assessing whether the disputed measures were necessary, must be given the opportunity to demonstrate that its assessment of the perceived threat to its essential security interests was reasonable under the circumstances.[233]

Adjudicators may further differ in identifying indicia for such substantive criteria. Adjudicators might, for example, conclude that States act 'reasonably' where their decisions appear to be well founded or rational.[234] Alternatively, the reasonableness of a decision could be assessed by reference to its 'reasonable', 'rational', or 'proportionate' connection to a State's public purpose, or the balance it achieves between individual and collective goals.[235] This indicates that analysis of reasonableness can take subjective

[231] *Uniya, Judgment, 19-Jun-2014 (ECtHR)*, para. 297. See, similarly, *Terem, Judgment, 18-Oct-2005 (ECtHR)*, para. 32.

[232] *Oil Platforms (Dissent/SO-Buergenthal), 6-Nov-2003 (ICJ)*, para. 38.

[233] Ibid, para. 37.

[234] See, for example, *Chassagnou, Judgment, 29-Apr-1999 (ECtHR-GC)*, paras 91–3; *Herrmann (Dissent/SO-Pinto De Albuquerque), 26-Jun-2012 (ECtHR-GC)*; *Binder, Award on Jurisdiction, 6-Jun-2007 (UNCITRAL)*, paras 427–8, 469; *Gustav Hamester, Award, 18-Jun-2010 (ICSID)*, paras 297–8.

[235] See, for example, *LG&E, Decision on Liability, 3-Oct-2006 (ICSID)*, para. 195 (a measure 'having a social or general welfare purpose ... must be accepted without any imposition of liability, except in cases where the State's action is obviously disproportionate to the need being addressed'). See, similarly, *Total, Decision on Liability, 27-Dec-2010 (ICSID)*, para. 123; *Electrabel, Award, 25-Nov-2015 (ICSID)*, paras 179–80.

or objective perspectives.[236] Instead of enquiring into whether the State had 'reasonable grounds' for making a decision,[237] for instance, the adjudicator could assess whether the State's decision fell within the range of 'reasonable measures expected from a well administered government in similar circumstances'.[238] Judge Kooijmans, for example, held in *Oil Platforms* that the State's assessment of a threat to its essential security interests was 'reasonable', given that '[a]ny other government finding itself in the same situation might have come to the same conclusion'.[239]

Adjudicators could alternatively defer to decisions that are rational or not arbitrary. The ECtHR in *Kopecky*, for example, noted that the Court had 'only limited power to deal with alleged errors of fact or law committed by the national courts', it being for domestic authorities 'in the first place to interpret and apply domestic law'.[240] The Court, finding 'no appearance of arbitrariness' in the domestic court judgments concerning the applicant's claim, held that there was 'therefore no basis on which the Court could reach a different conclusion on the applicant's compliance with the requirement in issue'.[241] As with testing for reasonableness, adjudicators may adopt different approaches to reviewing non-arbitrariness. In *Patrikova*, for example, the ECtHR held that

236 Compare, for example, *SD Myers (Dissent/SO-Schwartz), 12-Nov-2000 (UNCITRAL)*, para. 166 (the tribunal 'can take into account the way a government reasonably perceives a matter, rather than judging government conduct on the basis of hindsight'); *Scollo, Judgment, 28-Sept-1995 (ECtHR)*, para. 40 ('the Italian legislature was reasonably entitled to consider . . . that the means chosen were appropriate to achieve the legitimate aim'); *Electrabel, Award, 25-Nov-2015 (ICSID)*, para. 168 (applying 'an objective test in the circumstances prevailing at the relevant time'); para. 219 ('Whether the Tribunal, acting in Hungary's shoes, would have come to a different figure from Hungary is not the right question under the ECT's FET standard. The Tribunal is not a court of appeal. Rather, the question is whether Hungary, at the relevant time, acting in good faith, could have arrived at that figure in a rational manner'); *Philip Morris (Uruguay) (Dissent/SO-Born), 8-Jul-2016 (ICSID)*, para. 144 (adopting 'an objective consideration of the extent to which a governmental measure is rationally related to, or fairly advances, the state's articulated objectives').

237 See, for example, *Diallo, Merits Judgment, 30-Nov-2010 (ICJ)*, para. 74 ('It is for the State to demonstrate that the "compelling reasons" required by the Covenant existed, or at the very least could reasonably have been concluded to have existed'); *Lauder, Final Award, 3-Sept-2001 (UNCITRAL)*, paras 248–55, 285–6 ('[t]here is indeed sufficient evidence that the Media Council thought – or could think – that CNTS was violating the Media Law').

238 *Al Warraq, Final Award, 15-Dec-2014 (UNCITRAL)*, para. 627. See, also, *AES (Hungary), Award, 23-Sept-2010 (ICSID)*, paras 13.3.2–13.3.3; *Perenco, Decision on Jurisdiction and Liability, 12-Sept-2014 (ICSID)*, para. 591; *Suez-Interagua (Dissent/SO-Nikken), 30-Jul-2010 (ICSID)*, paras 36–43. See, further, Legg (2012), p. 116.

239 *Oil Platforms (Dissent/SO-Kooijmans), 6-Nov-2003 (ICJ)*, para. 45.

240 *Kopecky, Judgment, 28-Sept-2004 (ECtHR-GC)*, para. 56.

241 Ibid, para. 56. See, similarly: *Jahn, Judgment, 30-Jun-2005 (ECtHR-GC)*, paras 84–7; *Slivenko, Decision on Admissibility, 23-Jan-2002 (ECtHR-GC)*, paras 78–9.

domestic judicial decisions were 'arbitrary' because they had been issued by courts 'refusing to take into account [the] context and applying a formalistic approach'.[242] Other adjudicators have focused on whether decision-makers 'acted for wholly improper reasons'[243] or on a 'capricious, irrational or absurd' basis.[244]

Review for rationality may thus blend with the other bases for review in a mode of respect, including good faith, procedural, and reasonableness review. Borchard advocated this mixed approach to review, arguing that:

> Given good faith, a fair opportunity to the alien to be heard, and the absence of discrimination between native and foreigner, it would seem that the judgment of a municipal court interpreting municipal law is internationally conclusive, even if in error.[245]

Moreover, the combination of these forms of review will frequently lead to balancing by the adjudicator of a range of second-order reasons for deference (often alongside first-order reasons for decision). The *Philip Morris* ICSID tribunal observed, for example, that:

> investment tribunals should pay great deference to governmental judgments of national needs in matters such as the protection of public health. In such cases respect is due to the 'discretionary exercise of sovereign power, not made irrationally and not exercised in bad faith … [t]he sole inquiry for the Tribunal … is whether or not there was a manifest lack of reasons for the legislation'.[246]

The adjudicator may otherwise use rebuttable presumptions in its analysis. It could, for example, start from a presumption of good faith or reasonableness.[247] There may also be gradations within such standards of review. Reasonableness review might, for instance, prompt the adjudicator to require that a decision be *reasonable* or instead not *un*reasonable.[248] Such presumptions and gradations entail important differences, particularly in relation to the burden of proof. But

242 *Patrikova, Judgment, 4-Mar-2010 (ECtHR)*, para. 102.
243 *Invesmart, Award, 26-Jun-2009 (UNCITRAL)*, paras 487–9, 502–3.
244 *Enron, Award, 22-May-2007 (ICSID)*, para. 282.
245 Borchard (1919), p. 340.
246 *Philip Morris (Uruguay), Award, 8-Jul-2016 (ICSID)*, para. 399. See, also, para. 418 (whether the decision was 'taken against the background of a strong scientific consensus').
247 See, for example, *Interhandel (Dissent/SO-Lauterpacht), 21-Mar-1959 (ICJ)*, p. 111. See, further, Amerasinghe (2008), p. 93.
248 Compare, for example, *Pope & Talbot, Merits Award, 10-Apr-2001 (UNCITRAL)*, pp. 123–8 (requiring reasonableness); *Total, Decision on Liability, 27-Dec-2010 (ICSID)*, para. 214 (requiring that the decision was 'not unreasonable'). See, also, *Chassagnou (Dissent/SO-Zupančič), 29-Apr-1999 (ECtHR-GC)* ('it is much easier to say what is *not* reasonable than

all such approaches can nonetheless be grouped together under the mode of deference as respect because they all indicate situations in which the adjudicator selects qualitative criteria that, if met, mean that the domestic actor's judgment will attract deference, and the adjudicator will not consider all the available first-order reasons for decision to unsettle that judgment.

7.3.4 *Equivalence Review*

A further set of devices operating in a mode of respect are equivalence or *solange* doctrines. According to these devices, an international adjudicator accords respect to decisions adopted in legal systems ensuring equivalent protection to that which would govern the international adjudicator's own decision on the same issue.[249] This mode of deference thus focuses not on the qualities of an individual domestic decision as such, but rather the qualities of the system from which it has emerged. The ECtHR stated in *Bosphorus* to this effect that State compliance with the decisions of another international organisation (the European Union) would not be reviewed under the ECHR:

> as long as the relevant organisation is considered to protect fundamental rights . . . in a manner which can be considered at least equivalent to that for which the Convention provides.[250]

The Court held that such equivalence would generate a 'presumption' that the State had not violated the Convention, unless 'such presumption can be rebutted' by showing that 'in the circumstances of a particular case, it is considered that the protection of Convention rights was manifestly deficient'.[251]

Adjudicators adopting requirements of equivalence will only recognise State authority where it operates within constraints comparable to those applicable to the international adjudicator's own exercise of decision-making authority or comparable to some minimal international standards. Such adjudicators decline to defer to domestic decisions that they perceive to derive from systems with inadequate or unsatisfactory decision-making safeguards. Deference is denied in such circumstances on the basis of a view that empirically or normatively better decisions could be reached through international adjudication.

what *is* reasonable'). See, further, Poole (2009), p. 143; Ortino (2017); Kolb (2013), p. 875; Salgado (1986), p. 907.

249 See, generally, Bilkova (2014), p. 276; Tzanakopoulos (2012), p. 198; Lavranos (2008).

250 *Bosphorus, Judgment, 30-Jun-2005 (ECtHR-GC)*, para. 155.

251 Ibid, para. 156.

Equivalence review may seek comparability at the level of procedure or substance. Focusing on the procedures in place within a domestic system, for example, the *Invesmart* UNCITRAL tribunal held that:

> A decision to revoke a bank's licence, which takes place within a detailed national legal framework that includes administrative and judicial remedies, is not reviewed at the international law level for its 'correctness', but rather for whether it offends the more basic requirements of international law. Numerous tribunals have held that when testing regulatory decisions against international law standards, the regulators' right and duty to regulate must not be subjected to undue second-guessing by international tribunals. Tribunals need not be satisfied that they would have made precisely the same decision as the regulator in order for them to uphold such decisions.[252]

A domestic judicial decision might alternatively attract deference where the decision – or process leading to it – is consistent with certain principles or rules of international law.[253] The *GAMI* UNCITRAL tribunal, for example, held that it would 'give respectful consideration' to domestic judicial determinations on matters of international law 'insofar as [the domestic court] applies norms congruent with those of NAFTA'.[254] In *Azinian*, an ICSID Additional Facility tribunal used such equivalence review to defer to a domestic judicial decision that a contract was void under Mexican law, adopting that decision as the basis for holding that there was no contract to be expropriated.[255] The tribunal held that such finding of the local court had to be accepted, because 'the Claimants have neither contended nor proved that the Mexican legal standards for the annulment of concessions violate Mexico's Chapter Eleven obligations',[256] or that the domestic judicial decisions themselves constituted violations of the treaty.[257] Other investment tribunals have indicated that they would defer to domestic judicial decisions 'as long as no deficiencies, in procedure or substance, are shown in regard to the local proceedings which are of a nature of rendering these

252 *Invesmart, Award, 26-Jun-2009 (UNCITRAL)*, para. 501.

253 See, for example, *Liman Caspian Oil, Award, 22-Jun-2010 (ICSID)*, para. 431 (domestic judicial decisions 'have to be accepted' except if they are 'arbitrary, grossly unfair, unjust, idiosyncratic, discriminatory or lacking due process'); *Rachel Grynberg, Award, 10-Dec-2010 (ICSID)*, para. 7.1.11 ('BIT tribunals do not reopen the municipal law decisions of competent fora, absent a denial of justice'). See, similarly, *Swisslion, Award, 6-Jul-2012 (ICSID)*, para. 265; *Luigiterzo Bosca, Award, 17-May-2013 (UNCITRAL)*, paras 163, 198–200.

254 *GAMI, Final Award, 15-Nov-2004 (UNCITRAL)*, para. 41.

255 *Azinian, Final Award, 1-Nov-1999 (ICSID-AF)*, para. 100.

256 Ibid, para. 96.

257 Ibid, para. 99. See, similarly, *Waste Management (No. 2), Award on Jurisdiction, 26-Jun-2002 (ICSID-AF)*, para. 47; *Feldman, Award, 16-Dec-2002 (ICSID-AF)*.

deficiencies unacceptable from the viewpoint of international law, such as in the case of a denial of justice'.[258] As the *Unglaube* ICSID tribunal stated:

> under the Constitution and laws of Costa Rica, it is the Attorney General and the Supreme Court who are empowered to give authoritative and final interpretation of the law . . . it is not appropriate for this Tribunal to substitute an opinion of its own or make any finding of liability unless the Attorney General and the Court are found to have acted in a manner which is arbitrary, discriminatory or otherwise shocking to the conscience. The Tribunal does not find in the reasoning of the Attorney General or the Supreme Court any such abuse of their responsibilities.[259]

The ECtHR has also adopted approaches to deference signifying equivalence review. In *Mago*, for example, the ECtHR noted that a respondent State had 'consistently held that an occupancy right constitutes "possessions" within the meaning of Article 1 of Protocol No. 1', and held that '[a]s the position of the national authorities appears to be in accordance with international standards . . . the Court does not see any reason to depart from it'.[260] The ECtHR has similarly indicated that it may defer to domestic judicial decisions rendered after the initiation of ECtHR proceedings provided that they exhibit the qualities of relief that would be available to applicants before the ECtHR. Such deference arises where domestic courts acknowledge the alleged breach and award 'appropriate and sufficient' relief.[261] As the Court stated in *Doo*, 'when these conditions are satisfied . . . the subsidiary nature of the protective mechanism of the Convention preclude[s] examination of an application'.[262] To reach the threshold for such deference, domestic courts must 'acknowledge' the breach by referring to 'the principles established by the Court in relation to . . . the right to peaceful enjoyment of possessions'.[263] An adjudicator might alternatively adopt equivalence review by deferring to domestic decisions shown to reflect certain substantive values. A domestic decision could thus attract deference if it is non-discriminatory or otherwise not 'in breach of a fundamental right'.[264] Adjudicators might, alternatively, defer to domestic decisions that exhibit particular characteristics reflecting the perceived *telos* of the international regime,

[258] *Helnan, Award, 3-Jul-2008 (ICSID)*, paras 105–6.
[259] *Unglaube, Award, 16-May-2012 (ICSID)*, para. 253.
[260] *Mago, Judgment, 3-May-2012 (ECtHR)*, para. 78.
[261] *Khaynatskyy, Judgment, 9-Jan-2014 (ECtHR)*, para. 34; *Uniya, Judgment, 19-Jun-2014 (ECtHR)*, para. 280.
[262] *Doo, Judgment, 26-Nov-2013 (ECtHR)*, para. 41.
[263] See, for example, *Centro Europa, Judgment, 7-Jun-2012 (ECtHR-GC)*, para. 86; *Centro Europa (Dissent/SO-Steiner), 7-Jun-2012 (ECtHR-GC)*.
[264] *Dan Cake, Decision on Jurisdiction and Liability, 24-Aug-2015 (ICSID)*, para. 117.

including generality, clarity, or consistency.[265] The criteria for 'equivalence' may therefore differ, and it is possible that this approach to deference as respect will entail review that is less limiting of State decision-making authority than other approaches to deference as respect, particularly where the adjudicator engages in substantive review. Although equivalence review is positioned next to deference as control in the taxonomy, such approaches are more deferential than approaches in that mode because they entail at least some scope for second-order reasons to influence the adjudicator's analysis of the first-order reasons relevant to determining a given issue.

7.4 CONCLUSIONS

The three modes of deference reflecting a concurrent view of authority introduced in this chapter reflect different ways of managing overlapping domestic and international decision-making authority. In the mode of restraint, the adjudicator invokes second-order reasons to identify applicable first-order reasons for decision. In so doing, it structures its analysis to increase domestic decision-making authority. In a mode of reference, the adjudicator uses domestic decisions as reference points for the exercise of its own decision-making authority. In the mode of respect, domestic decision-making authority is recognised insofar as it is 'earned' including, for example, because domestic decisions were made in good faith or according to particular procedures. Each of these modes of deference nonetheless reflects a common view of the interface between domestic and international decision-making authority. When operating in the modes of restraint, reference or respect, international adjudicators exhibit a view that international adjudication is *complementary* to domestic decision-making processes. In these modes, international adjudication operates as 'a safety net in case of a failure of the domestic system, not an alternative to it'.[266] Domestic authority in these modes does not suspend or preclude international decision-making. It is instead analysed more comprehensively such that international authority can be exercised to *supplement* domestic decision-making, including to check that it has been exercised within certain bounds; is consistent with other decision-making data; or is consistent with particular procedural or normative values and safeguards.

265 Brunnée and Toope (2010), p. 20; Roth-Isigkeit (2017).

266 European Parliament Directorate-General for External Policies (2015), p. 50.

PART III

THE SYSTEMIC ROLE OF DEFERENCE IN INTERNATIONAL LAW

This part concludes the book by examining what approaches to deference reveal about the underlying structural features of international adjudication. Chapter 8 explores approaches to deference comparatively, to highlight how approaches have changed over time or differ by regime. Chapter 9 illustrates the systemic significance of differing approaches to deference. It demonstrates how the three types of authority introduced in Part II can be explained by reference to monist, dualist, and pluralist approaches to conceptualising the relationships between the international and domestic legal orders. Chapter 10 connects theory to practice, to draw out key lessons from the preceding analysis for policymakers, adjudicators, and litigants. It proposes a theory of deference founded on practice, but capable of continued evolution. Collectively, these chapters draw together the preceding analysis to reflect on the systemic function of deference in international adjudication.

8

Deference in Different Times and Contexts

The sheer diversity of approaches to deference identified in Part II is sufficient to dispel the concern that there is 'no established body of principles to deal adequately with the new realities of vertical and horizontal clashes of adjudicative competence'.[1] It leaves open, however, questions as to the extent to which international adjudicators exhibit preferences for some modes of deference over others. This chapter uses descriptive statistics to investigate how approaches to deference in international private property claims differ according to regime, and whether they have changed over time or according to context. The purpose of the chapter is not to engage in an exhaustive statistical, historiographical, sociological, or institutional analysis of deference, nor is it to suggest that particular contexts or institutional features have caused these courts and tribunals to adopt different approaches to deference.[2] Instead, the aim is to identify – based on the inductive, qualitative, review – whether some approaches to deference have been more prevalent than others in different times or contexts. The chapter consists of four Sections. Section 8.1 explains how the figures reported in this chapter were generated. Section 8.2 investigates regime-specific trends in approaches to deference. The section highlights differences in the frequency with which the modes of deference, and approaches to authority, were applied by adjudicators in each regime. It further examines the different approaches to deference exhibited by

[1] Douglas (2003), p. 236.

[2] It is important to note that this quantitative data has been produced through coding with significant levels of discretion, reflecting the conceptual focus of the analysis. This quantitative analysis has not been prepared in a way that would support prediction about future cases. On enumerative content analysis see, further, Berg and Lune (2014), p. 338; Webley (2010), p. 936; Hsieh (2005), p. 1278; Gerbic and Stacey (2005), p. 47; Winham (1969), p. 192; Silverman (2011), p. 64; Creswell and Plano Clark (2011), p. 231; Ngulube (2015), p. 13; Tarrow (2010), p. 89.

adjudicators at the ECtHR Grand Chamber and Committee/Chamber levels, and in ICSID and non-ICSID arbitral decisions. Section 8.3 emphasises the dynamic qualities of deference to investigate whether approaches to deference have changed over time. It identifies a rise in applications of modes of deference reflecting a concurrent view of authority and a dynamism in the approaches of adjudicators to selecting grounds for deference within the mode of deference as respect. Section 8.4 concludes.

8.1 COMPARING APPROACHES TO DEFERENCE IN DIFFERENT TIMES AND CONTEXTS

A key finding of the present study is that deference is ubiquitous across the selected subset of international decisions. To develop the results reported in this chapter, the 1,714 majority and dissenting/separate decisions of the PCIJ, ICJ, ECtHR, and investment treaty tribunals were coded as set out in Part I. This analysis captured all references by adjudicators to each of the modes of deference identified in Part II. International adjudicators applied at least one mode of deference in 726 of the 1,714 reviewed majority and separate/dissenting decisions (42 per cent of the analysed decisions).[3] Adjudicators in the four regimes differed, however, in the frequency with which they applied deferential reasoning. The ECtHR and investment treaty tribunals, for example, applied the various modes of deference in a greater proportion of their majority decisions than did either the PCIJ or ICJ.[4] One or more modes of deference were applied in 47 per cent of ECtHR decisions (222 out of 471 decisions); in 47 per cent of investment tribunal decisions (327 out of 689 decisions); in 38 per cent of ICJ decisions (8 out of 21 decisions); and in 35 per cent of PCIJ decisions (11 out of 31 decisions). It cannot be concluded from these results alone that the ECtHR is more deferential than adjudicators in the other three regimes. Instead, the results may simply reflect the types of case presented to these adjudicators for decision. They may also reflect the types of decision issued most frequently by the adjudicators in each regime. The PCIJ and ICJ, for instance, issued comparatively fewer decisions determining the merits of private property claims than did the ECtHR and investment treaty tribunals. The data may therefore not reflect differing positions as to whether deference to domestic decision-makers is appropriate *in principle*, but instead reflect the

3 All percentages in this chapter have been rounded to the nearest percentage point.

4 The proportion of adjudicators issuing dissenting and separate opinions who indicated they would have applied one or more modes of deference (n = 157) was relatively consistent for each regime: PCIJ 28 per cent (n = 16 of 58); ICJ 31 per cent (n = 31 of 101); ECtHR 32 per cent (n = 72 of 226); ISDS 32 per cent (n = 38 of 117).

reactions of adjudicators in each regime to differing stimuli. Non-applications of deference may merely reflect that deference was inapposite to the issues before the adjudicator, or otherwise that the litigating parties did not request adjudicators to consider deference.

To control for the different opportunities adjudicators in each regime had to consider deference, the cases were coded to record all *references to deference*, and not merely its application. This coding captured, in particular, adjudicative summaries of party requests for deference, even if such deference was not ultimately accorded by the international adjudicator. The analysis also captured decisions in which an adjudicator expressly declined to accord a State deference, and decisions in which an international adjudicator referred to the possibility of affording a State deference without ultimately doing so, usually because it determined the dispute on different grounds. This method meant that one decision could yield more than one 'observation' of deferential reasoning. A decision would yield three observations, for example, if an adjudicator accorded deference as submission to a domestic judicial decision, refused to accord deference as respect to a domestic administrative decision, and accorded deference as submission to a domestic policy decision.

Analysis of the 1,714 decisions using this method yielded 1,800 observed references to the possibility of deference. A total of 1,543 observations were recorded for majority decisions.[5] Of these, 65 per cent reflected the application of a mode of deference (n = 1,009),[6] with 35 per cent reflecting non-applications of a mode of deference (either references to deference without subsequent application, or rejections of deference) (n = 534).[7] A total of 257 observations were recorded for dissenting and separate opinions. Of these, 73 per cent reflected the application of a mode of deference (n = 187).[8] Adjudicative references to deference were thus often accompanied by application, rather than rejection, of deferential reasoning. These references to deference also indicate that adjudicators in some regimes referred more frequently to deference than others. The bulk of observations came from investment arbitration decisions (n = 997, or 55 per cent of all observed references) and ECtHR decisions (n = 644, or 36 per cent of the total). This

5 In majority decisions, PCIJ (n = 33 observations), ICJ (n = 29 observations), ECtHR (n = 547 observations), and ISDS (n = 934 observations).

6 By regime, the 1,009 observed applications in majority decisions comprised PCIJ (n = 11); ICJ (n = 11); ECtHR (n = 357); and ISDS (n = 630).

7 By regime, the 534 non-applications in majority decisions comprised PCIJ (n = 22), ICJ (n = 18), ECtHR (n = 190), and ISDS (n = 304).

8 By regime, the 257 observations from dissenting/SOs comprised PCIJ (n = 27), ICJ (n = 70), ECtHR (n = 97), and ISDS (n = 63).

means that particular care must be taken in analysing trends for the PCIJ and ICJ, given the low number of references to deference in private property decisions from those regimes (n = 60 for the PCIJ, and n = 99 for the ICJ).[9]

8.2 THE TREATMENT OF DEFERENCE IN DIFFERENT REGIMES

The analysis has thus far focused on how international courts and tribunals have mediated the interface between domestic and international decision-making authority. In particular, I have drawn out seven 'modes' or approaches to deference that exhibit different features and that result in different relationships between domestic and international decision-making. Empirical analysis of these modes in the cases under study indicates that approaches to deference differ by institutional setting. This section examines some of the differences in approach that were observed in the analysed cases. Subsection 8.2.1 examines the frequency with which adjudicators in each regime applied the seven modes of deference – and the conclusive, suspensive, or concurrent views of authority that underpin them – as introduced in Part II. Subsection 8.2.2 investigates how adjudicators identified domestic decision-makers to benefit from deference.

8.2.1 *Modes of Deference and Structures of Authority in Different Regimes*

Part II demonstrated that international adjudicative approaches to deference can be divided into seven different 'modes'. Each mode entails a different treatment by the international adjudicator of domestic decision-making and results in a different relationship between the international adjudicator and domestic actors. These modes, arrayed roughly from most to least deferential, are recalled in Figure 8.1. As noted earlier, the coding process returned a total of 1,196 observed *applications* of deference, 1,009 of which appeared in majority decisions. These applications of deference revealed that some adjudicators elect to apply particular modes of deference in a higher proportion than other modes. Figure 8.1 identifies the frequency of modes of deference, by regime, in the 1,009 observed applications of deference in majority decisions.

Figure 8.1 highlights several differences in the approaches of adjudicators to deference. The PCIJ did not, for example, apply the modes of abstention or

9 This also follows from the PCIJ and ICJ rendering fewer private property decisions than the ECtHR or investment tribunals. Interestingly, PCIJ and ICJ Judges indicated greater willingness to discuss deference in dissenting/separate (n = 97), compared to majority (n = 62), decisions.

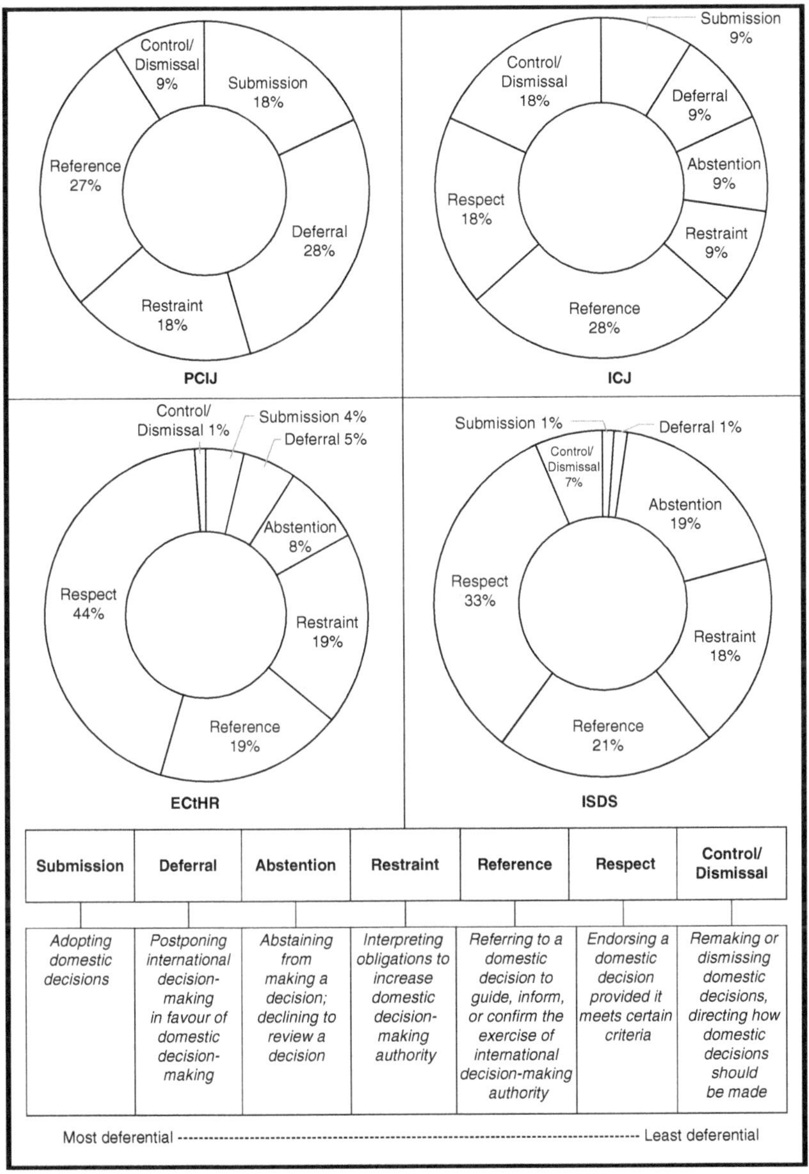

Submission	Deferral	Abstention	Restraint	Reference	Respect	Control/ Dismissal
Adopting domestic decisions	*Postponing international decision-making in favour of domestic decision-making*	*Abstaining from making a decision; declining to review a decision*	*Interpreting obligations to increase domestic decision-making authority*	*Referring to a domestic decision to guide, inform, or confirm the exercise of international decision-making authority*	*Endorsing a domestic decision provided it meets certain criteria*	*Remaking or dismissing domestic decisions, directing how domestic decisions should be made*

Most deferential -- Least deferential

FIGURE 8.1 Applications of modes of deference by adjudicators in each regime (majority decisions)

respect in any of its majority decisions. The Court's dominant modes of deference were instead deferral and reference (55 per cent of PCIJ observations). The ICJ's dominant modes, by contrast, were reference, respect, and control/dismissal (64 per cent of ICJ observations). The PCIJ and ICJ also applied deference in the modes of submission and deferral proportionately more frequently than did the ECtHR or investment treaty tribunals. The ECtHR and investment treaty tribunals presented broadly comparable profiles to one another. Investment tribunals, however, applied a mode of abstention comparatively more frequently than the ECtHR (19 per cent of observations, compared to 8 per cent). Analysis of non-applications of deferential reasoning also indicates regime-specific trends.[10] Investment treaty decisions accounted for 53 per cent (n = 320) of the 604 instances of adjudicators in both majority and dissenting/separate opinions referring to the possibility of a mode of deference without then adopting that mode to afford deference to a domestic decision-maker.

This analysis further reveals that the mode of deference as deferral comprised only 5 per cent of the total applications of deference by the ECtHR. This is perhaps surprising given that the ECHR expressly requires applicants to exhaust local remedies prior to their claim becoming admissible before the Court. As Chapter 6 explained, such a rule has the potential to prompt adjudicators to adopt a mode of deferral reflecting a suspensive view of authority. The data does not, however, support a conclusion that this ELR requirement is not being applied. Instead, it may reflect that the rule is most typically applied by the commission (pre-1998) or by a single judge in an admissibility procedure. For the reasons set out in Part I, neither of these categories of decision was the subject of empirical enquiry. This, coupled with the established status of the rule, means that local remedies will typically have been exhausted prior to the application being considered by the adjudicators whose decisions were analysed in this empirical study. Furthermore, even where ECtHR adjudicators at the Grand Chamber, Chamber, or Committee level apply the ELR requirement, they do not necessarily do so as a rule of deference. As explained in Chapter 6, the empirical study captures only instances in which an adjudicator emphasises the deference-achieving qualities of the rule. What the data reveals of the analysed decisions is that the ELR requirement, relative to other modes of deference, is infrequently applied in majority decisions expressly to achieve deference.

[10] This includes where the court/tribunal expressly refused to apply a requested approach to deference; where the court/tribunal noted a request for a particular approach to deference but applied a different approach (without expressly rejecting the requested approach); and instances where the court/tribunal noted the possibility of using an approach to deference but ultimately either did not decide the issue, or decided it on the basis of other (non-deferential) reasoning. See the Appendix for a breakdown of non-applications of deference by regime.

It is of, course, possible that adjudicators even in the same 'regime' might adopt different approaches to deference. As noted in Part I, both investment treaty tribunals and the ECtHR comprise decision-makers operating in institutionally distinct settings. Some commentators doubt, for example, whether investment treaty arbitration is a coherent 'regime' at all.[11] There is, as posited in Part I, also reason to expect that territorialised (non-ICSID) tribunals might differ in analysing deference to domestic decision-makers.[12] They might, for example, share greater links to domestic decision-making processes than do ICSID tribunals, which are comparatively more insulated from domestic law. The ECtHR also has distinct institutional layers, and it is possible that ECtHR adjudicators may approach issues of deference differently depending on their institutional position. As was explained in Chapter 2, Grand Chamber judges are likely to confront fewer questions of fact than judges at the Chamber and Committee level. They are also unlikely to confront questions of domestic decision-making authority in the role of a first-instance decision-maker, given that such questions are likely to have already been canvassed at the Committee or Chamber level. Figure 8.2 disaggregates each mode of deference as a proportion of observed applications of deference in majority decisions from the ECtHR Grand Chamber (n = 111 applications), ECtHR Committee or Chamber (n = 246 applications), ICSID investment tribunals (n = 379 applications), and non-ICSID[13] investment tribunals (n = 251 applications).

To investigate the possibility of intra-regime differences in approaches to deference, Figure 8.2 reveals that adjudicators at the different institutional layers of the ECtHR differed most in the frequency with which they applied the modes of deferral and respect.[14] The Grand Chamber proportionately applied the modes of deferral, abstention, restraint, and control/dismissal more frequently than adjudicators at the Chamber and Committee level. ECtHR adjudicators at the Chamber and Committee levels by contrast proportionately applied the mode of submission, respect, and reference more frequently than these modes were applied in Grand Chamber decisions. Investment arbitrators showed the greatest difference in the modes of respect

[11] See, for example, Salacuse (2010), p. 430; Gelinas (2005), p. 583; Pauwelyn (2014).

[12] See Chapter 2. See, further, on 'territorial' and 'non-territorial' arbitration, Kjos (2013).

[13] Including ICSID Additional Facility, UNCITRAL, LCIA or SCC arbitrations.

[14] The results reported in respect of the ECtHR's propensity to operate in the mode of control/dismissal are consistent with an empirical analysis of all pilot judgments and Article 46 judgments issued by the Court between 2004–16, which reports that the GC was proportionately more likely than Chambers of the Court to indicate specific remedial measures: Niedlispacher et al. (2018), p. 4.

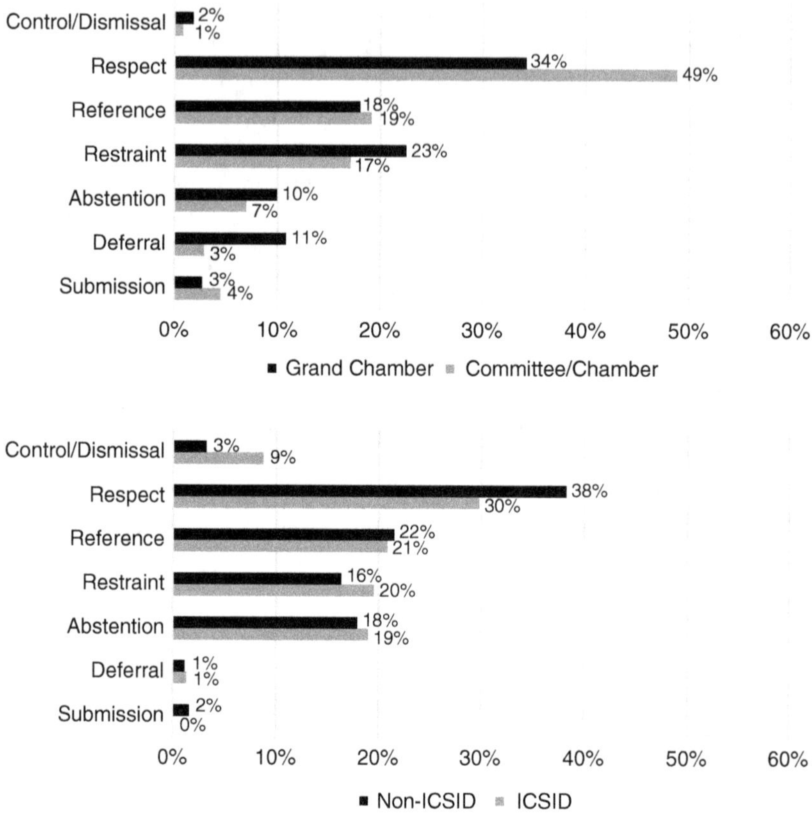

FIGURE 8.2 Frequencies of application of each mode of deference in Grand Chamber/non-Grand Chamber and ICSID/non-ICSID majority decisions

and control/dismissal. ICSID arbitrators adopted a mode of control/dismissal more frequently than non-ICSID arbitrators. The latter, by contrast, adopted the mode of respect more frequently than adjudicators in ICSID tribunals. They also accounted for all applications of the mode of submission in majority decisions for investment arbitrators. Figure 8.2 nevertheless reveals that – overall – there were not major differences between the approaches of investment treaty arbitrators in different institutional settings. This cuts against the hypothesis in Part I that territorialised and non-territorialised regimes might approach questions of deference differently.

As Part II indicated, different modes of deference reflect differing approaches to structuring authority. An adjudicator adopting the modes of submission or control/dismissal takes a conclusive view of domestic decision-making authority. Adjudicators in these modes use principles of trumping to regulate interactions between domestic and international decision-making authority. Adjudicators adopting the modes of deferral or abstention, by contrast, conceptualise decision-making authority in suspensive terms. They avoid determining conflicting claims to authority by delaying or denying conflict. Adjudicators operating in the modes of restraint, reference, and respect adopt concurrent approaches to analysing domestic decision-making authority. Such adjudicators view authority as conditional, and seek to balance or mediate – rather than override or foreclose – conflicting claims to authority. Figure 8.3 maps these conceptions of authority according to the application of different modes of deference in majority decisions. This tracks the discussion in Chapter 4, which grouped the modes of deference into four categories, as follows:

(i) 'conclusive domestic authority' (application of the mode of submission);
(ii) 'suspensive authority' (application of the modes of deferral or abstention);
(iii) 'concurrent authority' (application of the modes of restraint, reference or respect); and
(iv) 'conclusive international authority' (application of the mode of control/dismissal).

Figure 8.3 reveals the 'profiles' of authority analyses that underpin approaches to deference in each regime. This comparative analysis supports Chapter 2's observations related to the impact that institutional settings and claim structures have on adjudicative approaches to deference. The profiles indicate, in particular, a difference in approach between adjudicators determining State–State claims (the PCIJ and ICJ) and those adjudicating individual–State claims (the ECtHR and investment treaty tribunals). The ECtHR and investment tribunals disclosed relatively more conditional approaches to conceptualising decision-making authority, viewing it as concurrent more frequently than adjudicators in the other regimes. The ECtHR adopted this view of authority in 82 per cent of all applications of deference.[15] Investment tribunals similarly favoured modes of deference reflecting a concurrent view of authority, adopting modes reflecting such a view in 73 per cent of observed applications.[16] The PCIJ and ICJ, by

15 Majority decisions of the ECtHR adopted a conclusive view of authority in eighteen observed applications (5 per cent); a suspensive view in forty-seven observed applications (13 per cent), and a concurrent view in 292 observed applications (82 per cent).

16 Majority decisions of investment treaty tribunals adopted a conclusive view of authority in forty-eight observed applications (8 per cent); a suspensive view in 125 observed applications (20 per cent), and a concurrent view in 457 observed applications (72 per cent).

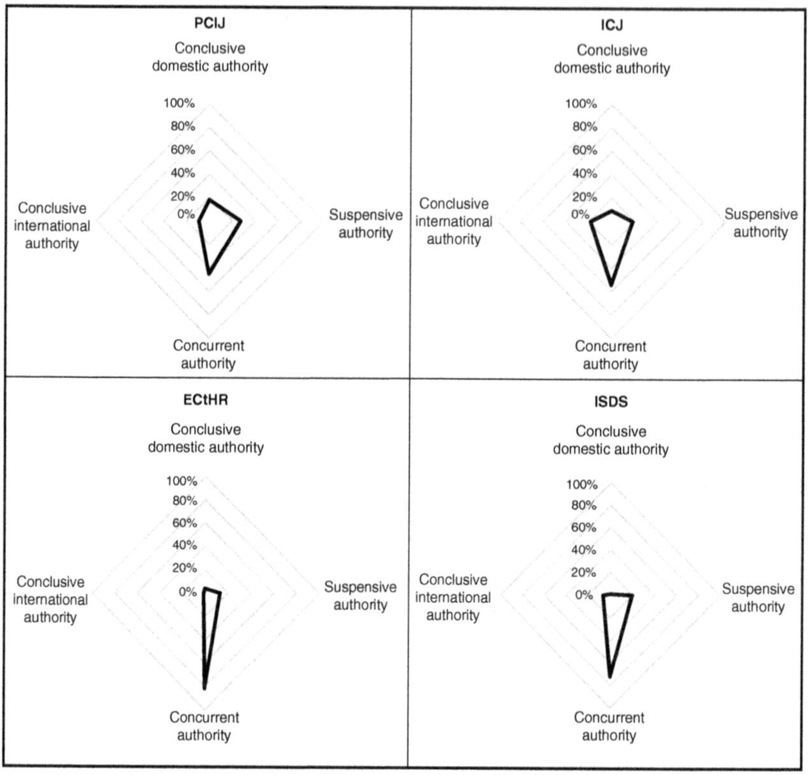

FIGURE 8.3 Approaches to structuring authority adopted by adjudicators in each regime (majority decisions)

contrast, adopted a concurrent view of authority in only 45 and 55 per cent of observed applications of deferential reasoning.[17] They displayed a greater tendency than adjudicators in the other two regimes to apply modes of deference reflecting other views of authority. The PCIJ adopted a suspensive view of authority in 27 per cent of observed applications of deference and a conclusive view of authority in 27 per cent of applications (18 per cent being in favour of domestic decision-making authority, and 9 per cent in favour of international authority). The ICJ, by contrast, adopted a suspensive view in 18 per cent of

[17] The limited number of observations for applications of deference in majority decisions (n = 11) for each court means care must be taken in appraising the significance of these results. PCIJ majority decisions adopted a conclusive view of authority in three applications (27 per cent), a suspensive view in three (27 per cent), and a concurrent view in five (46 per cent). ICJ majority decisions adopted a conclusive view in three (27 per cent), a suspensive view in two (18 per cent), and a concurrent view in six (55 per cent).

applications and a conclusive view in 27 per cent of applications (9 per cent being in favour of domestic decision-making authority, and 18 per cent in favour of international authority). The ECtHR and investment tribunals by contrast endorsed conclusive authority less frequently than adjudicators in the other regimes. Conclusive views of authority only constituted 5 per cent of all ECtHR's applications of deference and 8 per cent of all applications of deference recorded for investment tribunals. Investment treaty tribunals also disclosed an overall more mixed profile relative to other adjudicators. They were the second most frequent appliers of suspensive and concurrent forms of authority compared to adjudicators in the other regimes, and the third most frequent appliers of modes of deference reflecting conclusive approaches to authority. The profiles thus disclose important regime-specific trends, as well as differences between the approaches of adjudicators in different regimes to analysing domestic claims to decision-making authority. The systemic implications of these differing approaches to deference – including their impact on the domestic/international interface – are considered in more detail in Chapter 9.

8.2.2 *Into the Black Box: The Unitary State and its Decision-Making Organs*

The empirical study further revealed that international adjudicators frequently 'pierce the State's veil'[18] in analysing whether to defer to domestic decision-makers. In 94 per cent of the observed applications of a mode of deference, international adjudicators specifically identified a domestic decision-maker to benefit from the attribution of deference (n = 966). Adjudicators in only 6 per cent of observed applications either did not identify a specific domestic decision-maker to benefit from deference, or accorded deference by reference to 'the State' (n = 64).[19] Interestingly, investment tribunals adopted this latter approach more frequently (n = 53, or 10 per cent of their applications of deference) than other adjudicators (n = 11, or 3 per cent of the total applications of deference in the other three regimes). As might be expected in light of the discussion in Chapter 7, most of the instances in which adjudicators did not identify a specific domestic decision-maker to benefit from deference occurred in the mode of deference as restraint. Some 55 per cent of the total applications of deference to 'the State' rather than an identified domestic decision-maker occurred in this mode (n = 35). This reflects a large number of instances in

[18] Sadurski (2009), p. 421.

[19] This differs from total observed applications of deference, because sometimes in one application of deference an adjudicator identified more than one beneficiary for deference.

which adjudicators emphasised there would be a high threshold for breach – or margin of discretion – associated with the application of certain rules of international law, in order to accommodate State claims to decision-making authority. Such instances of deference focused on the room for manoeuvre an adjudicator could provide a State when interpreting the State's international obligations, and so could occur in the absence of identifying a specific domestic actor to benefit from the deference being accorded.

Where deference was accorded to a specific decision-maker rather than the State, various domestic actors benefitted from deference. For majority decisions, domestic judicial organs were the beneficiaries of deference in 47 per cent of the observed applications of deference (n = 482), and executive or legislative actors in 47 per cent of applications (n = 484). This indicates that international adjudicators have not tended to favour domestic actors of particular institutional types (judicial vs. executive/legislative) in according deference.[20] Different modes of deference nonetheless attached to the decisions of different domestic institutions. Figure 8.4 categorises the observed applications of deference according to the type of domestic decision-maker and the mode of deference that was applied by the international adjudicator. To control for the opportunity each adjudicator had to accord a specific mode of deference to a particular decision-maker, the figure splits up applications of deference by mode, as a proportion of the application for each mode.[21] This reveals that domestic courts benefitted most frequently relative to other domestic decision-makers from the application of the modes of submission, deferral, and reference. The modes of abstention and control/dismissal were each applied by reference to a range of different domestic decision-makers. By contrast, the modes of restraint and respect were applied most frequently to accord deference to non-judicial actors. This indicates that international courts and tribunals are comparatively more comfortable treating domestic court decisions as conclusive or suspensive; whereas they more frequently adopted modes of deference reflecting a concurrent view of authority in respect of domestic legislative or executive decisions (through restrained, or respectful, reasoning).

Various justifications were cited by adjudicators to justify deferring to these domestic decision-makers. Importantly, and different to existing accounts of

20 This is particularly interesting in light of the focus in existing literature on the utility of analogies from domestic approaches to judicial deference, all of which focus on a court's relationship with institutionally distinct decision-makers (administrative or legislative actors), rather than deference between more institutionally similar actors (courts). Additional issues associated with using such analogies as a basis for analysing international adjudicative deference are introduced in Chapter 9.

21 See the Appendix for raw totals per mode.

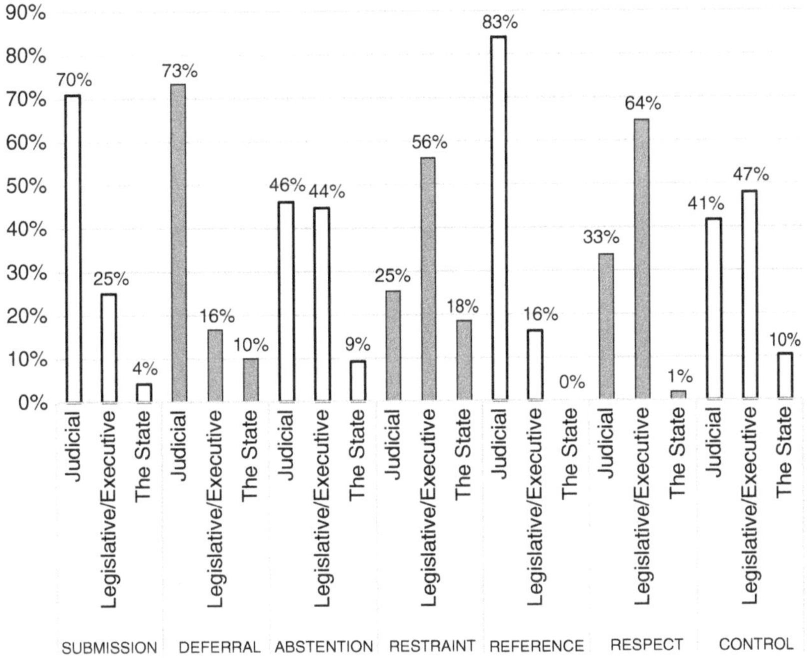

FIGURE 8.4 The decision-makers benefitting from the differing modes of deference (majority decisions)

deference, adjudicators did not rely merely on instrumental reasons to justify deference (for example, assessments of comparative expertise/competence and legitimacy). They also justified deference on prudential grounds (for example, to enhance the international adjudicator's legitimacy[22]), and non-instrumental grounds (for example, to signify empathy and respect for States[23]). A large number of the observed applications of deferential reasoning in majority decisions were not, moreover, accompanied by any explicit

22 *SD Myers (Dissent/SO-Schwartz), 12-Nov-2000 (UNCITRAL)*, para. 219 ('a finding of expropriation might contribute to public misunderstanding and anxiety about both this decision and the wider implications of the investment chapter of NAFTA').

23 See, for example, *Vistins (Dissent/SO-Bratza, Garlicki, Lorenzen, Tsotsoria and Pardalos), 25-Oct-2012 (ECtHR-GC)*, para. 6 (a State undergoing political transition 'may inevitably make mistakes' such that 'the State's margin of appreciation becomes wider'); *Glencore, Award, 27-Aug-2019*, para. 1458 ('States, and especially supervisory agencies, should enjoy deference. Supervisors are frequently required to take decision in short timeframes, making complex assessments of countervailing interests. Arbitral tribunals, sitting comfortably in the future, with full knowledge of the supervening events, must take the individual circumstances of each decision into consideration and avoid the temptation of using hindsight as the basis for assessing reasonableness').

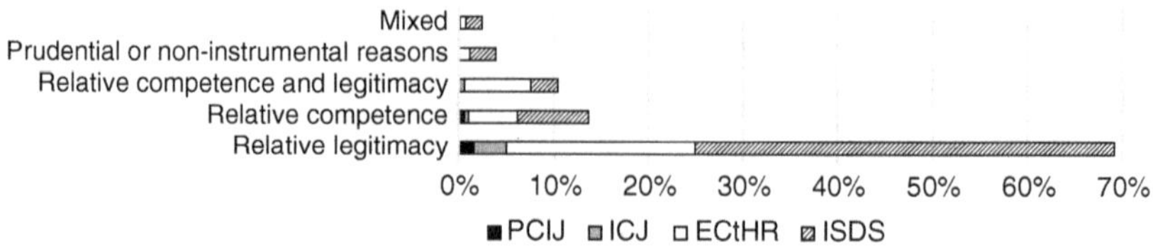

FIGURE 8.5 Justifications cited for according deference to domestic decision-making (majority decisions)

justification of the approach adopted by the adjudicator (n = 385, or 35 per cent of applications of deference).[24] In these instances, adjudicators referred to the need for 'deference' or a 'margin of appreciation' (or similar) but did not elaborate on what second-order reasons for deference supported the application of such deference to the facts before the adjudicator. This suggests that adjudicators frequently consider it unnecessary to justify *why* they are according deference to domestic decision-makers. This risks undercutting the transparency and predictability of approaches to deference, as well as the potential strategic benefits to adjudicators of according deference to States. Such silence may be due to deliberative compromises or drafting opacity, or because adjudicators view the attribution of deference to be uncontroversial or the reasons on which it is based to be self-evident. Adjudicators may, for example, judge it unnecessary to deal at length with the reasons for deference when the basis for deference has already been articulated by the parties in their oral or written submissions.

Examining the justifications cited by adjudicators (where such justification was provided) permits analysis of the types of reason that prompt international adjudicative deference. Figure 8.5 sets out the rationales most commonly cited by adjudicators in the analysed cases for according deference to domestic decision-makers.[25] It illustrates that, across the corpus of analysed decisions, the most commonly cited rationale for deference was the relative legitimacy of domestic decision-makers vis-à-vis international arbitrators (n = 485), usually on the grounds that it was not the court or tribunal's 'role' to second-guess domestic decision-making, or on the basis that deference allowed the court or tribunal to exhibit respect for the State's 'sovereignty' or the principle of subsidiarity. Regime-specific results, however, disclose variation as to the

24 No justification was provided in majority decisions as follows: PCIJ (n = 5, or 45 per cent of PCIJ applications); ICJ (n = 3, or 27 per cent of applications); ECtHR (n = 165, or 18 per cent of applications); ISDS (n = 212, or 34 per cent of applications).

25 This data reflects the justifications offered for deferring (or not deferring) in both applications and express non-applications of deference in majority and dissenting/separate opinions (n = 1,727).

rationales cited for according deference to domestic decision-makers. The ECtHR referred relatively more frequently to legitimacy *and* competence collectively to justify deference than adjudicators in the other regimes (n = 49). Considerations of relative legitimacy were most frequently invoked by investment tribunals to justify their approaches (n = 310). The PCIJ and ICJ did not invoke prudential or non-instrumental reasons for deference in either majority or dissenting/separate decisions, other than in one case where such reasons for deference were referred to in tandem with an analysis also of instrumental reasons ('mixed'). Adjudicators in the four regimes only occasionally adopted this latter approach of invoking instrumental, non-instrumental, and prudential reasons for deference in tandem ('mixed': n = 31).

These rationales for deference link to the accounts of authority introduced in Chapter 1. The preference exhibited by adjudicators for justifying approaches to deference on instrumental grounds indicates that international adjudicators predominantly defer (or say they are deferring) to domestic actors as an instrumental means of improving their decision-making, including as a means of producing a more empirically correct or normatively acceptable decision. As Chapter 1 indicated, however, some accounts of instrumental authority are more demanding than others. Some adjudicators, for instance, might be content to source legitimacy in an actor's legal credentials while others may require the actor to make decisions according to certain procedural or even substantive visions of legitimacy. The ECtHR's coupling of expertise/competence and legitimacy as the basis for according deference indicates, as foreshadowed in Chapter 1, that some accounts of authority recognise the normative epistemic authority (legitimacy) of actors only where they also hold empirical epistemic authority (expertise/competence). This discloses a relatively thicker conception of authority than that which informs the attribution of deference by adjudicators in the other regimes.

8.3 THE TREATMENT OF DEFERENCE OVER TIME

The frequency of, and approaches to, deference in international adjudication change over time. Adjustments to the jurisdictional and procedural features of international adjudicators will, for instance, impact their relative legitimacy and expertise vis-à-vis States. As international adjudicators gain jurisdiction over a wider range of topics and States, for example, they increasingly become generalists. While their expertise in interpreting and applying international law may increase, their expertise in national law or in the diverse and technical topics implicated in the disputes brought before them may decrease. Conversely, as adjudicators become more acquainted with particular types of disputes their authority to deal with them may improve, prompting a *decrease* in deferential reasoning over time.[26] Procedural adjustments may similarly impact deference. Procedures for party appointments of arbitrators, national judges, chambers, and judges ad hoc historically allowed disputing parties to select individuals as adjudicators on the basis that they held, inter alia, particular skills, knowledge or legitimacy relevant to a given dispute. Any adjustments to such procedures necessarily impact the balance of expertise and legitimacy between adjudicators and domestic officials. Equally, as international adjudicators confront 'backlash', the incidence of prudential deference may increase.[27] So, too, as States become repeat players before international courts and tribunals, adjudicators may begin to accord deference for non-instrumental reasons. This would include, for instance, deference accorded to States out of a sense of trust, or because the adjudicator begins to identify themselves with domestic officials endeavouring to apply protections for individuals as part of a broader epistemic community.[28] To explore the dynamic properties of deference, this section examines three trends observed in the analysed decisions.[29] Subsection 8.3.1 explores the frequency over time of applications of deference in international adjudicative decisions, Subsection 8.3.2 reports a rise in the application of modes of deference reflecting a concurrent view of authority, and Subsection 8.3.3 examines the dynamic features of the mode of respect.

8.3.1 *The Frequency of Deference over Time*

Analysis of deference in the analysed international private property decisions indicates that deferential reasoning has become *more* frequent over time. Most observed applications of deference in majority decisions date from the 1990s onwards with 97 per cent of all observed applications in majority decisions occurring between 1990 and 2019 (n = 977 out of 1,009 total observed applications). Raw totals are insufficient alone, however, to determine whether the increased number of observations per year is due to the increasing prevalence of deference in international adjudication. It may instead simply reflect an overall increase per year in the number of private property decisions rendered by international adjudicators, with the rise in deference indicating the

[26] Oesch (2003), p. 640.

[27] See, for example, Popelier and Van De Heyning (2017), p. 15; Gerards (2018a).

[28] Dan-Cohen (1994), p. 36.

[29] Results where appropriate are presented to permit the identification of jurisprudential shifts in the treatment of deference. This ensures that the quantitative analysis takes into account the qualitative approach developed in earlier chapters, to support the identification of jurisprudential shifts of legal – even if not numerical – significance.

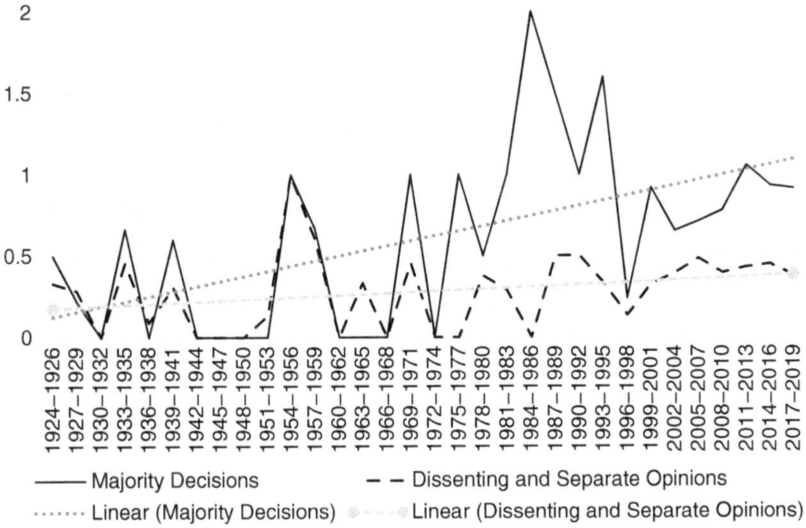

FIGURE 8.6 Applications of modes of deference over time (average per year: majority and dissenting opinions)

increased opportunities available to international adjudicators to examine domestic decision-making and, in so doing, to apply deferential reasoning. It is therefore necessary to analyse the relative frequency of deferential reasoning per decision. This can be measured by dividing the number of observed applications of deference per year by the number of decisions rendered that year. Figure 8.6 plots the relative frequency of observed applications of deference per decision over time. This analysis indicates that applications of deference in majority decisions peaked between 1984–9, with an average of two applications of deferential reasoning per decision in that period, and again in 1993–5. Average applications subsequently declined, but began to rise once more from 2004 onwards, dropping off again in more recent decisions. Since 2011, international adjudicators have applied some form of deference on average once in each majority decision. The trend lines indicate that the proportion of applications of deference per decision has increased overall over time for both majority and dissenting/separate decisions. This suggests that international adjudicators have become more deferential over time.

8.3.2 *The Rise of Concurrent Authority*

The connection between deference and authority makes it possible to explore whether the approaches of international adjudicators to deference disclose temporal shifts in how international adjudicators are conceptualising the structure of domestic decision-making authority. To investigate this issue, observed applications of the seven modes of deference were grouped by year, and categorised by reference to the structures of authority they represent according to the schema developed in Part II. As explained in more detail in that part, whereas the modes of submission, deferral, abstention, and control imply categorical views of authority (one decision-maker exercises their authority to the exclusion of the other), the modes of restraint, reference, and respect imply a more concurrent view of decision-making authority (both decision-makers work cooperatively or in tandem to exercise their decision-making authority). Figure 8.7 groups applications of the modes of deference according to whether they reflect a view of authority that is categorical (conclusive or suspensive) or concurrent. The figure reveals that, over time, adjudicators in the analysed decisions have opted to apply modes of deference reflecting a concurrent view of authority with more frequency than modes of deference reflecting a categorical view of authority.

Figure 8.7 indicates a rise from 1996 onwards in applications of modes of deference reflecting a concurrent view of authority. Given that this coincides with the increased issuance of decisions by both the ECtHR and investment treaty tribunals, Figure 8.8 isolates recorded observations of deference in majority decisions from these regimes. It illustrates the overall number of observed applications of modes of deference for the ECtHR (n = 357) and

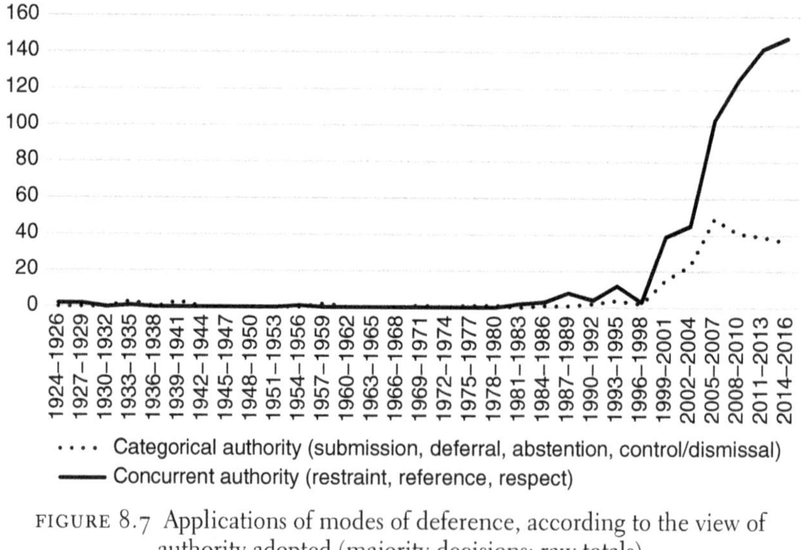

FIGURE 8.7 Applications of modes of deference, according to the view of authority adopted (majority decisions; raw totals)

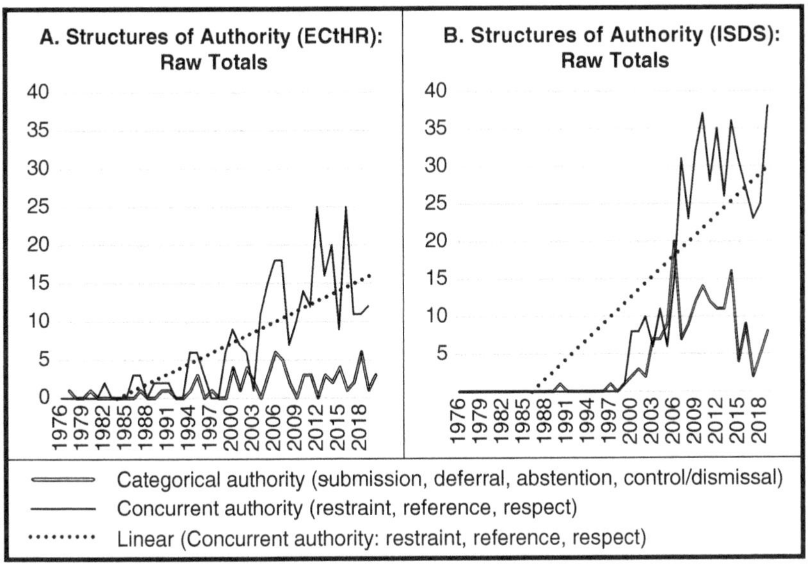

FIGURE 8.8 Structures of authority in ECtHR and investment tribunal decisions (raw totals: majority decisions)

investment tribunals (n = 630), according to the type of authority they represent. These graphs indicate that the propensity to adopt a particular view of authority has varied in both regimes, albeit more so in investment arbitration (Figure 8.8B) than for the ECtHR (Figure 8.8A).

To standardise the analysis of the structures of authority adopted by adjudicators in both settings, Figure 8.9 reports applications of each view of authority as a proportion of the total observed applications of deference per year. This figure reflects the proportion of decisions in which the ECtHR and investment tribunals adopted views of authority reflecting categorical approaches to analysing authority (the modes of submission, control/dismissal, deferral or abstention) or concurrent approaches (the modes of restraint, reference, or respect). The graphs in Figure 8.9 focus on the proportion in which these various approaches to authority were applied by adjudicators in the two regimes each year relative to other approaches to authority. Thus, for example, from 2011–13, the ECtHR applied a mode of deference fifty-eight times. Five of these recorded applications were instances in which the ECtHR applied a mode of submission, control/dismissal, deferral, or abstention. As these modes represent a categorical (conclusive or suspensive) view of authority, Graph A records that in that time period 9 per cent of observed applications (five out of fifty-eight) reflected this categorical view of authority. These graphs

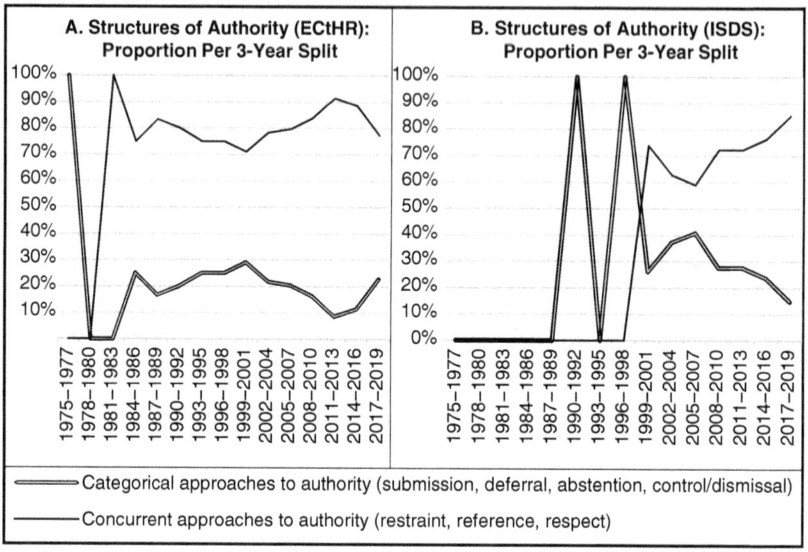

FIGURE 8.9 Structures of authority in ECtHR and investment tribunal decisions (proportion per three-year split: majority decisions)

indicate for both regimes a rise in the application of modes of deference exhibiting a concurrent view of authority relative to categorical views of authority over time. Approaches to authority began to diverge in investment arbitration decisions from 2005–7. Approaches diverged earlier in the decisions of the ECtHR (1991–2001) and from 2014 onwards appear to be reconverging (although concurrent approaches remain dominant, reflecting for example 77 per cent of applications of deference from 2017–19). Whereas the approach of the ECtHR shows a strong preference for concurrent approaches to authority (averaging 71 per cent of applications from 1975–2019; and 80 per cent from 1990–2019), this preference appears less strong for investment tribunals (averaging 50 per cent of applications from 1990–2019, but 70 per cent from 2008–19). These findings have systemic implications which are considered in more detail in Chapter 9.

8.3.3 *The Rise of Procedural Review*

Scholars have suggested that following increased critique and reform, the ECtHR began to favour procedural, rather than substantive, review of domestic decisions.[30] Chapter 7 linked such 'procedural' review to the mode of

30 See, especially, Arnardóttir (2015), p. 15; Spano (2018a), p. 9; Brems and Lavrysen (2013); Popelier and Van De Heyning (2017); Brems (2017); Huijbers (2017).

deference as respect, because it entails an international adjudicator determining that a domestic decision warrants deference conditionally, on the basis that a *proper procedure* was followed to make the decision. This approach differs to other possible approaches to deference as respect, including the attribution of deference because the decision was reached in good faith ('good faith review'), or because the decision exhibits particular qualities such as rationality or reasonableness ('substantive review'). Examining approaches to deference as respect over time provides a means to test the hypotheses of scholars that some adjudicators are increasingly favouring an approach to deference as respect that privileges procedural over substantive review.

Across the corpus of majority decisions, adjudicators were observed to apply a mode of respect 425 times in majority and separate/dissenting opinions. The mode of respect therefore comprised 35 per cent of all observed applications of deference (n = 1,196).[31] Most applications of a mode of respect focused on the substantive reasonableness or rationality of a decision or on *solange*/equivalence analysis (n = 166, or 39 per cent). This was followed by modes of respect focusing on the procedures associated with domestic decisions (n = 121, 28 per cent). Approximately 10 per cent of applications of a mode of deference as respect reflected good faith review (n = 44), and 22 per cent a mixed approach, combining elements of good faith review, procedural review and/or review for substantive reasonableness and rationality (n = 94). These aggregate results reveal that, collectively, international adjudicators exhibit some preference for a substantive – as opposed to procedural – approach to review in the mode of deference as respect. To examine whether a preference for procedural review has nonetheless manifested over time in different regimes, Figure 8.10A plots the observed applications of deference as respect over time in majority decisions (n = 369), beginning in 1990. This graph illustrates the dynamic quality of deference as respect. Figures 8.10B and 8.10C report regime-specific results based on observed applications of deference as respect in majority decisions from investment tribunals (n = 209, beginning in 1999) and the ECtHR (n = 158, beginning in 1982).

This regime-focussed analysis reveals that, whereas applications of procedural review increased in ECtHR decisions from 2010 to 2016, they have declined in more recent decisions, with applications of the mode of respect focusing increasingly on the substantive features of domestic decisions as a basis for deference (usually, reasonableness or rationality analysis). Applications of

[31] A mode of respect was applied in 369 of the 1,009 observed applications of deference in majority decisions (37 per cent); and in fifty-six of the 187 applications of deference in dissenting/separate decisions (30 per cent).

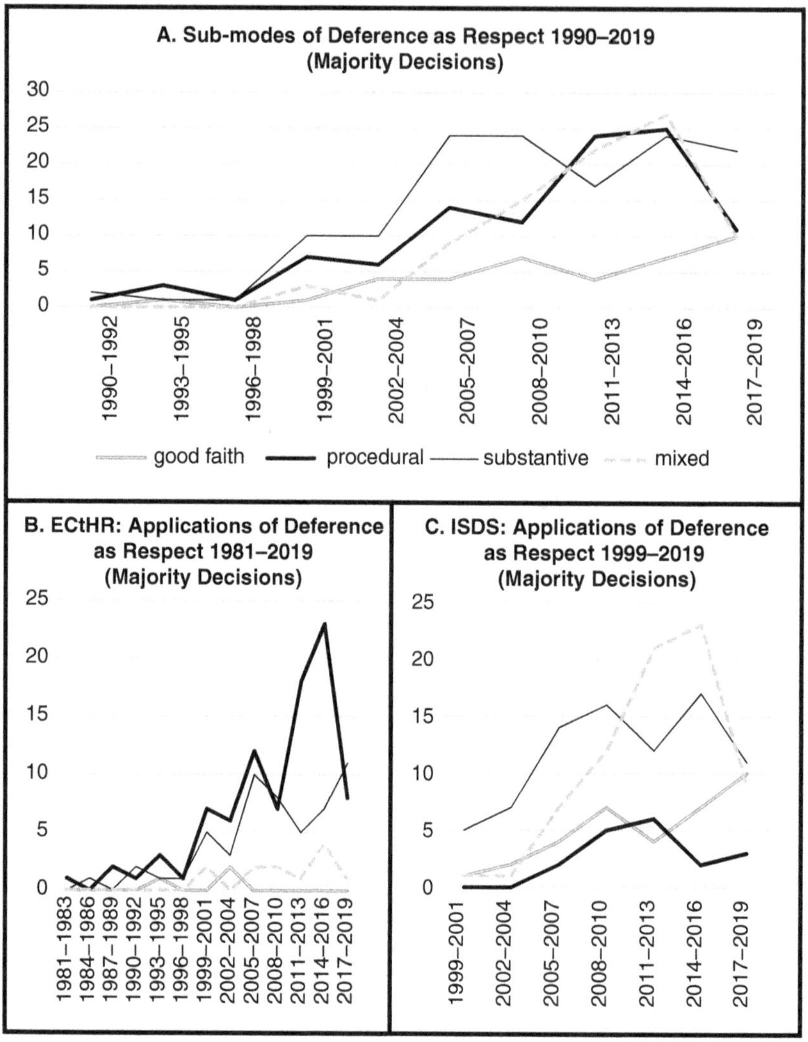

FIGURE 8.10 Grounds cited for according deference as respect (majority decisions)

procedural review have remained much less frequent in investment arbitration decisions over the same period. Decisions of investment tribunals instead indicate an increase in the application of a mixed mode of respect from 2004 to 2016, with good faith review becoming increasingly prevalent from 2013 onwards. For investment arbitrations, applications of a mode of deference focusing on the substantive rationality and reasonableness of domestic decisions peaked in 2008–10 and 2014–16. That mode of review was also more prevalent across the entire period compared to good faith review (both regimes), procedural review (for investment treaty tribunals), and mixed approaches to review (for the ECtHR).

Looking at the results in aggregate, it is also worth noting that the ECtHR most frequently deferred to domestic decisions made through particular processes (n = 89, or 56 per cent of applications of the mode of deference as respect in ECtHR majority decisions). Investment treaty tribunals have by contrast most frequently adopted a substantive view of the characteristics that will generate deference as respect for domestic decisions (n = 82, or 39 per cent of applications of the mode of deference as respect in investment majority decisions). As Chapters 1 and 4 demonstrated, this is significant because the different criteria applied in the mode of respect disclose an adjudicator's views as to how States ought to exercise their decision-making authority. A procedural approach, for example, indicates that the adjudicator links particular procedures with decision-making expertise and legitimacy. Such adjudicators might treat domestic decision-makers as expert authorities if they use particular procedures to reach their decisions. Alternatively, they may be considered legitimate authorities on the basis of a procedural view of legitimacy according to which some decision-making processes are considered normatively better than others. The above analysis reveals that the ECtHR is comparatively more likely than investment arbitrators to link a State's expertise or legitimacy to the procedural context within which it makes decisions. Investment tribunals, by contrast, exhibit a more substantive vision of expertise and legitimacy. Collectively, these results reveal that the grounds on which adjudicators accord 'respect' to domestic decisions differ both temporally and by regime.

8.4 CONCLUSIONS

This chapter analysed how adjudicators in the four regimes have selected between the seven modes of deference and the different structures of authority introduced in Part II. It used descriptive statistics to examine whether manifestations of 'deference' vary as to structure or frequency according to time and institutional context. Rather than providing an exhaustive account of how approaches to deference have changed over time or by regime, I have highlighted some key differences and changes in approaches to deference to emphasise the dynamic qualities of deference in international adjudication. This has served to demonstrate why a presentation of 'the' approach to deference in international adjudication is likely to be misleading. A static account of deference fails to account for its institutional, temporal, and contextual features. Deference is, instead, a dynamic tool of interface management. In addition to highlighting the dynamism of deference, the chapter has also illustrated its stability. Over the ninety-five years of analysed cases, deference has been consistently invoked to resolve conflicting claims to authority between international and domestic decision-makers. Deference is used to regulate a continued renegotiation of decision-making authority, in turn supporting the ongoing viability of international adjudication. It is to this systemic function of deference that Chapter 9 turns.

9

The Systemic Implications of Deference in International Adjudication

This chapter investigates the systemic role and implications of deference in international adjudication. Whereas Part II highlighted that approaches to deference *result in* different relationships between individual domestic and international decision-makers, this chapter shows that they also *result from* differing conceptualisations of the domestic/international interface. It demonstrates that the three conceptualisations of authority underlying the seven modes of deference introduced in Part II reflect distinct approaches to structuring the relationship between the international and domestic legal orders. Conclusive approaches to domestic decision-making authority disclose a monist view of that relationship, while suspensive approaches to authority reflect dualist structures, and concurrent approaches reveal pluralist paradigms. This analysis brings into focus the structural and systemic functions of deference in international adjudication.

The chapter is divided into two substantive sections. Section 9.1 demonstrates that much existing analysis of deference in international adjudication has been based on, without explicitly acknowledging, an assumed relationship between the domestic and international legal orders. This has precluded a comprehensive analysis of the structural implications of adjudicators adopting different approaches to deference in international adjudication. Section 9.2 proposes inverting the enquiry. Rather than starting from an assumption as to how deference *should* be structured, it shows how approaches to deference can instead be analysed and conceptually distinguished by reference to how they structure the interface between the international and domestic legal orders. Section 9.2 demonstrates that, conceptually, different modes of deference are better adapted to structuring the relations between decision-makers operating variously within the *same* (monist), *different* (dualist), or *blended* (pluralist) legal systems. This means that different approaches to deference hold systemic significance.

9.1 CONCEPTUALISING THE RELATIONSHIP BETWEEN INTERNATIONAL AND DOMESTIC DECISION-MAKERS: THE LIMITS OF RECOURSE TO DOMESTIC ANALOGIES

This section highlights the structural assumptions underlying the use of domestic analogies as a frame for analysing and critiquing approaches to deference in international adjudication. Subsection 9.1.1 notes that existing analyses of deference in international adjudication have focused almost exclusively on how international adjudicators might make better use of the approaches to deference applied in particular States in the context of judicial review under constitutional and administrative law. As Section 9.1.1 explains, this has made existing accounts of international adjudicative deference both blinkered and partial. More problematically, however, the use of such domestic analogies has been inadequately theorised. Subsection 9.1.2 demonstrates that domestic constitutional and administrative law approaches to deference are based on particular structural assumptions as to the relationship between the deferring adjudicator and the actor benefitting from deference. Using such analogies as a basis for analysing deference in international adjudication imports assumptions as to the structural relationship between domestic and international decision-makers, and the sources of domestic decision-making authority. Rather than embedding these assumptions into an analysis of international adjudicative deference, Section 9.2 shows instead how the enquiry can be productively inverted.

9.1.1 *Deference and Domestic Analogies*

Studies of deference in international adjudication have to date drawn heavily on domestic law analogies. Commentators invoke, in particular, analogies to domestic administrative and constitutional law approaches to deference.[1] Such accounts do not argue that domestic approaches provide a source of international law, but instead endorse particular approaches to deference by analogy to domestic practice. Commentators typically justify such recourse to domestic analogies by arguing that international adjudication functions analogously to domestic 'public law' adjudication.[2] Some

1 See, for example, von Bogdandy (2006), p. 226; Gardbaum (2009); Van Harten and Loughlin (2006), pp. 121–3; Henckels (2015), p. 12; Schill (2012), p. 15; von Bogdandy and Venzke (2014); Vadi (2018), pp. 31–54. On the use of constitutional analogies in the analysis of international law generally, see Ulfstein (2012); Cass (2001), pp. 51–2; Goldsmith III and Levinson (2009); Broude (2012), p. 527.

2 See, for example, Vadi and Gruszczynski (2013), p. 623; Van Harten (2007a); Katselas (2012), p. 139; Alter (2008b), p. 41; Henckels (2015); Ortino (2014); Burke-White and von Staden (2010), p. 285. On the difficulties of distinguishing 'public' and 'private' law disputes more generally,

scholars argue that international private property cases are akin to domestic administrative or constitutional disputes because they concern the exercise of public powers impacting private rights. They emphasise that such disputes concern the exercise of 'public' power, and derive from a 'vertical' power dynamic between the disputing parties.[3] Other scholars argue that international private property disputes are analogous to domestic public law disputes because they have the potential to impact third parties, including the public generally.[4]

Such uses of domestic analogies are unsurprising given that, as Crawford observes: '[O]ur thinking about law is infiltrated, marinated, drenched with the influence of national legal systems'.[5] Using domestic analogies can, however, be problematic. Domestic analogies can be biased, including because they are usually drawn from the domestic practice of particular, often western, States. They may also be blinkered. Scholars analysing deference in international adjudication have, for example, largely eschewed analogies to deference subsisting in other fields of domestic law. They have not invoked as the basis of analogy, for example, deference between the units of federalised systems or between sovereign States under private international law.[6] Existing analyses have also drawn almost exclusively from domestic approaches to deference between actors of different institutional types. This includes, in particular, a focus on the principles of deference applicable between judicial and non-judicial decision-makers.[7] As Chapter 8 noted, however, international adjudicators defer in equal measure to domestic judicial and non-judicial decision-makers. This may mean that the dominant focus on deference in domestic public law adjudication excludes from analysis other structures for analysing deference that could be equally or more analogous to the issues confronting international adjudicators grappling with questions of deference in international private property disputes. This could include, for instance, analysis of approaches to deference between judicial actors within the same – or different – domestic legal systems.

see Rosenfeld (2013), p. 125. For criticisms of such analogies, see Alvarez (2016); Schwobel (2012).

3 Roberts (2013), p. 63–4; Hepburn (2014), p. 710.

4 Schill (2010a), p. 405; Casini (2014), p. 408; Goldmann (2016); Burke-White and von Staden (2010), p. 285; von Bogdandy and Venzke (2014), p. 112.

5 Crawford (2006), p. 345.

6 See, however, reference to such analogies in Arangio-Ruiz (1990), para. 106; Klabbers et al. (2009), p. 31; Deneen (1930), p. 178; Ginsburg (2016), p. 205.

7 Inter-court deference is typically considered from the perspective of *national* judges deferring to *international* judicial decisions, and not vice versa. See, for example, Alford (2002); Kanetake and Nollkaemper (2016); Peters (2016).

Most proponents of domestic analogies accept that domestic approaches cannot be transported wholesale into international law, but must instead be adapted to fit the international setting. The use of domestic analogies to inform analysis of international adjudicative deference has typically not been accompanied, however, by detailed analysis of the structural assumptions on which such analogies are predicated. The importance of reflection on such structural assumptions is particularly pressing for any study of deference. This is because domestic approaches to deference derive from distinct structural relationships between the deferring decision-maker and the beneficiary of deference. Reliance on domestic analogies depends on such relationships mapping to those which subsist between international adjudicators and domestic decision-makers. The use of domestic analogies to analyse international adjudicative deference thus frequently starts from an (often unarticulated) assumption as to the structure of the relationship between domestic and international decision-makers, and the sources of State decision-making power.[8] Subsection 9.1.2 introduces the key structural and systemic assumptions imported into the analysis of international adjudicative deference through the use of domestic public law analogies.

9.1.2 *The Systemic Assumptions Underlying Domestic Deference Analogies*

Recourse to domestic analogies introduces several structural assumptions into analyses of international adjudicative deference. One such assumption concerns the source(s) of domestic decision-making authority and the nature of State sovereignty. A second assumption concerns the systemic relationship between domestic decision-makers and international adjudicators. This subsection considers these assumptions in turn, to highlight the difficulties associated with reliance on domestic analogies to develop and critique international adjudicative approaches to deference. In doing so, it sets the stage for Section 9.2, which proposes eschewing the structural assumptions and normative lens of domestic analogies. It examines instead what different approaches to deference in international adjudication themselves reveal about the structure of international law and its relationship to domestic legal orders.

8 See, similarly, Krisch (2010), p. 35. Shany, for example, develops 'pragmatic' principles yet bases them on a view of international-domestic conflict as a conflict between 'different normative orders': Shany (2007), pp. 21–2.

Like most systems of law, international law presupposes the existence of subjects of law (States), yet also brings those subjects into legal existence.[9] A question thus arises as to whether 'sovereignty *precedes* law or *results from* law'.[10] This affects whether State sovereignty is treated as a legal construct, according to which States derive their powers (sovereignty) from international law, or, rather, as a fact, in which case State powers subsist independently of international law. Hobbes, a proponent of the 'factist' view, took the view that that 'the sovereign is external to the normative system of law that emanates from it'.[11] Such a view of sovereignty adopts the perspective that 'international law is superior to the State in the sense that it sets a legal limit to the State's power, but not in the sense that this power is a delegation of international law'.[12] More radically, Schmitt contended that law cannot control the fact of sovereignty,[13] such that 'the sovereign stands outside the law'.[14] Kelsen, by contrast, adopted a 'legal' view, according to which sovereignty 'derives from and is recognized by the law'.[15] On this view, international law determines the validity of domestic legal orders and State competencies on the international plane.[16] Under the 'legal' view, international law provides a source of State rights, rather than merely a limitation on those rights.[17]

Without explicitly engaging with these debates, analogies to domestic public law approaches to deference implicitly take a particular view as to the nature of State sovereignty. Deference in domestic administrative law, for example, typically arises from an understanding that a court's role is to review 'whether the actions of administrative bodies have been exercised within the powers conferred by Parliament'.[18] The review function of the court derives, on this understanding, from a theory of delegation. A legislature is taken to delegate decision-making authority to another actor, with a court in turn having some power of control over that delegated decision-making authority.[19] Administrative law principles of deference derive from this structural relationship between decision-makers. Thus, for example, the United States' doctrine of *Chevron* deference prompts deference to administrative

9 Hart (1994), p. 149; Buchanan (2009); Cutler (2001), p. 137.
10 Crawford (2014), p. 75–6.
11 Crawford (2014), p. 77, referring to Hobbes (1996), p. 184.
12 de Visscher (1968), p. 104, quoting Anzilotti.
13 Schmitt (2005), p. 5.
14 Crawford (2014), p. 77.
15 Ibid, p. 78.
16 Broude (2012); Olivier (1988), p. 100; O'Connell (1960), p. 433.
17 Oppenheim et al. (1996), p. 12.
18 van Schooten and Sweeney (2003), p. 441.
19 Daly (2012), pp. 55, 60–1, 70, 189, 206.

interpretations of ambiguous statutes based on a view that the legislature intended the agency – and not the judiciary – to have authority to make reasonable interpretations to resolve the meaning of ambiguous text.[20] The role of the court is reduced to regulating permissible interpretations. It is only empowered to reject interpretations that are not reasonable (on the basis that these are outside the bounds of the legislature's delegation of power).[21] Judicial review on this model is directed towards ensuring that administrative officials exercise their power within the bounds of what has been delegated by parliament.[22]

Using administrative law analogies to analyse the relationship between international adjudicators and States thus implies a particular view of State sovereignty. Deference under administrative law presumes a vertical dynamic between decision-makers, with a 'legislature' at the top of an apex. The role of the court is to 'police the boundaries' stipulated by that legislature as constraints on the powers of other actors.[23] Using this paradigm to analyse international adjudicative deference presupposes a view that a State's competence (sovereignty) has been delegated from some higher authority and restricted in some way by that delegation.[24] In this administrative law paradigm, the international adjudicator would derive its approach to deference by reference to, for example, the intent of the original delegator of the State's power. An administrative law paradigm thus adopts a 'legal' view of State sovereignty, with the applicability of domestic administrative law approaches to deference in international adjudication implicitly relying on a perception that States hold 'delegated rather than original authority'.[25] The international adjudicator operating within such a paradigm might conclude, for example, that an international 'community' sits at the apex of the decision-making structure and use background principles of international law to analyse the issue of deference. It might conclude, for example, that the community intended the State to enjoy sovereignty only to the extent that it exercises such sovereignty 'reasonably'. In this structure, the adjudicator would consider itself empowered to police the boundaries of that delegated State sovereignty. It would hold power to review (and reject) exercises of

20 Krotoszynski Jr (2002), p. 736. See, similarly Daly (2012), p. 287 (discussing the position under English law).

21 Daniel (2017). See, for extension of this analysis to investment treaty arbitration, Katselas (2012), p. 140; Van Harten and Loughlin (2006), pp. 121–3; Van Harten (2007b), p. 372.

22 See, however, Young (2017) (analysing different approaches to conceptualising the role of courts in systems of constitutional and administrative review).

23 Daly (2011), p. 694.

24 Arangio-Ruiz (1996), p. 459.

25 Dyzenhaus (2011), p. 364.

sovereignty it deems to be unreasonable.[26] Such limits on a State's authority might be derived from certain theories about the nature of State sovereignty. In Locke's social contract theory, for example, legislative power is theorised to have been established by an agreement between individuals in a society in order to permit 'the preservation of the society, and (as far as will consist with the public good) of every person in it'.[27] With the delegation of legislative power from the people to a legislature, however, come certain implied limits. As Locke explains:

> [A]bsolute arbitrary power, or governing without settled standing laws, can neither of them consist with the ends of society and government, which men would not quit the freedom of the state of nature for . . . It cannot be supposed that they should intend, had they a power so to do, to give to any one, or more, an absolute arbitrary power over their persons and estates, and put a force into the magistrate's hand to execute his unlimited will arbitrarily upon them. This were to put themselves into a worse condition than the state of nature.[28]

According to this theory, the original delegation of legislative power to a State (from individuals in a state of nature) is effected for particular purposes. Those purposes, in turn, form implied limits on the scope of the delegated power. For Locke, the purpose of entering into a social contract was to escape a state of nature, and, with it, the arbitrary and non-transparent decision-making structures of primitive societies. Similar constraints might be supplied by other delegation-based theories of State sovereignty, including the recent debates about whether States exercise their powers as 'agents' or 'trustees' of their citizens.[29]

International adjudication could instead be analogised to domestic constitutional judicial review. International law in such a paradigm becomes akin to a domestic constitution. Constitutional and international obligations might be considered analogous because they provide sources of State power,[30] or 'constitute' political systems by manifesting the values of particular communities.[31] Alternatively, international law could be analogised to domestic constitutional law because international and constitutional courts perform similar roles in *constraining* domestic power.[32] This might include adjudication of 'evolutive' or 'living' obligations, or capacity to review State conduct for

26 Mullan (2006), p. 47; Ostrovsky (2005), p. 59.
27 Locke (1988), para. 131.
28 Ibid, para. 137.
29 See, for example, Benvenisti (2013); Tomuschat (2001).
30 van Asselt (2014); Stone Sweet (2009), p. 627.
31 See, generally, Letsas (2013); Burke-White and von Staden (2010), p. 294; Croquet (2010), p. 361; de Wet (2007).
32 See, especially, von Bogdandy (2006), p. 226; Gardbaum (2009).

breach of human rights.[33] The structure of international and constitutional obligations is also frequently analogised. Scholars argue, for example, that both bodies of law operate as a 'pre-commitment strategy', insulating certain rules from easy amendment to bind future generations.[34]

Differing to administrative analogies, constitutional analogies conceptualise State sovereignty not as delegated from another entity, but instead as akin to a prerogative power.[35] This view classifies State powers as original, rather than delegated: the State's powers constitute, and are not constituted by, the international legal order.[36] Constitutional analogies conceptualise international adjudicators as empowered to interpret and apply restrictions that States consensually adopt as a limit to their otherwise plenary powers. Without such limits, State powers – akin to prerogative powers – are conceptualised as 'a legally uncontrollable or non-justiciable area'.[37] In this paradigm, deferential review – particularly in the form of submission – might be favoured if State power is conceived to incorporate core sovereign functions that cannot be fettered.[38]

While they imply differing views as to the nature of State sovereignty, constitutional and administrative law analogies both share in common a structural assumption as to the systemic unity between international adjudicators and domestic decision-makers. Both analogies draw on approaches to deference that regulate conflicting claims to authority within unitary domestic systems, rather than conflicting claims to authority emanating from separate systems. Different analogies could, by contrast, be invoked as the basis for analysing deference in international adjudication. Private international law analogies, for instance, would supply a basis for addressing interactions between decision-making authority exercised by actors operating in separate legal orders. Analysis of comity and deference between federated units might similarly supply a basis for examining approaches to deference in autonomous but connected legal communities. Or, analysis of deference between domestic courts could supply a basis for examining deference between institutionally similar decision-makers within the same (or even separate) legal systems. Yet such approaches have been less frequently invoked as sources of inspiration to

33 See, further, von Bogdandy and Venzke (2014), p. 112; Legg (2012), p. 71; Croquet (2010), pp. 361–2; Letsas (2013); White (2000), p. 281; O'Donoghue (2013), p. 1028.

34 Staton and Moore (2011), p. 558; Dunoff (2006); Alter (2008b), p. 41; Schneiderman (1996), p. 514; Gardbaum (2009).

35 Daly (2012), p. 268; Lauterpacht (1930), p. 134; Arangio-Ruiz (1996), p. 459; Crawford and Brownlie (2012), p. 17.

36 Dupuy (1997), p. 3; Peters (2006), p. 581.

37 Dyzenhaus (2003), p. 24.

38 Miles (2010), p. 24.

inform approaches to deference to domestic decision-makers for international adjudicators.[39]

Increasingly, a growing body of scholarship has recognised the impact of these underlying systemic assumptions on the analysis of techniques capable of regulating diversity and fragmentation between *international* legal regimes. Several scholars argue that particular conflict-mediation techniques will be more appropriate for application within a unified international system, and others to fragmented sets of self-contained international legal regimes.[40] Section 9.2 considers the implications of this literature for the analysis of deference to domestic actors in international adjudication. In what follows, theories abut the relationship between the international and domestic legal orders are combined with the burgeoning literature on the nature of public international law as a legal system, to consider what different approaches to deference reveal about adjudicative perceptions as to the relationship(s) between the international and national orders.

9.2 DEFERENCE AS A LENS FOR MAPPING THE RELATIONSHIP BETWEEN THE INTERNATIONAL AND DOMESTIC LEGAL ORDERS

The relationship between domestic and international legal orders has traditionally been analysed through the lens of 'monist', 'dualist', and 'pluralist' theories of law. Like deference, these theories identify the '*hierarchy* as to which *institutions* have the final say and which *norms* have the superior status'.[41] Whereas deference regulates interactions between domestic and international decision-makers in practice, these theories provide a structural rationalisation to theorise that relationship in principle. The previous parts illustrated that deference can be used to allocate authority between decision-makers both vertically (upwards and downwards in hierarchies) and horizontally (laterally between peers). The application of deference therefore does not presuppose a particular structural relationship between decision-makers. Its manifestation may, nevertheless, indicate the structural assumptions made by international adjudicators concerning their relationships to domestic decision-makers. As such, instead of arguing from theory (monism/dualism/pluralism) to practice (deference), this section

39 Scholars have also suggested that in private (or commercial) forms of arbitration, there might be a 'no deference paradigm': Schill (2012); Roberts (2013). The structural analysis of deference in this book indicates that there is not – in principle – a reason to object to deference applying in such systems per se. The low use of deference in such settings may instead simply reflect the fewer opportunities afforded to adjudicators in such systems to grapple with questions of deference related to State decision-making. The issue is returned to in Chapter 10.

40 See, especially, Kuo (2013), p. 449; Krisch (2010), p. 76; Cohen (2010a), p. 49; Michaels and Pauwelyn (2010).

41 Kanetake (2016a), pp. 38.

examines how the enquiry can be productively inverted. Rather than deriving deference from an a priori conceptualisation as to the structure of the relationship between domestic and international law, it examines how international adjudicators manifest views on these conflicting theories through the adoption of different modes of deference. The analysis further inverts the usual use made of theories of monism, dualism, and pluralism. Instead of using such theories unidirectionally to analyse the reception of international law in different domestic legal systems, it uses such theories to analyse how *international* adjudicators interact with *domestic* actors and systems.

9.2.1 *Monism: Conclusive Authority and Trumping as a Means of Interface Mediation*

Monism adopts a unitary view of the relationship between the domestic and international legal orders. A theory of monism posits that the sources of international and domestic law are the same, and that these bodies of law regulate the same conduct, subjects, or subject matters.[42] Thus, monism envisages that all law – whether domestic or international – is a unified body of law.[43] Monists therefore conceptualise international and domestic law as subsisting within a single legal order.[44] According to monists, the international and domestic legal orders are 'coherent and consistent'.[45] Monists argue that both international and domestic law 'trace their validity as law from some system from which they are logically derived'.[46] To achieve coherence, monism entails hierarchy between the legal orders comprising the legal system. This requirement for hierarchy has prompted the development of two principal variants of monism. According to internationalist monism, international law is superior to domestic law.[47] Internationalist monists conceive of domestic law as 'derived by way of delegation from the international legal system'.[48]

42 See, further, Lauterpacht (1946), p. 47; Kelsen (2003), p. 404; Kammerhofer (2009), pp. 233–4; Somek (2007), p. 426.

43 See, especially, Kelsen (1960); Starke (1936); Wang (1937), pp. 187–8; Jones (1935), p. 7. See, also, Higgins (2009), p. 927; D'Alterio (2011), p. 414; Oppenheim et al. (1996), p. 54; Margolis (1955), pp. 117–18.

44 See, for example, Scelle (1984), p. 6 (Volume II) (in French); Thierry (1990); Cassese (1990).

45 Crawford and Brownlie (2012), p. 48.

46 Jones (1935), p. 7.

47 See, especially, Verdross (1971), p. 119; Kunz (1934); Kunz (1938). See, further, discussion in Kelsen (1960); Gordillo (2011), p. 1; O'Connell (1960), p. 432; Oppenheim et al. (1996), p. 54; Petersen (2009), p. 5.

48 Oppenheim et al. (1996), p. 54. See, for example, Kelsen (1960), p. 629; Verdross (1930) (in German). See, further, on Verdross' monism Simma (1995); Janzen (1935).

According to this view, international law authorises and legitimises the decision-making power of States,[49] albeit that they still hold some 'power to determine the individuals whose behavior forms the content of the obligations and rights established by international law'.[50] By contrast, under a theory of nationalist monism, domestic law takes primacy.[51] For nationalist monists, international law is derived from domestic law or from the sovereign will of the State.[52] Accordingly, international law binds the State only if it accepts that effect and incorporates the rules of international law into its own national legal order.[53] Most legal theorists accept that the choice between these variants is 'outside the science of law' and falls to be 'determined by political considerations'.[54]

Within a monist paradigm, decision-makers may need to select between two or more rules (or even decisions) that could govern a given situation. As Kelsen explained:

> [I]t is not possible to assume the simultaneous validity of two systems of norms regulating human behavior, if these systems are valid independently from each other and therefore may conflict with each other, the one prescribing that a certain action ought to be performed and the other that this action ought not to be performed. Two norms, one of which prescribes that A ought to be, and the other that A ought not to be, cannot be assumed as simultaneously valid, just as two judgments, the one of which asserts that A is, whereas the other declares that A is not, cannot be true together.[55]

Monists manage such conflicts by implying hierarchy into the relationship between rule creators or decision-makers, such as to permit one or other of the rules or decisions to prevail. The conflict between these rules or decisions is in effect a conflict between claims to the final authority to regulate or decide a given matter. Several tools are capable of mediating conflicting claims to authority within a monist system. These include approaches

49 Kwiecien (2011), p. 37; Crawford (2014), para. 271; Kammerhofer (2009), p. 242.

50 Kelsen (1960), pp. 629. See, also, O'Connell (1960), pp. 433–4; Scelle (1943), p. 21.

51 See, especially, Jellinek (1968) (in German). See, for further analysis of Jellinik's monism, Duncan (2004), pp. 513–16; Koskenniemi (2001), p. 200; Duguit (1917), pp. 123–4; Von Bernstorff (2012). See, also, Gordillo (2011), p. 1; O'Connell (1960), pp. 432, 437; Kelsen (1960), p. 629.

52 See, especially, Bergbohm (1877), p. 39 (in German); Jellinek (1968), p. 6 (in German). See, further, Kolb (2007).

53 See, further, Kelsen (1960), p. 630. Kelsen argues this means 'only the sovereignty of one state could be presupposed [which would] ... exclude the sovereignty of all other states': pp. 623–33; Duguit (1917), pp. 124–5.

54 Kelsen (1960), p. 640. Cf. however, Verdross (1923), pp. 33–4 (in German).

55 Kelsen (1960), p. 629.

focusing on 'status' (*lex superior*),[56] 'specificity' (*lex specialis*),[57] or 'temporality' (*lex posterior*)[58] to mediate conflict.[59] Such tools are tailored to regulate conflicts 'within a single legal system'.[60] As Michaels and Pauwelyn explain, this is because they:

> work smoothly only insofar as we can assume that (1) all legal rules in play coexist within a single overarching system and (2) the decision which rule to apply can be imputed, albeit by fiction, to a unitary lawmaker with a coherent legislative intent.[61]

The *lex specialis* rule, for example, presupposes a legislature with a unified legislative will. This is because the rule 'is grounded in the presumption that a legislator, in regulating a specific case, wants to carve out an exception from the general rules existing for a set of matters'.[62] All such rules presuppose a coherent organising principle that provides 'a common, objective standard' to identify rules capable of trumping others.[63]

Monist approaches to managing conflict depend on a conclusive view of authority. Such a view of authority closes off dialogue about authority, instead using trumping principles to manage conflict. This prompts the application of blunt tools of interface mediation. A decision either applies or not, a law is either binding or not. As argued in Part II, the modes of submission and control indicate that an international adjudicator is operating with such a conclusive view of authority. These modes are founded on hierarchy and supremacy between domestic and international decision-makers. They indicate that international adjudicators are treating one decision-maker as supreme in a given area, in a way which divests (or denies) the other decision-maker's authority. Whereas the mode of submission tracks the theory of nationalist monism, that of control reflects an approach of internationalist monism. Adjudicators in these modes collapse the structural boundaries between 'international' and 'national', adopting instead a unitary view of these orders to determine the conflicting claims to authority emanating from them.

56 This is a principle of trumping, according to which a 'higher' norm prevails.
57 This rule prompts application of the more detailed or specific norm.
58 The applicable norm would be that which was most recently enacted.
59 McLachlan (2005), p. 285. See, similarly, Michaels and Pauwelyn (2010), p. 23; Kammerhofer (2005), p. 126.
60 Cohen (2012b), p. 389.
61 Michaels and Pauwelyn (2010), p. 24. See, similarly, Ruse-Khan (2013), p. 310.
62 Michaels and Pauwelyn (2010), p. 25.
63 Ibid, p. 36.

9.2.2 *Dualism: Suspensive Authority and Non-Engagement as a Means of Interface Mediation*

The relationship between international adjudicators and domestic decision-makers could alternatively be conceptualised using a dualist paradigm. Under a theory of dualism, the international and domestic legal orders are conceptualised as operating on distinct planes.[64] Dualists typically conceptualise the domestic and international legal orders as separate on the basis that they derive from different legal sources, or regulate different subjects or subject matters.[65] Whereas, for example, international law might be conceptualised as governing the relations between States, domestic law might be considered to apply to persons within each State (a dualism of subjects).[66] For dualists, these separations mean that domestic and international claims to decision-making authority cannot conflict because 'the very nature of the disputes [each legal order] can decide is different'.[67] Dualists thus consider there to be a 'parallelism' between the international and domestic legal orders. These legal orders are treated as separate and independent, such that decisions made in one order do not impact decisions made in another. Each order is instead 'supreme in its own sphere',[68] with neither having 'hegemony over the other'.[69] This means that international and domestic law 'at most touch one another but never overlap'.[70]

The adoption by an international adjudicator of a dualist paradigm could designate one of two approaches. Dualism could, on a first understanding, merely designate that each order determines for itself the role of rules from the other order.[71] In this sense, all approaches to deference canvassed thus far could be characterised as 'dualist' perspectives, because they entail an international adjudicator determining by application of international law the role to be played by domestic decisions at the international level. A dualist

64 See, especially, Anzilotti (1928) (in Italian); Triepel (1923) (in French); Jessup (1956), pp. 96–7. See, also, Gaja (1992). The plurality of national legal orders means 'dualist' approaches are actually 'pluralist': Ulfstein (2012), p. 581. However, 'pluralism' commonly denotes a different type of interaction, and given acceptance of the term 'dualism' for designating the interaction described under that label here, the term 'dualism' has been selected for ease of reference.

65 O'Connell (1960), p. 436. See, also, Wang (1937), pp. 190–1; Margolis (1955), p. 119; Krisch (2017); Klabbers and Piiparinen (2013), p. 100.

66 Crawford and Brownlie (2012), p. 48. See, also, Shany (2007), p. 79.

67 El Hayek and Gilles (2014), p. 580. See, also, Arangio-Ruiz (1990), p. 342.

68 Oppenheim et al. (1996), p. 53.

69 Crawford (2014), para. 276.

70 Triepel (1899), p. 111, translation from Simma (1995), p. 44.

71 O'Connell (1960), p. 439; Crawford and Brownlie (2012), p. 48; Krisch (2010), pp. 291–2; Kanetake (2016a), p. 26.

approach could alternatively manifest as the view that domestic and international decision-makers occupy distinct zones of decision-making authority. Under this view, dualism focuses on the relationship of legal subjects to the law. A dualist approach to the relationship between international and domestic law denies that these bodies of law can 'conflict', because they regulate 'two mutually exclusive sets of relations that can never by any possibility be identical in content'.[72] The following discussion adopts this latter perspective of dualism. 'Dualism' is used to designate approaches to deference that respond to conflicting claims to authority by deferring or denying the existence of any such conflict.

Unlike the tools applied to regulate intra-system conflicts in a monist paradigm, the tools used to mediate conflicting claims to authority within a dualist paradigm presuppose (i) a lack of hierarchy between the different systems; and (ii) a lack of a uniform legislative intent 'under which different values could be balanced'.[73] The aims of inter- and intra-systems conflict rules are also different. In conflicts between systems, the decision-maker attempts to achieve 'coordination'.[74] By contrast, in conflicts within the one system the adjudicator attempts to achieve 'coherence'.[75] In the latter, intra- system conflicts, theories of monism will apply to prompt the use of tools to settle conflict that favour hierarchy or the pre-eminence of one decision-maker over another. In inter-system conflicts, by contrast, dualist approaches apply to recognise the existence of multiple systems and the potential for 'overlaps and intersections' between them.[76] Decision-makers in dualist systems operate in the absence of a formal hierarchy, and thus must mediate their relations as equals or decide to ignore one another altogether.[77]

The application of inter-system conflict rules, similarly to intra-system conflict rules, typically results in all-or-nothing approaches.[78] One system will apply to the exclusion of another. This is because such rules focus on 'maintain[ing] the internal integrity of each system by designating one or the other' as applicable to the matter in issue.[79] Inter-system conflict tools also

[72] Jones (1935), p. 5.
[73] Michaels and Pauwelyn (2010), p. 27. See, similarly, Dupuy and Viñuales (2013).
[74] Colangelo (2016), p. 34; Shany (2006), p. 76; Lehavi (2015).
[75] Colangelo (2016), pp. 17, 24.
[76] Ruse-Khan (2013), p. 332.
[77] Story (1834), p. 9; Steinhardt (1991), p. 523.
[78] Private international law conflict rules, for example, regulate relations between decision-makers in different national legal systems: Michaels and Pauwelyn (2010), p. 27; Ruse-Khan (2013), pp. 321–340; Fischer-Lescano and Teubner (2004), p. 1021; Colangelo (2009), p. 883; Jenks (1964), p. 442; Mann (1987), p. 437; Douglas (2003), p. 236.
[79] Michaels and Pauwelyn (2010), p. 31. See, similarly, Ruse-Khan (2013); Berman (2012), p. 249; Dupuy and Viñuales (2013).

foreclose dialogue about conflicting claims to authority. Rather than using *trumping* principles to preclude dialogue, however, dualist approaches typically instead favour *non-engagement*. Underlying non-engagement is a suspensive, rather than conclusive or concurrent, view of authority. Suspensive views of authority respond to conflicting claims to authority by deferring or denying the existence of such conflict altogether.

The clearest example of this approach to conflict is represented by the mode of deference as abstention. Adopting this mode, an international adjudicator delineates separate and exclusive zones of domestic and international decision-making authority. Doing so allows the adjudicator to adopt a perspective that there is not 'in fact a true conflict of norms at all'.[80] Such approaches avoid conflict by using principles of non-engagement. Using such an approach, an adjudicator would recognise – and so defer to – a domestic actor's claim to decision-making authority by declining to exercise its own authority on a given topic. Deference as deferral also signifies an inter-system view of conflict. Such a mode manifests a view of domestic and international decision-makers as 'alternatives' operating in a horizontal and non-hierarchical context.[81] Unlike the mode of abstention, the mode of deferral only temporarily uses non-engagement to manage the conflicting claims to authority emanating from such systems.

9.2.3 *Pluralism: Concurrent Authority and Dialogue as a Means of Interface Mediation*

Many scholars argue that monist and dualist conceptualisations of the relationship between domestic and international law are no longer empirically viable. They argue that the distinctions between domestic and international law have increasingly blurred, such that both bodies of law 'operate on the same terrain and regulate the same issues'.[82] These scholars propose pluralism as an alternative means of conceptualising the relationship between domestic and international law. Legal pluralism recognises that several legal systems may apply 'within a given space (whether territorial, personal, functional, or global)'.[83] Pluralists argue that, as the boundaries

80 McLachlan (2005), p. 286.

81 Shany (2006), pp. 15–19. See, further, Bjorklund (2007), p. 296 (fork-in-the-road clauses); D'Alterio (2011), p. 412 (*forum non conveniens*). Cf. Pauwelyn and Salles (2009) (*lis pendens* as regulating claims to authority in hierarchies); Verzijl (1965), p. 23.

82 Krisch (2017), p. 692. See, similarly, Bennouna (2014), p. 151; Nollkaemper (2013b); Klabbers and Piiparinen (2013), p. 101; Jennings (1998), p. 58.

83 Isiksel (2013), p. 163. See, similarly, McCorquodale (2013); Ellis (2011), p. 952; Merry (1988), p. 870; Kulick (2012), p. 78; López Escarcena (2014), p. 191; Krisch (2006), p. 11; Cohen (2010b), p. 274.

between the international and national blur, international and domestic actors will increasingly claim decision-making authority over the same subjects or subject matters.[84]

Decision-makers in a pluralist paradigm share overlapping or concurrent decision-making authority. Pluralist approaches recognise that wherever an issue of concurrent decision-making authority arises, it is for each decision-maker to decide 'when to claim authority or cede it to another level'.[85] Pluralists differ in whether they view pluralism as 'an ordering philosophy' or rather a 'diagnosis of disorder'.[86] As a diagnosis of disorder, pluralism encourages competition and contestation. This view of pluralism seeks to keep the relationships between actors in the pluralist order 'undetermined and thus ... open to redefinition over time'.[87] Other pluralists instead argue that pluralism can be managed.[88] As an ordering philosophy, pluralism prompts the development of principles to mediate conflicting claims to authority. Unlike monism, pluralism rejects the use of hierarchical principles to manage these conflicts.[89] Differing also from dualist approaches, pluralism aims to draw decision-makers 'into a shared social space' and so rejects the use of principles of non-engagement.[90] Pluralist approaches instead seek the settlement of conflicting claims to authority through the application of principles encouraging 'mutual respect', 'coexistence', and 'cooperation' rather than 'imposition' or non-engagement.[91]

An adjudicator taking a pluralist approach is more likely to view domestic and international decision-making authority as concurrent, and to seek to manage conflicting claims to authority flexibly. This prompts a less categorical approach to authority than that adopted in a monist or dualist paradigm. Adjudicators endorsing a pluralist paradigm conceptualise decision-making authority as shared, seeking to manage rather than preclude (monism) or

84 Nollkaemper (2013b); Klabbers and Piiparinen (2013), p. 98; Tamanaha (2008), p. 389; Crawford and Brownlie (2012), p. 50; Wismer (2006), p. 512; Berman (2008), p. 1158; Prost (2006); Krisch (2010), p. 294.

85 Krisch (2010), p. 76.

86 Isiksel (2013), p. 175. On pluralism as an 'ordering' philosophy, see, especially, Delmas-Marty (2009), pp. 2, 13–15.

87 McCorquodale (2013), p. 389. See, similarly, Krisch (2010), p. 225; Berman (2013b), pp. 668–9; Buchanan (2009).

88 Berman (2008), p. 1172. Others dispute this: Krisch (2010), p. 74; Walker (2002).

89 Greer and Wildhaber (2012), p. 681; Cohen (2010b), p. 274; McLachlan (2009), p. 229.

90 Berman (2008), p. 1172–3. See, similarly, McCorquodale (2013); Buchanan (2009); Krisch (2010), p. 288.

91 See, further, McLachlan (2009), p. 229; Benvenisti and Harel (2015), p. 57; Petersen (2009), p. 5; Krisch (2010), p. 69; Berman (2007), p. 321; Helfer and Slaughter (1997), p. 317; Tzanakopoulos (2012), p. 191.

suspend (dualism) particular claims to authority.[92] In a concurrent approach to authority, second-order reasons for recognising, and deferring to, another actor's authority take a non-exclusionary structure. The international adjudicator's own authority subsists alongside, rather than being displaced by or overriding, domestic decision-making authority. The modes of restraint, reference and respect facilitate this flexible approach to settling conflicting claims to decision-making authority. The mode of restraint, for example, encourages the international adjudicator to view themselves 'as part of a larger tapestry of decision-making in which they are not the only potentially relevant voice'.[93] The mode of reference reflects a similarly flexible approach to decision-making, implying 'a search for useable norms across the spectrum of domestic law and public international law'.[94] Finally, in the mode of respect, domestic and international claims to authority are leveraged to complement and supplement, rather than replace or foreclose, one another.[95] By adopting modes of deference reflecting a concurrent view of authority, international adjudicators assume the role 'of an arbiter or mediator between orders, rather than an advocate for one of them'.[96]

9.3 CONCLUSIONS

This chapter has deepened the conceptual analysis of deference to link deference to differing approaches to conceptualising the relationships between the domestic and international legal orders. Drawing on theories related to the structure of these relationships, I have developed a systemic theory of deference, according to which different approaches to deference not only reflect differing structures of authority but also fundamentally different approaches to conceptualising the relationship between the international and domestic legal orders or between particular decision-makers within those orders. Figure 9.1 redraws the taxonomy of deference first presented in Chapter 4 to account for these systemic features of deference. The figure develops the analysis of the various structures of authority introduced in Parts I and II to present a simplified depiction of the connection between structures

92 See, further, on 'shared' and 'shifted' authority Arnardóttir (2015), p. 3; Melish (2009), p. 439; Jachtenfuchs and Krisch (2016); Mowbray (2015), p. 340; Cohen (2012a), p. 1101; Peters (2016), p. 207; Bücheler (2015), p. 233; Hilson (2013), p. 319.

93 Berman (2008), p. 1152. See, similarly, Slaughter (2003), p. 192; Klabbers et al. (2009), pp. 32–3; Carter Jr (2008), p. 319.

94 Wismer (2006), p. 513; Slaughter (2003), p. 194.

95 Cassese (1990), p. 212; von Bogdandy (2006), p. 228; Crawford (2014), para. 267.

96 Krisch (2010), pp. 293–4. See, similarly, Koh (1997), p. 2655; Delmas-Marty (2009), p. 156.

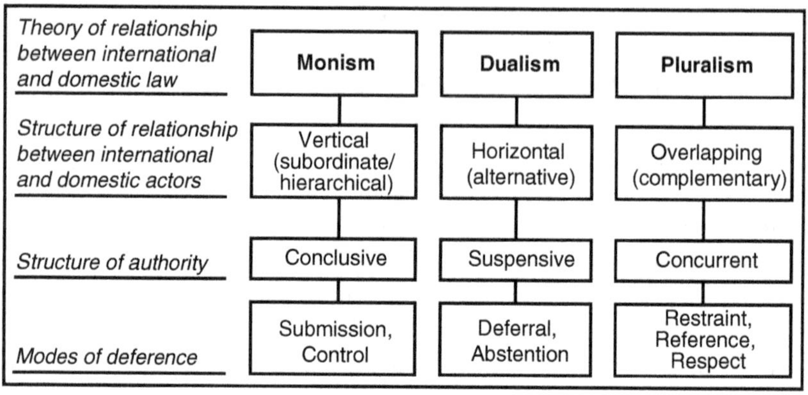

FIGURE 9.1 The connection between structures of law, structures of authority and modes of deference

of law, structures of authority, and modes of deference.[97] By bringing into focus these connections, the chapter has extended the conceptual cartography of deference, to demonstrate that the seven modes of deference identified in Part II reflect fundamentally distinct conceptualisations of the relationship between domestic and international decision-makers and the domestic and international legal orders.

[97] These approaches exist on a spectrum such that, in practice, adjudicative analyses may blur these boundaries.

10

Bringing Principles into Practice: Grappling with Deference in International Adjudication

This chapter draws together the preceding conceptual and empirical analysis of deference in international adjudication to explore how the principles discussed in the preceding pages might be used to inform approaches to deference in practice. This chapter does not develop a prescriptive approach to deference in international adjudication. Rather, it offers a *framework* to inform the analysis of deference in international adjudication. Section 10.1 addresses debates as to whether international adjudicative deference to domestic decision-makers is desirable at all. Section 10.2 examines whether approaches to deference should be 'fixed' in favour of some doctrinal approaches over others. Section 10.3 explores how a framework for analysing deference might be created, which allows evolution and malleability in approaches to deference while securing some level of predictability and transparency in practice. Section 10.4 concludes.

10.1 IS THERE A PLACE FOR DEFERENCE IN INTERNATIONAL ADJUDICATION?

Scholars studying international adjudicative deference to domestic decision-makers have suggested that such deference may be 'anathema' to the extent that international adjudication is analogised to a commercial or private adjudicative regime.[1] This explains why scholars studying deference in international adjudication have become so focused on deriving deference from analogies, and on a characterisation of international adjudication as a *public* rather than *private* means of dispute settlement. Chapter 9 addressed the pitfalls of drawing approaches to deference from a priori characterisations of a given adjudicative regime's 'character'. Instead, as explained in Part I, the

[1] See, especially, Roberts (2011); Schill (2012).

need for deference does not arise merely because a dispute settlement system is of a particular 'type'. Deference is instead a functional tool that will be required by *any* adjudicator confronted with overlapping and contested spheres of decision-making authority. The *character* of international adjudication as public, private, or somewhere in between, therefore offers little assistance for determining the role of deference in individual disputes. While scholars may be correct in suggesting that an institutional setting will inform adjudicative analysis of deference, this is not because it is 'public' or 'private' as a form of dispute settlement. The role for deference depends instead on more contextual factors, including the types of decision at issue and the qualities of the decision-makers that claim or could claim authority to settle those issues. The character of a regime cannot therefore be used to expand or preclude a role for deference ex ante.

Domestic law scholars have argued on different grounds that deference is in principle 'pernicious' and normatively undesirable. Allan, for example, argues that the fact-specific features of 'deference' mean that it is better subsumed into the judicial task of applying the law, such that 'no coherent doctrine of deference is feasible'.[2] As Allan explains, this view is underpinned by a perception that:

> Considerations of legitimacy are reflected in the proper standards and criteria of judicial review; and matters of competence and expertise are accommodated within the ordinary judicial process, wherein general principles of legality are applied to the particular case.[3]

For scholars adopting such a view, 'deference' necessarily implies an abdication by the court of its *obligation* to decide disputes by applying the law. Such views have also informed some international adjudicative analyses of deference. Arbitrator Garibaldi in *Glencore*, for example, rejected the Majority's deference to the State's regulatory decisions, on the basis that:

> [a] tribunal's duty is to apply the standard laid down in the applicable treaty, whatever that standard is and however it might be characterized . . . This is not to say that the Tribunal is free to impose its own conception of reasonableness or to ignore the circumstances . . . This and any other treaty standard must be interpreted and applied in good faith under the rules of the VCLT. But the interpretation and application process must be impartial, not influenced by any sense of deference to one party to the dispute or solicitude to the other.[4]

[2] Allan (2006), p. 672.
[3] Allan (2011), p. 97.
[4] *Glencore, Award, 27-Aug-2019*, para. 1458.

Such critiques of deference proceed from a view of law as determinate. They posit there to be one 'right' answer to the issues in dispute, with deference undermining the court's ability to provide this right answer.[5] Such a view of adjudication rejects that – in a particular case – it may be unclear *what* the right answer might be, or *who* has a better claim to the authority needed to make that decision. This 'casts the courts into a mechanistic role',[6] and in so doing limits the function to be played by deference in adjudicative decision-making processes.

The law is not, however, always as determinate or non-contestable as such views would indicate. Instead, deference typically arises in adjudicative situations exhibiting features that, for the most part, are denied by Allan's account. Accepting the contestability of law does not imply a theory of nihilism. The utility of deference does not depend on accepting that there are *no* right answers, or that 'rights are so incommensurable that it is never possible to balance competing rights and interests'.[7] Rather, it only requires recognition that (i) certain norms may permit more than one interpretation; (ii) the application of certain norms will not be clear cut in all circumstances; and/or (iii) a norm might have one interpretation or a clear-cut application, but another actor is, for some reason, better placed than the court or tribunal to decide on that interpretation or application. Norms can thus be indeterminate or contestable in respect of different situations involving overlapping authority to differing degrees. A need for some theory of deference will arise whenever at least *some* norms are indeterminate, contestable, or apply to matters in respect of which different actors may claim authority. These features indicate that deference is particularly likely to play an important role in international adjudication, and are returned to in Section 10.3.

10.2 CAN (OR SHOULD) APPROACHES TO DEFERENCE BE 'FIXED'?

As Chapter 8 indicates, approaches to deference fluctuate and evolve. This raises the question of whether, assuming there *is* a place for deference in international adjudication, approaches to deference should be 'fixed' to prefer some approaches to deference over others. This has been the focus of most of the literature on deference in international adjudication to date. Most commentators do not dispute that deference has a role to play in international

5 See, especially, Allan (2006), p. 678; Green (2010), p. 86; Letsas (2007); Benvenisti (1999), p. 844.

6 de Ville (2004), p. 586.

7 Young (2009), p. 576.

adjudication. They instead dispute its form and extent, and call for a more consistent approach to be taken to its analysis.[8] States, too, have shown increased interest in directing adjudicative approaches to deference through treaties and procedural rules. In 2012, for example, the High Level Conference on the Future of the European Court of Human Rights adopted the 'Brighton Declaration', which affirmed the Court's margin of appreciation doctrine and proposed the development of a preliminary reference procedure to support domestic courts and the ECtHR to engage in a closer dialogue about Convention rights.[9] Subsequently, in 2013, Protocol 15 to the European Convention on Human Rights opened for signature, to add a reference to subsidiarity and the margin of appreciation in the preamble of the Convention.[10] Protocol 16 was also opened for signature that year, to empower domestic courts to request advisory opinions from the Court concerning the interpretation and application of the Convention.[11]

Further reforms are also possible. Many reform discussions for both the ECHR and investment treaties have focused on approaches to deference falling within the modes of deferral and restraint. This has included, for example, increased interest in the role to be played by requirements to exhaust, or have recourse to, local remedies before filing international private property claims.[12] The 'Steering Committee for Human Rights' ('CDDH') that was set up to consider reforms for the ECHR has suggested, for example, that the Convention could be amended to introduce a new admissibility requirement according to which disputes that have been 'properly considered' by national courts would be inadmissible before the ECtHR unless the domestic court 'had manifestly erred in its interpretation or application of the Convention rights or the application raised a serious question affecting interpretation or application of the Convention'.[13] This proposal is motivated by a desire to give the Court

[8] See, for example, Vadi and Gruszczynski (2013), p. 632; Kratochvil (2011), pp. 324–5, 339; Gerards (2014); Chesney (2006), p. 1752; McGoldrick (2016), p. 39; Letsas (2006), pp. 711–12, 714; O'Donnell (1982), p. 478.

[9] Council of Europe (2012).

[10] Protocol 15 to the European Convention for the Protection of Human Rights and Fundamental Freedoms (2013/not in force) ETS 213 ('Affirming that the High Contracting Parties, in accordance with the principle of subsidiarity, have the primary responsibility to secure the rights and freedoms defined in this Convention and the Protocols thereto, and that in doing so they enjoy a margin of appreciation, subject to the supervisory jurisdiction of the European Court of Human Rights established by this Convention').

[11] Protocol 16 to the European Convention for the Protection of Human Rights and Fundamental Freedoms (2013/2018).

[12] See, for example, International Institute for Sustainable Development (2017); Leonhardsen (2014).

[13] Council of Europe Steering Committee for Human Rights, *CDDH Final Report on measures requiring amendment of the European Convention on Human Rights 15 February 2012, CDDH (2012)R74 Addendum I*, para. 28.

greater leeway to defer to national authorities, nevertheless ensuring it is still in a position to 'examine decisions of national courts where they clearly failed to apply the Convention and the Court's case law either properly or at all'.[14] States in some reform contexts have also emphasised the potential utility of endorsing approaches to deference reflecting a mode of submission. Morocco, for example, in its submission to UNCITRAL's Working Group III on investor–State dispute settlement reform has proposed that – where the applicable law is national law – any appellate body 'should be bound by the interpretation of domestic laws made by the competent courts of the host State'.[15] These, and other reform discussions, indicate increased appetite among States to give international courts and tribunals direction as to how to approach questions of deference. In making decisions about such reforms, such stakeholders may find inspiration in some of the hitherto under-considered approaches to deference set out in Part II.

Not all stakeholders agree, however, that embedding approaches to deference within treaty rules will be useful or successful. This is unsurprising given that scholars continue to debate how overlapping claims to authority should be settled even in established domestic legal systems.[16] During the drafting of Protocol 15, for example, the Court noted in a letter to the CDDH that inserting a reference to the margin of appreciation in the Convention without linking it to the Court's case-based development of that doctrine would be 'incomplete', given that the concept 'varies widely in its relevance and consequence from one context to another' and was not 'a given or a constant in every case'.[17] Locating deference within a specific doctrine may, moreover, overlook other approaches to deference. A striking finding from the empirical study is that many applications of deference were not labelled or signposted using the principles or doctrines of deference analysed in the bulk of contemporary literature on deference in international adjudication. While adjudicators may well be 'more deferential when confronted with a legal requirement to be that way',[18] the empirical study indicates that deference is applied even in the absence of a direction to that effect. It also indicates that much deference is achieved through ad hoc reasoning rather than through recourse to more established deference doctrines or principles. Indeed, while some adjudicators

14 Ibid, p. 38.

15 Government of Morocco (2020), 'Possible Reform of Investor-State Dispute Settlement (ISDS) – Submission from the Government of Morocco' UN Doc. A/CN.9/WG.III/WP.195, p. 5.

16 See, for example, Cohen-Eliya and Porat (2011); Berman (2008), p. 1152.

17 Milner (2014), p. 32.

18 Cross (2007), p. 7.

declined to accord deference by reference to primary (or secondary) rules of international law,[19] they most frequently sourced approaches to deference by reference to more general principles of international law or by reference to the role of the international court or tribunal vis-à-vis domestic decision-makers.

Many adjudicators, for instance, invoked broader principles of international law to inform their approaches to deference. In so doing, they disclosed underlying structural assumptions as to the relationship between domestic and international actors. Some adjudicators, for example, decline to accord States deference because they consider deference to be a 'radical departure' from the principle that international law is superior to domestic law.[20] Such a perspective, however, exhibits a particular approach to analysing the authority of international adjudicators vis-à-vis domestic actors and, in turn, deference. It is based on a view that deference forces international adjudicators to deny the superiority of international law over domestic decisions. This, however, is only the case if the adjudicator applies modes of deference exhibiting a conclusive or suspensive view of authority. As noted in Chapter 9, conclusive views of authority pit domestic and international claims to authority against one another, conceptualising them as inconsistent and in conflict. Suspensive views privilege non-engagement such that the 'breach of the rules of one system cannot be justified by reference to the rules of another'.[21] Both views result in treating deference to a domestic decision as akin to an order. As such, in each of these paradigms, deference may well appear inconsistent with the rule of international law that directs the international adjudicator to avoid giving superiority to domestic law or decision-making. Where claims to authority are analysed as concurrent, however, such analysis becomes inapposite. This is because concurrent approaches to authority permit a less categorical analysis of deference (and, in turn, of domestic decisions), disposing of the need to apply rules favouring trumping or non-engagement. In this latter paradigm, the recognition of a domestic actor's authority through deference does not trump or offset the exercise of the adjudicator's own authority: it is more akin to a request. This makes deference in such paradigms more reconcilable with international rules on the non-superiority of domestic

[19] In the 531 instances in which an adjudicator expressly declined to afford a State deference, 148 were justified by reference to the wording of a treaty provision, or applicable secondary rules of international law (including, in particular, rules concerning treaty interpretation and the prohibition on States invoking domestic law to escape international responsibility).

[20] Slaughter (2005), pp. 149–50. See, also, Watts (1996), p. 436; Nollkaemper (2011), p. 47; Kulick (2010), p. 182; Larson and Jenks (1965), pp. 383–4; Crawford and Brownlie (2012), pp. 59–60; De Dycker (2010), p. 489.

[21] Tomka et al. (2015), p. 15.

law or decision-making within the international system. Part of the problem associated with approaches to deference in international adjudication is that they frequently proceed from unstated assumptions as to the structural relationship between international adjudicators and domestic orders or actors. Adjudicators applying modes of deference as submission, deferral, abstention, and control will often do so due to a view that there is a hierarchy or structural disconnect between international and domestic law.

This indicates that States wishing to alter adjudicative approaches to deference may need to do more than tweak approaches at the level of doctrine or treaty text. They might, instead, need to engage in wider structural (and conceptual) reform. States wishing to encourage (or discourage) adjudicators from adopting certain modes of deference could therefore productively engage in their reform efforts with the practical impact of adjudicative conceptions of authority on the analysis of deference in practice. General direction at the level of principle, rather than one-size-fits-all doctrinal directions, might be better able to influence future adjudicative approaches to deference. This might include, for example, providing direction or cues to adjudicators to inform how they conceptualise the structural features of their relationship with domestic actors, to better assist them to navigate the plethora of approaches introduced in Part II that might be relevant to analysing relative domestic and international authority in a given case.

Even if doctrinal reconciliation of approaches to deference were possible, however, it may nevertheless be *undesirable*. This book has emphasised the malleable, 'chameleonic' nature of deference. The focus has differed from existing accounts of deference, which have sought to settle the question of how deference *should* be analysed doctrinally. This has included directions to adjudicators to adopt deferential proportionality analysis, good faith review under self-judging clauses, and margin of appreciation analysis.[22] This book has adopted a different focus. My primary aim has been to develop a framework linking approaches to deference *conceptually* in order to illuminate their function and cross-cutting implications. This analysis has highlighted that there is a greater connection between approaches to deference than is indicated by the disparate ways in which such approaches are labelled and have been analysed to date. All of the approaches to deference identified in this book perform a comparable function. They facilitate the articulation, negotiation, and settlement of conflicting claims to domestic and international decision-making authority in individual cases.

[22] See, for example, Henckels (2015); Schill and Briese (2009); Schill (2012); Arato (2014).

The space that deference carves out for such an analysis is systemically important regardless of what approach is ultimately adopted to settling those conflicts. Indeed, as Waldron argues: '[S]ometimes the point of a legal provision may be to start a discussion rather than to settle it.'[23] This book has developed a conceptual framework and theory of deference that respects the capacity for deference to structure and inform ongoing (and evolving) analysis of the role of domestic decision-making in international adjudication. This approach anticipates that the selection of an approach to deference within the contours of the framework is likely to remain contested. The desirable structure and scope of deference necessarily fluctuates depending on the identity of the entity appraising whether deference is due, the identity of the entity to which deference may be accorded, the issues to which deference relates, and the institutional and temporal context within which that appraisal takes place. Doctrinal reconciliation that tethers deference to particular devices risks stagnating debates about authority and depriving deference of its function. It also risks creating blunt, one-size-fits-all approaches that will be unsuited to mediating nuanced and difficult contests between domestic and international decision-making authority in practice. Instead, as a concept, deference has the qualities of an 'accordion' that can be 'contracted or released ad-hoc to fit almost any set of factors'.[24] As such, while seeking to bring clarity at the level of concept, I have avoided trying to settle approaches to deference at the level of device. Deference is necessarily (and desirably) flexible and dynamic.

10.3 TOWARDS A FRAMEWORK FOR ANALYSING DEFERENCE TO STATE DECISION-MAKING IN INTERNATIONAL ADJUDICATION

Even if deference remains unfixed to particular doctrines, however, it should not be analysed completely at random. Currently, much of the concern about international adjudicative deference to decision-making links to the ad hoc and unpredictable (and sometimes contradictory) approaches adopted by international adjudicators to these issues in practice. This reflects that adjudicators confront issues of deference in a rather ad hoc and pragmatic way, and are yet to develop overarching theories about when – and which approaches to – deference will be appropriate. The conceptual approach to analysing deference outlined in this book indicates that it *is* possible to develop a framework within which analyses of deference can take place, while remaining cognisant of the dangers of fixing such approaches too rigidly in advance. It

[23] Waldron (1994), pp. 539–40. See, also, Poirier (2002), pp. 136, 152.

[24] Benvenisti (2018), p. 252.

is to this task that this section is directed. The section proposes a series of analytical steps that are intended to clarify how adjudicators might use the conceptual and principled approach to deference developed in this book to analyse conflicting claims to decision-making authority in specific cases. The aim here is not to 'fix' deference or specify how it should apply in every scenario. Instead, the section explores how a more conceptual and systemic understanding of the *function* of deference can guide decisions as to its appropriate *manifestation*.

10.3.1 *Linking Deference to the Applicable Law*

Most international adjudicators derive their mandate from treaties. So, too, the law applicable to the international obligations of States typically derives (at least in part) from treaties and/or customary international law. Adjudicators might also rely on their procedural or inherent powers (including of competence-competence)[25] and/or rules or principles of general international law[26] to inform their approaches to deference. Adjudicators must respect the sources of law that delineate their adjudicative function. They must also correctly apply the applicable law. Such sources of law will therefore necessarily always be the starting point for any analysis of deference.[27] For the purposes of the following discussion, treaties will be used to illustrate the appropriate starting point for an international adjudicator's enquiry into the applicable approach to deference in a given case. Treaties are the focus of the following discussion because they will typically embed more restraints on an adjudicator's analysis of deference than comparable customary rules or general principles. Similar considerations can inform the analysis of deference where other such sources of law apply instead of (or as well as) a treaty. The applicable law may impact the analysis of deference in four key ways, which are examined in more detail in the following subsections.

25 See, for example, *Fraport, Award, 16-Aug-2007 (ICSID)*, para. 391 ('holdings of municipal legal institutions cannot be binding with respect to matters properly within the jurisdiction of this Tribunal'). See, similarly, *Soufraki, Award, 7-Jul-2004 (ICSID)*, paras 47–57. See, generally, on competence-competence powers Higgins (1968), p. 64; Grieves (1969), p. 109; Kolb (2013), p. 601; Heiskanen (1994), p. 70

26 Including, for example, rules of interpretation: *Loewen, Award on Jurisdiction, 5-Jan-2001 (ICSID-AF)*, para. 51; *Mobil, Decision on Liability and Quantum, 22-May-2012 (ICSID-AF)*, paras 251–5.

27 See, similarly, Henckels (2013); Schill (2012), p. 8; Allen (2005b), p. 416; Vandevelde (2011), p. 312; Alschner (2014); Croquet (2010); Ginsburg (2004); Lugato (2013); Mowbray (2010), p. 292; Paine (2019), p. 6; Moloo and Jacinto (2012).

10.3.1.1 Directions to Adopt (or Avoid) Particular Approaches to Deference

First, a treaty may specify that a particular mode (or doctrine) of deference is to be applied or that a particular approach should *not* be applied. Where this is the case, the international adjudicator must analyse whether the circumstances are such that this direction is applicable. Some approaches to deference are easier to encompass in treaties than others. States commonly, for instance, stipulate that international adjudicators should reflect modes of deferral in their decision-making. This could include, for instance, through treaty provisions requiring an exhaustion of local remedies before a dispute can be received by the international adjudicator. Self-judging clauses might similarly indicate to adjudicators that they should adopt particular approaches to deference. Adjudicators nevertheless retain discretion as to what modes of deference to adopt even in applying such clauses. Clauses with self-judging language, for example, have been interpreted to support approaches to deference across the taxonomy introduced in Part II, such that an adjudicator confronted with a self-judging clause might endorse (deference as submission), refer to as persuasive (deference as reference), or review only on grounds of good faith or reasonableness (deference as respect) certain State determinations. Such clauses nonetheless serve to indicate to an adjudicator that at least *some* deference might be appropriate. Where treaties provide guidance as to deference, however, it will usually be limited to specific issues or contexts. Treaty directives are therefore unlikely to resolve the question of whether deference is appropriate, or what approach to deference should be adopted, definitively for all circumstances in which deference might be relevant. Adjudicators therefore usually retain considerable discretion to adopt various approaches to deference in respect of issues for which partial or no treaty direction is provided.

A related question is whether *silence* indicates that *no* deference is appropriate. This has been the view adopted by some international adjudicators, particularly where 'deference' is equated with a particular doctrinal approach. Arbitrator Born in *Antaris*, for instance, argued that the Majority's deference to the State was inappropriate given that:

> [T]here is no reference to any 'margin of discretion' or analogous standard of deference in either of the Treaties providing a textual basis for the Tribunal's decision to abstain from a meaningful review of the Czech Republic's acts under the Treaties and, in particular, there is no reference to any such margin in either of the Treaties' fair and equitable treatment or nonimpairment

> protections. On the contrary, as noted above, both Treaties provide the investors unqualified protections of fair and equitable treatment.[28]

Interpretation of treaties in accordance with the VCLT may well preclude the application of particular *doctrines* or *approaches* to deference. The VCLT, for instance, arguably precludes the 'restrictive interpretation' of treaty provisions in favour of State sovereignty. As noted in Part II, this is because the VCLT requires a more neutral approach to be taken to treaty interpretation. Just because one particular approach to deference is excluded, however, does not mean that *deference* is not appropriate *at all*. While some *manifestations* of deference might be rejected through an interpretation of the treaty, it is questionable whether silence as to deference could foreclose *all* deference as such.[29] The appropriateness of deference instead depends on a close analysis of the treaty – consistent with the VCLT framework – to determine what exercises of authority might be required in its interpretation and application. Some common features of treaties will influence this analysis and are considered in turn in the following subsections.

10.3.1.2 Deference in Interpretation: The Role of Structural Discretion and Textual Flexibility

International law has frequently been characterised as vague and indeterminate.[30] Such indeterminacy results from a range of factors. All law is to some extent linguistically indeterminate.[31] No 'set of words, is so plain and clear that it will never need interpretation in the light of particular facts and circumstances'.[32] International law is particularly likely to suffer from linguistic indeterminacy because it is negotiated and drafted in different languages and applied to different legal cultures.[33] Treaties may also be drafted in deliberately vague terms or rely on vague rules of customary international law for interpretation.[34] International private property obligations exhibit particular linguistic indeterminacies. The concept of property

28 *Antaris, Dissent/SO (Born)*, 2-May-2018 (UNCITRAL), para. 50.
29 Cf. ibid, para. 47.
30 See, for example, Glashausser (2005), pp. 32–3; Tumonis (2012).
31 Most theorists agree that linguistic indeterminacy affects law, but differ as to the scope of the problem it poses. See, especially, Hart (1994), p. 128; Wolitz (2014), pp. 536, 540, 551–2; Mahoney (1990), p. 60.
32 Higgins (1981), pp. 1489–90.
33 Crawford (2014), p. 118.
34 Flexible language allows treaties to remain responsive to differing situations and future contingencies. States may also favour ambiguity because it defers disagreement on the content of legal standards at the point of negotiation, increasing the chances of successful treaty

is itself indeterminate.[35] Private property protections typically also embed linguistically indeterminate concepts. This includes references to 'public policy', 'good faith', 'reasonableness', and 'proportionality'.[36] International private property obligations may also be strategically ambiguous. The nature of property and its close connection to domestic political systems means that it may be difficult to achieve consensus on private property protections among diverse States.[37] While States may agree that it is desirable to protect property, they may draft obligations to secure flexibilities as to the structure or extent of that protection.

When interpreting a flexible obligation, an adjudicator could conceivably adopt one of several approaches that may open more or less scope for deference to a State. Suppose, for example, that there was an obligation requiring that 'States not deprive individuals of private property'. Questions of interpretation will arise in the analysis of what situations such an obligation prohibits. 'Deprivation', for example, could be interpreted to preclude various activities. So, too, exceptions to the rule could be alleged to be implicit in the obligation such that, for example, deprivations in times of emergency or for good reasons would not be prohibited. The adjudicator might refer to second-order reasons for deference in order to either (i) interpret the obligation more leniently, or (ii) give weight to the State's own interpretation of the obligation.[38] An adjudicator could, for example, determine that it has authority to complete or add precision to vague rules.[39] It might decide instead that any gap is to be filled by a political or national process, and thus either refer the question back to the State, determine the matter by reference to the State's interpretation, or interpret the obligation more flexibly to preserve the State's regulatory autonomy.[40] When interpreting flexible international obligations, therefore, adjudicators commonly use second-order reasons (and deference) to determine where final decision-making authority should lie.

This is not to suggest that international obligations, and international private property obligations in particular, are so indeterminate that they can be interpreted to support any desired proposition.[41] While an international

conclusion. See, generally, van Aaken (2008), p. 5; Poirier (2002), p. 106; Dunoff and Trachtman (1999), p. 34; Shelton (2008), p. 533.

35 Some theorists suggest that this is necessarily so, reflecting that private property rights must remain 'open to discussion and refinement over time': Poirier (2002), p. 103.

36 Shany (2005), p. 909.

37 See, further, Price (2000), p. 112; Allen (2005a), p. 3.

38 Grant (2017), p. 527.

39 See, for example, Venzke (2013b); Alvarez (2006), p. 476; Schill (2010b), p. 79; van Aaken (2008), p. 10.

40 See, for example, Maduro (2013), p. 548; Chen (2012), p. 26.

41 Cf Koskenniemi (2006).

rule may support any number of arguments, 'there comes a point at which a particular argument or interpretation becomes untenable'.[42] Interpretations of international obligations are bounded by what is considered an acceptable interpretation by the interpretive community.[43] International adjudicators are commonly empowered to make this distinction between justifiable and unjustifiable interpretations, including for private property protections. Such assessments are to be made by reference to the interpretive principles set out in the VCLT. The adjudicator nonetheless retains discretion under this framework to give a domestic decision-maker authority to decide certain matters autonomously (without interference by the adjudicator's own exercise of authority) or otherwise with minimal interference by an adjudicator (for example, by accepting decisions within certain margins or bounds).

Treaty provisions that allow adjudicators to select between 'right answers' might, for example, create particular scope for deference. An adjudicator interpreting such norms could exhibit deference by exercising restraint to give a State greater scope to make decisions lying outside of the international adjudicator's scrutiny. An adjudicator might, for instance, determine that the State has authority to choose what the provision requires such that the adjudicator will accept the State's choice without review (deference as submission), that the State's choice should be permitted within reasonable bounds (deference as restraint), that the State's choice should be treated as persuasive or influential in the adjudicator's analysis (deference as reference), or that the State should be permitted to make choices provided they are shown to be *in good faith*, through *particular procedures*, or consistent with certain *substantive criteria* (deference as respect). The possibility for such deference to a State's latent authority arises wherever an international obligation embeds structural leeway or flexibility. The important point is that treaty provisions will give adjudicators greater discretion to have recourse to principles of deference where they exhibit textual ambiguity.

10.3.1.3 Deference in Application: The Role of Substantive Contestability

International obligations may also be indeterminate at their point of application. That is, even if an obligation is free from textual ambiguity, it might 'only find concrete normative meaning through the formulation of value judgments

42 Crawford (2014), p. 131.
43 See, especially, Fish (1989); Johnstone (1990).

beyond the mere interpretation of the normative text'.[44] International private property obligations are particularly likely to give rise to such contestability in application. Property rights supply a useful example of such contestability because property is often said to be inherently contestable. Property is a 'socio-political institution',[45] such that private property disputes act as sites for 'a more basic dispute over the appropriate balance of rights and responsibilities between individuals and society itself'.[46] Private property protections also often embed additional contestable concepts. References to, for example, the 'public interest', implicate 'deeply held convictions and entrenched interests'.[47] The application of private property obligations often thus raises empirically or normatively contestable issues for decision. In applying such obligations, international adjudicators determining private property disputes are particularly likely to be confronted with a range of empirical and normative uncertainties resolvable only through fact-intensive or normative (including moral or political) judgments. Such judgments depend on empirical or normative epistemic authority. Some approach to deference will therefore be necessary wherever an adjudicator is required to assess a situation of 'epistemic leeway', such that the application of the norm is empirically or normatively contestable.[48]

Several scholars suggest that deference in the interpretation of an obligation will be based on distinct second-order reasons compared to deference in the application of an obligation. Rivers, for example, argues that deference in interpretation responds to another actor's normative epistemic authority (legitimacy), and deference in application to empirical epistemic authority (expertise).[49] It is better, however, to distinguish between deference in interpretation and application by reference to what work deference does in the reasoning process. As noted in Part II, deference in interpretation draws on second-order reasons for deference to identify and interpret the first-order reasons for decision. This explains why adjudicators applying relatively lenient obligations are likely to conclude that deference is already 'present in the standard as stated, rather than being additive to that standard'.[50] Deference in

44 Brems (1996), p. 295.

45 Lehavi (2010), p. 469.

46 Mahoney (2010), p. 1.

47 Krisch (2010), p. 244.

48 These features may also mean that deference is more likely to arise in primitive or heterogeneous regimes. This is because, as a system develops and integrates, consensus is likely to materialise in respect of matters that were previously contested. Conversely, as the subjects of the regime increase or homogeneity (and thus consensus) decreases, increased contestability and deference might be expected: Ostrovsky (2005), p. 51.

49 Rivers (2006), pp. 199–200.

50 *Glamis, Award, 8-Jun-2009 (UNCITRAL)*, para. 617.

application instead uses second-order reasons to suspend or foreclose the application of certain first-order reasons, or balance the adjudicator's analysis of those first-order reasons alongside applicable second-order reasons for decision. This brings into focus the impact of the structure and content of an obligation on the scope for deference in interpreting or applying it. As Elliott explains:

> when the burden under which the decision-maker is placed is especially light, adjudicative deference will have little, if any, role to play [in the application of the obligation], since in such circumstances the adjudicative task of the reviewing court involves the making of determinations that are unlikely to take it close to the limits of institutional competence or constitutional appropriateness.[51]

It also indicates that approaches to deference under the same obligation may differ over time. As obligations are interpreted and become more detailed and/or controlling, they may entail less scope for deference in interpretation but greater scope for deference in application.[52]

10.3.1.4 Deference in Context: Deference and Overlapping Authority Claims

The role for deference will also be determined by the subject matter regulated by the applicable law. A need for some approach to deference will arise wherever international adjudicators are empowered to decide empirically or normatively contestable matters *in respect of which domestic decision-makers might also expect to make determinations*. Once again, this indicates the particular scope for deference in the application of rules of international law concerning private property. Private property is a subject traditionally regulated at the domestic level. This means that international private property cases will raise facts in respect of which a domestic decision-maker also holds authority to make decisions.[53] This includes, for example, whether an individual holds a property interest; whether it is permissible to interfere with private property in pursuit of public policy objectives; and whether domestic

[51] Elliott (2015b), pp. 82–3. See, similarly, Shany (2005), p. 929.

[52] Several scholars argue that law becomes more certain over time. See, especially, Landes and Posner (1976), pp. 249–50; Holmes (1991), pp. 111–29. Others, by contrast, argue that legal certainty decreases over time because 'legal systems are biased in favor of unravelling those rules and principles': D'Amato (1983), p. 1.

[53] This feature distinguishes international private property disputes from many other international disputes, in which the international adjudicator is more likely to be in the position of first-instance decision-maker.

measures are consistent with domestic or even international law. Conflicting claims to authority are likely to arise wherever an international rule gives an international adjudicator some authority to determine one or more of these matters. All of these are issues for which the appropriate location of decision-making authority is likely to be contested. Where such matters are brought before them for decision, international adjudicators must decide whether to 'defer' to States by structuring their review to take into account existing domestic decisions or the possibility of future domestic decision-making on these topics. International adjudicators could take several approaches to this issue. They might refuse to recognise any role for domestic decision-makers; adopt domestic decisions as their own; or even defer making a decision pending the outcome of domestic processes. Selecting between such options becomes necessary whenever the adjudicator recognises that another actor has the capacity to make decisions of relevance to the matters in dispute before the adjudicator. Conversely, where there is only one decision-maker with a claim to authority in respect of a given issue 'deference' loses any utility.

Deference is therefore particularly likely to be relevant where a treaty puts into issue domestic decisions or matters likely to be regulated at the domestic level. As Chapter 4 noted, this means that the scope of an adjudicator's review will be closely tied to the possibility for deference in a given case. An adjudicator will usually require *some* approach to deference where public policy decisions, matters of domestic law, or domestic judicial decisions are relevant to the issues before it. Of course, adjudicators may foreclose a discussion of deference by rejecting that those elements form part of its enquiry, but where such topics are in issue a subsequent question arises as to whether the adjudicator or a domestic decision-maker is better equipped to address them. Whether this subsequent question arises will depend on the adjudicator's willingness to identify a domestic actor with overlapping authority to make a decision relevant to the matter before the international adjudicator.

This indicates that the scope for deference in the application of a given rule will turn on whether the adjudicator considers there to be a conflict (or overlap) between its own and another actor's authority. Take, for instance, a situation in which domestic courts have made determinations as to the interpretation of domestic law, or the domestic legality of particular conduct. If these matters are subsequently put before the international adjudicator for decision, a question will arise as to whether the adjudicator should defer to the existing domestic decisions (or the possibility of domestic courts making such decisions). A starting point for the analysis of the role of deference in such situations is the *perceived extent* of the overlap between domestic and international decision-making authority in respect of these issues.

One possibility is that there will be total overlap between the two exercises of decision-making authority because the international adjudicator perceives that it is tasked with determining a matter *identical* to that already determined by the domestic court. This might be the case, for instance, where the adjudicator is applying domestic law as the applicable law – and so must interpret what that law requires – but a domestic court has already performed that interpretation by reference to the facts now before the international adjudicator. In such circumstances, adjudicators might have recourse to tests akin to the 'triple identity' test to identify whether the domestic and international analyses are, properly speaking, 'identical'. Where they are linked to deferential reasoning, such tests are not applied to determine whether a party is 'bound' by the domestic decision as a matter of party autonomy,[54] but rather to determine the extent of the overlap between the domestic and international exercises of decision-making authority. These tests are unlikely to be satisfied where the adjudicator adopts a dualist understanding of the relationship between the domestic and international legal orders, as occurs in a deference as abstention mode. Indeed, many adjudicators operating in that mode note the difference between claims under domestic law and those under international law to justify their view that the former could not influence the latter and vice versa. Such overlaps may also arise in circumstances where the domestic court has made findings of fact that are directly in issue before the international adjudicator. This was the case, for example, in *Rompetrol*, where the tribunal treated as 'authoritative' domestic judicial findings of fact that 'national security was not the real motive for the interception but only a convenient device', and 'Rompetrol had not substantiated its claim of interference with its own business operations.'[55]

Another possibility is that a domestic court decision on a matter of *domestic* law (for example, whether a measure is consistent with domestic law or whether there is a property right under domestic law), will be relevant – but not coextensive with – a matter of *international* law before an adjudicator (for example, whether a measure is arbitrary, whether there has been an expropriation). In *Alghanim*, for example, a domestic court's finding that a tax was lawful under *domestic law* was considered to be *relevant* to whether the tax measure was arbitrary under *international law*, albeit in combination with other factors (such as the politically

54 See, for example, *Alghanim, Award, 14-Dec-2017* (ICSID), paras. 324–35.
55 *Rompetrol, Award, 6-May-2013 (ICSID)*, paras 256–61.

motivated nature of the measure).[56] In such circumstances, deference to the domestic court decision was significant to a component of the tribunal's analysis, but was not in itself dispositive of the overall enquiry because the assessment of arbitrariness was interpreted to entail other elements not already decided by the domestic court.[57] The overlap between the exercises of domestic and international decision-making authority was not therefore coextensive.

It might alternatively be the case that a domestic court is considered to have decided topics *completely different* to those before the international adjudicator. In *Maffezini*, for example, the tribunal rejected that a domestic decision was relevant to its analysis of attribution because this was a 'question of fact and law to be determined under the applicable principles of international law'.[58] Similarly, the *PNG Sustainable Development* tribunal held that a domestic court's decision on urgency was not coextensive with the tribunal's determination of urgency because it was made under domestic law, not under the international (ICSID) standard.[59]

The extent of perceived overlap will thus determine how decisive deference will be to the outcome in a given case. This settles the question of the *relevance* of deference but not its *structure* or *role* in the analysis. Recall that second-order reasons may exclude or influence the appraisal of first-order reasons for decision, depending on whether authority is viewed as akin to an order or a request. Assume for present purposes that second-order reasons for deference are treated as exclusionary (and so akin to an order), and that an adjudicator has been empowered to determine whether a measure is domestically unlawful. If the adjudicator decides that a domestic court has greater expertise in interpreting domestic law (superior authority), the domestic decision that the measure is domestically unlawful should be treated as having settled that question for the international adjudicator (such that it is, in effect, an order to the adjudicator to treat the decision as domestically unlawful). The second-order reasons for deferring to the domestic court (greater expertise/competence) would exclude the adjudicator's own analysis of the issue of domestic legality by reference to the facts of the case and its own interpretation of domestic law (first-order reasons). As the matter before the domestic court and that before the international adjudicator are coextensive, deference would have a significant impact on the outcome of such a dispute.

[56] *Alghanim, Award, 14-Dec-2017* (ICSID), paras 292, 317, 337.

[57] Ibid, paras 338–43, 354.

[58] *Maffezini, Decision on Jurisdiction, 25-Jan-2000 (ICSID)*, para. 82.

[59] *PNG Sustainable Development, Provisional Measures Decision, 21-Jan-2015 (ICSID)*, para. 168.

Suppose, however, that the adjudicator is instead tasked with determining whether the measure is arbitrary under international standards. The adjudicator might decide that domestic illegality is relevant to arbitrariness, but that an arbitrariness analysis may also take into view other features of a measure such as its rationality, predictability, or proportionality. In such circumstances, even where deference is treated akin to an order, the domestic court decisions will only cut off the adjudicator's analysis of some of the first-order reasons relevant to its overall enquiry. While the domestic court might be taken to have settled the question of domestic legality, this may be less true of the measure's rationality, predictability, or proportionality. Under Raz's exclusionary account of authority, the first order reasons relevant to assessing the rationality, predictability or proportionality of the measure are 'non-excluded' reasons: they are 'reasons that the [domestic court] was not meant to settle, because the [adjudicator] would better conform with reason by following their own judgment on those reasons' (or the judgment of another authority on those matters, such as a domestic legislature).[60] The categorisation of the types of authority required to decide a particular matter therefore requires nuance. The scope for deference will depend on the adjudicator's analysis of what issues it must determine as part of a given dispute, and its willingness to view domestic authority as relevant in some way towards those issues. The role to be played by deference will thereafter depend on the adjudicator's analysis of domestic authority. It is to this issue that the following subsection turns.

10.3.2 *Approaches to Analysing Relative Authority*

The factors examined earlier indicate when deference to another actor's authority *might* be relevant to an adjudicator's analysis. A second question arises as to whether – and to whom – an adjudicator might defer when these factors are present. This will depend on the adjudicator's analysis of the authority claims of other potential decision-makers. This will be influenced by how an adjudicator conceptualises 'authority', including what it considers to generate superior 'expertise' or 'legitimacy' for a given decision-maker, and the role of prudential and non-instrumental approaches to authority (either explicitly, or implicitly) in its reasoning process. How an adjudicator analyses deference will, moreover, be influenced by the level and detail at which it engages with questions of domestic authority. These issues are considered in more detail in the following subsections.

[60] Grant (2017), p. 518.

10.3.2.1 Identifying Actors to Benefit from Deference

Chapter 1 explored the theories of authority that might guide an adjudicator's analysis of whether deference should be given in recognition of another actor's 'authority'. That chapter introduced instrumental, prudential, and non-instrumental accounts of authority. As Chapter 3 noted, adjudicators may not in all cases expressly identify which of these accounts of authority they are following when they defer to a domestic actor in any particular case. Nevertheless, the reasons offered by adjudicators for deferring to domestic officials are important, because they signal what international adjudicators consider to be defensible reasons for deferring to other decision-makers in international disputes. Chapter 8 noted that, in the analysed cases, many adjudicators did not expressly signpost the reasons that motivated them to recognise the decision-making authority of domestic actors. Where adjudicators *did* identify reasons for recognising a domestic actor's authority, however, they predominantly focused on instrumental – rather than prudential or non-instrumental – second-order reasons for deference. That is, they typically linked deference to a recognition of the superior expertise and/or legitimacy of domestic officials. This is perhaps unsurprising, given that prudential and non-instrumental second-order reasons for deference might be more difficult to openly justify, including because they are more closely tied to an adjudicator's own interests or subjective values.

Even the concepts of 'legitimacy' and 'expertise', however, will differ by time, context, and perspective.[61] Whether any recognised 'legitimacy' or 'expertise' is sufficient to generate deference will also depend on relative assessments of the adjudicator's *own* expertise and legitimacy. To the extent that deference is motivated by instrumental second-order reasons, deference will be due only to the extent that a decision has been made by the application of a domestic actor's authority (judged by reference to their expertise or legitimacy), and provided that this authority exceeds that which the international adjudicator could bring to bear on the issue. Such assessments will fluctuate depending on a range of factors as canvassed in Chapter 2. An international court or tribunal's perception of its own legitimacy and expertise is, for instance, likely to be influenced by its historical and geographical context, institutional structure, personnel, claim structure, case load, and enforcement powers. Adjudicators appointed for their case-specific expertise –

[61] An additional work could be written on these social dimensions of 'expertise' and 'legitimacy', and on the types of expertise and legitimacy that find favour with adjudicators in decisions about deference. On the politics of expertise and legitimacy see, further, Kennedy (2005); Origgi (2018).

or expertise in particular domestic legal systems – might, for example, have less of a need for deference than a court or tribunal with a generalist bench. This was evident in the analysed cases. In *Fraport*, for instance, deference was justified on the basis that the tribunal 'had not been chosen for its knowledge of Philippine law'.[62] In *Eureko*, by contrast, the tribunal noted that it had been able to examine elements of Polish domestic law because it had 'the benefit of the exceptional knowledge and insight of its distinguished member who is steeped in Polish law'.[63] Arguments about *why* an adjudicator ought to recognise another actor's authority – and so defer to them – will thus have different traction in different times and contexts.

A related question is whether an international adjudicator analyses authority at a national, institutional, or personal level. Most States divide their decision-making authority between differently structured organs. This might include organs empowered to decide the content of laws or rules of general application, those empowered to apply rules to specific persons or cases, and those empowered to make policy decisions to support the development of domestic law. These different classes of decision-maker might be variously described as 'legislative', 'executive', 'administrative' or 'judicial', depending on their particular function and status within the domestic system. The label attached within a domestic system to a decision-maker will differ according to cultural and political context. This is why international rules on State responsibility take a unitary view of the State for the purposes of attributing State responsibility for the acts of State organs. The State as an international legal person is responsible for the acts of all of its organs, however designated.[64]

The *State* responding to an international private property claim will, nevertheless, comprise several *decision-makers*. Each of those decision-makers may have made decisions to which an international adjudicator could defer. These decisions may be more or less consistent with one another, or with the position taken by the State in response to the international claim. The attribution of deference will thus not always correlate with an adjudicator deciding in favour of a State's position in litigation. This is why, as explained in Chapter 3, 'deference' cannot be conflated with an overall successful outcome in the proceedings for one or other of the disputing parties.[65] It also means that, while responding States are particularly likely to seek deference, individuals may also seek deference to State decisions. The various decision-makers

62 *Fraport, Annulment Decision, 23-Dec-2010 (ICSID)*, paras 117, 236.

63 *Eureko, Partial Award, 19-Aug-2005 (UNCITRAL)*, para. 121.

64 See, especially, Crawford (2013).

65 Cf. Langford and Behn (2018). Prudentially, deference may also be used to soften adverse overall findings.

comprising a State might, for example, issue different decisions to which the litigating parties seek differing levels of deference depending on their position on the matters at stake in the litigation. The likelihood of this scenario arising depends on whether an adjudicator accords deference to 'the State' or instead to its constituent decision-makers.

Whether an international adjudicator accords deference to the *State*, or to a particular decision-maker within the State, is significant. It indicates the propensity of an adjudicator to open the 'black box' of the unitary State to consider its various institutional components.[66] This may impact the analysis of deference in individual cases. As observed in Chapter 5, for example, adjudicators applying the mode of control have analysed requests to control State decision-making authority differently depending on how they characterise the relationship between the State as regulator and the State as litigant. This has prompted differences in the analysis of deference depending on whether the State organ to be controlled has a judicial or an administrative/executive structure. So, too, an identity between the decision-maker to which deference could be given and the decision-maker whose decision a claim concerns might make adjudicative analyses of deference more likely to be particularly searching. Approaches to deference will thus likely differ depending on whether the domestic decision that could be deferred to by the adjudicator is the same decision that is alleged to breach international law. The timing of a State's decision in connection to the challenged decision will also influence the analysis of deference.[67] In such circumstances, the adjudicator might require that the second-order reasons justifying deference be particularly weighty or convincing. This reflects, as noted in Chapter 1, that in certain circumstances '*wrong* answers can be especially hazardous' and thus necessitate heightened thresholds for deference.[68]

The distinction between the State as regulator and as litigant, and between the State and its decision-making components, further influences the level of detail with which second-order reasons prompting deference may be analysed. If deference is accorded to the State as a unit, for example, any analysis of

66 Viñuales (2016). See, further, Cohen (2009); Sadurski (2009), p. 421; Ginsburg (2016), p. 204; Slaughter (1994), p. 728; Abbott (2008), p. 10; Kingsbury (1997), pp. 356–7.

67 *Pac Rim, Award, 14-Oct-2016 (ICSID)*, para. 8.31 ('As a general approach, deference should be given by an international tribunal to the unanimous interpretation of its own laws given in good faith by the responsible authorities of a State at a time before the emergence of the parties' dispute. There is a significant distinction to be drawn between an interpretation by the responsible bodies entrusted with governmental powers to be exercised at the time and non-authoritative interpretations, particularly when given by academic lawyers in a later arbitration. The former requires an element of deference').

68 Harowitz (2008), p. 1092.

specific institutional expertise/competence – including whether it was applied to make a particular decision – is likely to be general and limited in scope. These issues relate also to matters of institutional design. It might be expected, for example, that an international adjudicator more familiar with the particular structures of a State's domestic decision-making may be relatively better at analysing whether to attribute weight to State decisions on instrumental grounds than would an adjudicator unfamiliar with those processes or appraising them at a higher level of generality. Structural or organic linkages between international and domestic decision-makers may, therefore, be particularly likely to influence international adjudicative approaches to deference in practice. Analysis of deference will thus differ depending on whether it proceeds by reference to 'the State', or instead its various internal decision-making structures.

10.3.2.2 Formal versus Functional Approaches to Analysing Relative Authority

Once the decision-maker to benefit from deference has been identified, adjudicative approaches to deference will further be influenced by the approach the adjudicator adopts to analysing its own authority *relative* to that of the State (or domestic actor within the State). One important factor likely to influence approaches to deference will be whether the adjudicator attaches an assumption (or presumption) of authority to its own – or another actor's – decision. In practical terms, this will weight the analysis in favour of one decision-maker's authority. A second factor that will impact this analysis is the approach an adjudicator takes to structuring its analysis of relative authority. The following paragraphs introduce two such approaches, distinguishing between approaches to deference that link authority to particular *categories* of decision-making, and those that focus on the *context* of decision-making.

A formal approach to analysing relative authority would link authority (as derived from expertise and/or legitimacy) to particular institutional structures. Under a formal approach, each institutional structure would be conceptualised as holding *greater* decision-making expertise and/or legitimacy than other structures in respect of *particular* subjects.[69] Whereas, for example, a legislature might hold superior 'political' decision-making authority, adjudicators might be considered to be particularly equipped to exercise 'adjudicative' functions in respect of domestic or international law. Such approaches might inform deference by indicating that there are certain matters which a court or

[69] Carolan (2009), p. 18; Brown (1990), p. 1525.

tribunal ought not to consider at all, or in respect of which another decision-maker will be the source of more authoritative decisions. This approach relies on 'an *a priori* classification of forms or functions' to ground the analysis of deference.[70] As Carolan notes, under this approach:

> When faced with a question of disputed competences, the formalist court or commentator is concerned chiefly to identify and classify the task at hand. Once characterized as a legislative, executive, or judicial function, the task is allocated to the appropriate institution. The initial classification effectively exhausts the formalist enquiry.[71]

Numerous commentators have noted the limits of such formal approaches to analysing relative authority. These commentators note that the functions performed by different organs might overlap or be indistinguishable in practice.[72] This view has produced less formal, more functional, approaches to analysing relative authority. A functional approach does not allocate decision-making powers by reference to the formal structure (or identity) of a potential beneficiary of deference or the category of decision at issue, but rather by reference to the qualities and capacities required to make a decision about the matter at issue. Functional approaches recognise that decision-makers may be comparatively stronger (or weaker) at making particular types of decision. The capacities of different decision-makers to make a particular decision (correctly or legitimately) will differ *in each case* such that, in an ideal system, deference will be malleable enough to ensure that these decision-makers 'dovetail' with one another to leverage their respective decision-making strengths and minimise their respective weaknesses.[73]

Functional approaches allow adjudicators to appraise the strengths and weaknesses of decision-makers not by reference to their formal institutional designation or a specific decisional category, but instead by reference to their capabilities (both latent and exercised).[74] A functional approach makes the analysis of deference more nuanced. Rather than deciding that another actor should be deferred to in respect of an entire category of decisions, the

70 Carolan (2009), p. 201. See, also, King (2012), p. 121.
71 Carolan (2009), p. 23.
72 Ibid, p. 19; King (2012), pp. 122–9.
73 Hart Jr and Sacks (1994), p. 158; Westlund (2013), p. 467.
74 This would entail analysis of the matters highlighted in Chapter 1, including whether the adversarial structure, procedures or evidence-gathering powers of international adjudicators would make them better equipped to answer contested issues than other (domestic) decision-making procedures. So, too, the reasoning process of legal adjudication, the proximity of an adjudicator to a given dispute, or resourcing considerations might make international adjudication better suited to determine certain questions over others.

adjudicator adopting a functional approach to deference might instead decline to 'open their judicial review toolboxes fully on all occasions'.[75] Under such approaches, the focus is not merely on finding the *best decision-maker* for a given question, but also on producing the *best decision* for a given context. Whether an international adjudicator adopts a formalist or a functionalist approach to appraising domestic decision-making authority will impact their approaches to deference in practice. The more functional the analysis becomes, the less likely the adjudicator will be to select binary approaches to deference.

10.3.3 *Identifying 'Levers' for Deference: A Framework Approach*

The features just examined indicate the contours of a framework to guide analysis of deference in individual cases. The steps in this framework are set out in the following subsections, which, although they do not settle the issue of how deference should manifest, explain how a series of background levers might be deployed to guide that enquiry.

10.3.3.1 Step 1: Is Deference Relevant to the Adjudicator's Enquiry?

A first step is to examine whether deference might be relevant to a given enquiry. The features relevant to this assessment were addressed in Subsection 10.3.1. The propensity of an adjudicator to conclude from their analysis of the applicable law that deference *might be relevant* will depend on their willingness to identify indeterminacy in law, contestability in its application, and the availability of alternative sites for decision-making on the topics presented to them for analysis. The threshold question of whether deference is relevant at all will thus be heavily influenced by the legal and factual context, and the adjudicator's analysis of their role and authority vis-à-vis domestic actors. Litigants may nevertheless attempt to influence such appraisals by focusing on 'levers' relevant to increasing (or decreasing) the relevance of deference as part of their case strategy. A litigant might influence an adjudicator's analysis of whether deference *might be relevant*, for example, by increasing (or reducing) the adjudicator's perception that empirical uncertainty is associated with the matters at issue, or by raising (or not raising) normatively uncertain points for decision. States, for example, are typically more likely to be granted deference if they succeed in framing the issues in dispute as related to broad systemic questions, unsettled questions, or otherwise as raising issues of

75 Daly (2012), p. 281.

empirical or normative uncertainty. They may also increase the scope for deference by expanding the scope of review to encompass more domestic decisions, or more discretionary elements of analysis (for example, analysis of a measure's proportionality or reasonableness). Where a party wishes to avoid deference being relevant it should give consideration to: arguing that issues that might otherwise invite deference are outside the scope of review; framing submissions such that the issues in dispute appear more narrow or technical (and so do not appear to require particular expertise or any political or policy analysis but rather require only analysis suited to adjudicative decision-making); contesting the extent of overlap between domestic decisions and those decisions the adjudicator has been asked to make; and/or arguing that obligations impose objective, rather than subjective, requirements and so leave little leeway or discretion for State choices in implementation.

10.3.3.2 Step 2: Is Deference Appropriate and to Whom?

Once a decision has been made that deference *might* be relevant, a second step of analysis focuses on whether deference *is appropriate* and *to whom* it might attach. This will depend on how an adjudicator conceptualises 'authority', and how it assesses its own authority relative to that of domestic actors. The considerations relevant to this assessment were addressed in Subsection 10.3.2. This analysis will be impacted by the adjudicator's assessment of what makes a given decision-maker an 'authority' on a given topic. An adjudicator's professional background, institutional context, and procedural powers are all likely to factor into this assessment of whether they – or a domestic actor – holds superior authority to determine a given issue. The perceived acceptability of particular instrumental, non-instrumental, or prudential reasons for deference will also influence this analysis, or at least the way in which the adjudicator distils this analysis in their decision. A second issue impacting this analysis will be the level of detail with which an adjudicator engages with domestic decision-making. Approaches to deference will thus differ depending on the extent to which international adjudicators are willing to 'penetrate the surface of the state to interact with government decision-makers'.[76] A third issue impacting this analysis will be the level of separation the adjudicator perceives there to be between the State as regulator and the State as litigant. This will turn on an analysis of whether the domestic decision that could be deferred to is also the domestic decision being challenged, and/or whether the

[76] Helfer (2008), p. 131.

timing of the domestic decision indicates that it has been produced by the State in its role of litigant rather than regulator.

Litigants may again be able to influence this analysis. This could include, for example, through appointment of adjudicators cognisant or particularly trusting of a State's decision-making processes. Further, rather than requesting deference to a 'State', a litigant might be able to secure a more nuanced appraisal of relative authority by identifying specific domestic actors to whose decisions the adjudicator could defer. The more specific – and functional – the analysis of relative authority becomes, the more likely it is to account for the full gamut of circumstances relevant to appraising whether authority should be recognised in the context of a specific case.

10.3.3.3 Step 3: How Does the Adjudicator's Authority Compare to that of the Potential Beneficiary of Deference?

Having identified an actor to benefit from deference, an adjudicator needs to consider next how its own authority interacts with the authority of that actor. This will depend on the adjudicator's views as to the structural relationship between its own authority and that of a domestic actor: does the adjudicator view itself as exercising superior, inferior, distinct, or overlapping authority vis-à-vis the domestic actor? As the interface between domestic and international decision-making authority becomes increasingly blurred, a useful starting point for the analysis of deference might increasingly be for adjudicators to approach all claims to authority on a given topic as 'both legitimate and provisional'.[77] A formal approach to assessing relative authority could supply a starting point for such analysis, but more functional approaches should usually follow as a second step. Under this approach, the adjudicator would presume that domestic actors claiming authority have brought (or would bring) their expertise and legitimacy to bear in deciding a given issue. This presumptive starting point might derive from the domestic actor's formal institutional status or their specific decision-making competencies. The important point is that – where their authority overlaps with that of domestic actors – international courts and tribunals should not 'simply continue to insist that power should be exercised only in accordance with their views'.[78] While adjudicators might thus start from a presumption of 'deference', they must also imbue their analysis of whether deference is due with an attitude of 'distrust'.[79] The starting point of presumptive deference should be

[77] Carolan (2009), p. 183.
[78] Ibid, p. 188.
[79] Ibid, p. 187.

provisional. Complete deference to the initial decision-maker will no longer be appropriate insofar as the adjudicator itself holds authority (expertise/competence or legitimacy) that could be applied to improve the decision on the matter at issue.[80] An approach adopting the mode of deference as restraint, for instance, might indicate that the adjudicator should intervene to correct serious and obvious flaws in domestic decisions. An approach adopting the mode of deference as respect might allow the adjudicator to check that the process through which a decision has been made is at least as good as – if not better than – the process the adjudicator itself might use to determine the topic at issue. In analysing these issues, an international adjudicator must continue to 'have regard to its own relative limitations'.[81]

The balance struck by the adjudicator between these attitudes of 'deference' and 'distrust' will determine which modes of deference they are likely to favour in practice. As international and domestic decision-making authority increasingly overlap, this starting point for deference will mean that adjudicators will be particularly likely to adopt approaches to deference reflecting concurrent rather than conclusive or suspensive approaches to authority. This will produce a 'culture of justification' as introduced in Part II, rather than a culture of 'bare authority' or 'control'. The balance can nevertheless not be resolved in isolation from the particular facts and context of a given dispute. As the authority of international adjudicators increases or wanes over time, different mediations of their relationship with domestic actors will follow through deference. The authority of an international court or tribunal will depend on a range of factors, including applicable law, institutional design, adjudicative personnel, and applicable procedural rules. It is thus not possible to 'fix' deference once and for all. Equally, and as noted in Chapter 1, different situations may require qualitatively different, or weightier, second-order reasons to justify deference. An adjudicator might need to offer more or less justification when exercising its own authority depending on whether that exercise will touch on, second-guess, override, or prevent the exercise of domestic decision-making authority, or the exercise of domestic decision-making authority on particular or core sovereign functions.

10.4 CONCLUSIONS

Deference performs an important role in international adjudication as a tool to assist international adjudicators to grapple with uncertainty and with

80 Ibid, p. 188.
81 Ibid, p. 200.

overlaps between their own authority and that of domestic actors. The propensity of adjudicators to recognise a role for deference, and the form it subsequently takes, will depend on the openness of adjudicators to accepting uncertainty in the interpretation or application of international obligations, and to recognising the potential authority of other actors to settle such uncertainties once they have been identified. These features also indicate that, as the interface between domestic and international decision-making authority becomes increasingly blurred, adjudicators are likely to benefit from approaches to deference that permit more nuanced, and less categorical, analyses. In a contemporary international legal system, in which it is increasingly contended that something more than *bare* legal authority is required to justify the exercise of decision-making authority at both the domestic and international levels, international adjudicative deference is increasingly likely to rest on views of international and domestic decision-making authority as both contingent and contestable.

While the framework set out in this chapter can guide such analyses, the outcome of applying this framework will differ by time and context. The relative nature of the enquiry means that deference can never be fixed in advance for all relationships and contexts. One advantage of the approach to analysing deference set out in this chapter is that it entails a responsibility for each potential decision-making authority to be transparent about – and to justify – the basis for its decisions, such that other decision-makers can appraise whether such decisions should attract deference or not.[82] As Dyzenhaus observes, by requiring a decision-maker to 'justify the exercise of its power', and by requiring deference where a 'reasonable justification' of greater expertise or legitimacy is provided, the roles of each authority vis-à-vis others 'are made clearer'.[83] Such exercises of authority might, therefore, contribute to making decisions about deference more transparent and justifiable in the future.

82 Ibid, pp. 188–9.
83 Dyzenhaus, p. 255.

Conclusion

Deference as a Story of International Law and Adjudication

This book has investigated how deference manifests in international adjudication. It set out to analyse two questions. First, it sought to identify when and how international adjudicators defer to States in international private property claims. Second, it sought to examine the implications of deference in international adjudication, including of varying approaches to deference in different regimes and over time. In answering these two questions, the book has identified the structures of deference in international adjudication and the implications of deference for adjudication under public international law. It has developed a conceptual framework for understanding deference, to demonstrate that different modes of deference disclose differing approaches to dividing authority between domestic and international decision-makers. The study has also linked deference to several fundamental debates about the relationship between public international law and domestic law, and between private property rights and State interests. Pursuing these lines of analysis, the book used deference to tell a story of international law and adjudication. International private property claims have provided a useful setting for this story. Private property has been accorded longstanding protection under public international law, and is also subject to adjudication in differently structured regimes. By analysing approaches to deference in the private property cases of adjudicators in four such regimes, the study revealed the relationship between deference, State sovereignty, and power in international adjudication. It further identified how international adjudicators use deference to manage continuity and change, and to settle conflicting claims to authority.

A SOVEREIGNTY

The close connection between authority and deference means that deference can be used as a lens through which to study conceptualisations of State sovereignty in international adjudication. This book defined 'sovereignty' as autonomous decision-making authority. Each part of the book explored the relationship between deference and authority, bringing into focus the role of deference in delineating the contours of State sovereignty in international adjudication. Part I linked deference to the recognition of (superior) decision-making authority and introduced several theories of authority, each recognising authority on the basis of different second-order reasons. It illustrated that some theories of authority focus on instrumental reasons for deference, while, for others, deference will follow from prudential or even non-instrumental second-order reasons. This discussion expanded existing conceptual accounts of deference in international adjudication, which, to date, have focused almost exclusively on deference deriving from instrumental second-order reasons. The part further introduced the debate between theorists as to the structure of authority, according to which second-order reasons may take an exclusionary or non-exclusionary structure.

Part II drew on the conceptual framework developed in Part I to investigate how international adjudicators use deference to recognise the decision-making authority of domestic officials. Chapter 4 introduced seven different 'modes' of deference, exhibited by differing doctrines and devices. The chapter showed how these modes result in different relationships between international adjudicators and domestic decision-makers based on different views of authority. Whereas some modes reflect a view of authority founded on exclusionary second-order reasons, others instead structure authority in less exclusionary terms, leading to the recognition of concurrent authority between international and domestic decision-makers. Chapters 5 to 7 illustrated the application of these modes of deference in international private property cases, illuminating how international adjudicators use deference to structure their interactions with domestic decision-makers. This analysis connected approaches to deference hitherto seen as discrete, and developed the connection between authority and deference developed in Chapter 1 by reference to international case law. Building on this analysis, Part III illustrated how international adjudicators use the seven modes of deference to mediate, and even define, the boundaries of national and international decision-making authority. That part investigated how the balance between international and domestic decision-making authority has been negotiated over time and in different contexts, and the role played by deference in mediating this balance between international adjudicative and domestic decision-making authority. Deference assists international adjudicators to determine whether to assert their own authority over that of domestic decision-makers or, instead, to recognise the authority of domestic actors.

This analysis illustrated how international adjudicators use deference to articulate different views of the sources of sovereign decision-making authority. Where deference derives from second-order reasons related to the origin of a decision, an adjudicator operates in a culture of bare authority. In this culture of review, international adjudicators adopt a source-based view of authority: domestic decision-makers are accorded deference simply because they are an organ of a sovereign State, or because they have made particular categories of decision. By contrast, in a culture of justification, international adjudicators attribute and recognise authority due to the *qualities* of State decision-makers and their decisions. It is no longer sufficient for a domestic decision-maker to claim that it represents a domestic system or a particular institutional type of decision-making. It must also show how it has applied superior expertise or brought greater legitimacy to the making of a particular decision. Different approaches to deference thus impose fundamentally different criteria for recognition of a sovereign's claim to a right to decide and a right to be left alone. Whereas some approaches to deference stop analysis at the boundary of State decision-making, others investigate State claims to authority more deeply.

These different approaches to deference also influence the impact and quality of international adjudicative reasoning. As explored in Part II, if an international adjudicator elects to apply modes of deference reflecting a culture of justification, it must engage more closely with the components of the State and their decision-making processes. To attribute deference as respect, for example, adjudicators must articulate and identify the structures of decision-making and types of decision that they value. Such reasoning in turn incentivises States to structure and make decisions in particular ways.[1] Particular approaches to deference may thus assist international adjudicators to avoid the criticism that international adjudication removes claims from domestic systems and diminishes the quality of domestic decision-making.[2] Deference, instead, may prompt local improvement. A question arises, however, as to who is empowered to define the qualities that domestic decision-making ought to exhibit. It is this issue that the theme of power addresses.

B POWER

International adjudicators use deference to claim and exercise decision-making authority and to recognise or constrain the decision-making authority

[1] See, similarly, Puthuppally (2014), p. 86; Harowitz (2008), p. 1102; Schauer (2004), p. 1574.

[2] Butler (2013), p. 622; Ginsburg (2005), p. 119; Sepúlveda-Amor (2013), p. 566.

of States. Deference thus governs 'decisions about how decisions will be made, where, and by whom'.[3] It recognises the power of particular actors to make decisions, and also determines whether they may exercise that power free from the control of other actors. Deference performs this function in a range of ways. Some approaches to deference result in hierarchies, whereas others provide scope for shared exercises of decision-making power. Different approaches to deference thus 'articulate and consolidate a particular distribution of . . . power'.[4] From this perspective, deference has significant implications for the allocation of power in the international system.[5] Part II highlighted the approaches adopted by international adjudicators to these issues. Contrary to what might be expected, Part III revealed that international adjudicators rarely assert their own primacy to deny the authority of States altogether. Instead, they recognise zones of concurrent authority by which they acknowledge rather than displace State decision-making authority. The story of deference is therefore not one in which international adjudicators have claimed all power for themselves.

The conceptual analysis of deference further indicates that international adjudicative authority may owe as much to cessions of authority as it does to its assertion. Deference itself may function as a tool of power for international adjudicators. Prudential deference may be used by international adjudicators as a means of cementing their own authority by ceding authority strategically to other actors.[6] Deference might alternatively be used instrumentally to bolster international authority, by allowing adjudicators to avoid prematurely asserting their own expertise or legitimacy before it has developed.[7] Deference may thus assist international adjudicators to avoid backlash in periods of flux or development, while leaving open the possibility of asserting their authority over domestic actors once it is better established.

Deference also impacts the international balance of power between States, and domestic power and politics. Deference may, for instance, influence which States are more likely to be successful in international claims. A more developed State, for example, may have greater institutional capacity than a developing State and therefore be more capable of attracting deference for second-order reasons of empirical epistemic

3 Sloane (2009b), p. 519.
4 Koskenniemi (1997), pp. 570–1.
5 Johns (2009). My thanks to Professor Nikolas Rajkovic for encouraging me to consider this point.
6 Analysis of legitimation of *international* actors indicates a similar process, with international actors drawing on the established authority of other international actors to incrementally 'ratchet up' their own 'cachet' of legitimacy: Block-Lieb and Halliday (2007), p. 898.
7 Spano (2018b), p. 3.

authority (experise/competence).[8] Democratic States might similarly be granted deference on the grounds of normative epistemic authority (legitimacy) more frequently than other States.[9] Franck, for example, argued that: 'While expropriations by totalitarian regimes invite close scrutiny of their motives, open government invites judicial deference.'[10] This book has examined the conceptual basis on which commentators – and some adjudicators – might justify this position. It has also argued that different approaches to deference may impact the organisation of domestic structures of power. Deference may privilege, for example, decisions emanating from particular decision-making structures or institutions over others. It therefore creates an incentive for States to structure and exercise their domestic decision-making authority in particular ways.

This book has also illustrated the significance of adjudicators as a class of actors relevant to the study of power in international systems. Deference prompts international adjudicators to lift the State's veil to appraise its internal structure and the performance of its various organs. At the same time, it provides adjudicators with 'a *method* for resolving conflicts ... which is conceptually defensible and hence allows them to preserve their claim to neutrality'.[11] The identification of fundamentally different approaches to deference reveals the significance of the values and backgrounds of the individuals appointed to international courts and tribunals. This perspective opens pathways for future research. It might be expected, for instance, that approaches to deference will change as courts or tribunals are institutionally restructured or 'socialised' to attain greater familiarity with particular litigant States or domestic decision-making processes.[12] Such analysis may reveal an extended significance of the ongoing debates about how representative international adjudicators are of the States comprising the international system and of the litigants appearing before them.

C CONFLICT, CONTINUITY AND CHANGE

Deference responds to conflicting claims to authority. It is used by adjudicators to determine which institutions, in which legal orders, will have their decision-making power recognised in international claims.[13] It mediates the

[8] Henckels (2015), p. 42; Duhaime (2014), p. 314; Young (2005), p. 191; Spano (2018a), pp. 21–2.
[9] Dothan (2018).
[10] Franck (1998), p. 467.
[11] McHarg (1999), p. 672.
[12] Helfer (2008), p. 135; Koh (2003), p. 1502; Koh (1996), pp. 204–5.
[13] Greer (2010), p. 6; Stone Sweet (2009), p. 626; Klabbers et al. (2009), p. 22.

'hegemonic struggle'[14] between domestic and international decision-makers over the authority to decide the matters at issue in private property disputes. Part II introduced seven modes of deference used by international adjudicators to coordinate these conflicting claims to authority. Arraying these from most to least deferential, the part also distinguished between the various views of authority reflected by each mode. It illustrated that, whereas the mode of 'submission' signifies a view of domestic authority as conclusive, the modes of 'deferral' and 'abstention' adopt a suspensive view of domestic authority. By contrast, the modes of 'restraint', 'reference' and 'respect' manifest a view of concurrent authority and – at the end of the spectrum – the mode of 'control/dismissal' a conclusive view of authority in favour of international decision-making. Chapters 5 to 7 examined the approaches to settling conflicting claims to authority represented by each of these modes.

This analysis shows that deference is vital to the resolution of conflicting claims to authority in international adjudication. It assists adjudicators to settle controversies about the distribution of decision-making authority in the regimes in which they operate. Deference thus links to broader debates about fragmentation and regime conflict. As Chapter 9 argued, deference offers a proxy for studying how international adjudicators conceptualise their relationships to actors in other legal orders. This gives different approaches to deference systemic significance. Even if the PCIJ, ICJ, ECtHR and investment treaty tribunals function in self-contained regimes (a point doubted but not resolved in Chapter 2), Parts II and III revealed that they are using deference by reference to a conceptually similar logic. This shows that the concept of deference holds conceptual and functional unity despite its manifestation under different labels in different regimes and time periods.

The dynamic properties of deference, and its connection to authority, indicate that approaches to deference are likely to remain unsettled and highly contested. In fact, the role of deference is particularly likely to be contested in a context of increased globalisation and privatisation, where the boundaries between public/private and international/domestic are in constant flux. This is not necessarily undesirable. Even if it remains unfixed to particular doctrines or devices, deference can be used to stabilise this ongoing process of change. It is used by international adjudicators to negotiate and readjust the national/international interface dynamically as circumstances change. This book has demonstrated that part of the value of deference lies not in resolving but rather in creating space for debate about the relationships between States and international adjudicators. Deference has been flexibly used to manage

[14] Koskenniemi (2014), p. 46.

resistance, contestation, and feedback to the reach of international law. While conceptions of deference have exhibited significant change, the concept of deference has assisted adjudicators to secure continuity during phases of transition.

***

This is not the first study of deference, and it is unlikely to be the last. The application of deference in legal adjudication has been much discussed in both domestic and international scholarship. Despite the ubiquity of references to deference, however, the systemic operation and significance of deference across public international law has been underappreciated. While literature to date has accorded considerable attention to the need for deference to State policy choices in international adjudication, there has been little analysis of the full spectrum of approaches by which international adjudicators accord a role for domestic decision-making in international adjudication or of the full range of domestic decisions to which such deference might attach. There has also been little investigation of whether approaches to deference vary across international adjudicative regimes or over time. Through a wide-ranging empirical study covering four adjudicative mechanisms, this book has developed an empirically informed theory of deference applicable in the international adjudication of private property disputes. Through both temporal and cross-institutional comparison, the book has illuminated how international adjudicative perceptions of the international/domestic interface have changed over time and differ according to institutional setting. Investigating these issues, the book has examined the role of deference in managing conflicting claims to authority between domestic and international adjudicators in diverse institutional settings and different time periods.

Tracking these themes, the book has presented a theory of deference as an authoritative practice. It has demonstrated that different approaches to deference depend on an adjudicator's analysis of authority. Adjudicators recognise authority by reference variously to instrumental, prudential and non-instrumental second-order reasons. Approaches to deference further depend on an adjudicator's analysis of the structure of authority. Moving beyond a presentation of adjudicative reasoning as 'deferential' or 'non-deferential', the book has identified instead seven modes of deference reflecting different approaches to analysing these issues of authority. The book has identified conceptual connections between these modes, arguing that they reflect three distinct views as to the structure of authority. Conclusive and suspensive approaches to authority operate on the basis of *exclusionary* second-order reasons for deference. Deference in these approaches operates akin to an order, precluding or suspending the international adjudicator's own analysis of relevant first-order reasons for decision. Other approaches, by contrast, balance authority with other reasons for decision. Such approaches function in a manner more akin to a request, giving the international adjudicator comparatively more scope to exercise its own decision-making authority, albeit alongside or in recognition of the decision-making authority of domestic actors. International adjudicators thus do not exclusively operate in the position of the 'nosy neighbour' or 'Victorian lady' referred to in the Introduction. Their approaches to deference instead reflect a spectrum of personas. The selection between these personas depends on how adjudicators analyse the structural relationship between their own authority and that of domestic decision-makers.

By examining these approaches, the book has sought to extend the analysis of deference in existing accounts and to examine its cross-institutional and temporal manifestations and significance. It has highlighted the dynamic and political properties of deference, and examined what it reveals about the changing nature and structure of authority in international adjudication. In doing so, the book has brought into focus the implications of ostensibly technical debates concerning doctrinal techniques. Debates about deference act as a proxy for broader contestations of authority and debates about the appropriate balance of power in the international system. The significance of deference lies in its use by international adjudicators to articulate their views as to the relationships between national and international decision-makers, between national and international law, and between law and politics. While these interfaces remain in flux, so, too, will the approaches to deference used to manage them.

APPENDIX

Data Tables

The sections in this Appendix set out the data underlying the analysis in Chapter 8.

A 'OBSERVATIONS' OF DEFERENCE IN MAJORITY AND DISSENTING/ SEPARATE OPINIONS

		PCIJ	ICJ	ECtHR	ISDS	Total
Majority decisions	Applications	11	11	357	630	1009
	Non-applications	22	18	190	304	534
	Total observations	33	29	547	934	1543
Dissents/separate opinions	Applications	17	35	88	47	187
	Non-applications	10	35	9	16	70
	Total observations	27	70	97	63	257
Total		60	99	644	997	1800

B MODES OF DEFERENCE BY REGIME

(i) Applications of Deference; Majority Decisions

	Submission	Deferral	Abstention	Restraint	Reference	Respect	Control/ dismissal	Total
PCIJ	2	3	0	2	3	0	1	11
ICJ	1	1	1	1	3	2	2	11
ECtHR	14	19	28	67	67	158	4	357
GC	*3*	*12*	*11*	*25*	*20*	*38*	*2*	*111*
Non-GC	*11*	*7*	*17*	*42*	*47*	*120*	*2*	*246*
ISDS	7	8	117	115	133	209	41	630

(continued)

	Submission	Deferral	Abstention	Restraint	Reference	Respect	Control/ dismissal	Total
ICSID	3	5	72	74	79	113	33	379
Non-ICSID	4	3	45	41	54	96	8	251
Total	24	31	146	185	206	369	48	1009

(ii) *Non-Applications of Deference; Majority Decisions*

	Submission	Deferral	Abstention	Restraint	Reference	Respect	Control/ dismissal	Total
PCIJ	2	8	7	2	1	0	2	22
ICJ	2	9	4	0	1	0	2	18
ECtHR	0	138	2	0	2	48	0	190
GC	0	25	1	0	1	7	0	34
Non-GC	0	113	1	0	1	41	0	156
ISDS	45	87	56	62	7	17	30	304
ICSID	31	48	33	35	4	8	21	180
Non-ICSID	14	39	23	27	3	9	9	124
Total	49	242	69	64	11	65	34	534

C STRUCTURES OF AUTHORITY BY REGIME (APPLICATIONS OF DEFERENCE; MAJORITY DECISIONS)

	Conclusive domestic authority	Suspensive authority	Concurrent authority	Conclusive international authority	Total
PCIJ	2	3	5	1	11
ICJ	1	2	6	2	11
ECtHR	14	47	292	4	357
ISDS	7	125	457	41	630
Total	24	177	760	48	1009

D THE BENEFICIARIES OF DEFERENCE (APPLICATIONS OF DEFERENCE; MAJORITY DECISIONS)

		Total
Submission	Judicial decision	17
	Legislative/executive decision	6
	The 'State'	1
Deferral	Judicial decision	22
	Legislative/executive decision	5
	The 'State'	3
Abstention	Judicial decision	65
	Legislative/Executive decision	63
	The 'State'	13
Restraint	Judicial decision	48
	Legislative/executive decision	106
	The 'State'	35
Reference	Judicial decision	182
	Legislative/executive decision	35
	The 'State'	0
Respect	Judicial decision	128
	Legislative/executive decision	246
	The 'State'	7
Control	Judicial decision	20
	Legislative/executive decision	23
	The 'State'	5
Total	Judicial decision	482
	Legislative/executive decision	484
	The 'State'	64
Total		1030[1]

E JUSTIFICATIONS FOR DEFERENCE (MAJORITY AND SEPARATE/ DISSENTING DECISIONS; APPLICATIONS AND REJECTIONS OF DEFERENCE)

	PCIJ	ICJ	ECtHR	ISDS	Total
Relative competence	4	3	36	53	96
Relative legitimacy	11	24	140	310	485
Relative competence *and* legitimacy	0	4	49	20	73
Prudential reasons	0	0	2	4	6
Non-instrumental reasons	0	0	6	19	25
Mixed instrumental/non-instrumental/prudential reasons	0	1	4	12	17

[1] This differs from total observed applications of deference, because sometimes in one application of deference an adjudicator identified more than one beneficiary for deference.

F OBSERVATIONS OF APPLICATIONS OF DEFERENCE OVER TIME

	Majority decisions			Dissenting and separate opinions		
	Total number of reviewed decisions	Total observed applications of deference	Applications of a mode of deference per number of decisions that year	Total number of reviewed dissents/SOs	Total observed applications of deference	Applications of a mode of deference per number of dissents/SOs that year
1924–6	4	2	0.5	9	3	0.333333
1927–9	9	2	0.222222	14	4	0.285714
1930–2	0	0	0	0	0	0
1933–5	6	4	0.666667	11	5	0.454545
1936–8	7	0	0	11	1	0.090909
1939–41	5	3	0.6	13	4	0.307692
1942–4	0	0	0	0	0	0
1945–7	0	0	0	0	0	0
1948–50	0	0	0	0	0	0
1951–3	5	0	0	15	2	0.133333
1954–6	1	1	1	4	4	1
1957–9	3	2	0.666667	15	9	0.6
1960–2	0	0	0	0	0	0
1963–5	1	0	0	9	3	0.333333
1966–8	0	0	0	0	0	0
1969–71	1	1	1	11	5	0.454545
1972–4	0	0	0	0	0	0
1975–7	1	1	1	2	0	0
1978–80	2	1	0.5	8	3	0.375
1981–3	2	2	1	7	2	0.285714
1984–6	2	4	2	5	0	0
1987–9	6	9	1.5	6	3	0.5
1990–2	6	6	1	4	2	0.5
1993–5	10	16	1.6	6	2	0.333333
1996–8	21	5	0.238095	30	4	0.133333
1999–2001	59	54	0.915254	37	12	0.324324
2002–4	104	68	0.653846	36	14	0.388889
2005–7	214	152	0.71028	48	23	0.479167
2008–10	214	166	0.775701	46	18	0.391304
2011–13	172	181	1.052326	54	23	0.425926
2014–16	198	184	0.929293	45	20	0.444444
2017–19	159	145	0.91195	56	21	0.375
Total	1212	1009	(average: 0.832508)	502	187	(average: 0.37251)

G APPROACHES TO AUTHORITY OVER TIME (APPLICATIONS OF DEFERENCE; MAJORITY DECISIONS)

	Categorical					Concurrent			
	Sub-mission	Def-erral	Abst-ention	Control	Total	Rest-raint	Refe-rence	Respect	Total
1924–6	0	0	0	0	0	2	0	0	2
1927–9	0	0	0	0	0	0	2	0	2
1930–2	0	0	0	0	0	0	0	0	0
1933–5	2	1	0	0	3	0	1	0	1
1936–8	0	0	0	0	0	0	0	0	0
1939–41	0	2	0	1	3	0	0	0	0
1942–4	0	0	0	0	0	0	0	0	0
1945–7	0	0	0	0	0	0	0	0	0
1948–50	0	0	0	0	0	0	0	0	0
1951–3	0	0	0	0	0	0	0	0	0
1954–6	0	0	0	0	0	0	0	1	1
1957–9	1	1	0	0	2	0	0	0	0
1960–2	0	0	0	0	0	0	0	0	0
1963–5	0	0	0	0	0	0	0	0	0
1966–8	0	0	0	0	0	0	0	0	0
1969–71	0	0	1	0	1	0	0	0	0
1972–4	0	0	0	0	0	0	0	0	0
1975–7	1	0	0	0	1	0	0	0	0
1978–80	1	0	0	0	1	0	0	0	0
1981–3	0	0	0	0	0	0	1	1	2
1984–6	0	0	1	0	1	1	1	1	3
1987–9	0	0	1	0	1	3	3	2	8
1990–2	0	0	1	1	2	1	0	3	4
1993–5	1	0	3	0	4	4	3	5	12
1996–8	1	0	1	0	2	0	1	2	3
1999–2001	2	1	9	3	15	7	11	21	39
2002–4	0	5	15	3	23	8	16	21	45
2005–7	1	5	36	7	49	21	31	51	103
2008–10	1	2	27	11	41	40	27	58	125
2011–13	5	5	22	7	39	37	38	67	142
2014–16	5	1	23	7	36	30	35	83	148
2017–19	3	8	6	8	25	31	36	53	120
Total	24	31	146	48	249	185	206	369	760

H ECtHR STRUCTURES OF AUTHORITY (APPLICATIONS OF DEFERENCE; MAJORITY DECISIONS)

	Categorical approaches to authority	Concurrent approaches to authority	Total
1976	1	0	1
1977	0	0	0
1978	0	0	0
1979	1	0	1
1980	0	0	0
1981	0	0	0
1982	0	2	2
1983	0	0	0
1984	0	0	0
1985	0	0	0
1986	1	3	4
1987	0	3	3
1988	0	0	0
1989	1	2	3
1990	1	2	3
1991	0	2	2
1992	0	0	0
1993	1	0	1
1994	3	6	9
1995	0	6	6
1996	1	3	4
1997	0	0	0
1998	0	0	0
1999	4	6	10
2000	1	9	10
2001	4	7	11
2002	2	6	8
2003	0	1	1
2004	3	11	14
2005	6	15	21
2006	5	18	23
2007	2	18	20
2008	0	7	7
2009	3	10	13
2010	3	14	17
2011	0	12	12
2012	3	25	28
2013	2	16	18
2014	4	20	24
2015	1	9	10
2016	2	25	27

(*continued*)

	Categorical approaches to authority	Concurrent approaches to authority	Total
2017	6	11	17
2018	1	11	12
2019	3	12	15
Total	65	292	357

I ISDS STRUCTURES OF AUTHORITY (APPLICATIONS OF DEFERENCE; MAJORITY DECISIONS)

	Categorical approaches to authority	Concurrent approaches to authority	Total
1990	1	0	1
1991	0	0	0
1992	0	0	0
1993	0	0	0
1994	0	0	0
1995	0	0	0
1996	0	0	0
1997	1	0	1
1998	0	0	0
1999	1	1	2
2000	2	8	10
2001	3	8	11
2002	2	10	12
2003	7	6	13
2004	7	11	18
2005	9	6	15
2006	20	15	35
2007	7	31	38
2008	9	23	32
2009	12	32	44
2010	14	37	51
2011	12	28	40
2012	11	35	46
2013	11	26	37
2014	16	36	52
2015	4	31	35
2016	9	27	36
2017	2	23	25
2018	5	25	30
2019	8	38	46
Total	173	457	630

J APPROACHES TO DEFERENCE AS RESPECT (ECtHR AND ISDS APPLICATIONS OF DEFERENCE; MAJORITY DECISIONS)

	Good faith		Procedural		Substantive/equivalence		Mixed	
	ECtHR	ISDS	ECtHR	ISDS	ECtHR	ISDS	ECtHR	ISDS
1981–3	0		1	0	0	0	0	0
1984–6	0	0	0	0	1	0	0	0
1987–9	0	0	2	0	0	0	0	0
1990–2	0	0	1	0	2	0	0	0
1993–5	1	0	3	0	1	0	0	0
1996–8	0	0	1	0	1	0	0	0
1999–2001	0	1	7	0	5	5	2	1
2002–4	2	2	6	0	3	7	0	1
2005–7	0	4	12	2	10	14	2	7
2008–10	0	7	7	5	8	16	2	12
2011–13	0	4	18	6	5	12	1	21
2014–16	0	7	23	2	7	17	4	23
2017–19	0	10	8	3	11	11	1	9
Total	3	35	89	18	54	82	12	74

References

Aalberts TE and Venzke I (2017), 'Moving beyond Interdisciplinary Turf Wars: Towards an Understanding of International Law as Practice' in d'Aspremont et al. (eds.), *International Law as a Profession* (Cambridge University Press)

Abbott KW (2008), 'Enriching Rational Choice Institutionalism for the Study of International Law', *University of Illinois Law Review* 5

Abi-Saab G (1996), 'The International Court as a World Court' in Lowe and Fitzmaurice (eds.), *Fifty Years of the International Court of Justice* (Cambridge University Press)

Adede AO (1977a), 'International Law and Property of Aliens: The Old Order Changeth', 19 *Malaya Law Review* 175

(1977b), 'A Survey of Treaty Provisions on the Rule of Exhaustion of Local Remedies', 18 *Harvard International Law Journal* 1

Adler MH (1990), 'The Exhaustion of the Local Remedies Rule after the International Court of Justice's Decision in *ELSI*', 39 *International & Comparative Law Quarterly* 641

Ahdieh R (2004), 'Between Dialogue and Decree: International Review of National Courts', 79 *New York University Law Review* 2029

Ajevski M (2014), 'Unstable Identities: The European Court of Human Rights and the Margin of Appreciation', University of Oslo Faculty of Law Research Paper Series, Paper No. 2014-34

Akinsanya AA (1980), *The Expropriation of Multinational Property in the Third World* (Praeger)

Alexander L and Schauer F (1997), 'On Extrajudicial Constitutional Interpretation', 110 *Harvard Law Review* 1359

Alexy R (2009), *A Theory of Constitutional Rights* (Oxford University Press)

Alford R (2002), 'Federal Courts, International Tribunals, and the Continuum of Deference', 43 *Virginia Journal of International Law* 675

Allan TRS (2006), 'Human Rights and Judicial Review: A Critique of "Due Deference"', 65 *Cambridge Law Journal* 671

(2010), 'Deference, Defiance, and Doctrine: Defining the Limits of Judicial Review', 60 *University of Toronto Law Review* 41

(2011), 'Judicial Deference and Judicial Review: Legal Doctrine and Legal Theory', 127 Law Quarterly Review 96

Allars M (1994), 'On Deference to Tribunals, with Deference to Dworkin', 20 *Queen's Law Journal* 163

Allen T (2005a), *Property and the Human Rights Act 1998* (Hart)

(2005b), 'Transitional Justice and the Right to Property under the European Convention on Human Rights', 16 *Stellenbosch Law Review* 413

(2007), 'Compensation for Property under the European Convention on Human Rights', 28 *Michigan Journal of International Law* 287

(2010), 'Liberalism, Social Democracy and the Value of Property under the European Convention on Human Rights', 59 *International & Comparative Law Quarterly* 1055

Allison JWF (1994), 'Fuller's Analysis of Polycentric Disputes and the Limits of Adjudication', 53 *Cambridge Law Journal* 367

Allott P (1999), 'International Law and the Idea of History', 1 *Journal of the History of International Law* 1

Alschner W (2014), 'The Return of the Home State and the Rise of 'Embedded' Investor-State Arbitration' in Lalani and Lazo (eds.), *The Role of the State in Investor-State Arbitration* (Martinus Nijhoff)

Alter K (2008a), 'Agents or Trustees? International Courts in Their Political Context', 14 *European Journal of International Relations* 33

(2008b), 'Delegating to International Courts: Self-Binding vs. Other-Binding Delegation', 71 *Law & Contemporary Problems* 37

(2011), 'The Evolving International Judiciary', 7 *Annual Review of Law and Social Science* 387

(2014), *The New Terrain of International Law: Courts, Politics, Rights* (Princeton University Press)

Alter K, Helfer L and Madsen MR (2016), 'How Context Shapes the Authority of International Courts', 79 *Law and Contemporary Problems* 1

Alvarez JE (2006), *International Organizations as Law-Makers* (Oxford University Press)

(2016), 'Is Investor-State Arbitration "Public"?', 7 *Journal of International Dispute Settlement* 534

Alvik I (2010), 'The Hybrid Nature of Investment Treaty Arbitration: Straddling the National/International Divide' in Eriksen and Emberland (eds.), *The New International Law: An Anthology* (Martinus Nijhoff)

(2018), 'Protection of Private Property in the Early Law of Nations', 20 *Journal of the History of International Law* 217

Amaza IP (2012), 'Multiplicity of International Dispute Settlement Forums: Avoiding the Risk of Parallel Proceedings', 6 *Dispute Resolution International* 149

Ambrus M (2013), 'The European Court of Human Rights and Standards of Proof in Religion Cases', 8 *Religion and Human Rights* 107

Amerasinghe CF (2008), *Diplomatic Protection* (Oxford University Press)

American Bar Association (2016), *Investment Treaty Working Group: Task Force Report on the Investment Court System Proposal*

Anand RP (1963), 'The International Court of Justice and Impartiality between Nations', 12 *Indian Year Book of International Affairs* 12

(1965), 'The Role of Individual and Dissenting Opinions in International Adjudication', 14 *International & Comparative Law Quarterly* 788

(1969), *Studies in International Adjudication* (Oceana Publications Inc.)

Anthony R (1998), 'Which Agency Interpretations Should Get Judicial Deference? A Preliminary Inquiry', 40 *Administrative Law Review* 121

Anzilotti D (1928), *Corso Di Diritto Internazionale* (3rd edn, Athenaeum)

Arai Y (1998), 'The Margin of Appreciation Doctrine in the Jurisprudence of Article 8 of the European Convention on Human Rights', 16 *Netherlands Quarterly of Human Rights* 41

Arai-Takahashi Y (2002), *The Margin of Appreciation Doctrine and the Principle of Proportionality in the Jurisprudence of the ECHR* (Intersentia)

Arangio-Ruiz G (1990), 'Le Domaine Reserve: L'Organisation Internationale et Le Rapport Entre Droit International et Droit Interne', *Collected Courses of the Hague Academy of International Law*, vol. 225

(1996), 'The Plea of Domestic Jurisdiction before the International Court of Justice: Substance or Procedure?' in Lowe and Fitzmaurice (eds.), *Fifty Years of the International Court of Justice: Essays in Honour of Sir Robert Jennings* (Cambridge University Press)

Arato J (2014), 'The Margin of Appreciation in International Investment Law', 54 *Virginia Journal of International Law* 2

Arendt H (2006), *Between Past and Future: Eight Exercises in Political Thought* (Penguin Books)

Arnardóttir OM (2015), 'Organised Retreat? The Move from "Substantive" to "Procedural" Review in the ECtHR's Case Law on the Margin of Appreciation', European Society of International Law Conference Paper No. 4/2015

(2017), 'The "Procedural Turn" under the European Convention on Human Rights and Presumptions of Convention Compliance', 15 *International Journal of Constitutional Law* 9

Arndt JD (1959), 'International Court of Justice – Legal Effect, Constitutional and International, of the Connally Reservation', 28 *University of Kansas Law Review* 1

Ashforth BE and Gibbs BW (1990), 'The Double-Edge of Organizational Legitimation', 1 *Organization Science* 177

Atik J (2003), 'Repenser NAFTA Chapter 11: A Catalogue of Legitimacy Critiques', 3 *Asper Review of International Business and Trade Law* 215

Austin J (1885), *Lectures on Jurisprudence: Or, the Philosophy of Positive Law*, vol. 2 (5th edn, Lawbook Exchange Ltd)

Ayres L, Kavanaugh K and Knafl K (2003), 'Within-Case and Across-Case Approaches to Qualitative Data Analysis', 13 *Qualitative Health Research* 871

Baker P (2006), *Using Corpora in Discourse Analysis* (Continuum)

Balcerzak M (2004), 'The Doctrine of Precedent in the International Court of Justice and the European Court of Human Rights', 27 *Polish Yearbook of International Law* 131

Balkin JM (1996), 'A Night in the Topics: The Reason of Legal Rhetoric and the Rhetoric of Legal Reason' in Brooks and Gewirtz (eds.), *Law's Stories: Narrative and Rhetoric in the Law* (Yale University Press)

Banakar R and Travers M (eds.) (2013), *Law and Social Theory* (2nd edn, Hart)

Bankowski Z, MacCormick N, Summers R, and Jerzy W (1991), 'On Method and Methodology', in N MacCormick and R Summers (eds), *Interpreting Statutes: A Comparative Study* (Dartmouth)

Banks K (1999), 'NAFTA's Article 1110 – Can Regulation Be Expropriation?', 5 *NAFTA: Law & Business Review of the Americas* 499

Barkhuysen T and van Emmerik M (2009), 'Legitimacy of European Court of Human Rights Judgments: Procedural Aspects' in Huls et al. (eds.), *The Legitimacy of Highest Courts' Ruling* (TMC Asser Press)
Barnett M and Finnemore M (2004), *Rules for the World: International Organizations in Global Politics* (Cornell University Press)
Barrie G (1995), 'International Human Rights Conventions: Public International Law Applicable to the Protection of Rights', *Journal of South African Law* 66
Beck G (2007), 'The Idea of Human Rights between Value Pluralism and Conceptual Vagueness', 25 *Penn State International Law Review* 615
Bedjaoui M (1991), 'The "Manufacture" of Judgments at the International Court of Justice', 3 *Pace Yearbook of International Law* 29
Behn D, Langford M and Laudal Berge T (2018), 'Development or Democracy? Explaining Outcomes in Investment Treaty Arbitration, 38(3) *Northwestern Journal of International Law & Business* 333
Bellamy R (2014), 'The Democratic Legitimacy of International Human Rights Conventions: Political Constitutionalism and the European Convention on Human Rights', 25 *European Journal of International Law* 1019
Bemelmans-Videc M (2011), 'Guaranteeing the Authority and Effectiveness of the European Convention on Human Rights' AS/Jur 44 Committee on Legal Affairs and Human Rights
Benhabib S (2009), 'Claiming Rights across Borders: International Human Rights and Democratic Sovereignty', 103 *American Political Science Review* 691
Bennouna M (2014), 'The International Court of Justice: Bestriding Past and Present' in Gaja and Grote Stoutenburg (eds.), *Enhancing the Rule of Law through the International Court of Justice* (Brill)
Benvenisti E (1999), 'Margin of Appreciation, Consensus, and Universal Standards', 31 *New York University Journal of International Law and Politics* 843
(2013), 'Sovereigns as Trustees of Humanity: On the Accountability of States to Foreign Stakeholders', 107 *American Journal of International Law* 295
(2018), 'The Margin of Appreciation, Subsidiarity and Global Challenges to Democracy', 9 *Journal of International Dispute Settlement* 240
Benvenisti E and Harel A (2017), 'Embracing the Tension between National and International Human Rights Law: The Case for Discordant Parity', 15(1) *International Journal of Constitutional Law* 36
Berg BL and Lune H (2014), *Qualitative Research Methods for the Social Sciences* (8th edn, Pearson)
Bergbohm C (1877), *Staatsverträge Und Gesetze Als Quellen Des Völkerrechts* (Mattiesen)
Berman F (2013a), 'Fair and Equitable Treatment: A Rejoinder to Martins Paparinskis' EJIL: Talk!
Berman PS (2007), 'A Pluralist Approach to International Law', 32 *Yale Journal of International Law* 301
(2008), 'Federalism and International Law Through the Lens of Legal Pluralism', 73 *Missouri Law Review* 1149
(2012), *Global Legal Pluralism: A Jurisprudence of Law Beyond Borders* (Cambridge University Press)

(2013), 'Jurisgenerative Constitutionalism: Procedural Principles for Managing Global Legal Pluralism', 20 *Indiana Journal of Global Legal Studies* 665

Bernhardt R (1993), 'The Convention and Domestic Law' in Macdonald et al. (eds.), *The European System for the Protection of Human Rights* (Martinus Nijhoff)

Besson S (2009), 'The Authority of International Law – Lifting the State Veil', 31 *Sydney Law Review* 343

(2011), 'International Judges as Dispute-Settlers and Law-Enforcers: From International Law without Courts to International Courts without Law; A Reply to Anna Spain', 34 *Loyola of Los Angeles International and Comparative Law Review* 33

Bickel AM (1962), *The Least Dangerous Branch: The Supreme Court at the Bar of Politics* (Yale University Press)

Bilder R (1982), 'Some Limitations of Adjudication as an International Dispute Settlement Technique', 23 *Virginia Journal of International Law* 1

(2007), 'Adjudication: International Arbitral Tribunals and Courts' in Zartman (ed.), *Peacemaking in International Conflict: Methods and Techniques* (United States Institute of Peace)

Bilkova V (2014), 'The Standard of Equivalent Protection as a Standard of Review' in Gruszczynski and Werner (eds.), *Deference in International Courts and Tribunals: Standard of Review and Margin of Appreciation* (Oxford University Press)

Bjørge E and Miles CA (eds.) (2017), *Landmark Cases in Public International Law* (Hart)

Bjorklund A (2004), 'Waiver and the Exhaustion of Local Remedies Rule in NAFTA Jurisprudence' in Weiler (ed.), *NAFTA Investment Law and Arbitration: Past Issues, Current Practice, Future Prospects*

(2007), 'Private Rights and Public International Law: Why Competition among International Economic Law Tribunals Is Not Working', 59 *Hastings Law Journal* 241

Blades BW (2006) 'The Exhausting Question of Local Remedies: Expropriation under NAFTA Chapter 11', *Oregon Review of International Law* 31

Block-Lieb S and Halliday T (2007), 'Incrementalisms in Global Lawmaking', 32(3) *Brooklyn Journal of International Law* 851

Bodansky D (1999), 'The Legitimacy of International Governance: A Coming Challenge for International Environmental Law?', 93 *American Journal of International Law* 596

(2006), 'International Law in Black and White', 34 *Georgia Journal of International and Comparative Law* 285

(2007), 'The Concept of Legitimacy in International Law' in Wolfrum and Röben (eds.), *Legitimacy in International Law* (Springer)

(2012), 'Legitimacy in International Law and International Relations' in Dunoff and Pollack (eds.), Interdisciplinary Perspectives on International Law and International Relations: The State of the Art (Cambridge University Press)

Bodie TJ (1995), *Politics and the Emergence of an Activist International Court of Justice* (Greenwood Publishing Group)

Bodin J (1576), *Six Books of the Commonwealth* (translated by M.J. Tooley) (Blackwell Oxford)

Bomhoff J (2010), 'Genealogies of Balancing as Discourse', 4 *Law & Ethics of Human Rights* 109

Bonnitcha J (2014), *Substantive Protection under Investment Treaties: A Legal and Economic Analysis* (Cambridge University Press)

Borchard E (1919), *The Diplomatic Protection of Citizens Abroad* (Banks Law Publishing Co.)

Boyatzis RE (1998), *Transforming Qualitative Information: Thematic Analysis and Code Development* (Sage Publications)

Bradley C and Kelley J (2008), 'The Concept of International Delegation', 71 *Law and Contemporary Problems* 1

Brems E (1996), 'The Margin of Appreciation Doctrine in the Case-Law of the European Court of Human Rights', 56 *Zeitschrift für Ausländisches Öffentliches Recht und Volkerrecht* 230

(2017), 'The "Logics" of Procedural-Type Review by the European Court of Human Rights' in Brems and Gerards (eds.), *Procedural Review in European Fundamental Rights Cases* (Cambridge University Press)

Brems E and Gerards J (eds.) (2017), *Procedural Review in European Fundamental Rights Cases* (Cambridge University Press)

Brems E and Lavrysen L (2013), 'Procedural Justice in Human Rights Adjudication: The European Court of Human Rights', 35 *Human Rights Quarterly* 176

(2015), '"Don't Use a Sledgehammer to Crack a Nut": Less Restrictive Means in the Case Law of the European Court of Human Rights', 15 *Human Rights Law Review* 139

Brierly JL (1925), 'Matters of Domestic Jurisdiction', 6 *British Yearbook of International Law* 8

Briggs H (1960), 'Confidence, Apprehension and the International Court of Justice', 54 *American Society of International Law Proceedings* 25

Bring OE (1980), 'The Impact of Developing States on International Customary Law Concerning Protection of Foreign Property', 24 *Scandinavian Studies in Law* 97

Brisbane Telegraph (1927), 'League of Nations: How It Can Fail - University Lecture' (Trove)

Brölmann C (2007), 'Deterritorialization in International Law: Moving Away from the Divide Between National and International Law' in Nijman and Nollkaemper (eds.), *New Perspectives on the Divide Between National and International Law* (Oxford University Press)

(2013), 'The Permanent Court of International Justice and the International Rights of Groups and Individuals' in Tams and Fitzmaurice (eds.), *Legacies of the Permanent Court of International Justice* (Martinus Nijhoff)

Broude T (2012), 'The Constitutional Function of Contemporary International Tribunals, or Kelsen's Visions Vindicated', 4 *Goettingen Journal of International Law* 519

(2016), 'Selective Subsidiarity and Dialectic Deference in the World Trade Organization', 79 *Law and Contemporary Problems* 53

Brown C (2002), 'Review Essay – The Proliferation of International Courts and Tribunals: Finding Your Way through the Maze', 3 *Melbourne Journal of International Law* 453

Brown MB (2014), 'Expertise and Deliberative Democracy' in Elstub and McLaverty (eds.), *Deliberative Democracy* (Edinburgh University Press)

Brownlee K (2004), 'Obedience, Conformity, and Deference', 10 *Res Publica* 267

Brownlie I (1963), 'The Relations of Nationality in Public International Law', 39 *British Yearbook of International Law* 284

(1967),'The Justiciability of Disputes and Issues in International Relations', 42 *British Yearbook of International Law* 123

(1998), *Principles of Public International Law* (5th edn, Oxford University Press)

Brunnée J and Toope SJ (2000), 'International Law and Constructivism: Elements of an International Theory of International Law', 39 *Columbia Journal of Transnational Law* 19

(2010), *Legitimacy and Legality in International Law: An Interactional Account* (Cambridge University Press)

Bryman A and Burgess RG (eds.) (2000), *Analyzing Qualitative Data* (Routledge)

Buchanan A (2003), *Justice, Legitimacy, and Self-Determination* (Oxford University Press)

Buchanan A and Keohane RO (2006), 'The Legitimacy of Global Governance Institutions', 20 *Ethics & International Affairs* 405

Buchanan R (2009), 'Reconceptualising Law and Politics in the Transnational Constitutional and Legal Pluralist Approaches', 5 *Socio-Legal Review* 21

Bücheler G (2015), *Proportionality in Investor-State Arbitration* (Oxford University Press)

Bultrini A (2010), 'The European Convention on Human Rights and the Rule of Prior Exhaustion of Domestic Remedies in International Law', 20 *Italian Yearbook of International Law* 101

Burke-White WW (2008a), 'The Argentine Financial Crisis: State Liability under BITs and the Legitimacy of the ICSID System', 3 *Asian Journal of WTO and International Health Law and Policy* 199

(2008b), 'Proactive Complementarity: The International Criminal Court and National Courts in the Rome System of International Justice', 49 *Harvard International Law Journal* 53

Burke-White WW and von Staden A (2008), 'Investment Protection in Extraordinary Times: The Interpretation and Application of Non-Precluded Measures Provisions in Bilateral Investment Treaties', 48 *Virginia Journal of International Law* 307

(2010), 'Private Litigation in a Public Law Sphere: The Standard of Review in Investor-State Arbitrations', 35 *Yale Journal of International Law* 283

Butler N (2013), 'Possible Improvements to the Framework of International Investment Arbitration', 14 *Journal of World Investment & Trade* 613

Calvert C and Hayes J (2012), 'To Defer or Not to Defer? Deference and Its Differential Impact on First Amendment Rights in the Roberts Court', 63 *Case Western Reserve Law Review* 13

Candia G (2014), 'Comparing Diverse Approaches to the Margin of Appreciation: The Case of the European and the Inter-American Court of Human Rights' Pontificia Universidad Católica de Chile, Law School Working Paper Series, Paper No. 2014/01

Caporaso JA (2000), 'Changes in the Westphalian Order: Territory, Public Authority, and Sovereignty', 2 *International Studies Review* 1

Cardozo B (1947), 'Law and Literature' in Hall and Patterson (eds.), *Selected Writings of Benjamin Nathan Cardozo* (Fallon Publications)

Carolan E (2009), *The New Separation of Powers* (Oxford University Press)

Caron DD (1991), 'Comparative Analysis of International Dispute Resolution Institutions', 85 *Proceedings of the Annual Meeting (American Society of International Law)* 65

(1992), 'Reputation and Reality in the ICSID Annulment Process: Understanding the Distinction between Annulment and Appeal', 7 *ICSID Review – Foreign Investment Law Journal* 21

(1993), 'The Legitimacy of the Collective Authority of the Security Council', 87 *American Journal of International Law* 552

(2000), 'War and International Adjudication: Reflections on the 1899 Peace Conference', 94 *American Journal of International Law* 4

(2007a), 'Towards a Political Theory of International Courts and Tribunals', 24 *Berkeley Journal of International Law* 401

(2007b), 'The Iran-US Claims Tribunal and Investment Arbitration: Understanding the Claims Settlement Declaration as a Retrospective BIT' in Drahozal and Gibson (eds.), *The Iran-US Claims Tribunal at 25* (Oxford University Press)

(2012), 'Framing the Work of ICSID Annulment Committees', 6 *World Arbitration & Mediation Review* 173

(2014), 'International Claims and Compensation Bodies' in Romano et al. (eds.), *International Claims and Compensation Bodies* 279

(2015), 'The United Nations Compensation Commission: Understanding an Institution and the Three Phases of Its Work' in Feighery et al. (eds.), *War Reparations and the UN Compensation Commission: Designing Compensation After Conflict* (Oxford University Press)

Caron DD and Shirlow E (2015), 'Most-Favored-Nation Treatment: Substantive Protection' in Kinnear et al. (eds.), *Building International Investment Law: The First 50 Years of ICSID* (Wolters Kluwer)

(2018), 'Dissecting Backlash: The Unarticulated Causes of Backlash and its Unintended Consequences' in Ulfstein and Føllesdal (eds.), *The Judicialization of International Law – A Mixed Blessing?* (Oxford University Press)

(2019), 'Article 25(2)(b)' in Fouret et al. (eds.), *The ICSID Convention, Rules and Regulations: A Practical Commentary* (Edward Elgar)

Carter Jr W (2008), 'Rethinking Subsidiarity in International Human Rights Adjudication', 30 *Hamline Journal of Public Law and Policy* 319

Casas M (2016), 'Nationalities of Convenience, Personal Jurisdiction, and Access to Investor-State Dispute Settlement', 49 *International Law and Politics* 63

Casini L (2014), '"Down the Rabbit-Hole": The Projection of the Public/Private Distinction beyond the State', 12 *International Journal of Constitutional Law* 402

Cass D (1996), 'Navigating the Newstream: Recent Critical Scholarship in International Law', 65 *Nordic Journal of International Law* 341

(2001), 'The "Constitutionalisation" of International Trade Law: Judicial Norm-Generation as the Engine of Constitutional Development in International Trade', 12 *European Journal of International Law* 39

Cassese A (1990), 'Remarks on Scelle's Theory of "Role Splitting" (Dedoublement Fonctionnel) in International Law', 1 *European Journal of International Law* 210

Caudle S (2010), 'Qualitative Data Analysis' in Wholey et al. (eds.), *Handbook of Practical Program Evaluation* (Jossey-Bass)

Charlotin D (2017), 'US Court Declines to Set Aside Mesa *v.* Canada Award' IAReporter

Chen T (2012), 'The Standard of Review and the Roles of ICSID Arbitral Tribunals in Investor-State Dispute Settlement', 5 *Contemporary Asia Arbitration Journal* 23

Cheng B (2006), *General Principles of Law as Applied by International Courts and Tribunals* (1st edn, Cambridge University Press)

Chesney R (2006), 'Disaggregating Deference: The Judicial Power and Executive Treaty Interpretations', 92 *Iowa Law Review* 1723

Cheyne I (2014), 'Deference and the Use of the Public Policy Exception in International Courts and Tribunals' in Gruszczynski and Werner (eds.), *Deference in International Courts and Tribunals: Standard of Review and Margin of Appreciation* (Oxford University Press)

Christiano T (2010), 'Democratic Legitimacy and International Institutions' in Besson and Tasioulas (eds.), *The Philosophy of International Law* (Oxford University Press) 119

(2012), *Authority* (Stanford Encyclopedia of Philosophy)

Christie GC (1962), 'What Constitutes a Taking of Property under International Law?', 38 *British Yearbook of International Law* 307

Christoffersen J and Madsen MR (eds.) (2011), *The European Court of Human Rights between Law and Politics* (Oxford University Press)

(2013), 'Postscript: Understanding the Past, Present, and Future of the European Court of Human Rights' in Christoffersen and Madsen (eds.), *The European Court of Human Rights between Law and Politics* (2nd edn, Oxford University Press)

Christol C (1959), 'The Jurisdiction of the International Court of Justice', 33 *Southern California Law Review* 378

Clark I (2007), *International Legitimacy and World Society* (Oxford University Press)

Clayton R (2004), 'Judicial Deference and "Democratic Dialogue": The Legitimacy of Judicial Intervention under the Human Rights Act 1998', *Public Law* 33

(2006), 'Principles for Judicial Deference', 11 *Judicial Review* 109

Clayton R and Ghaly K (2007), 'Shifting Standards of Review', 12 *Judicial Review* 210

Coe Jr JJ (2003), 'Taking Stock of NAFTA Chapter 11 in Its Tenth Year: An Interim Sketch of Selected Themes, Issues, and Methods', 36 *Vanderbilt Journal of Transnational Law* 1381

Cohen HG (2009), 'Can International Law Work? A Constructivist Expansion', 27 *Berkeley Journal of International Law* 636

(2010), 'From International Law to International Conflicts of Law: The Fragmentation of Legitimacy', 104 *American Society of International Law Proceedings* 49

(2012a), 'Finding International Law, Part II: Our Fragmenting Legal Community', 44 *New York University Journal of International Law and Politics* 1049

(2012b), 'From Fragmentation to Constitutionalization', 24 *Pacific McGeorge Global Business & Development Law Journal* 381

(2015), 'International Precedent and the Practice of International Law' in Helfand (ed.) (Cambridge University Press)172

Cohen J (2010), 'Sovereignty in the Context of Globalization: A Constitutional Pluralist Perspective' in Besson and Tasioulas (eds.), *The Philosophy of International Law* (Oxford University Press)

Cohen M (1927), 'Property and Sovereignty', 13 *Cornell Law Quarterly* 8

Cohen-Eliya M and Porat I (2011), 'Proportionality and the Culture of Justification', 59 *American Journal of Comparative Law* 463

Colangelo AJ (2009), 'Universal Jurisdiction as an International "False Conflict" of Laws', 30 *Michigan Journal of International Law* 881

(2016), 'A Systems Theory of Fragmentation and Harmonization', 49 *International Law and Politics* 1

Collins D (2016), 'The Line of Equilibrium: Improving the Legitimacy of Investment Treaty Arbitration through the Application of the WTO's General Exceptions', 32 *Arbitration International* 575

Colwell B (2007), 'Deference or Respect? Status Management Practices Among Prison Inmates', 70 *Social Psychology Quarterly* 442

Contreras P (2012), 'National Discretion and International Deference in the Restriction of Human Rights: A Comparison Between the Jurisprudence of the European and the Inter-American Court of Human Rights', 11 *Northwestern Journal of International Human Rights* 28

Coquiz J (1977), 'The Problem of Jurisdiction of the International Court of Justice', 52 *Philippine Law Journal* 154

Costa J-P (2011), 'On the Legitimacy of the European Court of Human Rights' Judgments', 7 *European Constitutional Law Review* 173

Cottier T et al., (2017) 'The Principle of Proportionality in International Law: Foundations and Variations', 18 *Journal of World Investment & Trade* 628

Cotula L (2015), 'Property in a Shrinking Planet: Fault Lines in International Human Rights and Investment Law', 11 *International Journal of Law in Context* 113

(2017), 'Democracy and International Investment Law', 30 *Leiden Journal of International Law* 351

Craven M (2003), 'Unity, Diversity and the Fragmentation of International Law', 14 *Finnish Yearbook of International Law* 3

Crawford J (2002), *International Law as an Open System: Selected Essays* (Cameron May)

(2005), *The International Law Commission's articles on State Responsibility: Introduction, Text and Commentaries* (3rd edn, Cambridge University Press)

(2006), 'Multilateral Rights and Obligations in International Law', *Collected Courses of the Hague Academy of International Law*, vol. 319 (Brill)

(2013), *State Responsibility: The General Part* (Cambridge University Press)

(2014), 'Chance, Order, Change: The Course of International Law, General Course on Public International Law' in *Collected Courses of the Hague Academy of International Law*, vol. 365 (Hague Academy of International Law)

Crawford J and Brownlie I (2012), *Brownlie's Principles of Public International Law* (8th edn, Oxford University Press)

Crawford J and Koskenniemi M (eds.) (2012), *The Cambridge Companion to International Law* (Cambridge University Press)

Crema L (2010), 'Disappearance and New Sighting of Restrictive Interpretation(s)', 21 *European Journal of International Law* 681

Creswell JW and Plano Clark VL (2011), *Designing and Conducting Mixed Methods Research* (2nd edn, Sage Publications)

Croquet N (2010), 'The European Court of Human Rights' Norm-Creation and Norm-Limiting Processes: Resolving a Normative Tension', 17 *Columbia Journal of European Law* 307

Cross FB (2007), *Decision Making in the U.S. Courts of Appeals* (Stanford University Press)

Crow K (2017), 'A Taxonomy of Proportionality in International Courts' iCourts Working Paper Series, Paper No. 107

Cunliffe J and Reeve A (1999), 'Dialogic Authority', 19 *Oxford Journal of Legal Studies* 453

Cutler AC (2001), 'Critical Reflections on the Westphalian Assumptions of International Law and Organization: A Crisis of Legitimacy', 27 *Review of International Studies* 133

Czapiewska M (1990), 'General Principles of International Responsibility of the State for Nationalization of Foreign Investments as One of the Means of Their Protection', 2 *Sri Lanka Journal of International Law* 59

Çali B (2016), 'From Flexible to Variable Standards of Judicial Review: The Responsible Domestic Courts Doctrine at the European Court of Human Rights' in Arnardóttir and Buyse (eds.), *Shifting Centres of Gravity in Human Rights Protection: Rethinking Relations between the ECHR, EU, and National Legal Orders* (Routledge)

(2018), 'Explaining Variation in the Intrusiveness of Regional Human Rights Remedies in Domestic Orders', 16 *International Journal of Constitutional Law* 214

Çoban AR (2004), *Protection of Property Rights within the European Convention on Human Rights* (Ashgate)

d'Aspremont J (2012), 'The Permanent Court of International Justice and Domestic Courts: A Variation in Roles' in Tams and Fitzmaurice (eds.), *Legacies of the Permanent Court of International Justice* (Martinus Nijhoff)

(2020), 'The Control over Knowledge by International Courts and Arbitral Tribunals' in Schultz and Ortino (eds.), *Oxford Handbook of International Arbitration* (Oxford University Press)

d'Aspremont J and de Brabandere E (2011), 'The Complementary Faces of Legitimacy in International Law: The Legitimacy of Origin and the Legitimacy of Exercise', 34 *Fordham International Law Journal* 190

d'Aspremont J and Mbengue MM (2014), 'Strategies of Engagement with Scientific Fact-Finding in International Adjudication', 5 *Journal of International Dispute Settlement* 240

D'Alterio E (2011), 'From Judicial Comity to Legal Comity: A Judicial Solution to Global Disorder?', 9 *International Journal of Constitutional Law* 394

D'Amato A (1983), 'Legal Uncertainty', 71 *California Law Review* 1

D'Ascoli S and Scherr KM (2007), 'The Rule of Prior Exhaustion of Local Remedies in the International Law Doctrine and Its Application in the Specific Context of Human Rights Protection' 16(1) *Italian Yearbook of International Law* 117

Daly P (2011), 'Deference on Questions of Law', 74 Modern Law Review 694

Daly P (2012), *A Theory of Deference in Administrative Law: Basis, Application and Scope* (Cambridge University Press)

Dan-Cohen M (1994), 'In Defense of Defiance', 23 *Philosophy and Public Affairs* 24

Daniel J (2017), 'Scrutinizing Deference to Administrative Agencies', *The Regulatory Review*

Danilowicz W (1983), 'The Relation between International Law and Domestic Law in the Jurisprudence of the International Court of Justice', 12 *Polish Yearbook of International Law* 153

Davis H (1996), 'Democratic Disablement and the Right to Property in the European Convention for the Protection of Human Rights', 1 *Journal of Civil Liberties* 125

de Brabandere E (2012), 'Arbitral Decisions as a Source of International Investment Law' in Gazzini and de Brabandere (eds.), *International Investment Law: The Sources of Rights and Obligations* (Martinus Nijhoff)

(2015), *Investment Treaty Arbitration as Public International Law: Procedural Aspects and Implications* (1st edn, Cambridge University Press)

de Bustamente y Sirven AS (1924), 'The Permanent Court of International Justice', 9 *Minnesota Law Review* 122

De Dycker S (2010), 'Private International Law Disputes before the International Court of Justice', 1 *Journal of International Dispute Settlement* 475

de Londras F and Dzehtsiarou K (2015), 'Managing Judicial Innovation in the European Court of Human Rights', 15 *Human Rights Law Review* 523

de Schutter O and Tulkens F (2008), 'Rights in Conflict: The European Court of Human Rights as a Pragmatic Institution' in Brems (ed.), *Conflicts between Fundamental Rights* (Intersentia)

de Vattel E (1797), *The Law of Nations: Or, Principles of the Law of Nature Applied to the Conduct and Affairs of Nations and Sovereigns* (GG & J Robinson)

De Ville JR (2004), 'Deference as Respect and Deference as Sacrifice', 20 *South African Journal on Human Rights* 577

(2006), 'Deference and Différance: Judicial Review and the Perfect Gift', 9 *Potchefstroom Electronic Law Journal* 1

de Visscher C (1956), 'Reflections on the Present Prospects of International Adjudication', 50 *American Journal of International Law* 467

(1968), *Theory and Reality in Public International Law* (PE Corbett tr., Princeton University Press)

de Wet E (2007), 'The Emerging International Constitutional Order: The Implications of Hierarchy in International Law for the Coherence and Legitimacy of International Decision-Making', 10 *Potchefstroom Electronic Law Journal* 7

Delmas-Marty M (2009), *Ordering Pluralism: A Conceptual Framework for Understanding the Transnational Legal World* (Hart)

Demirkol B (2018), *Judicial Acts and Investment Treaty Arbitration* (Cambridge University Press)

Deneen C (1930), 'The Permanent Court of International Justice', 35 *Commercial Law League Journal* 178

Desierto DA (2012), *Necessity and National Emergency Clauses: Sovereignty in Modern Treaty Interpretation* (Martinus Nijhoff)

Dick JC (1978), 'The Bounds of Authority', 4 *Social Theory and Practice* 375

Dixon MJ (1996), 'Fairness in International Laws and Institutions by Thomas M. Franck', 55 *Cambridge Law Journal* 617

Dodge W (2006), 'Investor-State Dispute Settlement between Developed Countries: Reflections on the Australia-United States Free Trade Agreement', 39 *Vanderbilt Journal of Transnational Law* 1

Dolzer R (2002), 'Indirect Expropriations: New Developments?', 11 *New York University Environmental Law Journal* 64

Donoghue J (2012), 'The Role of the World Court Today', 47 *Georgia Law Review* 181

Donoho DL (2001), 'Autonomy, Self-Governance, and the Margin of Appreciation: Developing a Jurisprudence of Diversity within Universal Human Rights', 15 *Emory International Law Review* 391

Dothan S (2018), 'Margin of Appreciation and Democracy: Human Rights and Deference to Political Bodies', 9(2) *Journal of International Dispute Settlement* 145

Douglas Z (2003), 'The Hybrid Foundations of Investment Treaty Arbitration', 74 *British Yearbook of International Law* 151

(2009), *The International Law of Investment Claims* (Cambridge University Press)

(2014a), 'Property, Investment and the Scope of Investment Protection Obligations' in Douglas et al. (eds.), *The Foundations of International Investment Law: Bringing Theory into Practice* (Oxford University Press)

(2014b), 'International Responsibility for Domestic Adjudication: Denial of Justice Deconstructed', 63 *International & Comparative Law Quarterly* 867

Douglas Z, Pauwelyn J and Viñuales JE (eds.) (2014), *The Foundations of International Investment Law: Bringing Theory into Practice* (Oxford University Press)

Drezner D (2001), 'On the Balance between International Law and Democratic Sovereignty', 2 *Chicago Journal of International Law* 321

Dugard J (2004), 'Fifth Report on Diplomatic Protection' UN Doc. A/CN.4/538

(2005), 'Diplomatic Protection and Human Rights: The Draft Articles of the International Law Commission', 24 *Australian Year Book of International Law* 75

Duguit L (1917), 'The Law and the State', 31 *Harvard Law Review* 119

Duhaime B (2014), 'Subsidiarity in the Americas: What Room Is There for Deference in the Inter-American System?' in Gruszczynski and Werner (eds.), *Deference in International Courts and Tribunals: Standard of Review and Margin of Appreciation* (Oxford University Press)

Dumberry P and Stone J (2014), 'International Law, Whether You Like It or Not: An Analysis of Arbitral Tribunal Practice Regarding the Applicable Law in Deciding State Contracts Disputes under the ICSID Convention in the Twenty-First Century', 5 *Yearbook of International Investment Law and Policy* 477

Duncan K (2004), 'Revisiting the Rights of Man: Georg Jellinek on Rights and the State', 22 *Law and History Review* 493

Dunoff JL and Pollack MA (2012), 'International Law and International Relations: Introducing an Interdisciplinary Dialogue' in Dunoff and Pollack (eds.), *Interdisciplinary Perspectives on International Law and International Relations: The State of the Art* (Cambridge University Press)

Dunoff JL (2006), 'Constitutional Conceits: The WTO's "Constitution" and the Discipline of International Law', 17 *European Journal of International Law* 647

Dunoff JL and Trachtman J (1999), 'Economic Analysis of International Law', 24 *Yale Law Journal Online* 1

Dupuy P-M (1997), 'The Constitutional Dimension of the Charter of the United Nations Revisited', 1 *Max Planck Yearbook of International Law* 1

(1999), 'The Danger of Fragmentation or Unification of the International Legal System and the International Court of Justice', 31 *New York University Journal of International Law and Politics* 791

(2007), 'A Doctrinal Debate in the Globalisation Era: On the "Fragmentation" of International Law', 1 *European Journal of Legal Studies* 25

(2009), 'Unification Rather than Fragmentation of International Law? The Case of International Investment Law and Human Rights Law' in Dupuy et al. (eds.), *Human Rights in International Investment Law and Arbitration* (Oxford University Press)

Dupuy P-M and Viñuales JE (2012), 'Human Rights and Investment Disciplines: Integration in Progress' in Bungenberg et al. (eds.), *International Investment Law* (Nomos)

(2013), 'The Challenge of "Proliferation": An Anatomy of the Debate' in Romano et al. (eds.), *The Oxford Handbook of International Adjudication* (Oxford University Press)

Dworkin R (1977), *Taking Rights Seriously* (Duckworth)

(1986), *Law's Empire: Legal Theory* (Harvard University Press)

(1996), *Freedom's Law: The Moral Reading of the American Constitution* (Harvard University Press)

Dye VD (2013), '"Deference as Respect" in WTO Standard of Review', 12 *Journal of International Trade Law and Policy Information* 23

Dyson LJ (2006), 'Some Thoughts on Judicial Deference', 11 *Judicial Review* 103

Dyzenhaus D (1997), 'The Politics of Deference: Judicial Review and Democracy' in Taggart (ed.), *The Province of Administrative Law* (Hart)

(1998), 'Law as Justification: Etienne Mureinik's Conception of Legal Culture', 14 *South African Journal on Human Rights* 11

(2003), 'Humpty Dumpty Rules or the Rule of Law: Legal Theory and the Adjudication of National Security', 28 *Australian Journal of Legal Philosophy* 1

(2011), 'Positivism and the Pesky Sovereign' 22 *European Journal of International Law* 363

Dzehtsiarou K and Greene A (2011), 'Legitimacy and the Future of the European Court of Human Rights: Critical Perspectives from Academia and Practitioners', 12 *German Law Journal* 1707

Ederington LB (1997), 'Property as a Natural Institution: The Separation of Property from Sovereignty in International Law', 13 *American University of International Law Review* 263

Edwards R (2002), 'Judicial Deference under the Human Rights Act', 65 *Modern Law Review* 859

Egger P and Pfaffermayr M (2004), 'The Impact of Bilateral Investment Treaties on Foreign Direct Investment', 32 *Journal of Comparative Economics* 788

Ehlermann C-D and Lockhart N (2004), 'Standard of Review in WTO Law', 7 *Journal of International Economic Law* 491

El Boudouhi S (2015), 'A Comparative Approach of the National Margin of Appreciation Doctrine before the ECtHR, Investment Tribunals and WTO Dispute Settlement Bodies' RSCAS Global Governance Programme Paper No. 2015/27

El Hayek I and Gilles A (2014), 'Multifaceted Settlement of International Investments Disputes: Thoughts about the Variety of Instruments Claiming Their

Applicability to the Investment Dispute', 29 *ICSID Review – Foreign Investment Law Journal* 567

Eleftheriadis P (2010), 'The Law of Laws', 1(4) *Transnational Legal Theory* 597

Elias T (1983), *The International Court of Justice and Some Contemporary Problems: Essays on International Law* (Martinus Nijhoff)

Elliott M (2010), 'Proportionality and Deference: The Importance of a Structured Approach' in Forsyth et al. (eds.), *Effective Judicial Review: A Cornerstone of Good Governance* (Oxford University Press)

(2015a), 'Justification, Calibration and Substantive Judicial Review: Putting Doctrine in Its Place' in Wilberg and Elliott (eds.), *The Scope and Intensity of Substantive Review: Traversing Taggart's Rainbow* (Hart)

(2015b), 'From Bifurcation to Calibration: Twin-Track Deference and the Culture of Justification' in Wilberg and Elliott (eds.), *The Scope and Intensity of Substantive Review: Traversing Taggart's Rainbow* (Hart)

Ellis J (2011), 'General Principles and Comparative Law', 22 *European Journal of International Law* 949

Ely JH (1980), *Democracy and Distrust: A Theory of Judicial Review* (Harvard University Press)

Emberland M (2004), 'The Corporate Veil in the Jurisprudence of the Human Rights Committee and the Inter-American Court and Commission of Human Rights', 4 *Human Rights Law Review* 257

(2006), *The Human Rights of Companies: Exploring the Structure of ECHR Protection* (Oxford University Press)

(2007), 'The International Court of Justice and Companies: Is It Possible to Discern a "Structural Bias" at the Court Regarding Private Economic Enterprise?', 9 *International Community Law Review* 187

Endicott T (2001), 'International Meaning: Comity in Fundamental Rights Adjudication', 13 *International Journal of Refugee Law* 280

(2015), 'Comity among Authorities', 68 *Current Legal Problems* 1

Engle E (2012), 'The History of the General Principle of Proportionality: An Overview', 10 *Dartmouth Law Journal* 1

Enoch D (2014), 'A Defense of Moral Deference', 111 *Journal of Philosophy* 229

Esty D (2006), 'Good Governance at the Supranational Scale: Globalizing Administrative Law', 115 *Yale Law Journal* 1490

Evenson E (2001), 'Reforms Ahead: Enlargement of the Council of Europe and the Future of the Strasbourg System', 1 *Human Rights Law Review* 219

Ewing-Chow M (2001), 'Investor Protection in Free Trade Agreements: Lessons from North America', 5 *Singapore Journal of International and Comparative Law* 748

Eyffinger A (2007a), *The 1907 Hague Peace Conference* (JudiCap)

(2007b), 'A Highly Critical Moment: Role and Record of the 1907 Hague Peace Conference', 54 *Netherlands International Law Review* 197

Fachiri AP (1932), *The Permanent Court of International Justice: Its Constitution, Procedure and Work* (2nd edn, Oxford University Press)

Fahner JH (2013), 'Margin of Appreciation in Investor-State Arbitration: The Prevalence and Desirability of Discretion and Deference', 26 *Hague Year Book of International Law* 422

(2016), 'From Dispute Settlement to Judicial Review? The Deference Debate in International Investment Law' in Duchateau et al. (eds.), *Evolution in Dispute Resolution: From Adjudication to ADR?* (Eleven International Publishing)

Falk RA (1964), *The Role of Domestic Courts in the International Legal Order* (Syracuse University Press)

(1967), 'New Approaches to the Study of International Law', 61 *American Journal of International Law* 477

Fassbender B (2003), 'Sovereignty and Constitutionalism in International Law' in Walker (ed.), *Sovereignty in Transition* (Hart)

Fauchald OK (2008), 'The Legal Reasoning of ICSID Tribunals – An Empirical Analysis', 19 *European Journal of International Law* 301

Fawcett JES (1954), 'The Exhaustion of Local Remedies: Substance or Procedure?', 31 *British Yearbook of International Law* 452

Feldman M (2017), 'Investment Arbitration Appellate Mechanism Options: Consistency, Accuracy, and Balance of Power', 32 *ICSID Review – Foreign Investment Law Journal* 528

Feller AH (1935), *The Mexican Claims Commissions: 1923–1934, A Study in the Law and Procedure of International Tribunals* (Macmillan)

Fereday J and Muir-Cochrane E (2006), 'Demonstrating Rigor Using Thematic Analysis: A Hybrid Approach of Inductive and Deductive Coding and Theme Development', 5 *International Journal of Qualitative Methods* 80

Ferrari-Bravo L (1983), 'International and Municipal Law: The Complementarity of Legal Systems' in Macdonald and Johnston (eds.), *The Structure and Process of International Law: Essays in Legal Philosophy, Doctrine and Theory* (Martinus Nijhoff)

Ferrero G (1942), *The Principles of Power: The Great Political Crises of History* (Putnam's)

Finnis J (2011), *Natural Law and Natural Rights* (2nd edn, Oxford University Press)

Fischer-Lescano A and Teubner G (2004), 'Regime-Collisions: The Vain Search for Legal Unity in the Fragmentation of Global Law', 25 *Michigan Journal of International Law* 999

Fish S (1989), *Doing What Comes Naturally: Change, Rhetoric, and the Practice of Theory in Literary and Legal Studies* (Clarendon)

(2000), *Is There a Text in This Class? The Authority of Interpretive Communities* (11th edn, Harvard University Press)

Flanders CW (2009), 'Toward a Theory of Persuasive Authority', 62 *Oklahoma Law Review* 55

Føllesdal A (2009), 'Why the European Court of Human Rights Might Be Democratically Legitimate – A Modest Defense' 27 *Nordisk Tidsskrift for Menneskerettigheter* 289

(2013a) 'Much Ado About Nothing? International Judicial Review of Human Rights in Well-Functioning Democracies' in Føllesdal et al., *The Legitimacy of International Human Rights Regimes* (Cambridge University Press)

(2013b), 'The Principle of Subsidiarity as a Constitutional Principle in International Law', 2 *Global Constitutionalism* 37

(2016), 'Subsidiarity and International Human Rights Courts: Respecting Self-Governance and Protecting Human Rights – Or Neither?', 79 *Law and Contemporary Problems* 147

Foster C (2010), 'Burden of Proof in International Courts and Tribunals', 29 *Australian Year Book of International Law* 27

Foster GK (2011), 'Striking a Balance between Investor Protections and National Sovereignty: The Relevance of Local Remedies in Investment Treaty Arbitration', 49 *Columbia Journal of Transnational Law* 201

Foucault M (2007), *The Politics of Truth* (MIT Press)

Fragale AR et al. (2012), 'Appeasing Equals: Lateral Deference in Organizational Communication', 57 *Administrative Science Quarterly* 373

Francioni F (1999), 'Customary International Law and the European Convention on Human Rights', 9 *Italian Yearbook of International Law* 11

Franck S (2006), 'The Role of International Arbitrators', 12 *ILSA Journal of International & Comparative Law* 499

(2009), 'Development and Outcomes of Investment Treaty Arbitration', 50 *Harvard International Law Journal* 435

Franck TM (1988), 'Legitimacy in the International System', 82 *American Journal of International Law* 705

(1990), *The Power of Legitimacy among Nations* (Oxford University Press)

(1998), *Fairness in International Law and Institutions* (Oxford University Press)

(2006b), 'The Power of Legitimacy and the Legitimacy of Power: International Law in an Age of Power Disequilibrium', 100 *American Journal of International Law* 88

(2008), 'On Proportionality of Countermeasures in International Law', 102 *American Journal of International Law* 715

Fredman S (2006), 'From Deference to Democracy: The Role of Equality under the Human Rights Act 1998', 122 *Law Quarterly Review* 53

Freeman E (2003), 'Regulatory Expropriation under NAFTA Chapter 11: Some Lessons from the European Court of Human Rights', 42 *Columbia Journal of Transnational Law* 117

Friedheim RL and Kadane JB (1970), 'Quantitative Content Analysis of the United Nations Seabed Debate: Methodology and a Continental Shelf Case Study', 24 *International Organization* 479

Friedman S (1953), *Expropriation in International Law* (Stevens & Sons Limited)

Friedmann W (1964), *The Changing Structure of International Law* (Stevens & Sons Limited)

Frigo M (2000), 'Peaceful Enjoyment of Possessions, Expropriation and Control of the Use of Property in the System of the European Convention on Human Rights', 10 *Italian Year Book of International Law* 45

Frowein JA (1993), 'The Protection of Property' in Macdonald et al. (eds.), *The European System for the Protection of Human Rights* (Martinus Nijhoff)

Fry JD (2007), 'International Human Rights Law in Investment Arbitration: Evidence of International Law's Unity', 18 *Duke Journal of Comparative and International Law* 77

Fukunaga Y (2012), 'Standard of Review and "Scientific Truths" in the WTO Dispute Settlement System and Investment Arbitration', 3 *Journal of International Dispute Settlement* 559

Gaillard E (2010), *Legal Theory of International Arbitration* (Martinus Nijhoff)

Gaja G (1992), 'Positivism and Dualism in Dionisio Anzilotti', 3 *European Journal of International Law* 123

Gallie WB (1956), 'Essentially Contested Concepts', *Proceedings of the Aristotelian Society* (Harrison & Sons)

Galligan DJ (2010), 'Legal Theory and Empirical Research' in Cane and Kritzer (eds.), *The Oxford Handbook of Empirical Legal Research* (Oxford University Press)

Gardbaum S (2009), 'Human Rights and International Constitutionalism' in Dunoff and Trachtman (eds.), *Ruling the World? Constitutionalism, International Law and Global Government* (Cambridge University Press)

Garner JW (1929), 'The New Arbitration Treaties of the United States', 23 *American Journal of International Law* 595

Garrity-Rokous G and Brescia RH (1993), 'Procedural Justice and International Human Rights: Towards a Procedural Jurisprudence for Human Rights Tribunals', 18 *Yale Journal of International Law* 559

Gathii JT (2009), 'War's Legacy in International Investment Law', 11 *International Community Law Review* 353

Gelinas F (2005), 'Investment Tribunals and the Commercial Arbitration Model: Mixed Procedures and Creeping Institutionalisation' in Gehring and Cordonier Segger (eds.), *Sustainable Development in World Trade Law* (Kluwer Law International)

Gerards J (2004), 'Intensity of Judicial Review in Equal Treatment Cases, 51 *Netherlands International Law Review* 135

(2009), 'Judicial Deliberations in the European Court of Human Rights' in Huls et al. (eds.), The Legitimacy of Highest Courts' Rulings (TMC Asser Institute)

(2011), 'Pluralism, Deference and the Margin of Appreciation Doctrine', 17 *European Law Journal* 80

(2014), 'Diverging Fundamental Rights Standards and the Role of the European Court of Human Rights' in Claes and de Visser (eds.), *Constructing European Constitutional Law* (Hart)

(2017), 'Procedural Review by the ECtHR: A Typology' in Brems and Gerards (eds.), *Procedural Review in European Fundamental Rights Cases* (Cambridge University Press)

(2018a), 'The Draft Copenhagen Declaration and the Court's Dual Role – the Need for a Different Definition of Subsidiarity and the Margin of Appreciation' Strasbourg Observers

(2018b), 'Margin of Appreciation and Incrementalism in the Case Law of the European Court of Human Rights' 18 *Human Rights Law Review* 495

Gerards J and Senden H (2009), 'The Structure of Fundamental Rights and the European Court of Human Rights', 7 *International Journal of Constitutional Law* 619

Gerbic P and Stacey E (2005), 'A Purposive Approach to Content Analysis: Designing Analytical Frameworks', 8 *Internet and Higher Education* 45

Ghosh VN (2015), 'An Uncertain Shield – *Res Judicata* in Arbitration', 31 *Arbitration International* 661

Ghouri A (2014), 'On Genealogy of Proposals to Reform Investor-State Arbitration', 11 *Transnational Dispute Management* 1

Gibson C (2015), 'Beyond Self-Judgment: Exceptions Clauses in US BITs', 1 *Fordham International Law Journal* 38

Gibson JL, Caldeira GA and Baird V (1998), 'On the Legitimacy of National High Courts', 92 *American Political Science Review* 343

Gilmore G (1945), 'The International Court of Justice', 55 *Yale Law Journal* 1049

Ginsburg T (2004), 'Bounded Discretion in International Judicial Lawmaking', 45 *Virginia Journal of International Law* 631

(2005), 'International Substitutes for Domestic Institutions: Bilateral Investment Treaties and Governance', 25 *International Review of Law and Economics* 107

(2016), 'The Interaction between Domestic and International Law' in Kontorovich and Parisi (eds.), *Economic Analysis of International Law* (Edward Elgar)

Giorgetti C (2013), 'Is the Truth in the Eyes of the Beholder? The Perils and Benefits of Empirical Research in International Investment Arbitration', 12 *Santa Clara Journal of International Law* 263

Giustini A (1986), 'Compulsory Adjudication in International Law: The Past, the Present, and Prospects for the Future', 9 *Fordham International Law Journal* 213

Glashausser A (2005), 'Difference and Deference in Treaty Interpretation', 50 *Villanova Law Review* 25

Glenn HP (1987), 'Persuasive Authority', 32 *Revue de droit de McGill* 261

Goldhaber M (2016), 'A Matter of Perspective: Global Governance and the Distinction between Public and Private Authority (and Not Law)', 5 *Global Constitutionalism* 48

Goldsmith III JL and Levinson D (2009), 'Law for States: International Law, Constitutional Law, Public Law' 122(7) *Harvard Law Review* 1791

Gordillo LI (2011), *Interlocking Constitutions: Towards an Interordinal Theory of National, European and UN Law* (Hart)

Graham DE (1970), 'The Calvo Clause: Its Current Status as a Contractual Renunciation of Diplomatic Protection', 6 *Texas International Law Forum* 289

Grant JA (2017), 'Reason and Authority in Administrative Law', 76 *Cambridge Law Journal* 507

Grant K (2015), 'ICSID's Reinforcement?: UNASUR and the Rise of a Hybrid Regime for International Investment Arbitration', 52 *Osgoode Hall Law Journal* 1115

Green A (2010), 'An Absolute Theory of Convention Rights: Why the ECHR Gives Rise to Legal Rights That Cannot Conflict with Each Other', 16 *UCL Jurisprudence Review* 75

Green L (1988), *The Authority of the State* (Clarendon)

Greene RD (1927), 'The Permanent Court of International Justice', 7 *B.U.L. Review* 181

(1931), 'The Progress of the Permanent Court of International Justice', 6 *St. John's Law Review* 226

Greener J (2002), 'Constructive Expropriation and the Framework of Deferential Progressivism', 25 *Loyola of Los Angeles International and Comparative Law Review* 725

Greer S (2000), *The Margin of Appreciation: Interpretation and Discretion under the European Convention on Human Rights* (Council of Europe Publishing)

(2004), '"Balancing" and the European Court of Human Rights: A Contribution to the Habermas-Alexy Debate', 63 *Cambridge Law Journal* 412

(2010), 'The Interpretation of the European Convention on Human Rights: Universal Principle or Margin of Appreciation?', 3 *UCL Human Rights Review* 1

Greer S and Wildhaber L (2012), 'Revisiting the Debate about "Constitutionalising" the European Court of Human Rights', 12 *Human Rights Law Review* 655

Grieves FL (1969), *Supranationalism and International Adjudication* (University of Illinois Press)

Griffey B (2011), 'The "Reasonableness" Test: Assessing Violations of State Obligations under the Optional Protocol to the International Covenant on Economic, Social and Cultural Rights', 11 *Human Rights Law Review* 275

Grisel F (2014a), 'Precedent in Investment Arbitration: The Case of Compound Interest', 2 *Peking University Transnational Law Review* 217

(2014b), 'The Sources of Foreign Investment Law' in Douglas et al. (eds.), *The Foundations of International Investment Law* (Oxford University Press)

(2017), 'Competition and Cooperation in International Commercial Arbitration: The Birth of a Transnational Legal Profession', 51 *Law & Society Review* 790

(2020), 'Marginals and Elites in International Arbitration' in Schultz and Ortino (eds.), *Oxford Handbook of International Arbitration* (Oxford University Press)

Gross O and Ni Aolain F (2001), 'From Discretion to Scrutiny: Revisiting the Application of the Margin of Appreciation Doctrine in the Context of Article 15 of the European Convention on Human Rights', 23 *Human Rights Quarterly* 652

Grossman N (2009), 'Legitimacy and International Adjudicative Bodies'. 41 *George Washington International Law Review* 107

Gruszczynski L and Vadi V (2014) 'Standard of Review and Scientific Evidence in WTO Law and International Investment Arbitration – Converging Parallels?' in Gruszczynski and Werner (eds.), *Deference in International Courts and Tribunals: Standard of Review and Margin of Appreciation* (Oxford University Press)

Gruszczynski L and Werner W (eds.) (2014), *Deference in International Courts and Tribunals: Standard of Review and Margin of Appreciation* (Oxford University Press)

Guillaume G (1995), 'The Future of International Judicial Institutions', 44 *International & Comparative Law Quarterly* 848

(2011), 'The Use of Precedent by International Judges and Arbitrators', 2 *Journal of International Dispute Settlement* 5

Guthrie G (2010), *Basic Research Methods an Entry to Social Science Research* (Sage Publications)

Guzman AT (2008), 'International Tribunals: A Rational Choice Analysis', 157 *University of Pennsylvania Law Review* 171

Guzman AT and Meyer T (2008), 'International Common Law: The Soft Law of International Tribunals', 9 *Chicago Journal of International Law* 515

Habermas J (2015), *Between Facts and Norms: Contributions to a Discourse Theory of Law and Democracy* (Polity Press)

Haesler T (1968), *The Exhaustion of Local Remedies in the Case Law of International Courts and Tribunals* (AW Sijthoff)

Hall M and Wright R (2008), 'Systematic Content Analysis of Judicial Opinions', 96 *California Law Review* 63

Han SWD (2006), 'Decentralized Proliferation of International Judicial Bodies', 16 *Journal of Transnational Law and Policy* 101

Harbo T-I (2017), 'Introducing Procedural Proportionality Review in European Law', 30 *Leiden Journal of International Law* 25

Harding J (1962), 'The Nationalization of Canadian Property in Cuba under International Law', 2 *Western Law Review* 50

Harowitz P (2008), 'Three Faces of Deference', 83 *Notre Dame Law Review* 1061

Harris B (2003), 'Judicial Review, Justiciability and the Prerogative of Mercy', 62 *Cambridge Law Journal* 631

Hart HLA (1994), *The Concept of Law* (2nd edn, Clarendon)
Hart Jr HM and Sacks AM (1994), *The Legal Process: Basic Problems in the Making and Application of Law* (Foundation Press)
Hathaway O (2008), 'International Delegation and State Sovereignty', 71 *Law and Contemporary Problems* 115
Hayward B (2017), *Conflict of Law and Arbitral Discretion: The Closest Connection Test* (1st edn, Oxford University Press)
Heise M, (2000) 'Preliminary Thoughts on the Virtues of Passive Dialogue', 34 *Akron Law Review* 73
Heiskanen V (1994), 'Jurisdiction v. Competence: Revisiting a Frequently Neglected Distinction', 5 *Finnish Yearbook of International Law* 1
Helfer L (2003), 'Constitutional Analogies in the International Legal System', 37 *Loyola of Los Angeles International and Comparative Law Review* 193
(2008), 'Redesigning the European Court of Human Rights: Embeddedness as a Deep Structural Principle of the European Human Rights Regime', 19 *European Journal of International Law* 125
Helfer L and Alter KJ (2009), 'The Andean Tribunal of Justice and Its Interlocutors: Understanding Preliminary Reference Patterns in the Andean Community', 41 *New York University Journal of International Law and Politics* 871
Helfer L and Slaughter A-M (1997), 'Toward a Theory of Effective Supranational Adjudication', 107 *Yale Law Journal* 273
Henckels C (2012), 'Indirect Expropriation and the Right to Regulate: Revisiting Proportionality Analysis and the Standard of Review in Investor-State Arbitration', 15 *Journal of International Economic Law* 223
(2013), 'Balancing Investment Protection and the Public Interest: The Role of the Standard of Review and the Importance of Deference in Investor-State Arbitration', 4 *Journal of International Dispute Settlement* 197
(2014), 'The Role of the Standard of Review and the Importance of Deference in Investor-State Arbitration' in Gruszczynski and Werner (eds.), *Deference in International Courts and Tribunals: Standard of Review and Margin of Appreciation* (Oxford University Press)
(2015), *Proportionality and Deference in Investor-State Arbitration: Balancing Investment Protection and Regulatory Autonomy* (Cambridge University Press)
Henkin L (1990), 'International Law: Politics, Values and Functions', in *Collected Courses of the Hague Academy of International Law*, vol. 4 (Brill)
Henrard K (2012), 'A Critical Appraisal of the Margin of Appreciation Left to States Pertaining to "Church-State Relations" under the Jurisprudence of the European Court of Human Rights' in Vrielink et al. (eds.), *A Test of Faith? Religious Diversity and Accommodation in the European Workplace* (Ashgate)
Hepburn J (2014), 'Comparative Public Law at the Dawn of Investment Treaty Arbitration: Saar Papier Vertriebs GmbH *v.* Republic of Poland', 15 *Journal of World Investment & Trade* 705
(2016), 'Applicable Law in TPP Investment Disputes', 17 *Melbourne Journal of International Law* 368
(2017), *Domestic Law in International Investment Arbitration* (Oxford University Press)

Heringa AW (1996), 'The "Consensus Principle" – The Role of "Common Law" in the ECHR Case Law', 3 *Maastricht Journal of European and Comparative Law* 108
Hernández GI (2014), *The International Court of Justice and the Judicial Function* (Oxford University Press)
Hershovitz S (2003), 'Legitimacy, Democracy, and Razian Authority' 9 *Legal Theory* 201
Herz J (1941), 'Expropriation of Foreign Property', 35 *American Journal of International Law* 243
Hess G (2013), 'Qualitative Research on Legal Education: Studying Outstanding Law Teachers', 51 *Alberta Law Review* 925
Hey E and Mak E (2009), 'Introduction: The Possibilities of Comparative Law Methods for Research on the Rule of Law in a Global Context', 2 *Erasmus Law Review* 287
Hickman T (2005), 'Constitutional Dialogue, Constitutional Theories and the Human Rights Act 1998', *Public Law* 306
Higgins R (1968), 'Policy Considerations and the International Judicial Process', 17 *International & Comparative Law Quarterly* 58
(1981), 'Reality and Hope in International Human Rights: A Critique', 9 *Hofstra Law Review* 1485
(1982), 'The Taking of Property by the State: Recent Developments in International Law', in *Collected Courses of the Hague Academy of International Law*, vol. 176 (Brill)
(2009), *Themes and Theories* (Oxford University Press)
Hill N (1931), 'National Judges in the Permanent Court of International Justice', 25 *American Journal of International Law* 670
(1932), 'The Extension of the Jurisdiction of the Permanent Court of International Justice by Treaties', 10 *New York University Law Quarterly Review* 484
Hilson C (2013), 'The Margin of Appreciation, Domestic Irregularity and Domestic Court Rulings in ECHR Environmental Jurisprudence: Global Legal Pluralism in Action', 2 *Global Constitutionalism* 262
Hirsch M (2005), 'The Sociology of International Law: Invitation to Study International Rules in Their Social Context', 55 *University of Toronto Law Journal* 891
Hobbes T (1996), *Leviathan* (R Tuck ed., Cambridge University Press)
Hoexter C (2000), 'The Future of Judicial Review in South African Administrative Law', 117 *South African Law Journal* 484
Holmes OW (1991), *The Common Law* (Dover Publications)
Holstein J and Gubrium J (2000), 'The Constructionist Analytics of Interpretive Practice' in Denzin and Lincoln (eds.), *Handbook of Qualitative Research* (2nd edn, Sage Publications)
Holtermann J v. H and Madsen MR (2016), 'What Is Empirical in Empirical Studies of Law? A European New Legal Realist Conception' iCourts Working Paper Series, Paper No. 77
Hovius B (1985), 'The Limitation Clauses of the European Convention on Human Rights: A Guide for the Application of Section 1 of the Charter?', 17 *Ottawa Law Review* 213
Howell J (2006), 'Book Reviews: Property and the Human Rights Act 1998', 65 *Cambridge Law Journal* 728

Hsieh H-F (2005), 'Three Approaches to Qualitative Content Analysis', *Qualitative Health Research* 1277
Hudson MO (1928), 'The World Court: 1922–1928' World Peace Foundation Pamphlet Series 1
(1930), 'The Eighth Year of the Permanent Court of International Justice', 13 *International Conciliation* 193
(1931), 'The Independence of the Permanent Court of International Justice', 17 *American Bar Association Journal* 430
(1941), 'The Nineteenth Year of the Permanent Court of International Justice', 35 *American Journal of International Law* 1
(1945), 'The Twenty-Third Year of the Permanent Court of International Justice and Its Future', 39 *American Journal of International Law* 1
(1957), 'The Succession of the International Court of Justice to the Permanent Court of International Justice', 51 *American Journal of International Law* 569
Huijbers L (2017), 'Procedural-Type Review: A More Neutral Approach to Human Rights Protection by the European Court of Human Rights?' European Society of International Law, Conference Paper No. 6/2017
Huiping C (2008), 'The Investor-State Dispute Settlement Mechanism: Where to Go in the 21st Century?', 9 *Journal of World Investment & Trade* 467
Hull WI (1970), *The Two Hague Conferences and Their Contributions to International Law* (Kraus)
Hurd I (1999), 'Legitimacy and Authority in International Politics', 53 *International Organization* 379
Hurrelmann A and others (2005), 'Is There a Legitimation Crisis of the Nation-State?', 13 *European Review* 119
Hurst CJB (1943), 'The Permanent Court of International Justice', 59 *Law Quarterly Review* 312
Hussain I (1984), *Dissenting and Separate Opinions at the World Court* (Martinus Nijhoff)
Hyde CC (1930), 'The Interpretation of Treaties by the Permanent Court of International Justice', 24 *American Journal of International Law* 1
ICJ Registry (1976), *The International Court of Justice* (International Court of Justice)
Iluyomade BO (1977), 'Dual Claim and the Exhaustion of Local Remedies Rule in International Law', 10 *Vanderbilt Journal of Transnational Law* 83
International Institute for Sustainable Development (2017), *Exhaustion of Local Remedies in International Investment Law*
International Law Association (2000), 'Committee on Diplomatic Protection of Persons and Property', 69 *International Law Association Reports of Conferences* 604
(2006), 'Diplomatic Protection of Persons and Property', 72 *International Law Association Reports of Conferences* 353
Ishikawa T (2010), 'Third Party Participation in Investment Treaty Arbitration', 59 *International & Comparative Law Quarterly* 373
Isiksel T (2013), 'Global Legal Pluralism as Fact and Norm', 2 *Global Constitutionalism* 160
Jachtenfuchs M and Krisch N (2016), 'Subsidiarity in Global Governance', *Law & Contemporary Problems* 79

Jackson JH (2003), 'Sovereignty-Modern: A New Approach to an Outdated Concept', 97 *American Journal of International Law* 782

Jackson JL (2006), 'Broniowski *v.* Poland: A Recipe for Increased Legitimacy of the European Court of Human Rights as a Supranational Constitutional Court', 39 *Connecticut Law Review* 759

Jacob M (2011), 'Precedents: Lawmaking through International Adjudication', 12 *German Law Journal* 1005

Jacoby S (1936), 'Some Aspects of the Jurisdiction of the Permanent Court of International Justice', 30 *American Journal of International Law* 233

Janzen H (1935), 'The Legal Monism of Alfred Verdross', 29 *American Political Science Review* 387

Jellinek G (1968), *Die Rechtliche Natur Der Staatenverträge: Ein Beitrag Zur Juristischen Construction Des Völkerrechts* (Keip)

Jenks CW (1938), 'The Interpretation and Application of Municipal Law by the Permanent Court of International Justice', 19 *British Yearbook of International Law* 67

(1964), *The Prospects of International Adjudication* (Stevens & Sons Limited)

Jennings RY (1996), 'The Judiciary, International and National, and the Development of International Law', 45 *International & Comparative Law Quarterly* 1

(1998), 'The Role of the International Court of Justice', *British Yearbook of International Law* 1

(2002), 'Sovereignty and International Law' in Kreijen et al. (eds.), *State, Sovereignty, and International Governance* (Oxford University Press)

Jessup PC (1956), *Transnational Law* (Yale University Press)

Jhabvala F (1978), 'Declarations by Judges of the International Court of Justice', 72 *American Journal of International Law* 830

Jimenez de Arechaga E (1965), 'Diplomatic Protection of Shareholders in International Law', 4 *Philippine International Law Journal* 71

(1978), 'International Law in the Past Third of a Century', in *Collected Courses of the Hague Academy of International Law*, vol. 159 (Brill)

Johns F (2009), 'International Legal Theory: Snapshots from a Decade of International Legal Life', 10 *Melbourne Journal of International Law* 1

Johnson OT and Gimblett J (2011), 'From Gunboats to BITs: The Evolution of Modern International Investment Law', *Yearbook on International Investment Law and Policy* 649

Johnstone I (1990), 'Treaty Interpretation: The Authority of Interpretive Communities', 12 *Michigan Journal of International Law* 371

Jones JW (1935), 'The "Pure" Theory of International Law', 16 *British Yearbook of International Law* 5

Jowell J (2003), 'Judicial Deference and Human Rights: A Question of Competence' in Craig et al. (eds.), *Law and Administration in Europe: Essays in Honour of Carol Harlow* (Oxford University Press)

Juss SS (1994), 'Nationality Law, Sovereignty, and the Doctrine of Exclusive Domestic Jurisdiction', 9 *Florida Journal of International Law* 227

Kammerhofer J (2005), 'Unearthing Structural Uncertainty through Neo-Kelsenian Consistency: Conflicts of Norms in International Law' Papers of the European Society of International Law

(2009), 'Kelsen – Which Kelsen? A Reapplication of the Pure Theory to International Law', 22 *Leiden Journal of International Law* 225

Kanetake M (2016a), 'The Interfaces between the National and International Rule of Law: A Framework Paper' in Kanetake and Nollkaemper (eds.), *The Rule of Law at the National and International Levels: Contestations and Deference* (Hart)

(2016b), 'Subsidiarity in the Practice of International Courts' in Kanetake and Nollkaemper (eds.), *The Rule of Law at the National and International Levels: Contestations and Deference* (Hart)

Kanetake M and Nollkaemper A (eds.) (2016), *The Rule of Law at the National and International Levels: Contestations and Deference* (Hart)

Kanto M (2017), 'The Status of Municipal Law before the World Court in the Light of Recent Cases' in Maluwa et al. (eds.), *The Pursuit of a Brave New World in International Law* (Brill)

Kapeliuk D (2010), 'The Repeat Appointment Factor: Exploring Decision Patterns of Elite Investment Arbitrators', 96 *Cornell Law Review* 47

Katselas A (2012), 'Do Investment Treaties Prescribe a Deferential Standard of Review?', 34 *Michigan Journal of International Law* 87

Kaushal A (2009), 'Revisiting History: How the Past Matters for the Present Backlash Against the Foreign Investment Regime', 50 *Harvard International Law Journal* 491

Kavanagh A (2008), 'Deference of Defiance?: The Limits of the Judicial Role in Constitutional Adjudication' in Huscroft (ed.), *Expounding the Constitution: Essays in Constitutional Theory* (Cambridge University Press)

(2014), 'Proportionality and Parliamentary Debates: Exploring Some Forbidden Territory', 34 *Oxford Journal of Legal Studies* 443

Kawano M (2014), 'Decisions of the International Court of Justice on Disputes Concerning Internal Law' in Gaja and Grote Stoutenburg (eds.), *Enhancing the Rule of Law through the International Court of Justice* (Brill)

Kelsen H (1943), 'Compulsory Adjudication of International Disputes', 37 *American Journal of International Law* 397

(1960), 'Sovereignty and International Law', 48 *Georgetown Law Journal* 627

(2003), *Principles of International Law* (Lawbook Exchange)

Kennedy D (2005), 'Challenging Expert Rule: The Politics of Global Governance', 27 *Sydney Law Review* 5

Keohane RO, Moravcsik A and Slaughter A-M (2003),'Legalized Dispute Resolution: Interstate and Transnational' in Keohane (ed.), *Power and Governance in a Partially Globalized World* (Routledge)

King DB and Moloo R (2014), 'International Arbitrators as Lawmakers', 46 *International Law and Politics* 875

King JA (2008), 'Institutional Approaches to Judicial Restraint: Judging the Scientific and Medical Literature', 28 *Oxford Journal of Legal Studies* 409

(2012), *Judging Social Rights* (Cambridge University Press)

Kingsbury B (1997), 'The Concept of Compliance as a Function of Competing Conceptions of International Law', 19 *Michigan Journal of International Law* 345

(2011), 'International Courts: Uneven Judicialization in Global Order' in Crawford and Koskenniemi (eds.), *Cambridge Companion to International Law* (Cambridge University Press)

Kjeldgaard-Pedersen A (2010), 'The Evolution of the Right of Individuals to Seise the European Court of Human Rights', 12 *Journal of the History of International Law* 267

(2014), 'The Influence of the Concept of International Legal Personality on the Drafting of the PCIJ Statute', 16 *Journal of the History of International Law* 9

Kjos HE (2013), *Applicable Law in Investor-State Arbitration: The Interplay between National and International Law* (1st edn, Oxford University Press)

(2016), 'Domestic Courts under Scrutiny: The Rule of Law as a Standard (of Deference) in Investor-State Arbitration' in Kanetake and Nollkaemper (eds.), *The Rule of Law at the National and International Levels: Contestations and Deference* (Hart)

Klabbers J (2009), 'The Bridge Crack'd: A Critical Look at Interdisciplinary Relations', 23 *International Relations* 119

Klabbers J and Piiparinen T (2013), 'Normative Pluralism: An Exploration' in Klabbers and Piiparinen (eds.), *Normative Pluralism and International Law: Exploring Global Governance* (Cambridge University Press)

Klabbers J, Peters A and Ulfstein G (2009), *The Constitutionalization of International Law* (Oxford University Press)

Klager R (2010), 'Fair and Equitable Treatment: A Look at the Theoretical Underpinnings of Legitimacy and Fairness', 11 *Journal of World Investment & Trade* 435

Kleinlein T (2011), 'Judicial Lawmaking by Judicial Restraint? The Potential of Balancing in International Economic Law', 12 *German Law Journal* 1141

Knight, D (2018), *Vigilance and Restraint in the Common Law of Judicial Review* (Cambridge University Press)

Koessler M (1947), "Subject", "Citizen", "National", and "Permanent Allegiance"', 64 *South African Law Journal* 350

Koh HH (1996), 'Transnational Legal Process', 75 *Nebraska Law Review* 181

(1997), 'Why Do Nations Obey International Law?', 106 *Yale Law Journal* 2599

(2003), 'On American Exceptionalism', 55 *Stanford Law Review* 1479

Kolb R (2007), 'German Legal Scholarship as Reflected in Hague Academy Courses on Public International Law', 50 *German Yearbook of International Law* 201

(2013), *The International Court of Justice* (Hart)

(2015), 'The Jurisprudence of the Permanent Court of International Justice Between Utilitas Publica and Utilitas Singulorum', 14 *Law & Practice of International Courts and Tribunals* 16

Korowicz MS (1956), 'The Problem of the International Personality of Individuals', 50 *American Journal of International Law* 533

Korzun V (2017), 'The Right to Regulate in Investor-State Arbitration: Slicing and Dicing Regulatory Carve-Outs', 50 *Vanderbilt Journal of Transnational Law* 355

Koskenniemi M (1997), 'Hierarchy in International Law: A Sketch', 8 *European Journal of International Law* 566

(2001), *The Gentle Civilizer of Nations: The Rise and Fall of International Law, 1870–1960* (Cambridge University Press)

(2006), *From Apology to Utopia: The Structure of International Legal Argument* (Cambridge University Press)

(2014), 'What Is International Law For?' in Evans (ed.), *International Law* (Oxford University Press)

Kratochvil J (2011), 'The Inflation of the Margin of Appreciation by the European Court of Human Rights', 29 *Netherlands Quarterly of Human Rights* 324

Kratochwil F (1982), 'On the Notion of "Interest" in International Relations', 36 *International Organization* 1

Kriebaum U (2007), 'Regulatory Takings: Balancing the Interests of the Investor and the State', 8 *Journal of World Investment & Trade* 717

(2014), 'The Nature of Investment Disciplines' in Douglas et al. (eds.), *The Foundations of International Investment Law* (Oxford University Press)

Krisch N (2006), 'Introduction: Global Governance and Global Administrative Law in the International Legal Order', 17 *European Journal of International Law* 1

(2010), *Beyond Constitutionalism* (Oxford University Press)

(2017), 'Pluralism in International Law and Beyond' in d'Aspremont and Singh (eds.), *Fundamental Concepts for International Law: The Construction of a Discipline* (Edward Elgar)

Krotoszynski Jr R (1998) 'Constitutional Flares: On Judges, Legislatures, and Dialogue', 83 *Minnesota Law Review* 1

(2002), 'Why Deference? Implied Delegations, Agency Expertise, and the Misplaced Legacy of Skidmore', 54 *Administrative Law Review* 735

Kulick A (2010), 'The Integration of International Investment Law', 23 *Hague Year Book of International Law* 171

(2012), *Global Public Interest in International Investment Law* (Cambridge University Press)

Kumm M (2016), 'Sovereignty and the Right to Be Left Alone: Subsidiarity, Justice-Sensitive Externalities, and the Proper Domain of the Consent Requirement in International Law', 79 *Law and Contemporary Problems* 239

Kunz J (1934), 'The "Vienna School" and International Law', 11 *New York University Law Quarterly Review* 370

(1938), 'The Theory of International Law', 32 *American Society of International Law Proceedings* 23

(1960), 'The Nottebohm Judgment', 54 *American Journal of International Law* 536

Kuo M-S (2010), 'On the Constitutional Question in Global Governance: Global Administrative Law and the Conflicts-Law Approach in Comparison', 2 *Global Constitutionalism* 437

Kurtz J (2013), 'Building Legitimacy Through Interpretation in Investor-State Arbitration: On Consistency, Coherence and the Identification of Applicable Law' in Douglas et al. (eds.), *The Foundations of International Investment Law: Bringing Theory into Practice* (Oxford University Press)

(2015), 'Balancing Investor Protection and Regulatory Freedom in International Investment Law: The Necessary, Complex, and Vital Search for State Purpose' in Bjorklund (ed.), *Yearbook on International Investment Law & Policy 2013–2014* (Oxford University Press)

Kwiecien R (2004), 'In Defence of the Idea of State Sovereignty in International Law', 27 *Polish Yearbook of International Law* 87

(2011), 'Sir Hersch Lauterpacht's Idea of State Sovereignty – Is It Still Alive?', 13 *International Community Law Review* 23

(2012), 'Does the State Still Matter? Sovereignty, Legitimacy and International Law', 32 *Polish Yearbook of International Law* 45

Kyriakou N (2007), 'Reform of the Reform: The European Court of Human Right's Endless Quest for Efficient Justice', 5 *Hellenic Review of European Law* 385

Lamm V (2014), *Compulsory Jurisdiction in International Law* (Edward Elgar)

Land M (2015), 'Justice as Legitimacy in the European Court of Human Rights' in Grant Cohen and Grossman (eds.), *Legitimacy and International Courts* (Cambridge University Press)

Landes W and Posner EA (1976), 'Legal Precedent: A Theoretical and Empirical Analysis', 19 *Journal of Law and Economics* 249

Langford M and Behn D (2017), 'Managing Backlash: The Evolving Investment Treaty Arbitrator?', 29(2) *European Journal of International Law* 551

Larouer CJ (2009), 'In the Name of Sovereignty? The Battle over In Dubio Mitius Inside and Outside the Courts' Cornell Law School, Inter-University Graduate Student Conference Papers, Paper No. 22

Larson A and Jenks CW (1965), *Sovereignty within the Law* (Dobbs Ferry)

Lauterpacht E (1962), 'The Drafting of Treaties for the Protection of Investment', 3 *International & Comparative Law Quarterly Supplementary Publication* 18

(1991), *Aspects of the Administration of International Justice* (Cambridge University Press)

Lauterpacht H (1928), 'The Doctrine of Non-Justiciable Disputes in International Law', 24 *Economica* 277

(1930), 'The Absence of an International Legislature and the Compulsory Jurisdiction of International Tribunals', 11 *British Yearbook of International Law* 134

(1933), *The Function of Law in the International Community* (Oxford Clarendon)

(1946), 'The Grotian Tradition in International Law', 23 *British Yearbook of International Law* 1

(1949), 'Restrictive Interpretation and the Principle of Effectiveness in the Interpretation of Treaties', 26 *British Yearbook of International Law* 48

(2010), *The Development of International Law by the International Court* (1st edn, Cambridge University Press)

Lavranos N (2008), 'Towards a Solange-Method between International Courts and Tribunals?' in Broude and Shany (eds.), *The Shifting Allocation of Authority in International Law: Considering Sovereignty, Supremacy and Subsidiarity* (Hart)

Lazarus L and Simonsen N (2015), 'Judicial Review and Parliamentary Debate: Enriching the Doctrine of Due Deference' in Hunt et al. (eds.), *Parliaments and Human Rights: Redressing the Democratic Deficit* (Hart)

Leech NL and Onwuegbuzie AJ (2007), 'An Array of Qualitative Data Analysis Tools: A Call for Data Analysis Triangulation', 22 *School Psychology Quarterly* 557

(2008), 'Qualitative Data Analysis: A Compendium of Techniques and a Framework for Selection for School Psychology Research and Beyond', 23 *School Psychology Quarterly* 587

Legg A (2012), *The Margin of Appreciation in International Human Rights Law: Deference and Proportionality* (1st edn, Oxford University Press)

(2016), 'Human Rights, the Margin of Appreciation, and the International Rule of Law' in Kanetake and Nollkaemper (eds.), *The Rule of Law at the National and International Levels: Contestations and Deference* (Hart)

Legrand P (1998), 'On the Singularity of Law', 47 *Harvard International Law Journal* 517

Lehavi A (2010), 'The Global Law of the Land', 81 *University of Colorado Law Review* 425

(2015), 'Unbundling Harmonization: Public versus Private Law Strategies to Globalize Property', 15 *Chicago Journal of International Law* 452

Leigh GIF (1971), 'Nationality and Diplomatic Protection', 20 *International & Comparative Law Quarterly* 453

Leonhardsen EM (2012), 'Looking for Legitimacy: Exploring Proportionality Analysis in Investment Treaty Arbitration', 3 *Journal of International Dispute Settlement* 95

(2013), 'Navigating International Waters: Standards of Review in Investment Treaty Arbitration as Adjudicative Response' SSRN

(2014), 'Treaty Change, Arbitral Practice and the Search for a Balance: Standards of Review and the Margin of Appreciation in International Investment Law' in Gruszczynski and Werner (eds.), *Deference in International Courts and Tribunals: Standard of Review and Margin of Appreciation* (Oxford University Press)

Letsas G (2006), 'Two Concepts of the Margin of Appreciation', 26 *Oxford Journal of Legal Studies* 705

(2007), *A Theory of Interpretation of the European Convention on Human Rights* (Oxford University Press)

(2013), 'The ECHR as a Living Instrument: Its Meaning and Legitimacy' in Føllesdal et al. (eds.), *Constituting Europe* (Cambridge University Press)

Levit JK (2005), 'A Bottom-Up Approach to International Lawmaking: The Tale of Three Trade Finance Instruments', 30 *Yale Journal of International Law* 125

Lillich R and Weston BH (1988), 'Lump Sum Agreements: Their Continuing Contribution to the Law of International Claims', 82 *American Journal of International Law* 69

Lim E (2014), 'Of "Landmark" or "Leading" Cases: Salomon's Challenge', 41 *Journal of Law and Society* 523

Lissitzyn OJ (1951), 'The International Court of Justice: Its Role in the Maintenance of International Peace and Security', in *United Nations Studies* (Carnegie Endowment)

Little L (2009), 'Empowerment through Restraint: Reverse Preemption or Hybrid Lawmaking', 59 *Case Western Reserve Law Review* 955

Llewelyn K (1930), 'A Realistic Jurisprudence – The Next Step', 30 *Columbia Law Review* 431

Locke J (1988), *Two Treatises of Government* (P Laslett ed., Cambridge University Press)

López Escarcena S (2014), *Indirect Expropriation in International Law* (Edward Elgar)

Lourie G (2015), 'Diplomatic Protection under the State-to-State Arbitration Clauses of Investment Treaties', *Austrian Yearbook on International Arbitration* 511

Lowe V (1996), 'Res Judicata and the Rule of Law in International Arbitration', 8 *African Journal of International and Comparative Law* 38

Lugato M (2013), 'The Margin of Appreciation and Freedom of Religion: Between Treaty Interpretation and Subsidiarity', 52 *Journal of Catholic Legal Studies* 49

Madsen MR (2013), 'Towards a Sociology of International Courts' iCourts Working Paper Series, Paper No. 1

(2014), 'The International Judiciary as Transnational Power Elite', 8 *International Political Sociology* 332

(2015), 'The Legitimization Strategies of International Judges' in Bobek (ed.), *Selecting Europe's Judges* (Oxford University Press)

(2016), 'The Challenging Authority of the European Court of Human Rights: From Cold War Legal Diplomacy to the Brighton Declaration and Backlash', 79 *Law and Contemporary Problems* 141

(2018), 'Who Rules the World? The Educational Capital of the International Judiciary' iCourts Working Paper Series, Paper No. 127

Madsen MR and Dezalay Y (2002), 'The Power of the Legal Field: Pierre Bourdieu and the Law' in Banakar and Travers (eds.), *An Introduction to Law and Social Theory* (Hart)

Maduro MP (2013), 'In Search of a Meaning and Not in Search of the Meaning: Judicial Review and the Constitution in Times of Pluralism', *Wisconsin Law Review* 541

Magnaye J and Reinisch A (2016), 'Revisiting Res Judicata and Lis Pendens in Investor-State Arbitration', 15 *Law & Practice of International Courts and Tribunals* 264

Mahoney B (2010), 'The Greater Good or Property Rights? Resolving the Tension between Positive and Negative Civil Rights in Eminent Domain', SSRN

Mahoney P (1990), 'Judicial Activism and Judicial Self-Restraint in the European Court of Human Rights: Two Sides of the Same Coin', 11 *Human Rights Law Journal* 5

Makela F (2013), 'Acquired Expertise of Administrative Tribunals and the Standard of Judicial Review: The Case of Grievance Arbitrators and Human Rights Law', 17 *Canadian Labour & Employment Law Journal* 345

Malintoppi L (2006), 'Methods of Dispute Resolution in Inter-State Litigation: When States Go to Arbitration Rather than Adjudication', 5 *Law & Practice of International Courts and Tribunals* 133

Mamolea A (2014), 'Good Faith Review' in Gruszczynski and Werner (eds.), *Deference in International Courts and Tribunals: Standard of Review and Margin of Appreciation* (Oxford University Press)

Mann FA (1987), 'The Proper Law in the Conflict of Laws', 36 *International & Comparative Law Quarterly* 437

Mardikian L (2018), 'The Right to Property as Regional Custom in Europe', 9 *Transnational Legal Theory* 56

Margolis E (1955), 'Soviet Views on the Relationship between National and International Law', 4 *International & Comparative Law Quarterly* 116

Martin A (1947), 'Private Property, Rights, and Interests in the Paris Peace Treaties', 24 *British Yearbook of International Law* 273

Martinez-Fraga P and Reetz R (2015), *Public Purpose in International Law: Rethinking Regulatory Sovereignty in the Global Era* (Cambridge University Press)

Martinkute I (2016), 'The Delimitation of Contractual Rights and Property in International Investment Law', 1 *European Investment Law and Arbitration Review Online* 1

McCorquodale R (2006), 'International Community and State Sovereignty: An Uneasy Symbiotic Relationship' in Warbrick and Tierney (eds.), *Towards an 'International Legal Community'? The Sovereignty of States and the Sovereignty of International Law* (British Institute of International and Comparative Law)

(2013), 'Pluralism, Global Law and Human Rights: Strengthening Corporate Accountability for Human Rights Violations', 2 *Global Constitutionalism* 287

McCrudden C (2007), 'Judicial Comparativism and Human Rights' in Örücü and Nelken (eds.), *Comparative Law: A Handbook* (Hart)

McGoldrick D (2010), 'The Boundaries of Justiciability', 59 *International & Comparative Law Quarterly* 981

(2016), 'A Defence of the Margin of Appreciation and an Argument for Its Application by the Human Rights Committee', 65 *International & Comparative Law Quarterly* 21

McHarg A (1999), 'Reconciling Human Rights and the Public Interest: Conceptual Problems and Doctrinal Uncertainty in the Jurisprudence of the European Court of Human Rights', 62 *Modern Law Review* 671

McLachlan C (2005), 'The Principle of Systemic Integration and Article 31(3)(c) of the Vienna Convention', 54 *International & Comparative Law Quarterly* 279

(2008), 'Investment Treaties and General International Law', 57 *International & Comparative Law Quarterly* 361

(2009), *Lis Pendens in International Litigation* (Martinus Nijhoff)

McRae DM (1971), 'Sovereignty and the International Legal Order', 10 *Western Ontario Law Review* 56

Meagher D (2011), 'The Brennan Conception of the Implied Freedom: Theory, Proportionality and Deference', 30 *University of Queensland Law Review* 119

Melish T (2009), 'From Paradox to Subsidiarity: The United States and Human Rights Treaty Bodies', 34 *Yale Journal of International Law* 389

Menon PK (1989), 'Primary, Subsidiary and Other Possible Sources of International Law', 1 *Sri Lanka Journal of International Law* 113

Merges RP (2011), *Justifying Intellectual Property* (Harvard University Press)

Merrills JG (1969), 'The Justiciability of International Disputes', 47 *Canadian Bar Review* 240

(1988), *The Development of International Law by the European Court of Human Rights* (Manchester University Press)

Merry SE (1988), 'Legal Pluralism', 22 *Law & Society Review* 869

Michaels R and Pauwelyn J (2010), 'Conflict of Norms or Conflict of Laws? Different Techniques in the Fragmentation of International Law' in Broude and Shany (eds.), *Multi-Sourced Equivalent Norms in International Law* (Hart)

Mik C (2014), 'Book Review: Lukasz Gruscyznski, Wouter Werner (eds.), Deference in International Courts and Tribunals: Standard of Review and Margin of Appreciation', 34 *Polish Yearbook of International Law* 305

Milano E (2005), 'Diplomatic Protection and Human Rights before the International Court of Justice: Re-Fashioning Tradition?' in Curtin and Nollkaemper (eds.), *Netherlands Yearbook of International Law*, vol. 35 (TMC Asser Press)

Miles K (2010), 'International Investment Law: Origins, Imperialism and Conceptualizing the Environment', 21 *Colorado Journal of International Environmental Law and Policy* 1

Miller N (2002), 'An International Jurisprudence? The Operation of "Precedent" Across International Tribunals', 15 *Leiden Journal of International Law* 483

Milner D (2014),'Protocols No. 15 and 16 to the European Convention on Human Rights in the Context of the Perennial Process of Reform', 17 *Zeitschrift für europarechtliche Studien* 19

Mitchell A, Munro J and Voon T (2018), 'Importing WTO General Exceptions into International Investment Agreements: Proportionality, Myths and Risks', in *Yearbook on International Investment Law & Policy 2016–2017* (Cambridge University Press)

Moloo R and Jacinto J (2012), 'Standards of Review and Reviewing Standards: Public Interest Regulation in International Investment Law', *Yearbook of International Law and Policy* 539

Montt S (2012), *State Liability in Investment Treaty Arbitration: Global Constitutional and Administrative Law in the BIT Generation* (Hart)

Moon WJ (2012), 'Essential Security Interests in International Investment Agreements', 15 *Journal of International Economic Law* 481

Moore JB (1922), 'The Organization of the Permanent Court of International Justice', 22 *Columbia Law Review* 497

Morgenthau H (1940), 'Positivism, Functionalism, and International Law', 34 *American Journal of International Law* 260

Mosk RM (2003),'The Role of Facts in International Dispute Resolution', in *Collected Courses of the Hague Academy of International Law*, vol. 304 (Hague Academy of International Law)

Mosler H (1963), 'The Protection of Human Rights by International Legal Procedure', 52 *Georgetown Law Journal* 800

Mountfield H (2002), 'Regulatory Expropriations in Europe: The Approach of the European Court of Human Rights', 11 *New York University Environmental Law Journal* 136

Mowbray A (2010), 'A Study of the Principle of Fair Balance in the Jurisprudence of the European Court of Human Rights', 10 *Human Rights Law Review* 289

(2015), 'Subsidiarity and the European Convention on Human Rights', 15 *Human Rights Law Review* 313

Mulhern JP (1988), 'In Defense of the Political Question Doctrine', 137 *University of Pennsylvania Law Review* 97

Mullan DJ (2006), 'Deference: Is It Useful Outside Canada?', *Acta Juridica* 42

Müller E and Schneider P (2007), 'The ICJ 1945–2001: Empirical Findings about its Performance and Recommendations for an Improvement of its Efficiency', 3 *Review of International Law & Politics* 71

Mureinik E (1994), 'A Bridge to Where? Introducing the Interim Bill of Rights', 10 *South African Journal on Human Rights* 31

Murphy S (1991), 'The ELSI Case: An Investment Dispute at the International Court of Justice', 16 *Yale Journal of International Law* 391

(2013), 'International Judicial Bodies for Resolving Disputes between States' in Romano et al. (eds.), *Oxford Handbook on International Adjudication* (Oxford University Press)

Nafziger JAR (1984), 'Some Remarks on the Writing Style of the International Court of Justice' in Buergenthal (ed.), *Contemporary Issues in International Law: Essays in Honor of Louis B. Sohn* (N P Engel)

Nelken D (2004), 'Using the Concept of Legal Culture', 29 *Australian Journal of Legal Philosophy* 1

(2013), 'Comparative Sociology of Law' in Banakar and Travers (eds.), *Law and Social Theory* (2nd edn, Hart)

Newcombe A (2005), 'The Boundaries of Regulatory Expropriation in International Law', 20 *ICSID Review – Foreign Investment Law Journal* 1

Ngulube P (2015), 'Qualitative Data Analysis and Interpretation: Systematic Search for Meaning' in Mathipa and Gumbo (eds.), *Addressing Research Challenges: Making Headway for Developing Researchers* (Mosala-MASEDI Publishers & Booksellers)

Nicholson F (1965), 'The Protection of Foreign Property under Customary International Law', 6 *Boston College Industrial and Commercial Law Review* 391

Niedlispacher I (2018), *The Developing Remedial Practice of the European Court of Human Rights (Speaking Notes)* (Council of Europe)

Niedlispacher I et al. (2018), *The Developing Remedial Practice of the European Court of Human Rights (Handout)* (Council of Europe)

Nollkaemper A (2006), 'The Role of Domestic Courts in the Case Law of the International Court of Justice', 5 *Chinese Journal of International Law* 301

(2009), 'The Reception by the International Court of Justice of Decisions of Domestic Courts', 7(15)*Federalismi.it: Rivista di Diritto Pubblico Italiano* 1

(2011), *National Courts and the International Rule of Law* (Oxford University Press)

(2013a), 'Conversations Among Courts: Domestic and International Adjudicators' in Romano and Shany (eds.), *Oxford Handbook of International Adjudication* (Oxford University Press)

(2013b), 'Inside or Out' in Klabbers and Piiparinen (eds.), *Normative Pluralism and International Law* (Cambridge University Press)

Nourse V and Shaffer G (2014), 'Empiricism, Experimentalism, and Conditional Theory', 67 *Southern Methodist University Law Review* 141

O'Connell D (1960), 'The Relationship between International Law and Municipal Law', 48 *Georgetown Law Journal* 431

O'Donnell T (1982), 'The Margin of Appreciation Doctrine: Standards in the Jurisprudence of the European Court of Human Rights', 4 *Human Rights Quarterly* 474

O'Donoghue A (2013), 'International Constitutionalism and the State', 11 *International Journal of Constitutional Law* 1021

Oellers-Frahm K (2001), 'Multiplication of International Courts and Tribunals and Conflicting Jurisdiction – Problems and Possible Solutions', 5 *Max Planck Yearbook of United Nations Law* 67

Oesch M (2003), 'Standards of Review in WTO Dispute Resolution', 6 *Journal of International Economic Law* 635

Oldfather C, Bockhorst J and Dimmer B (2012), 'Triangulating Judicial Responsiveness: Automated Content Analysis, Judicial Opinions, and the Methodology of Legal Scholarship', 64 *Florida Law Review* 1189

Olivier M (1988), 'Aspects of the Establishment of Sovereignty and the Transfer of Government Authority', 14 *African Year Book of International Law* 85

Olynyk S (2012), 'A Balanced Approach to Distinguishing between Legitimate Regulation and Indirect Expropriation in Investor-State Arbitration', 15 *International Trade & Business Law Review* 254

Oppenheim L (1908), 'The Science of International Law: Its Task and Method', 2 *American Journal of International Law* 313

Oppenheim L, Jennings RY and Watts A (1996)*Oppenheim's International Law: Volume 1, Peace* (9th edn, Longman)

Orakhelashvili A (2003), 'Restrictive Interpretation of Human Rights Treaties in Recent Jurisprudence of the European Court of Human Rights', 14 *European Journal of International Law* 529

(2008), *The Interpretation of Acts and Rules in Public International Law* (Oxford University Press)

Origgi G (2018), *Reputation: What it Is and Why it Matters* (Princeton University Press)

Ortino F (2005), 'From "Non-Discrimination" to "Reasonableness": A Paradigm Shift in International Economic Law?' Jean Monnet Working Paper No. 01/05

(2014), 'The Investment Treaty System as Judicial Review' Dickson Poon School of Law Research Paper No. 2014–23

(2017), 'Investment Treaties, Sustainable Development and Reasonableness Review: A Case Against Strict Proportionality Balancing', 30 *Leiden Journal of International Law* 71

Ostrovsky A (2005), 'What's So Funny about Peace, Love, and Understanding? How the Margin of Appreciation Doctrine Preserves Core Human Rights within Cultural Diversity and Legitimises International Human Rights Tribunals', 1 *Hanse Law Review* 47

Owen H (1968), 'Compulsory Jurisdiction of the International Court of Justice: A Study of Its Acceptance by Nations', 3 *Georgia Law Review* 704

Paine J (2015), 'The Project of System-Internal Reform in International Investment Law: An Appraisal', *Journal of International Dispute Settlement* 1

(2019), 'Standard of Review (Investment Arbitration)' in Ruiz-Fabri(ed.), *Max Planck Encyclopedia of International Procedural Law* (Oxford University Press)

Pandya APG and Moody A (2010), 'Legitimate Expectations in Investment Treaty Arbitration: An Unclear Future', 15 *Tilburg Law Review* 93

Paparinskis M (2014), 'Analogies and Other Regimes of International Law' in Douglas et al. (eds.), *The Foundations of International Investment Law* (Oxford University Press)

Pappas M (2008), 'No Two-Stepping in the Laboratories: State Deference Standards and Their Implications for Improving the Chevron Doctrine', 39 *McGeorge Law Review* 977

Parker D (2013), 'Policing Procedure before Substance: Reforming Judicial Review of the Factual Predicates to Legislation', 99 *Virginia Law Review* 1327

Parlett K (2011), *The Individual in the International Legal System* (Cambridge University Press)

Paul JR (1991), 'Comity in International Law', 32 *Harvard International Law Journal* 1

Paulsson J (2005), *Denial of Justice in International Law* (Cambridge University Press)

Pauwelyn J (2014), 'At the Edge of Chaos? Foreign Investment Law as a Complex Adaptive System, How It Emerged and How It Can Be Reformed', 29 *ICSID Review – Foreign Investment Law Journal* 372

Pauwelyn J and Elsig M (2012), 'The Politics of Treaty Interpretation: Variations and Explanations across International Tribunals' in Dunoff and Pollack (eds.), *Interdisciplinary Perspectives on International Law and International Relations: The State of the Art* (Cambridge University Press)

Pauwelyn J and Salles LE (2009), 'Forum Shopping before International Tribunals: (Real) Concerns, (Im)Possible Solutions', 42 *Cornell International Law Journal* 77

Peaslee AJ (1931), 'Obligatory Jurisdiction of the Permanent Court of International Justice', 25 *American Society of International Law Proceedings* 48

Peat D (2013), 'The Normative Authority of Domestic Laws in International Law' ASIL Midyear Research Forum

Pendas DO (2012), 'Toward a New Politics? On the Recent Historiography of Human Rights', 21 *Contemporary European History* 95

Perry MJ (2003), 'Protecting Human Rights in a Democracy: What Role for the Courts?', *Wake Forest Law Review* 635

Perry SR (1989), 'Second-Order Reasons, Uncertainty and Legal Theory', 62 *Southern California Law Review* 913

Peter F (2019), 'Legitimate Political Authority and Expertise' in Sadurski et al. (eds.), *Legitimacy: The State and Beyond* (Oxford University Press)

Peters A (2006), 'Compensatory Constitutionalism: The Function and Potential of Fundamental International Norms and Structures', 19 *Leiden Journal of International Law* 579

(2013), 'Realizing Utopia as a Scholarly Endeavour', 24 *European Journal of International Law* 533

Peters B (2016), 'The Rule of Law Effects of Dialogues between National Courts and Strasbourg: An Outline' in Kanetake and Nollkaemper (eds.), *The Rule of Law at the National and International Levels: Contestations and Deference* (Hart)

Peters B and Schaffer JK (2013), 'The Turn to Authority beyond States', 4 *Transnational Legal Theory* 315

Peters P (1997), 'Exhaustion of Local Remedies: Ignored in Most Bilateral Investment Treaties', 44 *Netherlands International Law Review* 233

Petersen N (2009), 'The Reception of International Law by Constitutional Courts through the Prism of Legitimacy', 39 *Preprints of the Max Planck Institute for Research on Collective Goods*

Petersmann E-U (2014), 'Judicial Standards of Review and Administration of Justice in Trade and Investment Law and Adjudication' in Gruszczynski and Werner (eds.), *Deference in International Courts and Tribunals: Standard of Review and Margin of Appreciation* (Oxford University Press)

Petzold H (1993), 'The Convention and the Principle of Subsidiarity' in Macdonald, Matscher and Petzold (eds.), *The European System for the Protection of Human Rights* (Martinus Nijhoff)

Pinto M (2008), 'National and International Courts – Deference or Disdain?', 30 *Loyola of Los Angeles International and Comparative Law Review* 247

Pirker B (2014), 'Democracy and Distrust in International Law: The Procedural Democracy Doctrine and the Standard of Review Used by International Courts and Tribunals' in Gruszczynski and Werner (eds.), *Deference in International Courts and Tribunals: Standard of Review and Margin of Appreciation* (Oxford University Press)

Plato (2011), *The Republic* (Baker & Taylor)

Pocock JGA (1976), 'The Classical Theory of Deference', 81 *American Historical Review* 516

Poirier M (2002), 'The Virtue of Vagueness in Takings Doctrine', 24 *Cardozo Law Review* 93

Pollack MA (2014), 'Political Science and International Courts' in Romano et al. (eds.), *Oxford Handbook of International Adjudication* (Oxford University Press)

Poole T (2009), 'The Reformation of English Administrative Law', 68 *Cambridge Law Journal* 142

Popelier P and Van De Heyning C (2017), 'Subsidiarity Post-Brighton: Procedural Rationality as Answer?', 30 *Leiden Journal of International Law* 5

Posner EA (2004), 'The Decline of the International Court of Justice' University of Chicago, John M. Olin Law and Economics Working Paper Series, Paper No. 233

Posner EA and de Figueiredo MFP (2005), 'Is the International Court of Justice Biased?', 34 *Journal of Legal Studies* 599

Poulsen LNS and Aisbett E (2013), 'When the Claim Hits: Bilateral Investment Treaties and Bounded Rational Learning', 65 *World Politics* 273

Pratt T (2018), 'Deference and Hierarchy in International Regime Complexes', 72(3) *International Organization* 561

Price D (2000), 'Chapter 11 – Private Party vs Government, Investor-State Dispute Settlement: Frankenstein or Safety Valve?', 26 *Canada-United States Law Journal* 107

Prost M (2006), 'All Shouting the Same Slogans: International Law's Unities and the Politics of Fragmentation', 17 *Finnish Yearbook of International Law* 131

Prott LV (1970),'The Style of Judgment in the International Court of Justice', *Australian Year Book of International Law* 75

Puig S and Brown C (2012), 'The Secretary-General's Power to Refuse to Register a Request for Arbitration under the ICSID Convention', 27 *ICSID Review – Foreign Investment Law Journal* 172

Puthuppally C (2014), 'Science, Expertise and Due Deference', 5 *King's Student Law Review* 83

Radin M (1982), 'Property and Personhood', 34 *Stanford Law Review* 957

Ragni C (2014), 'Standard of Review and the Margin of Appreciation before the International Court of Justice' in Gruszczynski and Werner (eds.), *Deference in International Courts and Tribunals: Standard of Review and Margin of Appreciation* (Oxford University Press)

Raine T (2013), 'Judicial Review under the Human Rights Act: A Culture of Justification', 1 *North East Law Review* 81

Ramsey MD (1997), 'Escaping "International Comity"', 83 *Iowa Law Review* 893

Ratner S (2008), 'Regulatory Takings in Institutional Context: Beyond the Fear of Fragmented International Law', 102 *American Journal of International Law* 475

Raz J (1979), *The Authority of Law* (Oxford University Press)
(1986), *The Morality of Freedom* (Clarendon)
(1999), *Practical Reason and Norms* (Oxford University Press)
(2009), *Between Authority and Interpretation* (Oxford University Press)
Re E (1951), 'The Nationalization of Foreign-Owned Property', 36 *Minnesota Law Review* 323
Reid J (1972), 'The Judge as Law Maker', 12 *Journal of the Society of Public Teachers of Law* 22
Reinisch A (2011), 'Necessity in Investment Arbitration' in Dekker and Hey (eds.), *Netherlands Yearbook of International Law*, vol. 41 (TMC Asser Press)
Rivers J (2006), 'Proportionality and Variable Intensity of Review', 65 *Cambridge Law Journal* 174
(2014), 'The Presumption of Proportionality', 77 *Modern Law Review* 409
Roberts A (2011),'The Next Battleground: Standards of Review in Investment Treaty Arbitration', 16 *International Council for Commercial Arbitration Congress Series* 170
(2013), 'Clash of Paradigms: Actors and Analogies Shaping the Investment Treaty System', 107 *American Journal of International Law* 45
Roberts A and Braddock R (2016), 'Protecting Public Welfare Regulation Through Joint Treaty Party Control: A ChAFTA Innovation' EJIL: Talk!
Rogers C (2013), 'The Politics of International Investment Arbitrators', 12 *Santa Clara Journal of International Law* 223
Rogge K (1993), 'Fact-Finding' in Macdonald et al. (eds.), *The European System for the Protection of Human Rights* (Martinus Nijhoff)
Romano C (2002), 'International Justice and Development Countries: A Quantitative Analysis', 1 *Law & Practice of International Courts and Tribunals* 367
(2007), 'The Shift from the Consensual to the Compulsory Paradigm in International Adjudication: Elements for a Theory of Consent', 39(4) *NYU Journal of International Law and Politics* 791
(2013), 'The Rule of Prior Exhaustion of Domestic Remedies: Theory and Practice in International Human Rights Procedures' in Boschiero et al. (eds.), *International Courts and the Development of International Law* (TMC Asser Press)
Romano C, Alter K and Shany Y (2014), 'Mapping International Adjudicative Bodies, the Issues, and Players' in Romano et al. (eds.), *The Oxford Handbook of International Adjudication* (Oxford University Press)
Rook D (2001), *Property Law and Human Rights* (Blackstone Press)
Root E (1910), 'Basis of Protection to Citizens Residing Abroad', 4 *American Journal of International Law* 517
(1920), 'Permanent Court of International Justice', 6 *American Bar Association Journal* 181
Rosenau JN (1997), *Along the Domestic-Foreign Frontier: Exploring Governance in a Turbulent World* (Cambridge University Press)
Rosenfeld M (2013), 'Rethinking the Boundaries between Public Law and Private Law for the Twenty First Century: An Introduction', 11 *International Journal of Constitutional Law* 125
Rosenne S (1993), 'The International Court of Justice and International Arbitration', 6 *Leiden Journal of International Law* 297

(1995), *The World Court: What It Is and How It Works* (5th edn, Martinus Nijhoff)
(1997), *The Law and Practice of the International Court, 1920–1996*, vol. 1 (3rd edn, Martinus Nijhoff)
Roth-Isigkeit D (2017), 'The Blinkered Discipline? – Martti Koskenniemi and Interdisciplinary Approaches to International Law', 9 *International Theory* 410
Ruse-Khan HG (2013), 'A Conflict-of-Laws Approach to Competing Rationalities in International Law. The Case of Plain Packaging between IP, Trade, Investment and Health' 9 *Journal of Private International Law* 309
Sabahi B (2011), *Compensation and Restitution in Investor-State Arbitration* (Oxford University Press)
Sacerdoti G (2011), 'Precedent In The Settlement Of International Economic Disputes: The WTO and Investment Arbitration Models', in Rovine (ed.), *Contemporary Issues in International Arbitration and Mediation: The Fordham Papers (2010)* (Brill)
Sacriste G and Vauchez A (2007), 'The Force of International Law: Lawyers' Diplomacy on the International Scene in the 1920s', 32 *Law & Social Inquiry* 83
Sadl U and Olsen HP (2014), 'Empirical Studies of the Webs of International Case Law: A New Research Agenda' iCourts Working Paper No. 8
(2017), 'Can Quantitative Methods Complement Doctrinal Legal Studies? Using Citation Network and Corpus Linguistic Analysis to Understand International Courts', 30 *Leiden Journal of International Law* 327
Sadl U and Panagis Y (2015), 'What Is a Leading Case in EU Law? An Empirical Analysis', 40 *European Law Review* 15
Sadurski W (2009), 'Partnering with Strasbourg: Constitutionalisation of the European Court of Human Rights, the Accession of Central and East European States to the Council of Europe, and the Idea of Pilot Judgments', 9 *Human Rights Law Review* 397
Salacuse JW (2010), 'The Emerging Global Regime for Investment', 51 *Harvard International Law Journal* 427
Salacuse JW and Sullivan E (2005), 'Do BITs Really Work?: An Evaluation of Bilateral Investment Treaties and Their Grand Bargain', 46 *Harvard International Law Journal* 67
Salazar A (2010), 'NAFTA Chapter 11, Regulatory Expropriation, and Domestic Counter-Advertising Law', 27 *Arizona Journal of International and Comparative Law* 31
Saldaña J (2009), *The Coding Manual for Qualitative Researchers* (Sage Publications)
Sales P (2006), 'Property and Human Rights: Protection, Expansion and Disruption', 11 *Judicial Review* 141
Salgado RA (1986), 'Protection of Nationals' Rights to Property under the European Convention on Human Rights: Lithgow v. United Kingdom', 27 *Vanderbilt Journal of International Law* 865
Samuel G (2009), 'Interdisciplinarity and the Authority Paradigm: Should Law Be Taken Seriously by Scientists and Social Scientists?', 36 *Journal of Law and Society* 431

Sands P (2002), 'Searching for Balance: Concluding Remarks', 11 *New York University Environmental Law Journal* 198

Sassen S (2015), *Losing Control? Sovereignty in an Age of Globalization* (New York University Press)

Sasson M (2010), *Substantive Law in Investment Treaty Arbitration: The Unsettled Relationship between International Law and Municipal Law* (Kluwer)

Saul M (2016), 'Structuring Evaluations of Parliamentary Processes by the European Court of Human Rights', 20 *International Journal of Human Rights* 1077

Sauvant KP and others (2016), 'The Rise of Self-Judging Essential Security Interest Clauses in International Investment Agreements' Columbia FDI Perspectives on Topical Foreign Direct Investment Issues, No. 188

Sayeed S (2005), 'Beyond the Language of "Deference"', 10 *Judicial Review* 111

Scelle GAJ (1943), *Manuel Élémentaire de Droit International Public* (Loviton)

(1984), *Précis de droit des gens* (Editions du CNRS)

Schabas WA (2015), *The European Convention on Human Rights: A Commentary* (1st edn, Oxford University Press)

Scharpf FW (2002), *Governing in Europe: Effective and Democratic?* (Oxford University Press)

Schauer F (1977), 'Article 10 and Freedom of Expression: An Examination of Deference to National Authority under Article 10 of the European Convention on Human Rights', 3 *Poly Law Review* 25

(2004), 'Deferring', 103 *Michigan Law Review* 1567

(2008), 'Authority and Authorities', *Virginia Law Review* 1931

Schermers HG and Blokker N (2011), *International Institutional Law: Unity within Diversity* (Martinus Nijhoff)

Schill SW (2010a), 'Crafting the International Economic Order: The Public Function of Investment Treaty Arbitration and Its Significance for the Role of the Arbitrator', 23 *Leiden Journal of International Law* 401

(2010b), 'The Multilateralization of International Investment Law: Emergence of a Multilateral System of Investment Protection on Bilateral Grounds', 2 *Trade, Law and Development* 59

(2011), 'System-Building in Investment Treaty Arbitration and Lawmaking', 12 *German Law Journal* 1083

(2012), 'Deference in Investment Treaty Arbitration: Reconceptualizing the Standard of Review through Comparative Public Law' Society of International Economic Law, Online Proceedings Working Papers, Paper No. 2012/33

(2016), 'The European Commission's Proposal of an "Investment Court System" for TTIP: Stepping Stone or Stumbling Block for Multilateralizing International Investment Law?', 20 *ASIL Insights*

Schill SW and Briese R (2009), '"If the State Considers": Self-Judging Clauses in International Dispute Settlement', 13 *Max Planck Yearbook of United Nations Law* 61

Schmitt C (2005), *Political Theology: Four Chapters on the Concept of Sovereignty* (G Schwab tr., University of Chicago Press)

Schneiderman D (1996), 'NAFTA's Takings Rule: American Constitutional Comes to Canada', 46 *University of Toronto Journal* 499

(2008), *Constitutionalizing Economic Globalization: Investment Rules and Democracy's Promise* (Cambridge University Press)

(2010), 'Judicial Politics and International Investment Arbitration: Seeking an Explanation for Conflicting Outcomes', 30 *Northwestern Journal of International Law & Business* 383

Schreuer C (1996), 'International and Domestic Law in Investment Disputes. The Case of ICSID', 1 *Austrian Review of International and European Law* 89

Schreuer C et al. (2009) *The ICSID Convention: A Commentary* (2nd edn, Cambridge University Press)

Schrijver N (2000), 'The Changing Nature of State Sovereignty', 70 *British Yearbook of International Law* 65

Schultz T and Dupont C (2015), 'Investment Arbitration: Promoting the Rule of Law or Over-Empowering Investors? A Quantitative Empirical Study', 25 *European Journal of International Law* 1147

Schultz T and Ridi N (2017), 'Comity and International Courts and Tribunals', 50 *Cornell International Law Journal* 577

Schwebel SM (1996), 'The Treatment of Human Rights and of Aliens in the International Court of Justice' in Lowe and Fitzmaurice (eds.), *Fifty Years of the International Court of Justice: Essays in Honour of Sir Robert Jennings* (Cambridge University Press)

Schweigman D (2001), *The Authority of the Security Council under Chapter VII of the UN Charter: Legal Limits and the Role of the International Court of Justice* (Kluwer Law International)

Schwobel CEJ (2012), 'Whither the Private in Global Governance?', 10 *International Journal of Constitutional Law* 1106

Scott C (2008), 'Diverse Persuasion(s): From Rhetoric to Representation (and Back Again to Rhetoric) in International Human Rights Interpretation' Comparative Research in Law & Political Economy Research Paper No. 04/2008

Scott JB (1926), 'The Permanent Court of International Justice – Its Origin and Nature', 15 *Georgetown Law Journal* 297

Seidman LM (2004), 'The Secret Life of the Political Question Doctrine', *John Marshall Law Review* 441

Semertzi, A (2014), 'The Preclusion of Direct Effect in the Recently Concluded EU Free Trade Agreements', 51 *Common Market Law Review* 1125

Sepúlveda-Amor B (2013), 'International Law and National Sovereignty: The NAFTA and the Claims of Mexican Jurisdiction', 14 *Journal of World Investment & Trade* 613

Shaffer G (2008), 'A New Legal Realism: Method in International Economic Law Scholarship' in Picker et al. (eds.), *International Economic Law: The State and Future of the Discipline* (Hart)

Shaffer G and Ginsburg T (2012), 'The Empirical Turn in International Legal Scholarship', 106 *American Journal of International Law* 1

Shany Y (2003), *The Competing Jurisdictions of International Courts and Tribunals* (Oxford University Press)

(2005), 'Toward a General Margin of Appreciation Doctrine in International Law?', 16 *European Journal of International Law* 907

(2006), 'Jurisdictional Competition between National and International Courts: Could International Jurisdiction-Regulating Rules Apply?', in *Netherlands Yearbook of International Law*, vol. 37 (TMC Asser Press)

(2007), *Regulating Jurisdictional Relations between National and International Courts* (Oxford University Press)

(2009a), 'No Longer a Weak Department of Power? Reflections on the Emergence of a New International Judiciary', 20 *European Journal of International Law* 73

(2009b),'National Courts as International Actors: Jurisdictional Implications', 15 *federalismi.it* 1

(2016) 'Stronger Together? Legitimacy and Effectiveness of International Courts as Mutually Reinforcing or Undermining Notions' in Grossman et al. (eds.), *Legitimacy and International Courts* (Cambridge University Press)

Shelton D, (2003) 'The Boundaries of Human Rights Jurisdiction in Europe', 13 *Duke Journal of Comparative and International Law* 95

(2007) 'An Introduction to the History of International Human Rights Law' George Washington Law School, Public Law and Legal Theory Working Paper Series, Paper No. 346

(2008) 'Form, Function, and the Powers of International Courts', 9 *Chicago Journal of International Law* 537

Sherwood Dunn F (1932), *The Protection of Nationals: A Study in the Application of International Law* (Johns Hopkins Press)

Shirlow E (2014a), 'Taking Stock: Assessing the Implications of the Kadi Saga for International Law and the Law of the European Union', 15 *Melbourne Journal of International Law* 534

(2014b), 'Deference and Indirect Expropriation Analysis in International Investment Law: Observations on Current Approaches and Frameworks for Future Analysis', 29 *ICSID Review – Foreign Investment Law Journal* 595

(2014c), 'Les Laboratoires Servier, S.A.A., and others *v.* Republic of Poland: Defining the Nature of the Police Powers 'Defence' and the Deference Applicable in Regulatory Expropriation Cases', 29 *ICSID Review – Foreign Investment Law Journal* 559

Sik KS (1982), 'Nationality and (Public) International Law', 29 *Netherlands International Law Review* 100

Silverman D (2011), *Interpreting Qualitative Data: A Guide to the Principles of Qualitative Research* (4th edn, Sage Publications)

Simma B (1985), 'Self-Contained Regimes', in *Netherlands Yearbook of International Law*, vol. 16 (TMC Asser Press)

(1995), 'The Contribution of Alfred Verdross to the Theory of International Law', 6 *European Journal of International Law* 33

(2011), 'Foreign Investment Arbitration: A Place for Human Rights?', 60 *International & Comparative Law Quarterly* 573

(2012), 'The International Court of Justice and Scientific Expertise', 106 *Proceedings of the Annual Meeting (American Society of International Law)* 230

Simma B and Alston P (1988) 'The Sources of Human Rights Law: Custom, Jus Cogens, and General Principles', 12 *Australian Year Book of International Law* 82

Simma B and Pulkowski D (2006), 'Of Planets and the Universe: Self-Contained Regimes in International Law', 17 *European Journal of International Law* 483

Singh N (1989), *The Role and Record of the International Court of Justice* (Martinus Nijhoff)
Slaughter A-M (1994), 'Liberal International Relations Theory and International Economic Law', 10 *American University Journal of International Law and Policy* 717
(2003), 'A Global Community of Courts', 44 *Harvard International Law Journal* 191
(2005) *A New World Order* (Princeton University Press)
Sloane R (2009a), 'Breaking the Genuine Link: The Contemporary International Legal Regulation of Nationality', 50 *Harvard International Law Review* 1
(2009b), 'More Than What Courts Do: Jurisprudence, Decision and Dignity – In Brief Encounters and Global Affairs', 34 *Yale Journal of International Law* 517
Smith AM (2004), '"Judicial Nationalism" in International Law: National Identity and Judicial Autonomy at the ICJ', 40 *Texas International Law Journal* 197
Sohn L and Baxter RR (1961), 'Responsibility of States for Injuries to the Economic Interests of Aliens', 55 *American Journal of International Law* 545
Somek A (2007), 'Kelsen Lives', 18 *European Journal of International Law* 409
Soper P (2002), *The Ethics of Deference: Learning from Law's Morals* (Cambridge University Press)
Sornarajah M (1994), *The International Law on Foreign Investment* (Cambridge University Press)
(2011), 'Mutations of Neo-Liberalism in International Investment Law', 3 *Trade, Law and Development* 203
Spano R (2018a), 'The Future of the European Court of Human Rights – Subsidiarity, Process-Based Review and the Rule of Law', *Human Rights Law Review* 1
(2018b), *The Evolving Remedial Practice of the European Court of Human Rights (Speaking Notes)* (Council of Europe)
Spiermann O (2003), 'A Permanent Court of International Justice', 72 *Nordic Journal of International Law* 399
(2005), *International Legal Argument in the Permanent Court of International Justice: The Rise of the International Judiciary* (Cambridge University Press)
Sprankling JG (2012), 'The Emergence of International Property Law', 90 *North Carolina Law Review* 461
(2013), 'The Global Right to Property', 52 *Columbia Journal of Transnational Law* 44
(2014), *The International Law of Property* (Oxford University Press)
Sunstein C (2007), 'If People Would be Outraged by their Ruling, Should Judges Care?', 60 *Stanford Law Review* 155
Starke JG (1936), 'Monism and Dualism in the Theory of International Law', 17 *British Yearbook of International Law* 66
Staton JK and Moore WH (2011), 'Judicial Power in Domestic and International Politics', 65 *International Organization* 553
Steiner A (1936), 'Fundamental Conceptions of International Law in the Jurisprudence of the Permanent Court of International Justice', 30 *American Journal of International Law* 414
Steinhardt R (1991), 'The Privatization of Public International Law', 25 *George Washington Journal of International Law and Economics* 523

Steininger S (2018), 'What's Human Rights Got to do with It? An Empirical Analysis of Human Rights References in Investment Arbitration', 31 *Leiden Journal of International Law* 33

Stephan PB (2002), 'Courts, Tribunals, and Legal Unification – The Agency Problem', 3 *Chicago Journal of International Law* 333

Steyn JvZ (2005),'Deference: A Tangled Story', *Public Law* 346

Stone Sweet A (2009), 'Constitutionalism, Legal Pluralism, and International Regimes', 16 *Indiana Journal of Global Legal Studies* 621

Stone Sweet A and Brunell T (2013), 'Trustee Courts and the Judicialization of International Regimes', 1 *Journal of Law and Courts* 61

Stone Sweet A and Grisel F (2009), 'Transnational Investment Arbitration: From Delegation to Constitutionalization?' in Dupuy et al. (eds.), *Human Rights in International Investment Law and Arbitration* (Oxford University Press)

(2014), 'The Evolution of International Arbitration: Delegation, Judicialization, Governance' in Mattli and Dietz (eds.), *International Arbitration and Global Governance* (Oxford University Press)

(2017), *The Evolution of International Arbitration: Judicialization, Governance, Legitimacy* (1st edn, Oxford University Press)

Stone Sweet A and Mathews J (2008), 'Proportionality Balancing and Global Constitutionalism', 47 *Columbia Journal of Transnational Law* 72

Story J (1834), *Commentaries of the Conflicts Law, Foreign and Domestic* (Hiliard Gray)

Sucker F (2014], 'Including a General Public Interest Clause in WTO Agreements: A Way Forward in Trade Linkage Debates' Society of International Economic Law Conference Paper Series, Working Paper No. 2014/19

Sumption J (2011), 'Judicial and Political Decision-Making: The Uncertain Boundary', 16 *Judicial Review* 301

(2013), '27th Sultan Azlan Shah Lecture: The Limits of Law' www.supremecourt.uk/docs/speech-131120.pdf

Sylvest C (2010), 'Realism and International Law: The Challenge of John H. Herz', 2 *International Theory* 410

Tamanaha B (2008), 'Understanding Legal Pluralism: Past to Present, Local to Global', 30 *Sydney Law Review* 375

Tams CJ (2013), 'The Contentious Jurisdiction of the Permanent Court' in Tams and Fitzmaurice (eds.), *Legacies of the Permanent Court of International Justice* (Martinus Nijhoff)

Tarrow S (2010),'Bridging the Quantitative-Qualitative Divide' in Brady and Collier (eds.), *Rethinking Social Inquiry: Diverse Tools, Shared Standards* (2nd edn, Rowman & Littlefield)

Tasioulas J (2010), 'The Legitimacy of International Law' in Besson and Tasioulas (eds.), *The Philosophy of International Law* (Oxford University Press)

Teitelbaum R (2007), 'Recent Fact-Finding Developments at the International Court of Justice', 6 *Law & Practice of International Courts and Tribunals* 119

Telman DAJ (2014), 'International Legal Positivism and Legal Realism' in Kammerhofer and d'Aspremont (eds.), *International Legal Positivism in a Post-Modern World* (Cambridge University Press)

Thayer J (1893), 'The Origin and Scope of the American Doctrine of Constitutional Law', 7 *Harvard Law Review* 129

Thierry H (1990), 'The Thought of Georges Scelle', 1 *European Journal of International Law* 193
Thirlway H (2006), 'The Drafting of ICJ Decisions: Some Personal Recollections and Observations', 5 *Chinese Journal of International Law* 15
Thomas CA (2013), 'The Concept of Legitimacy and International Law' London School of Economics and Political Science, Law, Society and Economy Working Papers, Paper No. 12/2013
(2014), 'The Uses and Abuses of Legitimacy in International Law', 34 *Oxford Journal of Legal Studies* 729
Tierney B (2004), 'The Idea of Natural Rights – Origins and Persistence', 2 *Northwestern University Journal of International Human Rights* 2
Tipson F (1977), 'From International Law to World Public Order: Who Studies What, How, Why', 4 *Yale Studies in World Public Order* 39
Titi A (2014), *The Right to Regulate in International Investment Law* (1st edn, Nomos)
Titi C (2017), 'Refining the Expropriation Clause: What Role for Proportionality?' in Chaisse (ed.), *China-European Union Investment Relationships: Towards a New Leadership in Global Investment Governance?* (Cambridge University Press)
Tomka P, Howley J and Proulx V-J (2015), 'International and Municipal Law before the World Court: One or Two Legal Orders?', *Polish Yearbook of International Law* 11
Tomuschat C (2001), *International Law: Ensuring the Survival of Mankind on the Eve of a New Century* (Martinus Nijhoff)
Trakman LE (2012), 'Choosing Domestic Courts over Investor-State Arbitration: Australia's Repudiation of the Status Quo', 35 *UNSW Law Journal* 979
(2014), 'Investor-State Arbitration: Evaluating Australia's Evolving Position', 15 *Journal of World Investment & Trade* 152
Tremblay LB (2005), 'The Legitimacy of Judicial Review: The Limits of Dialogue between Courts and Legislatures', 3 *International Journal of Constitutional Law* 617
Triepel H (1899), *Völkerrecht und landesrecht* (CL Hirschfeld)
(1923), 'Les Rapports Entre Le Droit Interne et Le Droit International', in *Collected Courses of the Hague Academy of International Law* (Brill)
Tryon JL (1912), 'A Permanent Court of International Justice', 22 *Yale Law Journal* 203
Tumonis V (2012), 'Judicial Creativity and Constraint of Legal Rules: Duelling Cannons of International Law', 20 *University of Miami International & Comparative Law Review* 93
Tyler TR (2006), 'Psychological Perspectives on Legitimacy and Legitimation', 57 *Annual Review of Psychology* 375
Tzanakopoulos A (2012), 'Judicial Dialogue in Multi-Level Governance: The Impact of the Solange Argument' in Fauchald and Nollkaemper (eds.), *The Practice of International and National Courts and the (De-)Fragmentation of International Law* (Hart)
Ulfstein G (2012), 'The Relationship between Constitutionalism and Pluralism', 4 *Goettingen Journal of International Law* 575
(2013), 'International Courts and Judges: Independence, Interaction, and Legitimacy', 46 *New York University Journal of International Law and Politics* 849
Ulmer SS (1963), 'Quantitative Analysis of Judicial Processes: Some Practical and Theoretical Applications', *Law and Contemporary Problems* 164

Vadi V (2010), 'Critical Comparisons: The Role of Comparative Law in Investment Treaty Arbitration', 39 *Denver Journal of International Law and Policy* 67

(2015), 'Proportionality, Reasonableness, and Standards of Review in Investment Treaty Arbitration' in Bjorklund (ed.), *Yearbook on International Investment Law & Policy 2013–2014* (Oxford University Press)

(2016), *Analogies in International Investment Law and Arbitration* (Cambridge University Press)

(2018), *Proportionality, Reasonableness and Standards of Review in International Investment Law and Arbitration* (Edward Elgar)

Vadi V and Gruszczynski L (2013), 'Standards of Review in International Investment Law and Arbitration: Multilevel Governance and the Commonweal', 16 *Journal of International Economic Law* 613

Vaismoradi M, Turunen H and Bondas T (2013), 'Content Analysis and Thematic Analysis: Implications for Conducting a Qualitative Descriptive Study', 15 *Nursing and Health Sciences* 398

Valcke C (2004), 'Comparative Law as Comparative Jurisprudence – the Comparability of Legal Systems', 52 *American Journal of Comparative Law* 713

van Aaken A (2008), 'Between Commitment and Flexibility: The Fragile Stability of the International Investment Protection Regime' University of St. Gallen Law School, Law and Economics Research Paper Series, Working Paper No. 2008-23

van Asselt H (2014), 'Review Essay: Pluralism, Informality and Transnational Environmental Law Beyond Constitutionalism: The Pluralist Structure of Postnational Law', 3 *Transnational Environmental Law* 173

van Banning TRG (2002), *The Human Right to Property* (Intersentia)

van Coller EH (2006), 'Proportionality Review – the Battle between Community Standards and English Domestic Law', 39 *Comparative and International Law Journal of Southern Africa* 469

van den Hout T (2008), 'Resolution of International Disputes: The Role of the Permanent Court of Arbitration – Reflections on the Centenary of the 1907 Convention for the Pacific Settlement of International Disputes', 21 *Leiden Journal of International Law* 643

van der Vyver JD (1998), 'Universality and Relativity of Human Rights: American Relativism', 4 *Buffalo Human Rights Law Review* 43

Van Harten G (2007a), *International Treaty Arbitration and Public Law* (Oxford University Press)

(2007b), 'The Public-Private Distinction in the International Arbitration of Individual Claims against the State', 56 *International & Comparative Law Quarterly* 371

(2012), 'Arbitrator Behaviour in Asymmetrical Adjudication: An Empirical Study of Investment Treaty Arbitration', 50 *Osgoode Hall Law Journal* 211

(2013), *Sovereign Choices and Sovereign Constraints: Judicial Restraint in Investment Treaty Arbitration* (Oxford University Press)

(2014), 'Judicial Restraint in Investment Treaty Arbitration: Restraint Based on Relative Suitability', 5 *Journal of International Dispute Settlement* 5

Van Harten G and Loughlin M (2006), 'Investment Treaty Arbitration as a Species of Global Administrative Law', 17 *European Journal of International Law* 121

van Reenen TP (1995a), 'Major Theoretical Problems of Modern Comparative Legal Methodology (2); the Comparability of Positive Legal Phenomena', 28 *Comparative and International Law Journal of South Africa* 407

(1995b), 'Major Theoretical Problems of Modern Comparative Legal Methodology (1): The Nature and Role of the Tertium Comparationis', 28 *Comparative and International Law Journal of Southern Africa* 175

van Schooten H and Sweeney J (2003), 'Domestic Judicial Deference and the ECHR in the UK and Netherlands', 11 *Tilburg Foreign Law Review* 439

Vandevelde K (2011), 'Model Bilateral Investment Treaties: The Way Forward', 18 *Southwestern Journal of International Law* 307

(2013), 'Rebalancing through Exceptions', 17 *Lewis & Clark Law Review* 449

Vaughan A (2013), 'Minimum Interference Versus Rationality: The New Battleground in HRA Proportionality?', 18 *Judicial Review* 416

Venzke I (2011), 'The Role of International Courts as Interpreters and Developers of the Law: Working out the Jurisgenerative Practice of Interpretation', 34 *Loyola of Los Angeles International and Comparative Law Review* 99

(2012), *How Interpretation Makes International Law: On Semantic Authority and Normative Twists* (Oxford University Press)

(2013a), 'Understanding the Authority of International Courts and Tribunals: On Delegation and Discursive Construction', 14 *Theoretical Inquiries in Law* 381

(2013b), 'Between Power and Persuasion: On International Institutions' Authority in Making Law', 4(3) *Transnational Legal Theory* 354

(2014), 'Post-Modern Perspectives on Orthodox Positivism' in d'Aspremont and Kammerhofer (eds.), *International Law Positivism in a Post-Modern World* (Cambridge University Press)

(2016), 'Contemporary Theories and International Law-Making' in Brölmann and Radi, *Research Handbook on the Theory and Practice of International Lawmaking* (Edward Elgar)

Verdross A (1923), *Die Einheit des rechtlichen Weltbildes auf Grundlage der Völkerrechtsverfassung* (Mohr)

(1930), 'Die Rechtstheorie Hans Kelsens', 59 *Juristische Blätter* 423

(1971), 'Domestic Jurisdiction under International Law', 3 *University of Toledo Law Review* 119

Vermeer-Künzli A (2007), 'The Protection of Individuals by Means of Diplomatic Protection: Diplomatic Protection as a Human Rights Instrument' (PhD thesis, Leiden University)

Verzijl JHW (1965), *The Jurisprudence of the World Court: A Case by Case Commentary* (A W Sijthoff)

Viñuales JE (2008), 'State of Necessity and Peremptory Norms in International Investment Law', 14 *Law & Business Review of the Americas* 79

(2014), 'Sovereignty in Foreign Investment Law' in Douglas et al. (eds.), *The Foundations of International Investment Law* (Oxford University Press)

(2016), 'International Investment Law and Natural Resource Governance' in Kulovesi and Morgera (eds.), *Research Handbook on International Law and Natural Resources* (Edward Elgar)

(2017), 'Seven Ways of Escaping a Rule: Of Exceptions and Their Avatars in International Law' in Bartels and Paddeu (eds.), *Exceptions in International Law* (Oxford University Press)

Voeten E (2011), 'Politics, Judicial Behaviour, and Institutional Design' in Christoffersen and Madsen (eds.), *The European Court of Human Rights between Law and Politics* (Oxford University Press)

(2012), 'International Judicial Independence' in Dunoff and Pollack (eds.), *Interdisciplinary Perspectives on International Law and International Relations: The State of the Art* (Cambridge University Press)

Von Bernstorff J (2012), 'Georg Jellinek and the Origins of Liberal Constitutionalism in International Law', 4 *Goettingen Journal of International Law* 659

von Bogdandy A (2006), 'Constitutionalism in International Law: Comment on a Proposal from German', 47 *Harvard International Law Journal* 226

von Bogdandy A and Venzke I (2011), 'Beyond Dispute: International Judicial Institutions as Lawmakers', 12 *German Law Journal* 979

(2014), *In Whose Name?: A Public Law Theory of International Adjudication* (Oxford University Press)

von Papp K (2013), 'Clash of "Autonomous Legal Orders": Can EU Member State Courts Bridge the Jurisdictional Divide between Investment Tribunals and the ECJ? – A Plea for Direct Referral from Investment Tribunals to the ECJ', 50 *Common Market Law Review* 1039

von Rosenvinge DA (2010), 'Creating a Working Vocabulary of Sovereignty: Language at the International Court of Justice' Comparative Research in Law & Political Economy Paper No. 05/2010

von Staden A (2012), 'The Democratic Legitimacy of Judicial Review beyond the State: Normative Subsidiarity and Judicial Standards of Review', 10 *International Journal of Constitutional Law* 1023

(2016a), 'Subsidiarity, Exhaustion of Domestic Remedies, and the Margin of Appreciation in the Human Rights Jurisprudence of African Sub-Regional Courts', 20 *International Journal of Human Rights* 1113

(2016b), 'Subsidiarity in Regional Integration Regimes in Latin America and Africa', 79 *Law and Contemporary Problems* 27

Voon T (1999), 'Multinational Enterprises and State Sovereignty under International Law', 21 *Adelaide Law Review* 219

Waldock H (1965), 'Human Rights in Contemporary International Law and the Significance of the European Convention', 11 *International & Comparative Law Quarterly Supplementary Publication* 1

Waldron J (1994), 'Vagueness in Law and Language: Some Philosophical Issues', 82 *California Law Review* 509

(2006), 'The Core of the Case against Judicial Review', 115 *Yale Law Journal* 1346

(2013), 'Democracy and Human Rights: Good Companions' in Kinley et al. (eds.), *Human Rights* (Edward Elgar)

Walker N (2002), 'The Idea of Constitutional Pluralism' 65 Modern Law Review 317

(2013), 'Universalism and Particularism in Human Rights: Trade-Off or Productive Tension?' in Kinley and others, *Human Rights: Old Problems, New Possibilities* (Edward Elgar)

Walliman N (2011), *Research Methods: The Basics* (Routledge)

Wang S (1937), 'The Relation of International Law to Municipal Law', 10 *China Law Review* 179

Waschefort G (2012), 'Beyond Fragmentation: An Issues-Based Approach to "Human Rights"', 37 *South African Yearbook of International Law* 61

Watts A (1996), 'Nationality of Claims: Some Relevant Concepts' in Lowe and Fitzmaurice (eds.), *Fifty Years of the International Court of Justice: Essays in Honour of Sir Robert Jennings* (Cambridge University Press)

Webb P (2013), *International Judicial Integration and Fragmentation* (Oxford University Press)

Webber GCN (2010), 'Proportionality, Balancing and the Cult of Constitutional Rights Scholarship', 23 *Canadian Journal of Law and Jurisprudence* 179

Weber M (1947), *The Theory of Social and Economic Organization* (Oxford University Press)

Weber M and Roth G (1979), *Economy and Society: An Outline of Interpretive Sociology* (University of California Press)

Webley L (2010), 'Qualitative Approaches to Empirical Legal Research' in Cane and Kritzer (eds.), *The Oxford Handbook of Empirical Legal Research* (1st edn, Oxford University Press)

Weeramantry C (1996), 'Some Practical Problems of International Adjudication', 17 *Australian Year Book of International Law* 1

Wehland H (2019), 'Domestic Courts and Investment Treaty Tribunals: The Effect of Local Recourse Against Administrative Measures on the Breach of Investment Protection Standards', 36 *Journal of International Arbitration* 207

Weiner A (2003), 'Indirect Expropriations: The Need for a Taxonomy of "Legitimate" Regulatory Purposes', 5 *International Law FORUM du droit international* 166

Wellens K (1996), *Economic Conflicts and Disputes before the World Court (1922–1995): A Functional Analysis* (Kluwer Law International)

Wellhausen RL (2016), 'Recent Trends in Investor–State Dispute Settlement', 7 *Journal of International Dispute Settlement* 117

Westlund AC (2013), 'Deference as a Normative Power', 166 *Philosophical Studies: An International Journal for Philosophy in the Analytic Tradition* 455

Wheatley S (2011), 'A Democratic Rule of International Law', 22 *European Journal of International Law* 525

White G (1961), *Nationalisation of Foreign Property* (Stevens & Sons Limited)

White GE (1986), 'From Realism to Critical Legal Studies: A Truncated Intellectual History', 40 *Southwestern Law Journal* 819

White MD and Marsh EE (2006), 'Content Analysis: A Flexible Methodology', 55 *Library Trends* 22

White N (2000), 'The United Nations System: Conference, Contract or Constitutional Order?', 4 *Singapore Journal of International and Comparative Law* 281

Wildhaber L (1983), 'Sovereignty and International Law' in Macdonald and Johnston (eds.), *The Structure and Process of International Law: Essays in Legal Philosophy, Doctrine and Theory* (Martinus Nijhoff)

Wilson MM (1977), 'Federal Court Stays and Dismissals in Deference to Parallel State Court Proceedings: The Impact of Colorado River', 44 *University of Chicago Law Review* 641

Winham GR (1969), 'Quantitative Methods in Foreign Policy Analysis', 2 *Canadian Journal of Political Science* 187

Wismer P (2006), 'Bring Down the Walls! – On the Ever-Increasing Dynamic between the National and International Domains', 5 *Chinese Journal of International Law* 511

Wittgenstein L (2010), *Philosophical Investigations* (P Michael, S Hacker and J Schulte eds., GEM Anscombe tr., 3rd edn, Wiley-Blackwell)

Wolfrum R (ed.) (2008), *Legitimacy in International Law* (Springer)

Wolitz D (2014), 'Indeterminacy, Value Pluralism, and Tragic Cases', 62 *Buffalo Law Review* 529

Worster WT (2008), 'Competition and Comity in the Fragmentation of International Law', 34 *Brooklyn Journal of International Law* 119

Wortley BA (1956), 'Observations on the Public and Private International Law Relating to Expropriation', 5 *American Journal of Comparative Law* 577

Wouters J and Hachez N (2009), 'When Rules and Values Collide: How Can a Balanced Application of Investor Protection Provisions and Human Rights Be Ensured?', 3 *Human Rights and International Legal Discourse* 301

Yackee JW (2012), 'Controlling the International Investment Law Agency', 53 *Harvard International Law Journal* 391

Yalkin T (2009), 'International Investment Arbitration: Poisoned at the Root?', British Institute of International and Comparative Law Annual Conference on Business and Law

Young AL (2009), 'In Defence of Due Deference', 72 *Modern Law Review* 554

(2010), 'Deference, Dialogue and the Search for Legitimacy', 30 *Oxford Journal of Legal Studies* 815

(2014), 'Will You, Won't You, Will You Join the Deference Dance?', 34 *Oxford Journal of Legal Studies* 375

(2017), *Democratic Dialogue and the Constitution* (Oxford University Press)

Young E (2005), 'Institutional Settlement in a Globalizing Judicial System', *Duke Law Journal* 103

Yourow HC (1996), *The Margin of Appreciation Doctrine in the Dynamics of European Human Rights Jurisprudence* (Kluwer Law International)

Zammit Borda A (2013), 'A Formal Approach to Article 38(1)(d) of the ICJ Statute from the Perspective of the International Criminal Courts and Tribunals', 24 *European Journal of International Law* 649

Zarbiyev F (2012), 'Judicial Activism in International Law – A Conceptual Framework for Analysis', 3 *Journal of International Dispute Settlement* 247

Zeitler HE (2005), 'Good Faith' in the WTO Jurisprudence – Necessary Balancing Element or an Open Door to Judicial Activism?', 8 *Journal of International Economic Law* 721

Zglinski J (2018), 'The Rise of Deference: The Margin of Appreciation and Decentralized Judicial Review in EU Free Movement Law', 55 *Common Market Law Review* 1341

Zyberi G (2013), 'The International Court of Justice and the Rights of Peoples and Minorities' in Tams and Sloan (eds.), *The Development of International Law by the International Court of Justice* (Oxford University Press)

Index

For EU product safety concerns, contact us at Calle de José Abascal, 56–1°, 28003 Madrid, Spain or eugpsr@cambridge.org.

www.ingramcontent.com/pod-product-compliance
Lightning Source LLC
LaVergne TN
LVHW011702200926
848484LV00004B/1041
9781108490979